HADRIAN'S

'This is a magisterial volume . . . and the author is to be congratulated on his achievement.'

Professor Roger Ling, *Antiquaries Journal*

'Hingley has written *the* historiographical account of Hadrian's Wall for this generation and, I suspect, beyond: it is one of the most important books ever to have been written on Hadrian's Wall.'

Professor David Breeze, *Britannia*

'Hingley's book is nothing short of a will to relevance for Roman archaeology, for its living spirit to be resurrected in research that animates past with present. This is a book with a story, a playful joining of analytical and narrative forms that should be emulated. It is a book to be read tucked up in bed after a day of trekking along the Wall, or in preparation or remembrance of a visit.'

Professor Katheryn Lafrez Samuels, *Antiquity*

HADRIAN'S WALL: A LIFE

RICHARD HINGLEY

OXFORD
UNIVERSITY PRESS

OXFORD
UNIVERSITY PRESS

Great Clarendon Street, Oxford, OX2 6DP,
United Kingdom

Oxford University Press is a department of the University of Oxford.
It furthers the University's objective of excellence in research, scholarship,
and education by publishing worldwide. Oxford is a registered trade mark of
Oxford University Press in the UK and in certain other countries

First published 2012
First published in paperback 2015

Published in the United States of America by Oxford University Press
198 Madison Avenue, New York, NY 10016, United States of America

British Library Cataloguing in Publication Data
Data available

Library of Congress Cataloging in Publication Data
Data available

ISBN 978-0-19-964141-3 (Hbk.)
ISBN 978-0-19-870702-8 (Pbk.)

For Michael Shanks

PREFACE

The rain comes pattering out of the sky,
I'm a Wall soldier, I don't know why.
W. H. Auden (1937)

This preface explains something of my own motivation and also provides a background to the project from which this book arose. Although I was born in Oxfordshire, I was taken to see the Wall by my mother when I was ten. My father was born in Edinburgh, and this gave me an early interest in the borders of England and Scotland. After living in southern England until the age of 17, I studied for my degree in Durham from 1976 to 1979, just after the retirement of Eric Birley, whom I met on only one occasion. John Mann's teaching inspired me to visit and study the Wall. I moved back south—to Southampton, Oxford, and Warwick—for a decade before working for Historic Scotland in Edinburgh in 1989. Living in south-eastern Scotland for ten years, I regularly travelled across the line of Hadrian's Wall, at Corbridge and Newcastle, when I visited friends and family. During this time, I was also responsible for looking after the remains of Scotland's Roman Wall (the Antonine Wall), which drew me back to the topic of Roman frontiers. The enthusiasm of David Breeze, head of the Ancient Monument Inspectorate at the time, reinforced this; he has remained a constant source of help and advice ever since. In 1999, I crossed the line of Hadrian's Wall again to take up a lectureship at Durham University and, as the archaeologist teaching Roman Britain, I have become increasingly involved with the monument. I am on the Committee that oversees the Word Heritage Site and served on the organizing Committees for two major events held in Newcastle in 2009, the Limes Congress and the Hadrian's Wall Pilgrimage.

In the early 2000s, I discussed the Wall with Michael Shanks of Stanford University, California, since we were both thinking of conducting research on the monument. In 2005, I began to consider a project on the after-life of the Wall with two of my colleagues at Durham, Rob Witcher and Divya Tolia-Kelly. We prepared a major research grant application for the Arts and Humanities Research Council's Landscape and Environment initiative, for a project entitled *Tales of the Frontier: political representations and cultural practices inspired by Hadrian's Wall*. We were successful in obtaining funding and we appointed Claire Nesbitt as the Post Doctoral Researcher. *Tales of the*

Frontier ran from September 2007 to August 2009 and has already resulted in a number of publications.[1] The project produced a travelling exhibition, *The Archaeology of Race*, which has toured *Segedunum* (Wallsend), Carlisle, and Durham.[2] I am grateful to my three colleagues for their input and also to others who assisted with advice and contributions, including Lindsay Allason-Jones, Paul Bidwell, Anthony Birley, John Bonehill, Roger Bland, David Breeze, Rob Collins, Barry Cunliffe, Hella Eckardt, Dimitris Grigoroupolis, Ian Haynes, Sheila Hingley, Nick Hodgson, Edward Impey, Adrian James, Sophia Labadi, David Mattingly, Nigel Mills, Andrew Parkin, Renato Pinto, Georgina Plowright, Aileen Ribeiro, John Richardson, Darrell Rohl, Chris Scarre, Bryan Scott, Michael Shanks, Sam Smiles, Christina Unwin, Phiroze Vasunia, Jeff Veitch, Peter Wells, Ben Westwood, Christopher Witmore, Tony Wilmott, and Pete Wilson. Stephen Daniels was the programme director for AHRC and has provided constant support and helpful advice for this research, while Sam Smiles has supplied many reflections on engravings of the monument. The ideas behind this book have been discussed at a number of conferences during the past five years.[3]

This book arises from my research for *Tales of the Frontier*, which focused on historical representations of the Wall. The research and publication could not have been undertaken without the generous support of AHRC, both in terms of the original funding of *Tales of the Frontier* and also for the additional funding of a Research Fellowship from January to April 2011 that enabled me to complete the writing of this book. I am also most grateful for the comments that the anonymous reviewers provided on both the grant applications and also for two sets of anonymous comments on my book proposal. In the meantime, Durham University's partnership project with Stanford University at Binchester Roman fort (County Durham) has enabled the development of another major project with Michael Shanks. The perspective developed in this book has been explored in particular during various discussions with Michael and with Rob Witcher, David Breeze, Paul Bidwell, and Christina Unwin; I am particularly grateful to all for their continuing help and inspiration. I am also

---

[1] Published articles include Hingley (2010a); Hingley (2010b); Hingley and Hartis (2011); Hingley and Nesbitt (2008); Nesbitt and Tolia-Kelly (2009); Tolia-Kelly (2010); Tolia-Kelly and Nesbitt (2009); Witcher (2010a); Witcher (2010b); Witcher, Tolia-Kelly and Hingley (2010), and Daniels and Cowell (2011).

[2] Tolia-Kelly (2010); Tolia-Kelly and Nesbit (2009).

[3] Including the Arbeia Conference (South Shields, UK, 2006); the Royal Geographical Conferences in London (2008) and Nottingham (2009); imperialism conferences at Durham (US, 2008), Dartmouth (US, 2009), and Berlin (Germany, 2010); the Theoretical Archaeology Group at Durham (UK, 2009); the AHRC Bringing Landscapes to Life Workshop at the National Trust (London, 2011); during research visits to Campinas (Brazil, 2008) and Santiago de Compostela (Spain, 2009); and in lectures at Durham (UK, 2010), Cambridge (UK, 2011), Newcastle (UK, 2011), and St Andrews (UK, 2011).

extremely grateful to Lindsay Allason-Jones, Paul Bidwell, Anthony Birley, David Breeze, Nick Hodgson, Sam Smiles, Christina Unwin, and Pete Wilson for providing such useful and detailed comments on earlier drafts of the entire text. My thanks also to Hilary O'Shea, Desiree Kellerman, and Marilyn Inglis for considerable help with the production of this book.

Richard Hingley, Shadforth, Durham,
August 2011

Arts & Humanities
Research Council

CONTENTS

List of Figures

1

A Living Wall

Hadrian's Wall is a living wall . . .
Hunter Davies (1974), 155

ANIMATING THE WALL

Hadrian's Wall was constructed in the AD 120s and maintained for almost three centuries before ceasing to operate as a Roman frontier during the fifth century (Figure 1.1). Its scale and complexity means that it is one of the most important ancient monuments in the British Isles and one the most complex and well-preserved frontier works that once defined the boundaries of the Roman empire. Today, this Roman Wall is very popular with visitors and makes a substantial contribution to the economy of northern England. It has its own brand that promotes the marketing of produce derived from 'Hadrian's Wall Country'. The Wall is also the foremost element of The Frontiers of the Roman Empire World Heritage Site, a transnational designation that includes Roman frontier monuments in England, Germany, and Scotland. Hadrian's Wall is celebrated, conserved, and protected as an iconic Roman frontier, a massive physical barrier that defined the northern boundary of *Britannia* for much of the period of Roman rule.

In Roman terms, the life cycle of Hadrian's Wall came to an end when it ceased to be used for the purpose of defining and protecting the northern boundaries of the empire. This primordially Roman identity is the reason why the Wall is protected, managed, and interpreted for the public today. It is fundamental to the archaeological excavations undertaken on the Wall (Figure 1.2), studies which produce the information provided for the thousands of visitors to the Roman remains. Although a second Roman frontier structure, the Antonine Wall, runs between the Clyde estuary and the Firth of Forth in Scotland,[1] Hadrian's Wall is by far the best-known Roman monument in Great Britain.

---

[1] Breeze (2006c).

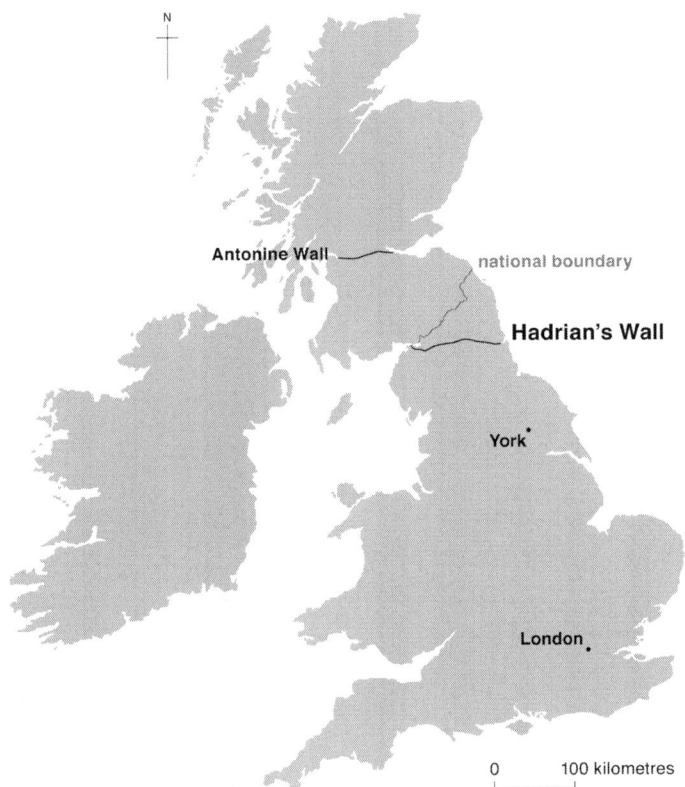

Fig. 1.1. A map of Roman Britain, showing the locations of Hadrian's Wall, the Antonine Wall, York, and London, and the national boundaries between England and Scotland. Drawn by Christina Unwin.

Despite the fact that Hadrian's frontier is often addressed as *the* Roman Wall, the ending of its Roman phase only completed one stage in its lengthy history.[2] Its substantial remains have long formed a dramatic physical link to the Roman past both for the people who live close to its line and for those who visit it.[3] Although robbing of stone from the monument began at least as early as the seventh century, the highly impressive remains of the stone curtain Wall—with its regular turrets and milecastles—survive, particularly in the upland sections of its course.[4] In addition, the accompanying elements

---

[2] cf. Bender (1998), 9.   [3] Whitworth (2000).
[4] Although the curtain Wall has been extensively cleared and reconstructed since the nineteenth century.

Fig. 1.2. An archaeological excavation underway on the Roman fort at Vindolanda. The reconstructed sections of curtain Wall, and turf and timber Wall are visible behind the excavations. Photograph by Richard Hingley, 2011.

of this Wall—the impressive northern ditch and the truly monumental earthwork called the 'Vallum'—continue to mark this complex linear frontier structure along much of its course. Accompanying these linear features, the ruins of the forts and towns that sheltered to the south of the Wall remain visible. These elements of the Wall have gradually been eroded, destroyed, and fragmented over the centuries, but enough of this substantial and extensive monument survives for it to have been inscribed as a World Heritage Site in 1987.

These physical traces have long formed the backdrop for the lives of the communities living along the line of the Wall, while the remains have impressed visitors for centuries. Knowledge of the monument appears to have been fairly widespread in medieval times and by the late sixteenth century the Wall had become a source of fascination for antiquaries who marvelled at its scale and significance.[5] Since this time, the Wall has been explored, mapped, depicted, and described. It has been drawn upon and used in texts and

[5] Shannon (2007).

Fig. 1.3. The detail of William Hole's image of 'aged *Pictswall*' taken from the map of Northumberland in Michael Drayton's *Poly-Olbion* (1622). This is a rare example of an image that recreates the Roman Wall as a living spirit. Reproduced by permission of Bodleian Library, Bookstack Mal 13[2].

illustrations for a variety of purposes.[6] By referencing the remains of the Wall, writers, illustrators, and film producers have brought its remains into a lively encounter with the present, as the following two examples help to demonstrate.

In 1622, the English poet Michael Drayton imagined this monument as a living spirit of place that he called 'aged *Pictswall*'—a title that drew upon the medieval name for Hadrian's Wall. In Drayton's poem about Northumberland, this aged spirit (Figure 1.3) articulates his significant role during the medieval border wars between England and Scotland; he calls himself 'the longest liv'd monument'.[7] Drayton's creation of *Pictswall* expresses the Wall's physical and conceptual significance at this particular time, since King James had inspired a relative state of peace on the border as a result of his joint rule of the formerly independent kingdoms of England and Scotland. The surviving

---

[6] The remains of the Wall have been drawn upon, for example, by poets, novelists, painters, illustrators, schoolteachers, antiquaries, archaeologists, cartoonists, journalists, politicians, heritage managers, urban planners, and military men.

[7] Drayton (1622), 158.

Fig. 1.4. A workman involved in the excavation of the Roman fort at South Shields in the 1870s. Reproduced by permission of the Great North Museum and Society of Antiquaries of Newcastle upon Tyne, Hadrian's Wall Photograph Collection, 6525.

remains of the Wall remained a notable feature of the landscape and the aged spirit recalls his former role, which subsumes the defence of the northern frontier of both the Roman province of *Britannia* and the medieval kingdom of England. *Pictswall*'s claim to continued life draws on his surviving military role in the defence of the frontier.

Three hundred and fifty years later, Hunter Davies published a popular account of Hadrian's Wall that once again aimed to animate its remains. On the crags in the centre of the Wall's line, Davies came across a group of men clearing and consolidating the impressive remains of the curtain Wall. They were clearing the tumbled stones and earth away from the faces of the Wall and finishing it with a concrete top. This operation also revealed the buried remains of the monument adding to the Roman turrets that had been discovered during the previous century. Observing this clearing and restoration, Davies noted that 'Hadrian's Wall is a living wall, not just for the local inhabitants, but for tourists and archaeologists, a living, breathing, expanding, growing wall'.[8] The human lives tied in to the uncovering and consolidation of the remains emphasized the Wall's living credentials (Figure 1.4). In different

[8] H. Davies (1974), 155.

Fig. 1.5. The 'Living Frontier' event at Corbridge on 30 May 2009. Photograph by Rob Witcher, 2009.

ways, Davies and Drayton viewed the monument as a living entity and as a vital spirit of place. Numerous other poets, antiquaries, novelists, travel writers, and artists have drawn upon this metaphor of the living Wall, using Roman structures and objects to narrate tales of the past.

As Hunter Davies has demonstrated, animating the Wall involves the people who have been involved in uncovering, maintaining, mapping, and interpreting its remains. The encouragement of tourism over the past decade has generated events based upon these impressive archaeological remains along the length of the Wall, including regular re-enactments to attract visitors to particular parts of the monument (Figure 1.5). An innovative project, *Illuminating Hadrian's Wall*, which took place on 13 March 2010, involved the entire line of the frontier being illuminated after dark by torches lit by thousands of people. Such events serve to illustrate the main theme of this book—that the disuse of the Wall as a Roman frontier during the early fifth century represented only one form of ending. From early medieval times to

Fig. 1.6. The reconstructed section of curtain Wall at the Roman fort and visitor centre at Vindolanda, showing the stone curtain Wall from immediately behind, and the reconstructed turf rampart to the left of the image. Photograph by Richard Hingley, 2011.

the present day, people have made use of the Wall, recreating it as a vital element of the landscape of northern England for their own times and telling many different stories that have kept its remains alive.

The Wall has not only been commemorated through text, image, and performance; many parts of the monument have been physically recreated. From the late sixteenth century, information on its character has been uncovered and collected by generations of antiquaries. From the mid-nineteenth century, a programme of archaeological research focused attention on uncovering the Wall's structure and chronological sequence. At the same time, there was a growing concern to protect and manage the Wall's remains, to defend it from the stone-robbing and attrition that had been ongoing since early medieval times. Many of the antiquaries and archaeologists who lavished attention on the Wall focused their studies on providing a fuller and more detailed documentation of its Roman identity, history, and character. Archaeological work has helped to uncover, display, consolidate, map, and interpret the Wall, creating far more of the monument for the visitor to see.

At the same time, some entirely new elements have been added to its structure. During his visit to the Wall, Hunter Davies saw a newly constructed section of the curtain Wall at Vindolanda, which was being built to provide visitors with an idea of the original appearance of the monument (Figure 1.6). Davies observed that, for the 'first time in almost two thousand years, here was a workman building Hadrian's Wall'.[9] In reality, the rebuilding of the physical fabric of this stone Wall had been underway at least since the early eighteenth

[9] H. Davies (1974), 121.

century, although it is true that the Vindolanda Trust was the first organization in post-Roman times to build an entirely new section of curtain Wall, albeit on the line of the Stanegate.

As a result of various forms of consolidation and rebuilding, Hadrian's Wall has become a composite monument. The impressive sections to visit and explore have been uncovered and consolidated mainly over the past 160 years. But the Wall is also a structure that contains, at its core, traces of the Roman Wall that was built on the orders of the Emperor Hadrian during the early second century. This book explores the variety of ways in which Hadrian's Wall has continued to develop—as a concept and also as a composite structure—since its disuse as a Roman frontier.

CHOROGRAPHY

In order to address the continuing life of the Wall, I shall consider the significance of certain places along its line through an approach to its chorography. Chorography is an analytical concept that has its origins in the ancient Mediterranean world and which was used by a number of early modern scholars in their accounts of the landscapes of England. Howard Marchitello observed that chorography delineates 'topography not exclusively as it exists in the present moment, but also as it has existed historically', since the approach is based on the idea that the character of the land described in particular places persists through time.[10] William Camden was the first antiquary to explore the history and structure of the Wall in detail and the first English translation of his book *Britannia*, published in 1610, was subtitled 'A Chorographicall description'. Michael Drayton was deeply influenced by Camden's account of the Wall and produced his own poetic chorography of England, which included the spirit of aged *Pictswall*. The influence of Camden's and Drayton's chorographical writings can be traced in later accounts of the Wall and these have carried elements of their approach through time.[11]

In early modern times, chorography had a close relationship with growing notions of landed property across England. As a method, it drew upon the history of the past of particular places to help to justify the local aristocracy's emphasis on lineage and rights to landed estates.[12] In modern works, the

---

[10] Marchitello (1997), 78, 85.

[11] In 1649, William Gray published a volume entitled *Chorographia, or a survey of Newcastle upon Tyne*. This is the first history of Newcastle, which claimed an origin for the town in Roman times and also includes references to the Roman Wall. Later accounts that draw broadly on the chorographical tradition include: Hutton (1802); J. C. Bruce (1851); Forster (1899); Kipling (1906); H. Davies (1974); and Breeze (2006a).

[12] Swann (2001), 101–7.

concept has been adopted for quite different reasons, since it can act as a means of eroding certain dominant forms of historical thinking in which time is perceived in entirely linear terms.[13] Archaeologists often construct time-scales in order to isolate the past from the present, so that it can identified, defined, and analysed.[14] The approach pursued here emphasizes a rather different understanding of both past and present. Christopher Witmore has argued that time is not necessarily a given parameter along which change can be placed in an orderly and defined sequence; instead, it is a quality that emerges from the particular involvement of archaeologists with the landscapes they study.[15] The acts of archaeological engagement through which materials from the past are uncovered and explored can, in Witmore's terms, be seen to create eddies in the flow of time, as encounters with ancient objects, sites, and texts link ancient materials to contemporary ideas and interests. For example, Hunter Davies was brought into an immediate engagement with Hadrian's Wall through the activities that were uncovering turrets and sections of the curtain Wall, revealing elements of the monument that had been invisible for centuries.

In his book '*In Comes I*', Mike Pearson argues that 'Chorographical writing creates complex and unexpected relations from and within the landscape of the autobiographical subject, through processes analogous to non-linear, hypertextual linkages.'[16] Pearson uses excursions to a number of specific places in North Lincolnshire to link topography and experience, history, and identity, 'and as a means to elaborate the social, cultural and environmental conditions within which performance is enacted'. W. G. Sebald's novel, *The Rings of Saturn*,[17] used a broadly comparable approach to illustrate, with considerable elegance, how visits to certain places in coastal East Anglia—including a hospital, a beach, a diesel train, and a churchyard—captured and directed his memories of some of the events of his own life.

This book explores themes related to specific places along the length and breadth of Hadrian's frontier, including buildings, landscape features, archae-ological sites, and artefacts (Figure 1.7). A focus on place emphasizes that the past and the present often effectively flow into one another.[18] It explores archaeological engagement with the Wall, but also addresses the ways that artists and popular writers have drawn on these ancient remains as a source of inspiration to directly link the past and the present.[19] The particular places and objects are material features and include a modern place of pilgrimage, a medieval priory, a Roman hypocaust, a Victorian painting, a reconstructed

---

[13] cf. Ulmer (1994), 33.
[14] cf. Pearson and Shanks (2001), 114; Blain and Wallis (2007), 33–4.
[15] Witmore (2007), 205–10.
[16] Pearson (2006), 9.   [17] Sebald (2002).
[18] cf. Hicks and McAtackney (2007), 17.
[19] cf. Ricoeur (1984), 227.

Clayton Wall on Whin Sill

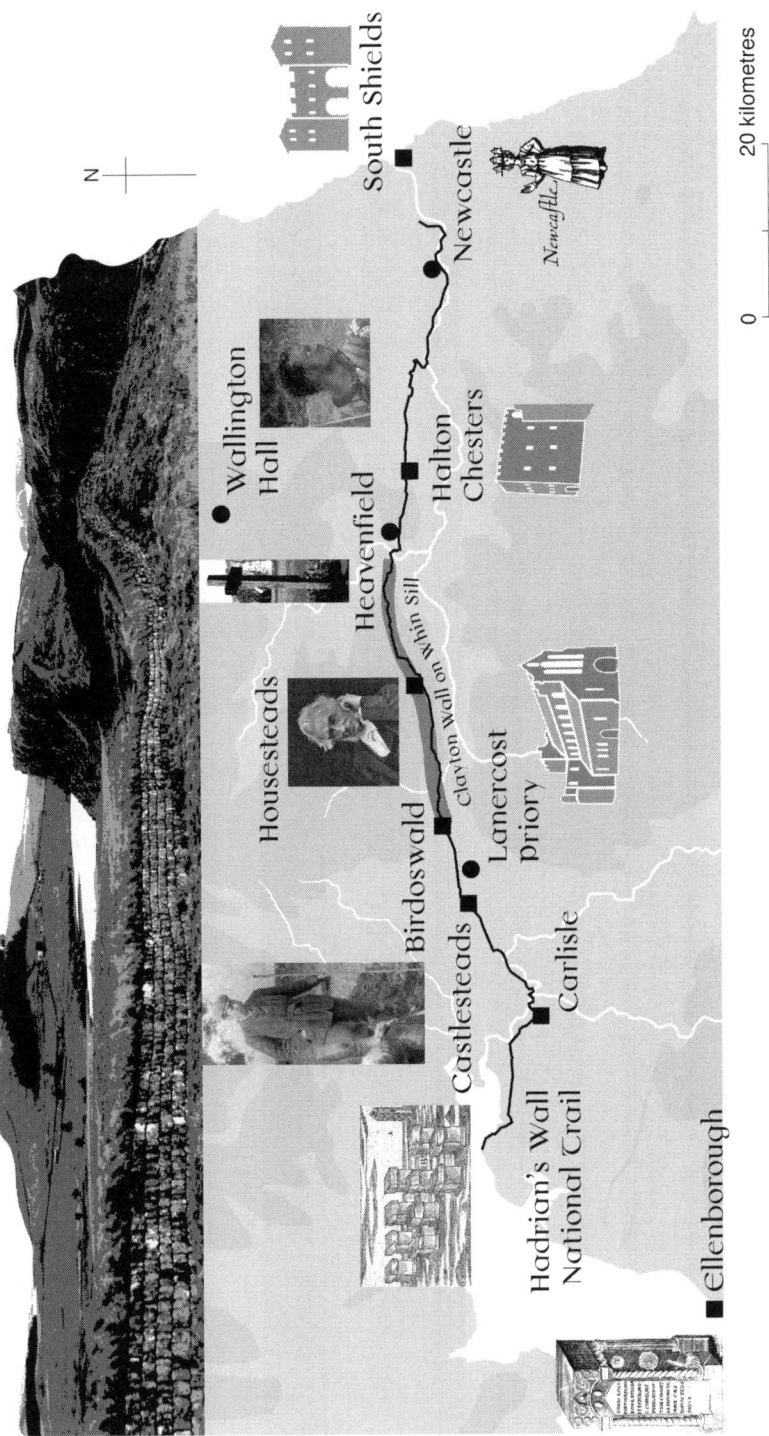

Fig. 1.7. The places mentioned in the Chapter titles 3 to 15. Drawn by Christina Unwin.

Roman gateway, and the Hadrian's Wall Path National Trail. These features form links that are used to narrate particular themes. The main focus is upon the efforts of people throughout the ages to maintain, rebuild, visit, and portray the Wall by using knowledge of its original nature and role as a Roman frontier. The book focuses deeply upon the Wall's life history, aiming to emphasize the myriad ways in which its material presence connects the activities that have taken place along its line over the past 1,800 years.[20] Unlike a person, the Wall has never died, but it has evolved, aged, been deconstructed and rejuvenated through writings, images, and in the reconstruction of its physical form. The Wall has provided, and provides, a source of inspiration in a wide variety of media, precisely because it helps to project important ideas that draw the past into an intimate engagement with the present.[21] Those who have visited, depicted, excavated, and described Hadrian's Wall have used various techniques to create this living engagement but, through a process of reinterpretation, the monument's material form has also been constantly reconstructed, reconstituted, and altered.

A COMPOSITE ROMAN WALL

The focus on the history of the Wall's post-Roman life in this book is *certainly not* intended to undermine the monument's vitally important Roman credentials. The aim of this book is to demonstrate that the Wall's Roman identity has been fundamental to its continuing vitality throughout the centuries, including its role and significance in the region, nation, and world today. At the same time, the monument has acquired a range of broader associations as a result of its long and complex sequence of use. It is a composite Wall, but with a Roman identity at the core of its living spirit.

The processes through which knowledge of the Wall has been created—the result of centuries of antiquarian and archaeological work—constitutes one of the key themes addressed here. This includes a consideration of why the Wall was built, its relationship with the other frontiers of the Roman empire, and its contemporary significance as a heritage icon.[22] Importantly, this book also seeks to explore the extent to which arguments about the meaning of the Wall, and its function and purpose in Roman times, can help to keep its significance alive in the present. Archaeological excavations are real-time living engagements with the Wall and are appreciated by the public in these terms. Similarly, disagreements over the function and role of Hadrian's Wall

---

[20] cf. Witmore (2007), 210.
[21] cf. Gazin-Schwartz and Holtorf (1999), 3–4.
[22] cf. Breeze and Jilek (eds. 2008).

keep the subject alive by stressing the requirement for additional research, excavation, and lively debate.

The first stage in this narration of the Wall's life is the exploration of the Roman period of its history. The structure and history of the Wall will be described through an account of its various components. Subsequently, three chronological sections successively address the medieval Picts' Wall, the Roman Wall of the eighteenth and nineteenth centuries, and the twentieth-century monument known as Hadrian's Wall. The study concludes with an assessment of the nature of the Wall as an inclusive monument in its twenty-first-century landscape.

2

Hadrian's Wall

[Hadrian] built a wall for eighty miles, which was to separate the
barbarians from the Romans.

Historia Augusta, de vita Hadriani (XI, 2)[1]

INTRODUCTION

This chapter provides a short summary of the archaeological information for
Hadrian's Wall. It draws on a variety of published accounts, particularly the
extremely useful two volumes of the *Research Framework* for the Wall, which
contains a number of review articles written by experts on the archaeology of
the Wall.[2] An outline of information about the Wall will be presented in order
to address its construction, form, and use in Roman times. This will provide a
background to the ways in which Hadrian's Wall was drawn upon after
Roman times. In subsequent chapters, the growth of knowledge of the Wall
will be assessed in some detail, building on the outline of the physical structure
and history presented here.

In AD 43, the Roman Emperor Claudius (10 BC–AD 54) mobilized an invasion
of Britain after a century or more of contact and diplomacy between the tribal
leaders of south-eastern Britain and the expanding Roman state.[3] A large
Roman army crossed the Channel from Gaul and Lowland Britain was
gradually subdued during the middle and late first century AD. This conquest
occurred through the use of diplomacy and armed violence directed against
some of the peoples of Britain.[4] The area of Britain through which the Wall
was later to be constructed was gradually assimilated into the Roman province

---

[1] For this translation, see A. Birley (2005, 121), 223.
[2] This publication is referred to in abbreviated form in this book as RFa; RFb. For other recent
accounts of the Wall, see Appendix 1.
[3] J. Creighton (2000).
[4] Mattingly (2006).

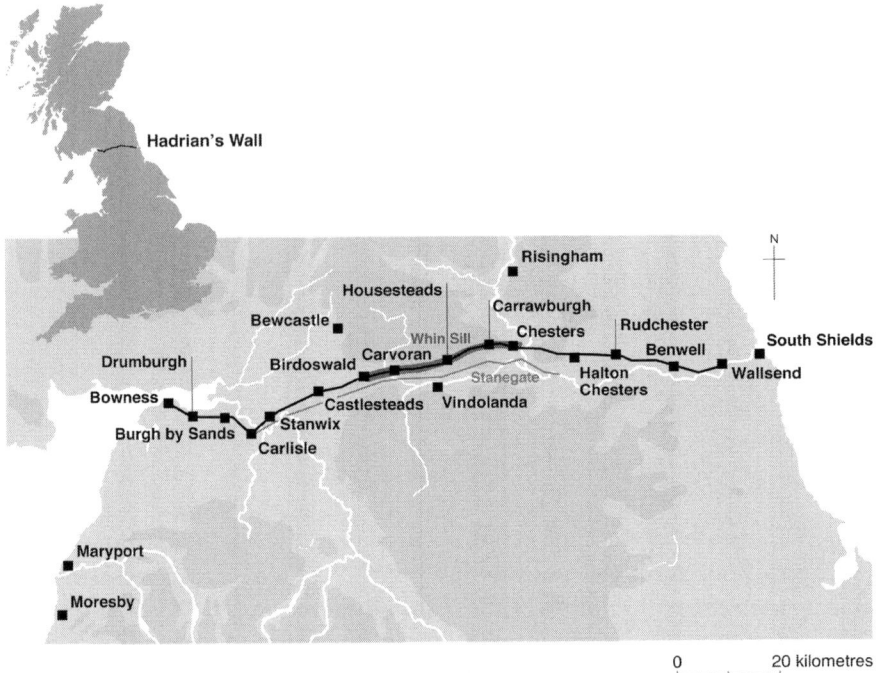

Fig. 2.1. A map of Hadrian's Wall showing the forts, outpost forts, Stanegate, and the location of the 'Clayton Wall' (shown as a thicker line). Drawn by Christina Unwin.

of *Britannia* during the later first century. The earliest Roman activity at Carlisle commenced at least as early as AD 72–3, as indicated by the dendrochronological dating of timbers incorporated in the south rampart of a turf and timber fort.[5] A fortified military road, the 'Stanegate', was constructed just to the south of the line on which the Wall was later to be built (Figure 2.1).[6] A number of Roman forts were established along this road, including at Carlisle, Vindolanda, and Corbridge. At Vindolanda, occupation probably began during the late first century, and excavations have produced important information, including the famous letters sent to and from soldiers serving at the fort during the decades before the Wall was constructed.[7]

We know very little about the indigenous context within which these Roman activities took place. The homes and settlements of the local people have been recognized and excavated in some numbers (Figure 2.2), but the relationship between these people and the Roman army and administration remains unclear.[8] Substantial areas of land will have been confiscated

---

[5] RFa, 29.   [6] ibid., 13–18.   [7] R. Birley (2009), 65–71.
[8] Hingley (2004), 328; RFa, 5–9, 149–52.

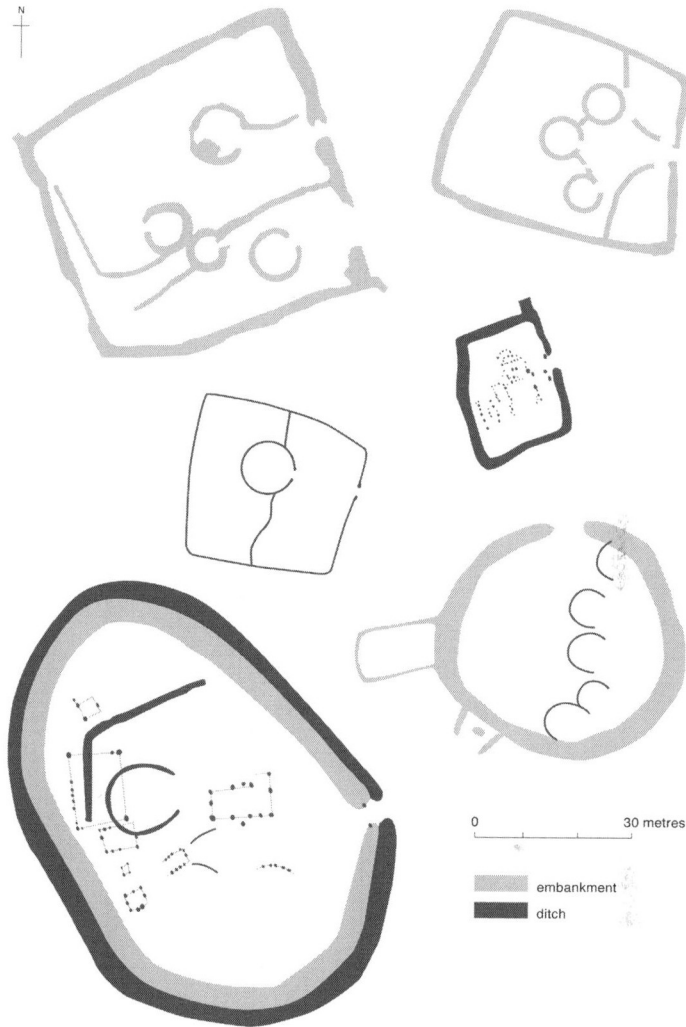

Fig. 2.2. Examples of some 'native settlements' from the landscape to either side of Hadrian's Wall. Drawn by Christina Unwin, after Hingley 2004, 340.

during the construction of the Roman military infrastructure. Roman roads, camps, and forts were enforced without discussion or negotiation—indeed, violence was probably commonplace during the conquest of Britain.[9] It is likely that the Roman army did very much whatever it wanted across this landscape, prior to, during, and after the construction of the Wall.

[9] cf. Mattingly (2006).

IDENTITY AND ORIGIN

The Emperor Hadrian (76–138), who visited Britain in AD 122, may well have travelled northwards and visited the site of the eastern end of his proposed Wall.[10] Latin inscriptions clearly indicate the construction of a number of the elements of the Wall during the reign of Hadrian.[11] The attribution of the monument to this emperor was, however, only firmly established during the early twentieth century, since from the sixth century its construction had often been attributed to later Roman emperors and military commanders. In fact, as R. G. Collingwood pointed out, at least six ancient writers attributed the Wall to Septimius Severus (146–211) and only one referred to Hadrian.[12] Most English antiquaries argued that the curtain Wall was built by Severus, drawing on the weight of the classical textual evidence.[13] Some of the early writers related the Wall to Hadrian, drawing on the information from the fourth-century source called the *Historia Augusta* (see above). The name 'Hadrian's Wall' was widely adopted by archaeologists during the early twentieth century as a result of the scholarly study of the stratigraphy of certain sites along the Wall.[14] Prior to this, the monument was known by various names, including the medieval title 'Picts' Wall' and the eighteenth-century term 'Roman Wall'.

The recent discovery of the 'Ilam Pan', or the 'Staffordshire Moorlands Pan' presents additional information about the Wall (Figure 2.3).[15] A man with a metal-detector came across this artefact in 2003 at Ilam in Staffordshire and its discovery has raised a number of important issues. The 'Pan' is a copper-alloy bowl, originally fitted with a handle missing on discovery. It has complex decoration and incised text that relates it directly to the Wall. It is one of three surviving pans that commemorate the Wall through the inclusion of the names of Roman forts at the west end of the monument. The other two pans, the Rudge Cup and the Amiens *Patera*,[16] also include a schematic rendering of Hadrian's Wall that is missing from the Ilam Pan. The importance of this new discovery is that its inscription contains a record of the Wall, terming it '*val(l)i*'.[17] Roger Tomlin and Mark Hassall suggest that these vessels may have been 'souvenirs' of the west end of the Wall, perhaps suggesting that the monument was already famous in Roman times.[18] The inscription on the

---

[10]   A. Birley (1997), 130–1; Breeze (2009a), 90. For a detailed account, see A. Birley (2005), 120–2.

[11]   RFa, 152.

[12]   Collingwood (1921a), 44–5; Maxfield (1982), 62.

[13]   Collingwood (1921a), 42–5.   [14]   Maxfield (1982).

[15]   Breeze (in press); Tomlin and Hassall (2004), 344–5.

[16]   Rivet and Smith (1979), 232–3.

[17]   Tomlin and Hassall (2004), 345.

[18]   ibid., 344 n. 47; Breeze (in press).

Fig. 2.3. The Ilam Pan. Reproduced by permission of Stuart Laidlaw of the Institute of Archaeology, University College London, by courtesy of the Portable Antiquities Scheme.

Ilam Pan confirms the evidence of the *Notitia Dignitatum* and the Antonine Itinerary that the Wall was originally called '*vallum*'.[19] Tomlin and Hassall have even suggested that the reading of the Ilam Pan inscription may refer to *vallum Aelium*, or 'the Wall of Hadrian'.[20] Although this is uncertain, if this reading is accurate, 'Hadrian's Wall' is a literal translation of the monument's Roman name.

The Wall formed part of Hadrian's policy of bringing the expansion of the Roman empire to an end; fortifications were also built along the German frontier at this time.[21] The Roman fort at Newcastle was called *Pons Aelius* ('Hadrian's Bridge'), a reference to a bridge constructed possibly around the time of the emperor's visit.[22] It has been suggested that there may well have been a monumental statue of Hadrian set up at the east end of the Wall at the same time as the bridge was built.[23] Anthony Birley has argued that Hadrian directly planned the construction of the monument, possibly modelling it on the wall erected by Dionysus I at Syracuse and the Long Walls of Athens.[24]

A good deal of evidence has been collected about the sequence of the building of the various elements of the Wall and this is considered in greater detail in Chapter 12. The complex of the Wall may well have taken eight to ten years to complete and there appear to have been a number of changes of plan

---

[19] Paul Bidwell (pers. comm.).
[20] Tomlin and Hassall (2004), 345; cf. N. Hodgson (2009b), 5.
[21] A. Birley (1997), 130–1.   [22] Rivet and Smith (1979), 441.
[23] A. Birley (1997), 132–4; cf. RIB 1051.   [24] cf. Breeze (2009a).

during the construction, including the narrowing of the width of the stone structure that formed the curtain Wall and the moving of forts onto the line of the Wall.[25] Initially, it would appear that the curtain Wall was to have been built on a broad foundation around ten Roman feet (2.9 metres) wide. Sections of the Wall were constructed to this gauge and broad foundations were laid out in a number of places.[26] Sometime during the construction of the monument a decision was taken to reduce the width of the curtain Wall to provide a narrow wall of around eight Roman feet (2.4 metres) in width and the structure is even narrower than this in some places. It was not originally intended to place the forts on the line of the Wall but to maintain the pre-existing forts along the Stanegate in the hinterland as the main bases for the troops.[27] However, prior to AD 126 it appears that a decision was made to construct forts at regular intervals along the Wall's course and transfer the garrisons onto the Wall. Wall scholars today call this 'the fort decision'.[28]

The Wall and the installations along its line—including the stone curtain itself, together with the associated forts, milecastles, and *vici*—were built of local materials such as sandstones, timber, turf, and tile. All the stone was obtained from small quarries excavated close to the Wall's line.[29]

ANATOMY

The idea of *the* Wall sounds fairly simple, but the monument actually includes a number of distinct elements (Figure 2.4), the best-known and most impressive of which is the substantial stone curtain Wall,[30] which remains highly visible along some parts of its course (Figure 2.5). This standing Wall has often dominated perceptions of the monument and continues to do so today.[31] Elsewhere, these remains have been flattened by cultivation and urban development although substantial remains of the foundations of the curtain Wall are sometimes found during excavation (Figure 2.6). Reconstructions show how it might once have looked (Figure 2.7), although it should be stated that there are a number of uncertainties about the construction of the upper parts of Hadrian's stone Wall. The original height is not known, since it does not survive to its full elevation anywhere along its line. Several pieces of information have been put together to suggest an original elevation of around 3.6 metres.[32] Owing to the fact that the upper level is not preserved, it is

---

[25] RFa, 34–41.   [26] ibid., 37–8.   [27] ibid., 34.
[28] N. Hodgson (2009b), 19; but for some problems with this idea, see Crow (2004b), 127–9.
[29] RFa, 39; Hill (2006), 39.
[30] RFa, 36–41; Breeze (2006a), 53–8.
[31] Witcher (2010a), 143.   [32] Breeze (2006a), 56.

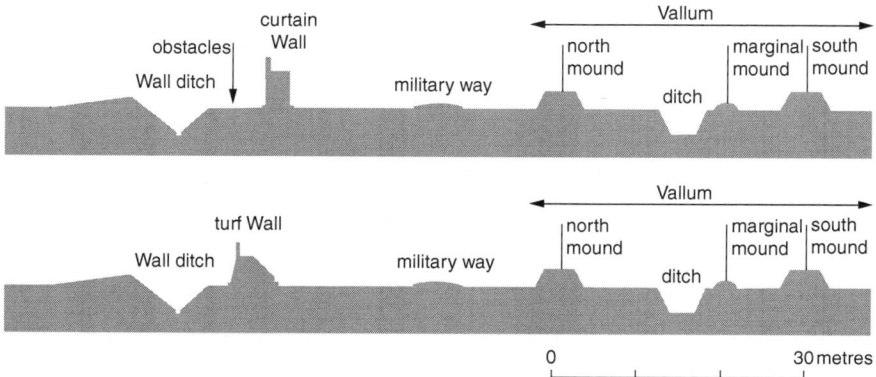

Fig. 2.4. Profiles of the major feature that make up Hadrian's Wall at two points along its course. Drawn by Christina Unwin, after Maxfield 1982, Figure 2.

Fig. 2.5. The curtain Wall on Housesteads Crags. This section of curtain Wall was heavily reconstructed during the nineteenth century and is often called the 'Clayton Wall'. Photograph by Richard Hingley, 2011.

unclear whether there was a walkway along the top or crenellations to defend those Roman soldiers who may have patrolled its line.[33]

The Wall was built by soldiers from three Roman legions—the *II Augusta*, the *VI Victrix*, and the *XX Valeria Victrix*—possibly with the assistance of labourers drawn from the civil communities of southern Britain. Stones that commemorate the building of the Wall have been found in large numbers that

---

[33] RFa, 39; Bidwell (2008); Breeze (2008a), 1.

Fig. 2.6. Foundations of the curtain Wall under excavation at Buddle Street, Wallsend. The Wall's foundations are visible under excavation and evidence for the collapse of the foundation is evident. At the end of this section on the right, a reconstruction of the curtain Wall is visible. The ditch was to the left of the curtain Wall but is not visible in this photograph. Reproduced by permission of Tyne and Wear Museum Services.

have fallen out of the face of the curtain Wall (Figure 2.8).[34] The 211 centurial stones discovered to date attest to the construction of the curtain Wall by Roman legionary detachments, each under the command of a centurion. Five building inscriptions set up by builders from the *civitates* of southern Britain have also been found along the line of the Wall, naming *Civitas Catuvellaunorum, Civitas Dumnoniorum,* and *Civitas Durotrigum Lendiniensis*[35] It is often supposed that these date from the later history of the structure, but

---

[34] RFa, 43–4.   [35] RIB, n. 1672, 1673, 1843, 1844, and 1962.

Fig. 2.7. The outer face of the modern reconstruction of the curtain Wall just to the north-west of the Roman fort and visitor centre at Wallsend. Photograph by Richard Hingley, 2010.

building inscriptions in general are rare on the Wall after the third century and there is no specific evidence to indicate that the *civitas* inscriptions were not incorporated into the curtain Wall during the second century.[36] It would appear that native peoples from certain parts of the province were used as labourers, providers of material, or as forced levies during the Wall's initial construction or at some stage in its later history.[37]

The Wall was of relatively high standard, with care taken to achieve an impressive finish in areas where large squared stones were needed, such as fort and milecastle gateways.[38] Elsewhere, its faces were of squared stones, defined as 'squared rubble' by David Breeze, sometimes set in mortar.[39] The core of the Wall was of clay or soil and stones. The curtain Wall appears to have undergone programmes of repair throughout the Roman period and evidence for the rebuilding of the stonework has been found on a number of sites along its length, although modern excavation has been conducted in a few locations and additional work is required to provide a fuller picture of its construction and reconstruction.[40] It has been suggested that a substantial rebuilding of the

---

[36] Fulford (2006). Although it has been pointed out to me that the character of the *civitas* inscriptions is quite distinct from that of the central inscriptions, which could well indicate a difference in date.

[37] Hill (2006), 114.   [38] RFa, 38.

[39] Breeze (2006a), 54.   [40] RFa, 39–40.

The stone images show inscriptions with these visible texts on their museum labels:

RECORD OF BUILDING WORK BY THE civitas
OF THE DUROTRIGIAN PEOPLE
OF LINDINIS (ILCHESTER)

'THE SIXTH COHORT, THE CENTURY
OF LOUSIUS SUAVIS (built this)'

'THE NINTH COHORT, THE CENTURY OF
PAULIUS APER (built this)'

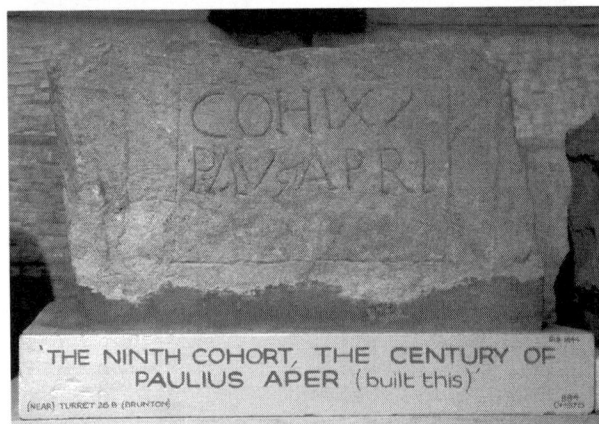

Fig. 2.8. Three Roman stones that commemorate the building of Hadrian's Wall: (top) A building stone from Hadrian's Wall that mentions the Durotrigian people of Lindinis; (middle) A centurial stone that mentions 'The Sixth Cohort of the Century of Lousius Suavis [built this]; (bottom) A centurial stone that mentions 'The Ninth Cohort of the Century of Paulius Aper [built this]'. Photographs by Richard Hingley, 2011, reproduced by permission of English Heritage and the Trustees of the Clayton Collection.

Fig. 2.9. The milecastle at Cawfields (*MC 42*), photographed from the south and showing the gates that gave access through the milecastle and the curtain Wall. Photograph by Richard Hingley, 2010.

Wall was conducted in the Severan period,[41] followed by more limited and makeshift repairs during the later third and fourth centuries.[42]

At intervals of around one Roman mile, fortified gateways with accommodation, today called milecastles, were built.[43] These were attached to the curtain Wall and contained two entrances that may have permitted passage through the line of the frontier (Figure 2.9). There are around eighty milecastles along the length of the monument that included regular passages through the curtain Wall in the original plan. It only became evident during the mid-nineteenth century that there were regular gateways through the Wall, but during the 1930s it was argued that the very few causeways across the ditch in front of the milecastles suggested that it was not possible to cross the curtain Wall at these points, despite the regular provision of gates.[44] Careful fieldwork has nevertheless suggested that many, if not all, milecastle gateways may have originally been accompanied by causeways across the ditch, which makes much more sense in terms of the original plans for the Wall.[45]

[41] Crow (1991), 55; A. Birley (2005), 183.
[42] Bidwell (1999b), 25–6.   [43] RFa, 45–7.
[44] Breeze (2008a), 3.   [45] Welfare (2000).

Fig. 2.10. The Roman turret on Hadrian's Wall at Willowford (*T 48a*). Photograph by Richard Hingley, 2010.

With the addition of the turrets, the milecastles form a regular sequence of small installations integrated into the fabric of the curtain Wall; two turrets usually occur between each pair of milecastles (Figure 2.10).[46] The milecastles and turrets are labelled using a system devised by R. G. Collingwood in 1929, in which each milecastle is numbered from east to west along the line of the Wall (e.g. *M 1*). The turrets are then annotated with an 'a' or a 'b', dividing the curtain Wall into sections one-third of a mile long (e.g. *T 1a*). Many of the turrets appear to no longer have been occupied by the late second or the early third centuries, although some may have survived into the fourth.[47]

Although the stone elements of Hadrian's Wall are, perhaps, the most visible elements of the linear frontier today, visitors can see far more of the linear earthworks that accompanied the frontier system.[48] These include the turf Wall, the northern ditch, the upcast mound, and the so-called Vallum. Some sections of the Wall were originally built in turf,[49] an element that was first recognized in 1895 during excavations close to Birdoswald (Cumbria).[50] Initially, the turf Wall formed the western counterpart to the curtain Wall from the river Irthing westwards to Bowness-on-Solway.[51] It may have been built in turf due to a lack of limestone to mix mortar along the western part of the Wall's route or because of the scarcity of good-quality stone. It was

---

[46] RFa, 47–9.   [47] ibid., 49.   [48] Wilmott and Bennett (2009), 72.
[49] Breeze (2006a), 58–62.   [50] Haverfield (1899a), 342.   [51] RFa, 41–3.

replaced by a stone curtain Wall along this section fairly soon after its initial construction. In some places, as around Birdoswald, the curtain Wall that replaced the turf Wall was built on a rather different alignment.

In front of the curtain Wall, along almost its entire length was a substantial generally V-shaped ditch with an average width of around 8.5 metres.[52] This is often the best-preserved part of the Wall complex today.[53] The ditch was evidently variable in form and the only gaps in its course are at the entrances through the Wall (mainly at the forts and milecastles), along the crags in the central section where it was evidently not required, and at the points where the curtain Wall ran along the line of the River Eden and on the Solway shore. A bank, called the 'upcast mound', is often visible to the north of the ditch. Since 1998, a number of excavations on the berm between the Wall and ditch have located systems of obstacles, which appear to have been intended to prevent access to the curtain Wall from across the ditch.[54] These were probably forked branches, set into pits that appear to be an original feature of the construction. The discovery of the obstacles has been used to argue that the Wall formed a standard military defensive line, with a walkway protected by a parapet with merlons and embrasures,[55] as shown in the reconstruction at Wallsend. This is uncertain, however, and other authors have argued that the Wall had no walkway or crenellations—a lively debate that will be considered in Chapter 14.[56]

Regular gates occurred in the line of the stone curtain Wall at the milecastles and forts, but at least two additional gateways at Port Gate and the Maiden Way are known, which do not appear to be accompanied by fortifications to the south.[57] Another feature, lying to the south of the frontier system, is the Vallum (Figure 2.11). This appears to have run along the entire length of the Wall westwards from Newcastle.[58] This structure is unique to Hadrian's Wall and the word 'Vallum' was probably the name used in Roman times for the entire frontier works, signifying a rampart, and not the earthwork complex that is attributed to this name today.[59] Antiquaries adopted this name for the earthworks and this remains in use today, although this structure is actually a ditch with two accompanying banks. The Vallum was constructed soon after, if not at the same time as, the building of the curtain Wall.[60] It is generally located just to the south of the Wall, although in its central section it diverges southwards from the Wall line as a result of the topography.[61] Although it appears to have consisted of a substantial central ditch with individual banks to each side, the Vallum varies in form along its length.[62] The relationship of

[52] Breeze (2006a), 62.   [53] RFa, 44–5.   [54] ibid., 45.
[55] ibid., 39   [56] Hill and Dobson (1992); Breeze (2008a).
[57] RFa, 49–50.   [58] Breeze (2006a), 84.   [59] Wilmott (2008), 119.
[60] RFa, 51.   [61] Wilmott (2008), 120.   [62] Breeze (2006a), 85.

Fig. 2.11. An engraving of the Vallum at Moss-kennel, just to the east of Housesteads. From J. C. Bruce 1863, 114.

the Vallum to the topography shows that it was not strictly defensive, since it ignores naturally defensible features such as bogs and hills.[63] It is likely that it defined the military zone of the Wall by forming a boundary on its south side.[64] It should be noted, however, that none of the other Roman frontier systems in Britain or overseas is known to have a comparable earthwork to define an internal zone.

Indeed, the function of the Vallum has been long contested. Francis Haverfield noted the competing views of the Vallum, including the nineteenth-century concept that it was a military work of Hadrian intended to guard the Wall from southern incursion, or that it represented a pre-Roman earthwork that was built between two tribes sometime prior to the Roman invasion.[65] He observed that, 'It has not, like Stonehenge, been attributed to the Apalachian Indians, not explained, like that, as an orrery or a theodolite, but has provoked almost as much curiosity as the great stones on the Wiltshire downs, and has defied that curiosity as successfully.' Although the Vallum does not represent a clearly defensive structure, this does not mean that it had no role in controlling movement. Eric Birley told a story about the excavation of the Vallum causeway at Benwell, recalling that someone slipped into the ditch and had to be rescued by ladder due to the steepness of the sides.[66] At

---

[63] Wilmott (2008), 125.   [64] Breeze (2006a), 86.
[65] Haverfield (1899a), 339.   [66] David Breeze (pers. comm.).

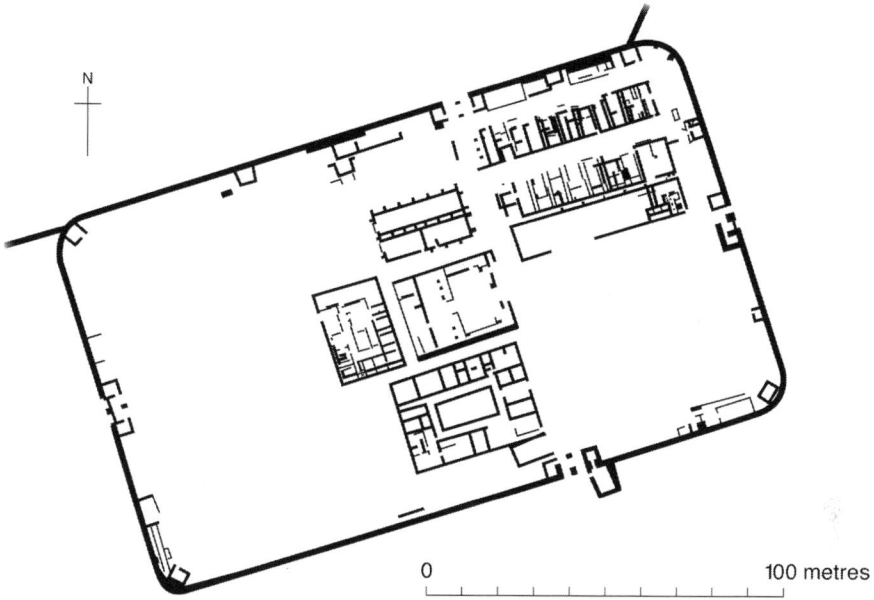

Fig. 2.12. An archaeological plan of the Roman fort at Housesteads, showing the main Roman features in the interior of the fort. Drawn by Christina Unwin, after Rushworth (2009), 2.

Black Carts, the Vallum ditch before silting was probably around 10 metres wide and over 6 metres deep.[67]

Another important element of the frontier is the Roman military way, which connected the forts, milecastles, and turrets along the Wall's line. One peculiarity is that it appears from stratigraphic evidence that this road was not built until the mid to late second century,[68] raising the problem of how communication passed along this line during the construction of the Wall and its initial occupation.

Eighteen forts are situated in close proximity to the Wall line (Figure 2.12); many were actually integrated into the curtain Wall while a few are located some way to the south. The gates in their northern defences allowed access across the curtain Wall. The chronology of the Hadrian's Wall forts demonstrates that not all are exactly contemporary with the construction of the curtain Wall and details of the chronological development of this system have emerged as a result of excavation since the nineteenth century.[69] It would appear that many are secondary to the construction of the curtain Wall and a 'fort decision' to move them up to the Wall may have been made during the reign of Hadrian.[70] It is possible that it was not initially intended to position forts on the line of the Wall and that the military units stationed at the milecastles would have observed and reported actions in the surrounding landscape.

[67] Wilmott (2008), Figure 2.   [68] RFa, 53; Breeze (2006a), 89.
[69] RFa, 63.   [70] ibid., 34.

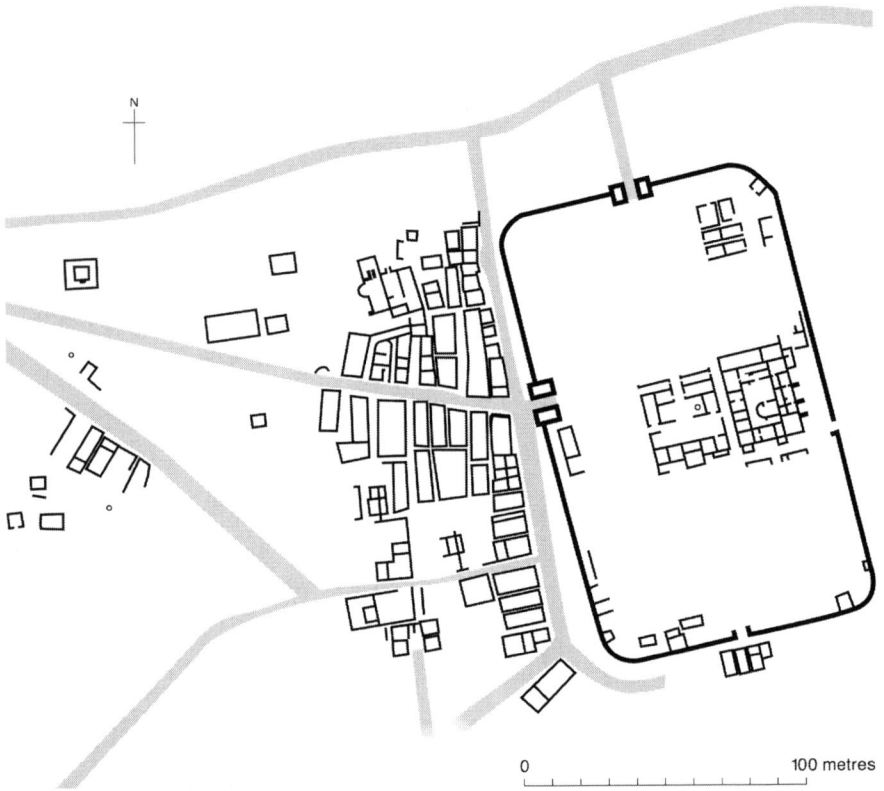

Fig. 2.13. A plan of the Roman fort and *vicus* at Vindolanda in the third and fourth centuries. Drawn by Christina Unwin, after *RFa*, Figure 29.

These forts are often associated with extensive *vici* (civil settlements; Figure 2.13). Unfortunately, excavation on the Wall has focused mainly on the curtain Wall, milecastles, and forts, and little modern work has been undertaken on the *vici*;[71] indeed only at Vindolanda has substantial modern excavation occurred.[72] Recent geophysical surveys show that some of these *vici* were very large.[73] Latin inscriptions providing evidence for the religious beliefs of the soldiers and settlers are commonly found at the extensive settlements represented by the forts and *vici* that developed during the Roman occupation of the Wall. Two substantial towns developed in close proximity to the Wall at Corbridge and Carlisle during the second to fourth centuries.[74] Corbridge was a highly impressive civil settlement with substantial and highly ornamented temples, while Carlisle may well have become a *civitas* capital during the period of Roman rule.

To the west, a series of five forts with milecastles and turrets continued the line of the Wall along the Solway coast.[75] Antiquarian authors mentioned elements of this building scheme, which was explored during the late

---

[71] RFb, 14.   [72] R. Birley (2009).   [73] RFa, 158–60.
[74] ibid., 22–6; Burnham and Wacher (1990), 51–62.   [75] RFa, 56–62.

nineteenth and throughout the twentieth centuries.[76] Its inclusion into the frontier results in the combined length of the Wall being around 120 miles. At the eastern end of the line, the fort at South Shields supplemented the Wall-forts to the south of the River Tyne. Three forts located some way north of the Wall—Birrens, Netherby, and Bewcastle—are usually defined as 'outpost forts',[77] while later forts were built at Risingham and High Rochester.[78] To the south, a network of forts and roads was connected to the Hadrian's Wall frontier.

FUNCTION

The specific reasons for the building of the Wall will not be discussed in any detail here, since these will be addressed in Chapters 12 and 14.[79] The *Historia Augusta* states that the Wall was built to separate the barbarians from the Romans and this is the only classical text that provides any idea of Hadrian's motivation for creating the structure. This text was written over two centuries later than the construction of Hadrian's Wall and although it cannot necessarily be considered a directly relevant source, Anthony Birley has argued that it contains comments copied from a lost biography of Hadrian that constitute direct evidence for the emperor's motivation.[80] The *Historia Augusta* does not, however, provide any further idea of the reasons for the construction.

Ideas about the purpose of the Wall have been discussed since the sixth century, and these will be explored in subsequent chapters. Part of the problem with trying to determine the function of Roman military frontiers is that the distribution of soldiers on frontier lines was seldom discussed in classical texts and, as a result, all modern ideas are dependent on inference from knowledge of the classical world, the archaeological remains of Roman frontier works, and on speculation.[81] A popular idea that persisted from the sixth to the nineteenth century was that the Wall was a solely defensive structure, built to keep barbarian northerners out of the Roman province towards the end of the period of imperial control in Britain. In the post-Roman era, this idea was reported by Gildas and Bede and dominated discussions about the Wall until the early twentieth century.[82] Consequentially, Victorian excavators uncovered and discussed what they considered to represent evidence for the burning and destruction of the Wall, reflecting ideas of the overthrow of the frontier during armed conflict with barbarians. Such evidence is often interpreted in different ways today.

---

[76] E. Birley (1961), 127; Collingwood (1931), 57; Bellhouse (1969).
[77] Breeze (2006a), 97. [78] ibid., 100. [79] cf. Breeze (2008a); Bidwell (2008).
[80] A. Birley (1997), 134. [81] Isaac (2000), 376–7. [82] Breeze (2008a), 1–3.

Many contemporary specialists consider that the Roman army in the 120s probably had no need to protect *Britannia* physically from invasion, since the system of roads and forts they had already constructed clearly demonstrate their domination across the landscape of central Britain. As a counter to the defensive argument, it has been claimed that the Wall acted as a way of observing the landscape and of controlling and monitoring people entering and leaving the province.[83] Parallels can be drawn with the function of the Berlin Wall before its demolition and with the role of the Israeli Separation Wall today.[84] It has also been suggested that Hadrian's Wall constituted an imperial statement of military and cultural might, planned and constructed on the instructions of the emperor.[85] Perhaps the Wall was intended to symbolize Roman identity at the frontier of the empire and to integrate soldiers from a variety of ethnic backgrounds into a coordinated imperial project that involved the construction, maintenance, and manning of a monumental frontier.[86]

These ideas will be discussed in later chapters, exploring how interpretations of the purpose of Hadrian's Wall interacted at certain times in the past with current cultural concerns. It remains clear, however, that the purpose of the Wall continues to elude us—its role is a contentious issue that continues to animate discussion.

ROMAN HISTORY

Hadrian's Wall was maintained for almost three centuries, during which time it was subjected to considerable changes. It appears to have remained in use, possibly until the early fifth century, but Hadrian's Wall should not be viewed as a monolithic structure, fixed in time and unchanging—it continued to evolve and develop throughout its Roman phase of occupation. Inscriptions mention the construction and reconstruction of various buildings in the forts along the Wall throughout its Roman period of life.[87] As we have seen, there were major phases of reconstruction of the curtain Wall, especially under Severus. The societies that developed along the Wall lived in ways that had a deep impact upon the landscape as the result of its occupation and cultivation.

During the late nineteenth century and the first sixty years of the twentieth, archaeologists established a number of 'Wall-periods' to address the history of the development of the Wall. These have since been abandoned, because they were defined in terms of the known historical events, an idea that is no longer fashionable in Roman archaeology. Since the 1980s an alternative approach supposes that each site (fort, milecastle, town) on the Wall has its own

---

[83] Collingwood (1921b); Breeze (2006a), 108.
[84] Breeze (2008a), 3.   [85] Hingley (2008c), 26–7.
[86] Hingley and Hartis (2011).   [87] RFa, 152–4.

particular history, each site with a different sequence. Nick Hodgson has recently explored the idea of reinvigorating the Wall-periods on the basis of the evidence for the communities that lived in the forts and associated settlements.[88] He has defined four phases, basing his argument on the works of David Breeze, John Dobson, and John Mann. Here they are slightly modified, with the first and second phases added below to represent the Wall's construction and its apparent abandonment during the period of the construction and use of the Antonine Wall:

(1) building of Hadrian's Wall during the 120s;
(2) abandonment during the construction and use of the Antonine Wall, from the 140s to late 150s;
(3) from the abandonment of the Antonine Wall to *c.*180;
(4) the Wall as reorganized from *c.*180 to the late third century;
(5) the Wall from 260–73 to the mid-late fourth century; and
(6) the Wall in the later fourth century and beyond.

Hadrian's Wall was largely abandoned for a time in the 140s when the Antonine Wall was built further north, but was reoccupied and recommissioned, probably in the late 150s, perhaps when the northern Wall was abandoned.[89] The third of these phases witnessed the recommissioning of the frontier, which may have commenced in AD 158 since an inscription from the Newburn area (Wall Mile 8 or 9) appears to provide evidence for the repair of the stone curtain Wall at this time.[90] It is assumed that other forts and installations that had been decommissioned in the 140s were recommissioned around this time, although the evidence for this is sparse. In the fourth period, Hadrian's Wall was reorganized and the substantial communities developed in the *vici* associated with the forts along its line.[91] There is some evidence for such civil settlements outside forts by the late second century, but the most impressive remains are third century in date.[92] At this time particular military units appear to have become permanently associated with individual forts along the Wall, represented by numerous Latin inscriptions. The *Notitia Dignitatum* records the names of many of these Roman forts,[93] information supplemented by the three *paterae* considered above, and by evidence from inscriptions. At this stage, a formerly mobile army became linked to this frontier and changes within forts attest to the gradual development of particular communities in extensive settlements spaced out along the Wall.

[88] N. Hodgson (2008), 11–13.
[89] ibid., 14.
[90] RFa, 152. N. Hodgson (2011) describes this stone, which was found in 1751 and has subsequently been lost, in detail and assesses its significance.
[91] N. Hodgson (2008), 15.
[92] RFb, 15.
[93] N. Hodgson (2008), 15; Rivet and Smith (1979), 220.

During Phase 5, it is argued that the *vici* went into 'drastic decline' around the end of the third century and that the practice of setting up dedicatory inscriptions largely ceased.[94] Further assessment is required, however, to address whether the evidence for the decline of *vici* at this time is fully conclusive. Nevertheless, new building work in the forts does indicate that these places continued into the late fourth century. It is known that the curtain Wall was repaired twice just to the west of the fort of Wallsend, probably initially in the mid-third century.[95] It has also been proposed that the building inscriptions set up by workers from the *civitates* of southern Britain are likely to date to the third or the fourth centuries although, as we have seen, there is no clear evidence to indicate that these are not second century in date. The available evidence appears to suggest that the curtain Wall was maintained in operational order throughout the third and early fourth centuries, although further excavation is required to confirm this.

After the mid fourth century the forts along the Wall were no longer maintained in their earlier forms;[96] plans of fort buildings cease to be so easily recognizable and fortifications are sometimes encased in earth ramparts or subject to running repairs. Some forts may have been abandoned during the late fourth century, but communities survived at others into the fifth century and even beyond. At Vindolanda, South Shields, and Birdoswald the evidence suggests that the Roman forts continue to be occupied beyond the end of Roman rule.[97] At Birdoswald the Phase 6 remains are defined by the excavator as 'non-Roman' and involved the erection of timber structures over a granary and earlier roads.[98] Two phases of building are represented and Tony Wilmott suggests that occupation may have ended around AD 520. A comparable sequence occurs at South Shields around the south-west gate, while a number of other Roman forts in central Britain may have continued to be occupied. It is possible that at some sites along the Wall the descendants of the Roman military units continued to be supplied locally.[99]

In the later phases of some of these forts, evidence has been found for Christianity, particularly at Vindolanda where occupation may well have continued until at least the early seventh century.[100] It is even possible that Gildas heard tales of the role and function of the Roman Wall from the descendants of the communities who lived along its line and that these informed his writing in the early sixth century. By this time, the Wall was no longer in use, but its substantial remains left a dramatic memorial of its former role and significance.

---

[94] N. Hodgson (2008), 18.   [95] Bidwell and Griffiths (1999).
[96] N. Hodgson (2008), 20.   [97] RFa, 167–70; Wilmott (2010).
[98] RFa, 167.   [99] ibid., 169.   [100] R. Birley (2009), 169.

PART I

Picts' Wall

The first section of this book considers the evidence for the Picts' Wall, addressing accounts from the sixth century to the late seventeenth. From medieval times, the monument that we know today as Hadrian's Wall was often addressed as the 'Picts' Wall',[1] Gildas and Bede commented that it had been built during the final phase of Roman rule in order to protect the lowland Britons from the attack of the Scots, Irish, and Picts, and this presumably explains why it was known by this name. The 'Picts' Wall' is, however, a strange name for a Roman monument. Indeed, William Hutton observed that the Picts 'had no concern with the Wall except to pull it down'.[2] A clue to this naming of the monument may be contained in a letter written during the late sixteenth century, probably by the curate of Haltwhistle, Christopher Ridley, in which the author refers to 'one wall builded betwixt the Brittons & Pightes (which we call the *Kepe Wall*) builded by the Pightes'.[3] This appears to record a local legend that the Wall, or at least one element of it, was the work of the Picts rather than of the Romans.[4] From the late sixteenth century, it was becoming increasingly apparent that the Wall dated to Roman times and, as a result, by the 1730s it commonly came to be known as the 'Roman Wall'. Despite this, some authors continued to use its old name during the eighteenth and nineteenth centuries, particularly when thinking about invasion or immigration from the north and west.

[1] Shannon (2007). [2] Hutton (1802), 1.
[3] E. Birley (1961), 3. [4] Bates (1895), 7–8.

3

Heavenfield: Christian Inspirations

'The Groans of the Britons' of the early half of the second century would
have been a tale fitted to move the heart of the modern Englishman.

John Collingwood Bruce (1875), xi

INTRODUCTION

Travelling west along the line of Hadrian's Wall, just before reaching the River
Tyne at Chollerford, the visitor arrives at Heavenfield. A large modern wood-
en cross marks this site of Christian pilgrimage by the side of the road running
just to the south of the Wall (Figure 3.2). The primary interest relates to the
Christian site and very little of the Roman Wall is visible here today. All that
can be seen are the slight traces of the northern ditch, running across the field
behind the cross and subtle traces of the Vallum by the roadside to the south.[1]
Beyond the line of the ditch of Hadrian's Wall is the small eighteenth-century
church of St Oswald's, reached by a footpath that crosses the field. Although it
contains no obviously early medieval material, this building may well be on

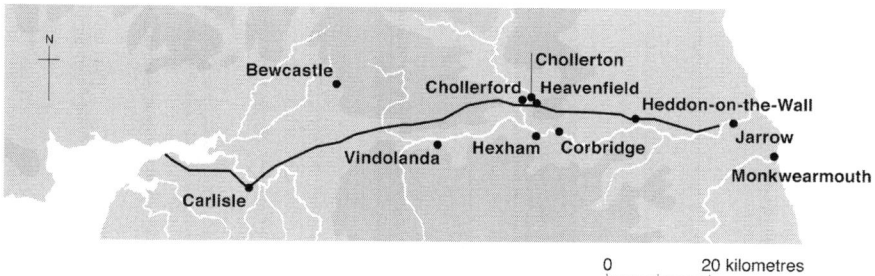

Fig. 3.1. Places mentioned in Chapter 3. Drawn by Christina Unwin.

[1] Breeze (2006a), 187.

Fig. 3.2. The modern wooden cross and the post-medieval church at Heavenfield. Photograph by Richard Hingley, 2011.

the site of an Anglo-Saxon church constructed at this place of pilgrimage.[2] It is probable that Heavenfield is a sacred site of considerable antiquity, since a battle fought in AD 635 possibly took place in the vicinity, as described in Bede's account.

Heavenfield remains a significant place today, visited on the first Saturday in August by the Annual Pilgrimage travelling from Hexham Abbey to celebrate the cult of St Oswald.[3] The church has also become the focus for another pilgrim route, since Heavenfield is at the end of St Oswald's Way, a long-distance footpath from Lindisfarne. This is one of Britain's newest long-distance paths, conceived by a local vicar to establish a short trail linking the places that had connections with the saint.[4] There are tales connected with this piece of ground. In the church, a Roman altar with an illegible inscription has a socket-hole in the top which is attributed with King Oswald's raising of the original cross; the information on display reads, 'For centuries [the] exact position [was] made known by a large stone cross set upon a Roman altar

---

[2] Frodsham (2004), 74, but see Corfe (1997).

[3] Paminter notes that an annual pilgrimage from Hexham to Heavenfield is still held on St Oswald's day (2007, 126).

[4] *The Guardian* (2008); Paminter (2007).

which stood south of the church.' It has even been suggested that Oswald's wooden cross was inserted into this hole.[5] This may constitute an example of the Christianization of a Roman altar. Tim Eaton has pointed out that those who reused the altar might have taken the plant scroll at the base to indicate that it was originally a Christian monument.[6] Bede's account (iii. 2) does not, however, support the idea that Oswald's cross was erected on top of this altar, since it refers to the cross being stood in a hole in the earth. Indeed, the date of the Christianization of this altar is uncertain; another Roman altar was reused as the base of a medieval cross in Corbridge market place.[7]

As a locus for medieval and modern pilgrimage, Heavenfield attracts visitors for spiritual and religious reasons. In this chapter, the writings of Gildas and Bede are used to argue that the Wall had a particularly Christian association, since these authors viewed it as the final work of a lost empire that had introduced Christianity to Britain. Today the accounts of Gildas and Bede are considered to be mythical. Since they contain little relevant historical or archaeological information, they are not usually addressed in publications concerning Hadrian's Wall written during the past century. If mentioned at all, Gildas and Bede are usually dismissed without very much consideration. For example, in his study of antiquarian research on the Wall, Eric Birley does not mention Gildas but suggests that Bede qualifies for inclusion because he provides some precise figures for the width and height of the Wall.[8] Birley's comments suggest that archaeological endeavour involves the measurement and description of ancient remains and the construction of ideas of chronology and function. In this context, the only comments made by Bede of relevance are the ones that give details of the monument's physical dimensions, since the Wall was better preserved in his day.

A rather different approach is taken in this chapter. The writings of Gildas and Bede indicate that during the centuries following the ending of Roman rule, at least some educated people in Lowland Britain retained an impression of the origin and history of the Wall. Bede's and Gildas' accounts are important in themselves, since they provide significant interpretations of the Wall, but they also had a sustained impact on later work.[9] Gildas and Bede had no exact information regarding the date of the Wall, describing it as a late Roman or immediately post-Roman construction. They attested to the armed defence of the Wall-walk against northern marauders, an idea that is no longer accepted by many archaeologists.[10] Gildas may have depended for much of his information about the Wall on local legends,[11] but these writings cannot simply be dismissed as irrelevant to the history of the Wall.

---

[5] For this idea, see Whitworth (2000), 12.   [6] Eaton (2000), 73–4.
[7] ibid., 75.   [8] E. Birley (1961), 1.   [9] Maxfield (1982), 63.
[10] e.g. Breeze (2008a).   [11] Jones (1996), 49–50.

GILDAS AND THE 'GROANS OF THE BRITONS'

A century before the battle of Heavenfield, Gildas had discussed the Roman Wall in his work *De Excidio Britonum* (*The Ruin of Britain*). It is unclear when this was written and a date of around AD 540 has been suggested,[12] although it may have been produced a few decades earlier.[13] It is uncertain where Gildas lived but it was possibly in the south of Britain. It is often observed that he was a preacher or a prophet, rather than a historian,[14] and that his comments on the history of Britain do not have credibility since he focuses on events that can be used negatively to enhance his moralizing message.[15] Gildas' narrative was presumably based on oral sources,[16] although he may have had access to a few relevant classical accounts.[17] Gildas strongly criticizes the activities of the Britons and exhorts them to reform their ways in order to forestall God's wrath.[18] He includes a general account of Britain's past, dealing with the Roman conquest and control of the island and giving particular prominence to the introduction of Christianity (Gildas, 8–12). The departure of the Romans is related to the reign of the Emperor Maximus (Magnus Maximus) who, by taking his retinue to Gaul, left Britain effectively independent of Roman rule (Gildas, 13). The classical texts available today suggest that in AD 383 the Roman commander Maximus raised a revolt and took an army to the continent before being defeated by the Emperor Theodosius in 388.[19] Roman rule in Britain actually appears to have continued for two decades after Maximus' defeat but, although Gildas was aware of the significance of Maximus, he does not appear to have had access to a detailed account of events in Britain during the late fourth and early fifth centuries.

Gildas' account presents some information on the history and structure of the two Roman Walls of Britain, probably derived from oral history and folklore.[20] He states that once the Romans had left Britain under Maximus, the Scots and the Picts attacked and that the British sent a request to Rome for aid (Gildas, 14). According to Gildas, Rome sent a legion to assist them and also instructed the Britons to construct a wall (*murus*) to link the two seas but, since this was the work of a 'leaderless and irrational mob' and was made of turf rather then stone, it proved to be ineffective (Gildas, 15, 3). Again, under pressure after the old enemies broke through the frontier, the British requested aid resulting in the Romans building a wall (*murus*) of stone that linked towns (*urbes*) that happened to be located there 'out of fear of the enemy' (Gildas, 18, 2).[21] Gildas mentioned that the Romans drew on public and private funds

---

[12] Morris (1978), 1; Jones (1996), 44–6.   [13] Kerlouégan (2004).
[14] Sims-Williams (1995a), 2; Jones (1996), 43.
[15] cf. Dumville (1984), 64; Sutherland (1984), 157.   [16] Morris (1978), 3.
[17] Higham (1991), 4–5.   [18] Jones (1996), 124.   [19] Casey (2002), 89–90.
[20] Collingwood (1921a), 46–7.   [21] See Sims-Williams (1995a), 18, n. 78.

(*sumtu publico privatoque*) for building this Wall and made the 'wretched inhabitants' (*miserabilibus indigenis*) cooperate with them in their work (Gildas, 18.2).

When the Scots and the Picts attacked again, they seized the whole north of Britain right up to the Wall (Gildas, 19, 1–2). Gildas (2) observes:

> A force was stationed on the high towers to oppose them, but it was too lazy to fight, and too unwieldy to flee; the men were foolish and frightened, and they sat about day and night, rotting away in their folly. Meanwhile there was no respite from the barbed spears flung by their naked opponents, which tore our wretched countrymen from the walls and dashed them to the ground. Premature death was in fact an advantage to those who were thus snatched away; for their quick end saved them from the miserable fate that awaited their brothers and children.

The towns and the 'high wall' (*muroque celso*) were abandoned and the 'miserable remnants' of the population sent a letter for further aid to the Roman commander 'Agitius' containing 'the groans of the British' (*gemitus Britannorum*; Gildas 20, 1–2).[22] This plea remained unanswered.[23]

AN EASTERN COMMENT ON THE WALL

Procopius, a contemporary of Gildas from the eastern Roman empire, presented a very different view of the Wall.[24] This suggests that even in the sixth century, some Romans still regarded Britain as under its sovereignty. In *De bello Gothico* (2.6.27–29), Procopius recorded that when Belisarius was negotiating with the Gothic King Vitigis in 537, the royal emissaries offered to surrender Sicily. Belisarius responded:

> 'That everything we have said is true none of you can be unaware. But so that we may not seem to be contentious, we give up to you Sicily, which is of such great size and such wealth, without which, indeed, it is not possible for you safely to possess Libya'. And Belisarius said: 'And we agree that the Goths should have the whole of Britain, which is much larger than Sicily and has long since been subject to the Romans. For it is proper to make an equal return to those who first do a good deed or perform a kindness'.[25]

Procopius appears to have possessed little current information about Britain. Later in *De bello Gothico* (4.20), it is indicated that he thought that it consisted

---

[22] cf. Higham (1991), 3.

[23] This unsuccessful appeal to the Romans was presumably made to Aetius and may have occurred between 446 and 454 (A. Birley 2005, 464).

[24] I am grateful to Anthony Birley for drawing my attention to this passage.

[25] For this translation and the comments in the following paragraph, see A. Birley (2005), 464.

of two islands, Brettania ($B\rho\epsilon\tau\tau\alpha\nu\acute{\iota}a$), 'to the west about in line with the far end of Spain', and Brittia ($B\rho\iota\tau\tau\acute{\iota}a$), 'towards the rear of Gaul' (4.20.5). After a lengthy anecdote about a sister of a king of the Angili of Brittia, who was betrothed to the son of a king of the Varni (4.20.11–41), Procopius told a story about the Wall: 'in this island of Brittia the men of old built a long wall, cutting off a large part of it.' To the east of the Wall the climate was healthy, many people lived there, and the land was fertile; but to the west it was said that people could not survive for more than half an hour in a land infested with snakes (4.20.42–47). Finally, he feels obliged to add 'a story which bears a very close resemblance to mythology' that the souls of the dead are brought to Brittia (4.20.47–55).

Anthony Birley has suggested that Procopius' comments may well represent a late fifth- or early sixth-century traveller's tale about the Wall.[26] These ideas were picked up by the Victorian antiquary John Collingwood Bruce to address a folktale related to a place called 'Bogle Hole' on the Wall, as explored in Chapter 10.

BEDE'S 'WRETCHED BRITONS' AND THEIR WALLS

Bede was a Northumbrian monk who lived at the monastery of Jarrow, finishing his work *The Ecclesiastical History of the English People* in AD 731.[27] Part of his account addresses the Roman Walls and draws directly on Gildas and other sources,[28] including the classical author Orosius.[29] Gildas' attribution of the two Walls to the end of the Roman period suggests that their earlier history had been forgotten,[30] a tradition built upon by Bede who probably had some personal experience of the Wall since he described its structure in some detail (Bede, i. 12).[31]

Like Gildas, Bede sought to derive morals from history. He refers to physical features of the past, including three Roman Walls, in order to make connections between past and present.[32] In this context, he stressed the supposed conversion of the Britons to Christianity during the Roman period and the inclusion of Britain in a Christian empire prior to its loss in the fifth century. Bede addresses the mythical conversion of the Britons by Eleutherius, bishop of the Church at Rome, at the request of the (apocryphal) King Lucius during the second century (Bede, i, 4).[33] The loss of religious faith as a result of the

---

[26] A. Birley (2005), 465.   [27] Colgrave (1969), xvii–xx.

[28] Colgrave and Mynors (eds. 1969), 44–5 n 2; Sims-Williams (1995b), 5.

[29] Wallace-Hadrill (1988), 18; Shannon (2007), 4.

[30] Collingwood (1921a), 46.   [31] cf. Colgrave and Mynors (eds. 1969), 44–5 n. 2.

[32] cf. Higham (2006), 170.   [33] ibid., 86.

invasion of Lowland Britain by pagan incomers is, therefore, blamed on the Britons.[34] Bede's writings on Hadrian's Wall are to be seen in this context, since the Christian faith of the people occupying this part of Britain became threatened as a result of the overthrowing of the frontier. Conflicts on this frontier in the Roman and immediately post-Roman periods had an immediate relevance to Bede, since his early life was characterized by the attempts of the Christian kings of Northumbria to conquer and control peoples to the north and west.[35]

Bede's account of Roman Walls in Book I of the *Ecclesiastical History* describes the remains of three distinct fortifications. He recorded that Severus, an African by race, became emperor in AD 189. After settling troubles in the wider empire and in Britain he decided to separate the part of the island over which he had regained control from the unconquered tribes, not by building a 'wall' (*murus*) but through the construction of a 'rampart' (*uallum*) (Bede i.5). Bede draws on Vegitius and notes that a wall is made of stone but a rampart is made of sods cut from the earth.[36] He described how Severus constructed a great ditch (*magnam fossam*) from sea to sea and a very strong rampart (*firmissimumque uallum*) that was fortified by numerous towers along its line (Bede, i. 5).[37] It appears from Bede's subsequent comments that this ditch and rampart followed the line of the monument that we know as Hadrian's Wall. Indeed, it appears to have been the earthwork now known as the Vallum that Bede had in mind when commenting on a ditch and rampart,[38] although the source of his comment about towers is unclear. Bede's term *uallum* was, in turn, taken up by William Camden when he wrote, in the first detailed account of the Wall, that the Emperor Severus built a '*Vallum* or Rampier . . . of turffes' along this line.[39] The modern use of the term 'Vallum' to describe these earthworks derives from Bede and from Camden.

Later in the first book, Bede observes that, after the departure of the Romans from Britain, the Britons asked Rome for aid because of the ravages of the Irish and Picts and because they were ignorant of the practice of war (Bede, i. 12). After driving the enemy out, the Romans urged the Britons to build a wall for protection, while the legions returned home. This is the second Wall described by Bede; he notes that, because it was built of turf, it was ineffective. He also records that its remains are still visible between *Peanfahel* or *Penneltun* (Kinneil) and *Alcluith* (Dumbarton), representing the monument today known as the Antonine Wall.[40] After further incursions from the north,

---

[34] ibid., 87.   [35] Colgrave (1969), xxvii–xxviii.
[36] Wallace-Hadrill (1988), 11–12.
[37] These observations draw upon the classical author Orosius' observations (7.17). For a translation of Orosius' observations on the Wall, see A. Birley (2005), 200.
[38] Collingwood (1921a), 47.   [39] Camden (1610), 790–1.
[40] Colgrave and Mynors (eds. 1969), 42–3 n. 1.

another Roman legion was dispatched to Britain and drove back the barbarians, building the third fortification, a strong wall (*murum*) of stone in a straight line between the towns or fortifications (*urbes*) on the line of Severus' Vallum (Bede, i. 12). Bede drew on Gildas in suggesting that this latest Wall was built at public and private expense (*sumtu publico priuatoque*) and with the help of the Britons. He referred to the Wall as 'famous' (*famosum*) and notes that its remains were still highly visible (*conspicuum*), describing it as eight feet wide and twelve feet high.

Bede then described the inability of the Britons to defend this latest Wall against the attacks of the Irish and the Picts: 'The cowardly defenders were wretchedly dragged from the walls and dashed to the ground. In short they deserted their cities, fled from the walls, and were scattered. The enemy pursued and there followed a massacre more bloodthirsty than ever before. The wretched Britons were torn in pieces by their enemies like lambs by wild beasts.' As in Gildas' account, the turf Wall is viewed as a British construction and the stone Wall as having been built by the Romans with the assistance of the Britons. Its overthrow is viewed as a result of the inability of the Lowland Britons to defend themselves.

The Walls are not described in any great detail either in the accounts of Gildas or Bede. Bede appears to have drawn a distinction between the monuments known today as the curtain Wall and the Vallum. He also appears to have distinguished between the towers along the line of Severus' Wall and the later *urbes* that existed when the latest Wall was built. This has been taken to indicate that he was aware that the Wall of Severus had been subject to considerable alteration between the early third and the early fifth centuries.[41] Bede's description of the curtain Wall suggests that he had visited the remains himself and it has been argued that, if any of the Latin inscriptions along its line were still visible in the eighth century, he did not read them, since they would have provided a more exact date for the construction of the monument.[42] It is possible that all the Latin inscriptions had been obscured by this time.

Later in his ecclesiastical history, Bede discusses the battle of Heavenfield. Narrating the events of AD 635, he describes the actions of King Oswald of Northumbria, who defeated the king of the Britons, Cædwalla (Bede, iii, 1–2). About to engage in battle, Oswald set up the 'sign of the holy cross' and prayed to God to send heavenly aid in this time of dire need; it is clear from the narrative that this was a wooden cross. Bede recalled that the place of Oswald's victory was still known and that the brethren of the church at *Hagulstad* (Hexham) travelled there once a year on the day before the anniversary of the king's death to celebrate his cult. Innumerable miracles of healing were known

---

[41] Colgrave and Mynors (eds. 1969), 44 no. 1.   [42] Whitworth (2000), 45.

to have occurred there and people were still in the habit of cutting splinters of wood from the cross and putting them in water for sick men or animals to drink. Bede states that this place is called 'Hefenfeld' and notes that it is close to the Roman Wall on its north side and that a church had recently been built here (Bede, iii, 2).

Bede's 'Hefenfeld' is very possibly the location of the modern cross and eighteenth-century church at Heavenfield. The Christian emphasis in Bede's account of the battle suggests, however, that his observations should be assessed critically. The defeated Cædwalla was a Christian king and Christianity was only recently established among Oswald's followers.[43] The story of Heavenfield appears to have more to do with creating an origin myth for Christianity rather than being a straightforward account of a historical battle, while it also claims the remains of the Wall for the English and illustrates the continuing tactical and military significance of the Roman works.[44] The significance of Oswald's victory is that it was deemed to have been fundamental to the success of Christianity in Northumbria, an issue of deep concern to Bede and his followers.[45] It is, therefore, not entirely clear that the location today called Heavenfield is the site of the place of pilgrimage, or the church mentioned by Bede.[46] Indeed, it has long been supposed that the battle may have been fought 10 or 12 kilometres to the south of modern Heavenfield but that the army may have mustered at this place.[47] The Pilgrimage to the modern church and cross was revived in 1927 from the ancient practice mentioned in Bede, providing a further demonstration of the power of this tradition.[48]

THE LASTING INFLUENCE OF GILDAS AND BEDE

These writings had a deep impact upon later ideas about Hadrian's Wall, partly due to their dramatic style recounting the dying days of Roman Britain and partly as a result of the general scarcity of classical texts that addressed the construction, use, and desertion of the structure. Significant issues arise from these accounts that re-emerge in tales told of the frontier in later times. Five themes will be introduced here which will be discussed in later sections of this book: the Wall's Christian associations; the dating of the curtain Wall to the late fourth or early fifth century; the idea that the Wall was built for and at least partly by the southern Britons; the supposedly defensive character of the

---

[43] Orton and Wood (2007), 171.   [44] Rob Collins (pers. comm.).
[45] Frodsham (2004), 74.   [46] Orton and Wood (2007), 171.
[47] Corfe (1997), 66.   [48] ibid.

Wall as a line of fortification; and the suggestion that urban sites occurred along its line.

It is unclear from Bede whether King Oswald raised his cross on a site close to the Wall for reasons that related directly to a supposed Christian identity for this monument or whether the battle was fought here purely for strategic reasons. It is possible, however, that the deeply Christian interpretation of the decline and fall of Roman power in Britain present in the writing of Gildas prompted Oswald and his followers to associate the remains of the Wall with the Christian identity of the population of the Wall-zone in late Roman times.[49] The archaeological evidence for late- and immediately post-Roman Christianity on Hadrian's Wall is limited but increasing,[50] including signifi-cant information from Vindolanda.[51] Communities appear to have been living well into the fifth century and probably beyond at Roman forts along the Wall and in its hinterland. They may have been the source of Gildas' knowledge for the post-Roman history of the Wall, with their memories of the construction and function of the monument.[52]

The associations between Christianity and the Wall in the post-Roman period appear to be more extensive than just one location at Heavenfield. Early medieval churches in southern Britain were often built on the site of Roman remains, or include Roman stones within their structures, possibly drawing on a religious association of stone-built Roman remains with the idea of the introduction of Christianity into Britain in Roman times.[53] Paul Bidwell has made the intriguing suggestion that the landscape of Roman ruins across the Wall-zone was crucial to the programme of stone church building con-ducted during the seventh and eighth centuries.[54] This was a recognizably Roman landscape with a comparable range of monuments—including stone bridges, temples, and the large mausoleum at Corbridge—to those of Italy and southern Gaul. St Wilfrid, bishop of Hexham, will have seen such structures during his visits to the continent and clearly drew upon these Roman ruins when he arranged for the construction of his new monastery at Hexham in the 670s. Indeed, churches built in the classical Mediterranean style would have been in harmony with the Roman landscape of the Wall and Bidwell has proposed that this provides the context for stone churches constructed at Hexham, Monkwearmouth, and Jarrow.

There are a number of additional potentially early church sites along the line of the Wall close to Carlisle,[55] including the outpost fort at Bewcastle, where the eighth-century cross has recently been directly related to the former

---

[49] cf. Higham (1991), 12.   [50] RFa, 169; Wilmott (2010), 14–15.
[51] R. Birley (2009), 169–72.   [52] Matt Chesnais (pers. comm.).
[53] T. Bell (2005), 19–20; cf. Eaton (2000).
[54] Bidwell (2010), 131–4; Paul Bidwell (pers. comm.); cf. Eaton (2000), 127.
[55] T. Bell (2005), 88.

Fig. 3.3. The Bewcastle cross from the south-east. Photograph by Richard Hingley, 2011.

Roman presence at the site (Figure 3.3).[56] The ecclesiastical establishments at Corbridge, Chollerford, and Heddon-on-the-Wall were also built close to the surviving remains of the Wall using Roman material.[57] Medieval churches were also constructed using inscribed stones from the Wall and there are a number of churches along its line that were fitted with fonts, stoups, or *piscinae* made from Roman altars, such as those at St Giles at Chollerton

[56] Orton and Wood (2007).   [57] Whitworth (2000), 10–14.

and St Andrew in Corbridge. Tim Eaton has proposed that these objects were reused because of their Roman origins and Latin inscriptions.[58] Perhaps the Roman identity of this landscape of ruins was being recreated as a result of the construction of Christian buildings throughout early medieval and medieval times.[59]

Gildas and Bede provided a date for the construction of the curtain Wall during the late fourth or fifth century. From an archaeological perspective, this is an error,[60] since by the early twentieth century antiquarian and archaeological research had conclusively demonstrated that it was built during the early second century AD. This does not, however, make the writings of Gildas and Bede irrelevant.[61] This received dating for the Wall to the late Roman period deeply influenced many accounts of the monument until the early eighteenth century. At this time, antiquaries drew upon classical texts and Roman inscriptions collected from the Wall to argue that Severus had built the curtain Wall. Subsequently, antiquaries tended to emphasize the building of the Wall by a succession of Romans, including the general Agricola, the Emperor Hadrian, and finally Septimius Severus. Nevertheless, these authors continued to quote Bede and Gildas when addressing the last phase of the use of the Wall during the abandonment of Britain by the Romans. It was not possible for antiquaries to write out entirely such powerful ideas concerning the purpose of the monument, and the writings of Gildas and Bede on the late Roman history of the Wall continued to be quoted in scholarly texts during the second half of the nineteenth century.[62]

In the accounts of Gildas and Bede, the Britons living to its south have a role, if only a subservient one, in the building of the curtain Wall. The idea that Britons helped to build and man the Wall became important from the late sixteenth century, when English commentators began to think about their identity apart from the Scots and the Irish. Indeed, the idea of a Lowland British contribution to the construction of the Wall provided English scholars with a clear genetic connection with these people. It also labelled those who lived beyond the Wall as disruptive barbarians and, from a literal reading of Gildas and Bede, as pagans. From the late sixteenth century, however, the English did not always identify themselves with the ancient British population of Lowland Britain, often claiming Teutonic ancestry instead.[63] Despite this, the spatial and perceived genetic association between ancient Britons living to the south of the Wall and the contemporary English was often upheld from the Renaissance to Victorian times and beyond.[64] This is one reason for the

---

[58] Eaton (2000), 67–72.   [59] Paul Bidwell (pers. comm.).
[60] Stevens (1941b), 359.   [61] E. James (2001), 96; Stevens (1941b), 353.
[62] e.g. J. C. Bruce (1875), xi–xii.
[63] Floyd-Wilson (2002); Kidd (1999), 99–122; Williams (2008).
[64] Hingley (2008a).

development of the concept that the Wall represented the geographical (or metaphorical) boundary of English identity, a theme that will be considered in the following chapter.

The idea that the Lowland Britons helped to construct the Wall remained current for a long time in antiquarian writings and popular culture. In 1857, William Bell Scott produced a painting for Wallington Hall (Northumberland), the Trevelyan family home near Newcastle, entitled *Building of the Roman Wall*, an image that is discussed in detail in Chapter 9. Drawing on the accounts of Gildas and Bede, it depicts subdued Britons put to use as labourers under the control of Roman officers. This painting is the first of a series representing local history that finishes with the Industrial Revolution in Victorian Tyneside.[65] In the background of the Roman painting, barbarous Picts or Caledonians threaten the progress on the Wall. Soldiers and civilians from across the empire, including Britons, are involved in building the Wall, while Picts or Caledonians attack it—a topic that will be considered further in Chapter 9. The Wall scholar John Collingwood Bruce also reflected on the role of the Britons in the construction of the Wall, observing that: 'Had they an historian amongst them, "The Groans of the Britons" of the early half of the second century would have been a tale fitted to move the heart of the modern Englishman.'[66] Other Edwardian illustrations of the Wall projected the writings of Gildas and Bede in visual form.

In modern times, the suggestion that Britons helped to build the Wall has found some support.[67] C. E. Stevens suggested that the five stones from the Wall recording the activities of British *civitates* in the construction works related to rebuilding activities on the Wall in AD 369 and that Gildas' account recalled the memory of the rebuilding and manning of Hadrian's Wall by British soldiers at this time.[68] As has been shown above, these stones could equally well date to the second century,[69] but their evidence does support Gildas' and Bede's contention that the Britons helped to construct, or to reconstruct, the Wall.[70]

The accounts of Gildas and Bede portray the Wall as directly defensive, built to counter the armed attacks on the province by peoples from the north. This focus on armed defence is a recurring motif in images of the Wall through time, although it has no support from the available classical texts.[71] Many archaeologists today see the Wall as a line of observation and means to control

---

[65] R. Trevelyan (1994), 56–7.   [66] J. C. Bruce (1875), xi.

[67] cf. Abbatt (1849), 10–11.

[68] Stevens (1941a), 148–9; see Wallace-Hadrill (1988), 18; cf. Breeze and Dobson (2000), 235–46.

[69] Fulford (2006).

[70] Stevens (1941b), 359.

[71] Nick Hodgson (pers. comm.) has pointed out to me that no other specific functions for the Wall are provided by the classical texts.

Fig. 3.4. A painting by Robert Spence titled *Night Attack* (1912–14). Reproduced by permission of the Great North Museum and Society of Antiquaries of Newcastle upon Tyne.

the movement of people.[72] The idea of the manning of a fortified military boundary has, however, proved incredibly resistant to change from the sixteenth to the early twentieth centuries, being particularly emphasized in troubled times, for instance in Victorian and Edwardian artworks.[73] In Robert Spence's *Night Attack*, a heavily defended fort on the Wall is subject to armed attack from northern barbarians (Figure 3.4), an idea that draws deeply on Gildas and Bede and one that is reflected in Rudyard Kipling's influential novel, *Puck of Pook's Hill* (1906). Nick Higham has argued that Gildas'

---

[72] Collingwood (1921b); Breeze (2008a).
[73] Chapters 12 and 14 discuss the development of a less directly defensive explanation for the Wall during the twentieth century.

writings on the defensive nature of Hadrian's Wall are 'rather Kiplingesque' drawing on the fact that the accounts of Gildas and Bede have long had a deep influence on the defensive interpretations of Hadrian's Wall.[74] These Edwardian images project imperial concerns by drawing on the work of early medieval authors who addressed the Wall. Earlier ideas derived from the Wall were transformed for contemporary times, emphasizing the considerable power of the monument in the making of myths.

Gildas and Bede both wrote about certain Roman places on the Wall as '*urbes*'. Colgrave and Mynors translated Bede's use of this Latin term as 'fortifications',[75] although it is more usual to translate it to refer to walled cities or walled towns. This term was to prove significant from the late sixteenth century, since the concept of an urban civilization along the line of Hadrian's Wall was developed from this time.[76] At various times, antiquaries have interpreted the forts and the milecastles as the remains of former towns or cities. This idea survived until the late nineteenth century, since prior to this time excavators had interpreted the central headquarters buildings of the Roman forts at Chesters, South Shields, and Hardknott (Lake District) as the *fora* (public squares) of small Roman cities. It was not until the late nineteenth century, when the results of a number of excavations on sites along the Roman frontiers in Britain and Germany were available, that archaeologists began to argue that the majority of the Roman 'stations' along the line of Hadrian's Wall were military rather than civil establishments. This was part of the gradual comprehension of what are now termed the 'civil' and 'military' areas of Roman Britain.[77] The concept of urban centres along the Wall has been subsequently revived by the discovery of extensive *vici* (civil settlements) located outside the gates of the forts.[78] As a result, the urban status of these places is now being emphasized once more as part of a broader agenda that is stressing the nature of the Roman army as a community, a topic explored in greater detail in Chapter 15.

The study of Roman inscriptions that attested to the construction and reconstruction of the Wall gradually led to the overturning of Gildas' and Bede's interpretations of the monument, but their accounts still remained. Ideas derived from Bede and Gildas survived well into the early twentieth century in popular writings. Certain writers, novelists, and artists have drawn upon the powerful image of imperial and provincial decline presented by the early medieval authors in order to recreate an imaginative Roman Britain for the requirements of the Victorian and Edwardian periods. Accounts of the history and sequence of the Wall and its landscape should not dismiss the

---

[74] Higham (1991), 4.
[75] Colgrave and Mynors (eds. 1969), 45; cf. Campbell (1978), 34–7.
[76] cf. Higham (1991), 7.
[77] Haverfield (1906); cf. Hingley (2008a), 319.   [78] RFa, 65.

significance of the writings of Gildas and Bede; indeed, the distinction between 'fact' and 'fiction' in the study of the Wall's history is not always entirely clear cut.

SUMMARY: A CHRISTIAN MONUMENT

Bede's and Gildas' accounts of the Wall had a significant impact upon later works, while Procopius' observations were rarely referenced. These texts were attractive to later authors and artists, partly because they overlaid a moral story onto the history and sequence of the Walls, projecting ideas that, by the early twentieth century, were often being undermined by archaeological research. From a strictly archaeological point of view, the five themes identified above may appear to have little to do with the structure and history of Hadrian's Wall itself. It is important to remember, however, that the attitudes projected in the writings of Gildas and Bede have helped to create the monument that people visit and read about today, including the site at Heavenfield and the ecclesiastical establishments in the landscape of the Wall. The sequence of activity at Heavenfield—including the use of the Roman altar in the church, the location of the eighteenth-century church, and the erection of the modern wooden cross, together with the development of the pilgrimage footpath—all draw upon the memory of this place and they have created eddies in time.

As a place of memory, Heavenfield is closely connected with ideas of the victory of the Christian religion in the early medieval North, but it is important to bear in mind the influence of Bede's writing on later generations. The elaborations and changes that have been made as a result of the reception of Bede's story throughout time, separating him from the construction of the Church at Heavenfield, cannot be known. There is an absence of archaeological evidence to link St Oswald to this particular place; an archaeological project conducted at this site might provide relevant information. Apart from the slight traces of the Roman Wall, the Roman altar, and a few other additional Roman stones kept at the church, the physical remains at Heavenfield are entirely eighteenth-century and later in date. Legends, oral history, and folklore clearly influence the ways that people respond to and influence the material world. Additional examples of the interrelationship between archaeology and myth will be studied in subsequent chapters.

4

Lanercost Priory: The Wall
and the English border

The mid fourth century Roman frontier is still the border between
England and Scotland.

John Morris (1978, 4)

INTRODUCTION

This chapter will review the formation of the northern frontier of the kingdom
of England from the eleventh to the later sixteenth century. Through a study of
the physical and symbolic roles of the Wall, the origins of the concept linking
this Roman monument to the delimitation of the northern boundary of
England will be explored. This theme draws upon a significant location
along the Wall's line, Lanercost Priory (Cumbria). Lanercost is a medieval
religious house that was founded during the later twelfth century, in the
contested borderlands between England and Scotland (Figure 4.2). The Priory
is in the guardianship of English Heritage and visitors may explore the
impressive remains of the church and associated buildings. The construction
of the Priory drew both physically and conceptually upon the remains of the

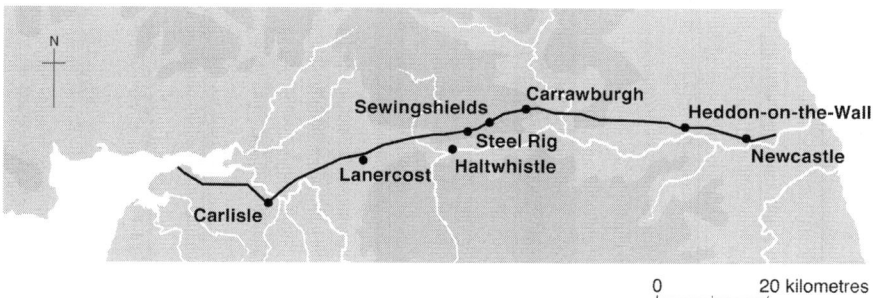

Fig. 4.1. Places mentioned in Chapter 4. Drawn by Christina Unwin.

Fig. 4.2. A view of the Priory church at Lanercost, from the north-west. Photograph by Richard Hingley, 2011.

Picts' Wall located 700 metres to the north. During the late sixteenth century, the buildings of the converted Priory were the home of Christopher Dacre, one of the Elizabethan gentlemen responsible for the maintenance of order along England's northern frontier.[1]

The surviving remains of the Picts' Wall at Lanercost and elsewhere were of considerable significance at this time. Keith Robbins has argued that the high visibility of the physical remains of the Wall along its central section has suggested that a frontier in this region of the English–Scottish border was perceived as 'natural' from medieval times.[2] The fabric of the Wall appears to have been very well preserved during the medieval period, as much of its stone was not robbed until the sixteenth century or later.[3] In 1599, William Camden explored a ruined but well-preserved Wall and wrote that in the wastes in the upland sections of its course, 'I my selfe have beheld with my owne eyes on either side, huge peeces thereof standing for a great way together, only wanting their battlements'.[4] Evidently, much of the stonework of the curtain Wall remained in place. Although medieval maps of England indicate the Wall's approximate location, often showing a set of battlements along its top (Figure 4.3), George Lily's map, printed in Rome in 1546, portrays a ruin with gateways and gaps (Figure 4.4). William Shannon has suggested that Lily's depiction of the Wall may have been based on a description of its remains that he derived from Polydore Vergil, although this is unsubstantiated.[5]

---

[1] Summerson (2004).   [2] Robbins (1998), 25.
[3] Eaton (2000), 25–6.   [4] Camden (1610), 793.
[5] Shannon (2007), 26–7.

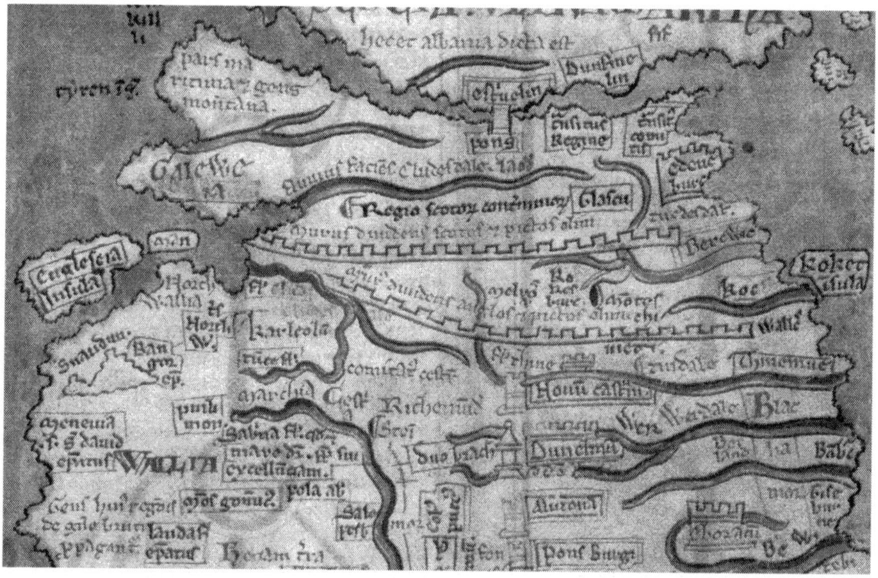

Fig. 4.3. An excerpt from Mathew Paris' 'Map A', *c.*1250 of Great Britain, showing the two Roman Walls of Britain. Reproduced by permission of the British Library, Cotton Ms, Claudius D.VI, fol. 12v.

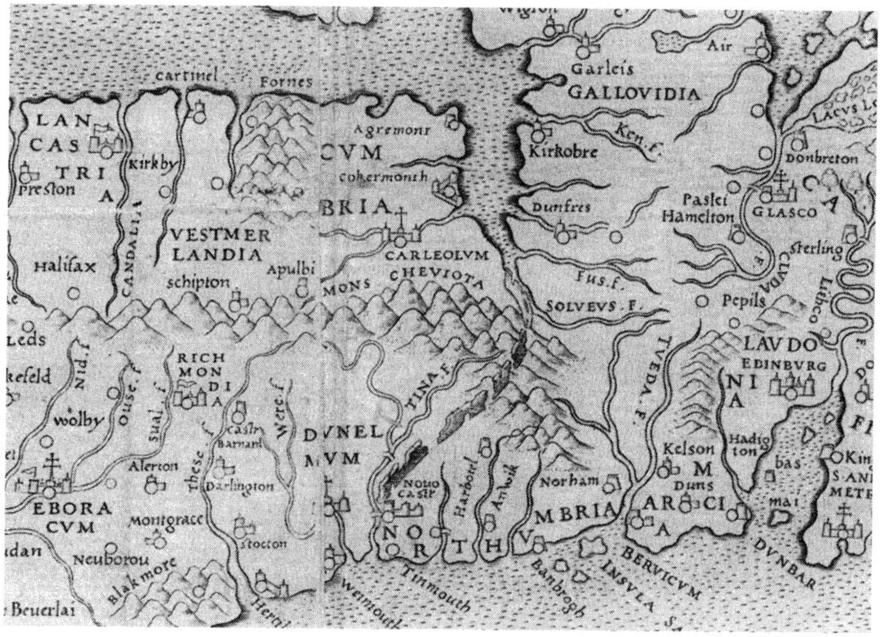

Fig. 4.4. An excerpt from George Lily's map of Britain, apparently showing details of the Roman Wall. Reproduced by permission of the British Library, Maps K. Top 5.1.

As a result of its geographical location, monumental form, and genealogical ancestry, the Picts' Wall became a powerful signifier of the division of the English nation from the Scots.[6] Early descriptions of the Wall, drawn from Gildas and Bede, viewed it as an amalgamated effort, built by the Romans with the assistance of the Lowland Britons and undertaken during and immediately after the decline of Roman rule. This supposed British contribution to the monument helped to project its value as a signifier of the identity of those living in its vicinity. Such an association was reinforced by the location of the Wall close to the northern frontier of England and, presumably, also reflected the physical impact of the curtain Wall and Vallum, which will have continued to restrict the movement of people across this line.

ESTABLISHING THE NORTHERN
FRONTIER OF ENGLAND

The frontier between England and Scotland gradually took form during the tenth to twelfth centuries (Figure 1.1). To the east, this border appears to have been settled approximately where it is located today when Scotland conquered Lothian during the tenth century.[7] In the west, it was defined in 1092, when William Rufus annexed Carlisle from the kingdom of the Scots, creating a new Anglo-Scottish border along the Solway Firth and River Esk.[8] To interpret the potential conceptual significance of the surviving remains of the Wall in medieval and early modern times, it is useful to consider the contentious and disputed character of this frontier zone. In a cross-cultural survey of frontiers in history, Daniel Power argued that such phenomena may have represented lines or zones in different historical situations. Although physical fortifications defining lines in the landscape—for example, Hadrian's Wall in Britain, the Great Wall of China, or the Berlin Wall in Germany—occur in some historical and geographical contexts, many frontiers are represented by zones rather than by clearly demarcated lines.[9] The frontiers of the Roman empire, for example, were not necessarily absolute definitions of the limits of imperial territory.[10] The network of Roman forts and roads to the north and south of Hadrian's Wall may demonstrate that this frontier constituted a zone rather than a single line of defence. Although it is possible that there was a specific legal definition of the exact location of the Roman frontier, we cannot

[6] Hingley (2010a), 26.   [7] Ellis (1988), 4.
[8] Summerson (2000), 2.   [9] Power (1999), 2–6.
[10] Whittaker (1994), 8–9.

know exactly where this may have been located.[11] Despite this, the monumental presence of the curtain Wall focused the attention of commentators onto its remains during the medieval and early modern periods.

Addressing the frontiers of late medieval England, Steven Ellis has explored the nature of the borders with Wales, Scotland, and Ireland as zones rather than as specific lines of demarcation.[12] In particular, the border between England and Scotland was an ill-defined, fluid, and contentious frontier territory during much of the late medieval period, until the late sixteenth century.[13] The character of this frontier appears to have been partly a result of the nature of the economy and settlement of this area. Robert Woodside and Jim Crow have drawn upon the archaeological evidence and historical sources to suggest that this upland area of Whin Sill was a place of seasonal settlement, characterized by groups of shielings that were probably associated with townships located in the valley of the South Tyne.[14] In the landscape on the northern border between England and Scotland, a distinctive border 'Reiver society' developed from the late thirteenth century to the early seventeenth.[15] Throughout much of this time, the borderlands between England and Scotland were disputed through fighting and cattle-raiding.[16] This frontier zone was sometimes called the 'debatable lands', reflecting its character as disputed territory on the border of the two kingdoms.[17]

The English part of this frontier zone contained the physical remains of the Roman Wall, a feature drawn upon in both conceptual and physical terms. William Shannon has argued that during medieval times, the Wall made 'a contribution to growing ideas of nation amongst the English, and perhaps among the Scots too'.[18] Although there was no clear and coherent concept of English nationhood prior to the late sixteenth century,[19] this does not undermine the medieval significance of the Picts' Wall. Shannon mentions a number of texts and representations to support his argument that the Wall was well known in medieval times. During the 1320s, Ranulph Higden drew on Bede to refer to 'the famous wall' (*murus ille famosus*) in his account of the history of Britain.[20] Medieval maps dating from the thirteenth to sixteenth centuries mark the line of the Wall in different ways.[21] The maps drawn by Matthew

---

[11] David Breeze (pers. comm.). Speidel (1998) has noted that the *praetensio* of the Wall, which appears to have included the Risingham and High Rochester outpost forts, in effect extended the Roman 'frontier' to make it run along a line not unlike the modern boundary between England and Scotland (Anthony Birley pers. comm.).

[12] Ellis (1999); cf. W. Ferguson (1977), 10.

[13] Ellis (1999), 176; Meikle (2004).

[14] Woodside and Crow (1999), 62–70.

[15] Crow (2007), 324; McCord and Thompson (1998), 65–139.

[16] Frodsham (2004), 87–94, 100–1.

[17] Lamont and Rossington (2007), 1–2.

[18] Shannon (2007), 3.   [19] Helgerson (1992).

[20] Babington (1869), 68; see Shannon (2007), 3, 8.   [21] Shannon (2007), 21–8.

Paris around 1250 comprise 'Map A' and 'B', which mark two Roman Walls, and 'Map C' and 'D' that show only one Wall (Figure 4.3). The name *murus pictorum* (Picts' Wall) is marked on Map C, while Map A and B state *murus dividens anglos et picots* ('the wall divided English and Picts').[22] Matthew Paris was a monk based at St Albans and may well have visited the remains of Hadrian's Wall during his travels.[23] The so-called 'Gough Map' of Britain, dating to around 1360, shows an extensive series of roads to the south of the Wall, but few to the north in Scotland or across most of Wales.[24] It presents an image of England as a settled land, while Scotland and much of Wales appear wild and tractless, reinforcing the vision of barbarism beyond the Wall derived from the accounts of Gildas and Bede. The Picts' Wall was also represented on printed maps of Britain during the sixteenth century.[25]

Military and religious actions that occurred across this frontier zone indicate the continued significance of the remains of the Picts' Wall. The castle at Newcastle upon Tyne was built in AD 1080, probably from stone derived from the Wall or from the Roman fort within which it was constructed.[26] Carlisle Castle and the other castles built close to the line of the Wall during the eleventh to fifteenth centuries incorporated stones from the Wall and, on occasions, the physical structures of the former Roman fortification were exploited in their construction.[27] Such actions represented the pragmatic use of available stone and the physical remains of the ruined Roman frontier structures, but they may also demonstrate the conscious recognition of the significance of the surviving Roman remains, re-establishing a frontier imbued with considerable antiquity.

Lanercost Priory provides a particularly well-researched case study for the reuse of the remains of the Wall. Until the late 1150s the area in which the Priory was located continued to owe allegiance to the Scottish Crown.[28] The Priory's establishment, possibly in 1169,[29] was a political act to assist the consolidation of the newly established frontier between England and Scotland. The proximity of the Priory to the Roman Wall may have drawn on the idea of an earlier border here. The Stanegate probably give this area a particular significance, since it continued to provide communication between Newcastle and Carlisle, just inside the border of the kingdom of England.[30] The records that make up the Lanercost *Cartulary* mention the Roman Wall (*murus*) on thirteen occasions.[31] William Pearson mentioned that the medieval documents surviving from the Priory contained a rhyme that refers to the Roman Wall.[32] The Priory buildings were constructed, at least in part, from

[22] Shannon (2007), 23.   [23] ibid., 24.   [24] Birkholz (2004), 114.
[25] Shannon (2007), 26–30.   [26] Whitworth (2000), 20; McCord and Thompson (1998), 25.
[27] Whitworth (2000), 20–1.   [28] Summerson (2000), 2.   [29] ibid., 4–5.
[30] ibid., 4.   [31] Todd (1997), 21.   [32] W. Pearson (1708), 62.

stones derived from the Wall,[33] including a number of Roman inscriptions that were built into its fabric.

According to its foundation charter, the remains of the Picts' Wall defined the northern limit of the Priory's lands.[34] Archaeological excavation undertaken in 1932 and again in 2004 indicated that a substantial section of the Roman curtain Wall on Hare Hill had been robbed, probably during the construction of the Priory buildings, and was later rebuilt to form the boundary to the Priory's lands, possibly during the fourteenth century.[35] The 1932 excavations suggested that the Roman turret here (*T 53a*) may have been left standing when this section of curtain Wall was robbed, perhaps because it was used as a border watchtower or beacon.[36] This awareness of the location of the Roman *murus* suggests that the reconstructed boundary wall may have reflected the location and character of the Picts' Wall, representing the rebuilding of the earlier monument.[37]

THE NIGHT WATCH

At certain times, the frontier zone that separated the independent kingdoms of England and Scotland was subject to considerable unrest.[38] In particular, documentary sources show that the border defences were in a very poor state by the middle of the sixteenth century.[39] At this time a serious attempt was made to control these unsettled lands through a system of night watches. This network stretched across the whole extent of a border zone that was many kilometers wide. Probably based on a method of surveillance originating in the earlier history of the frontier, this system involved stationing local men at certain significant points across an extensive area of the border landscape, including hills and fords, who would raise the alarm if marauders were sighted.

The remains of the Roman curtain Wall may have been utilized at a number of locations and two structures along its line may also have been associated with the night watch, although little systematic fieldwork has been undertaken to explore this idea. The Roman turret at Hare Hill may have been reused for the watch, while a small medieval building close to the present car park at Steel Rigg may have been a watchtower built behind the surviving remains of the

---

[33] Hill (2000); Whitworth (2000), 18; B. Young (2000), 85.
[34] Todd (2006), 58–9.
[35] Simpson and McIntyre (1933), 262–7; Hodgson and McKelvey (2006), 54.
[36] Simpson and McIntyre (1933), 266.
[37] Hodgson and McKelvey (2006), 54–5.
[38] Ellis (1999); Meikle (2004).
[39] Merriman (1984), 29.

Fig. 4.5. The excavation of a medieval peel tower on Steel Rigg, showing work undertaken by F. G. Simpson in 1911. Reproduced by permission of the Great North Museum and Society of Antiquaries of Newcastle upon Tyne.

Roman curtain Wall. F. G. Simpson has noted that this small structure was found in 1911, '208 yd. to the east' of the Steel Rigg Turret, recording that it was found 'abutting upon the inner face of the Wall and [was] similar in plan and size to a turret' (Figure 4.5).[40] When the building was excavated, some pieces of green glazed pottery were found, demonstrating its medieval date. It probably formed part of the original peel tower, after which the neighbouring farmhouse 'Peel' and the adjacent Peel Crag were named. Peel towers were built throughout the borderlands on the English-Scottish frontier to provide defence and safety for the occupants of this troubled area.[41] Faint traces of a slight platform just behind the curtain Wall mark the site of the tower today and the spoil heaps of the 1911 excavation are also visible. The photograph from the original excavation demonstrates that the south face of the Roman curtain Wall had been partly demolished at this point, but after the excavations it was carefully rebuilt and no trace of medieval robbing is now visible. Noting that this was probably a stone farmhouse constructed behind the partly demolished line of the Roman Wall, Jim Crow has suggested that pottery from the site is fourteenth-century.[42]

[40] Simpson (1976), 109.
[41] Woodside and Crow (1999), 58.
[42] Crow (2004a), 119.

Alan Whitworth has proposed that this particular building might still have been used as a watchtower in 1552 when a night watch was established in the area of Thorngrafton and the Bradley Beacons, presumably following the line of the Wall.[43] The fact that the structure does not occupy the more prominent and defensible position at Steel Rigg or Peel Crag led Jim Crow to suggest that the building was probably no more than a farm.[44] The range of visibility would have been extended if the peel tower had been built 150 metres along the line of the curtain Wall to the east, but Crow's comments do not explain the building's similarity to a Roman Wall turret or its exact location in relation to the curtain Wall. It is clear from the surviving documents that the night watch was stationed at several points along the curtain Wall, and this tower would have constituted one station in the watch. The potential fourteenth-century date of the Peel Crag building may support the idea that the night watches of the sixteenth century were based on earlier practices.[45]

Mid sixteenth-century documents related to the watch record two cases in which the Wall is mentioned. These records include, 'the ORDER of the Watch from the Waull within the Carrow-burgh [Carrawburgh] to North Tyne', and 'The Watch to be kept on the Wall at Welton-burne', which was held close to Heddon-on-the-Wall.[46] The key factor behind the use of the remains of the curtain Wall at Carrawburgh and Thorngrafton was presumably its topographic location on the top of the crags, which provided formidable elevated vantage points for the watch.[47] Further east, the remains of the Roman Wall at Heddon probably also formed a useful lookout point for the watch and the same is true at Hare Hill close to Lanercost. Across the border region, the watches monitored a large area of the landscape, including a network of places that extended both far to the north and to the south of the Picts' Wall. The Wall may have been a convenient local landmark, but its substantial remains probably continued to serve as a barrier to raiding.

There is no evidence that medieval activity along the line of the Wall involved any physical rebuilding of its surviving structures. The construction of the peel tower at Peel Crag and the possible reuse of the Roman turret at Hare Hill are not directly connected with the watch by any of the available

---

[43] Whitworth (2000), 23; J. Hodgson (1840), 118–19, n. t; 328, n. n. The original document described the watch as 'from the *kings-hill* to the *Craw-cragge*' (reproduced in Nicolson 1705, 241), which presumably means the area from Sewingshields to the west.

[44] Crow (2004a), 119. Lindsay Allason-Jones (pers. comm.) has pointed out that it is also possible that this was a Roman turret that had been reused in medieval times. Woodside and Crow (1999), 58.

[45] It is recorded that, when the watches were appointed in 1552, the 'articles of discipline were established or revived' (Ridpath 1776, 574).

[46] Nicolson (1705), 256–7, 280.

[47] Rushworth (2009), 329. Lindsay Allason-Jones (pers. comm.) notes that when Hadrian's Wall Heritage Ltd. held the 'Illuminating Hadrian's Wall' event in 2010, the lights were more visible to the north of the Wall than to the south.

documentary material. It is possible, however, that some of the local gentlemen who took charge of the planning of the watch during the mid sixteenth century were aware of the precedent of the Roman operations across this landscape. Indeed, local tales may have retained some memory of the origins of the Wall as a means for watching the area to the north and for preventing raiding and invasion.

PROPOSING A CIVIL FRONTIER

There was a further decline in the security of the border during the final two decades of the sixteenth century.[48] Lawlessness was rife across the border zone and there was fear of an invasion of England from the north.[49] After the Dissolution of the monasteries by Henry VIII, Lanercost had become the private home of the Dacres, an important local family. Christopher Dacre inherited the house at Lanercost from his father, who had converted it from the remains of the Priory.[50] Christopher may have been the author of a late sixteenth-century letter sent to Queen Elizabeth, entitled *The Epystle to the Queen's Majestie*.[51] This letter proposed the building of a new linear fortification, along the frontier of the kingdom from Berwick to Carlisle.[52] The contested and ill-defined nature of this border zone in Tudor times drew attention to the practical significance of the impressive surviving remains of the Picts' Wall.

That Christopher Dacre was the author of the *Epystle* is supported by the fact that he made at least one other proposal to fortify the border.[53] In 1583 he suggested that two new fortifications should be built and that a 'dyke or defence' should be built from Bowness, 'towne to towne throughout the said border to the boundes of the middle marches'.[54] Although in this context he does not mention the Picts' Wall as a source for the dyke, the observation that the fortification should link towns draws upon Bede's observation of the strong wall of stone that formed the last of the three lines of Roman fortification. Dacre noted that such a barrier would be 'to the most advantage of defence and saving of chardge best serveth be first made and finished with a nightly watch upon the same, whereby the enimyes and malefactours shall not by any meanes enter or escape without a sufficient forewarning to the said true

---

[48] Newton (2006), 67–8.   [49] Merriman (1984), 29–30.
[50] Summerson (2000), 43–9.
[51] Merriman (1982), 613; Merriman (1984), 31. An alternative suggestion is that Lord Hunsdon, Warden of the East March between 1577 and 1594, may have written the *Epystle* (Woodside and Crow 1999, 68).
[52] Bain (1894), xxii.   [53] Merriman (1982), 613; Merriman (1984), 30.
[54] Quoted in Merriman (1984), 30.

subiectes'.[55] This proposal links the practice of the night watch to the creation of a linear frontier, a concept drawing upon the Picts' Wall that was further developed in the *Epystle*.

The *Epystle* is a lengthy document proposing the construction of an ambitious new fortification along the entire length of the frontier of the kingdom.[56] The full document is in the National Archives of the British Library (SP 59/42) and is more fully discussed elsewhere.[57] It may date to the troubled year of 1587, which witnessed the execution of Mary, Queen of Scots.[58] The proposed scheme, which was never carried out, would have involved a substantial linear rampart partly inspired by earlier linear fortifications and partly by contemporary military planning. The author quotes a number of historical parallels for the fortification, including a frontier built by Julius Caesar against the Helvetii, a Greek frontier work, and the 'Pightes wall in Northomberlande'.[59] By making this equation, the author places the contemporary English in the guise of the classical Romans who had built the Picts' Wall and the contemporary Scots in the place of the Picts and Caledonians who attacked it.[60]

The Picts' Wall provided a particularly valuable example for this scheme since it was thought to be partly a British construction, and 'is heare at home, within your Majesties domynions'.[61] Drawing on the accounts of Gildas or Bede, the author remarked:

> The Romaynes were at the travalye to make this wall and that at that tyme to be defended from the dayly and daungerous incurtyous of the valyaunte barberous Scottyshe nation; but the cuntry them selves was at the cherge of the makinge of yt, which they were contented to doe as well for their owne more safftie, as by compulsoine of the Roymaynes, who were their maysters.

That the new fortification was to be built by the local population indicates that the author of the *Epystle* was aware of the writings of Gildas and/or Bede. This proposal uses the Picts' Wall to provide a precedent for the building of the new fortification by the local population with the support of the Elizabethan state.[62]

The *Epystle* also suggests that the establishment of this frontier might help to create a civil society in this unsettled zone. The new fortification would mean that the Scots would be 'utterlye excluded' and the borders which now lay 'waste and not Inhabyted, shalbe made as tenantable Lande as any your Majestie hathe within the myddeste of your Realme'.[63] A number of structures called 'skonces' were to be 'planted the one from other amyle at the leaste';

---

[55] Merriman (1984), 30.
[56] Bain (1894), 300–2; E. Birley (1961), 23–4; Merriman (1984), 25–9.
[57] Hingley (2008a), 90–3.   [58] Bain (1894), xxii; Merriman (1984), 25.
[59] quoted in Bain (1894), 300–1.   [60] Hingley (2008a), 91–5.
[61] cf. Bain (1894), 301.   [62] Hingley (2008a), 91.
[63] Quoted by Merriman (1984), 27.

each of these should have a thousand acres of adjoining ground, rented out as
1*d*. per acre. Marcus Merriman has observed that the term 'skonse' was in
common usage by the end of the sixteenth century and generally meant a
small fort, particularly one built to defend a pass, castlegate, or ford.[64] It was
suggested that men would be specially chosen to live in these skonses and
regard this as a 'perfermente, and a good bargaine'.[65]

Marcus Merriman has suggested that behind this proposed fortification, a
revitalized border society would arise, ready and able to defend the frontier
against any threat from the north. The comments in the *Epystle* regarding
making the land tenantable reflect the contemporary government policy of
settling contentious border areas, a concept that drew upon imperial Roman
parallels.[66] In 1571 there was a plan for the establishment of an English colony
in the Ards peninsular of Ireland, which explored the potential of the land for
colonization and cultivation.[67] The proposal in the *Epystle* for the establishment of 'skonses' behind the new fortification along the English border was
promoted by a comparable desire to create a civil society in this lawless zone.
The *Epystle* provides a concrete proposal to establish civility in the relatively
unsettled English frontier zone—to plant the area and make it economically
self-sustaining. It drew upon the politics of the frontier region as a 'Debatable
land', and also the character of the night watch which had strived to try to keep
order in this area during the unsettled times of the sixteenth century.

Eric Birley has noted that there is no indication that the author of the
Epystle had read Camden's *Britannia* (1586) with its fairly detailed account
of the Wall.[68] He also argues that the author had no direct experience of
the monument since it was recorded as at least sixteen feet thick. Some of the
details provided in the letter suggest, however, that its author had a very good
knowledge of the Roman Wall and that the mistaken measurement was merely
an oversight.[69] That the 'skonses' were to be positioned at least a mile apart
presumably draws directly upon the structures along the Wall now known as
'milecastles'. The curate of Haltwhistle, Christopher Ridley, was the first to
note, probably in 1572, that fortifications occurred along the line of the Wall at
intervals of approximately one mile.[70] The use of term 'skonse' may suggest
that some of the milecastles were still well preserved at this time, since the
term was often used for structures that were built to defend passes, suggesting
that the gateways of some milecastles were still visible. The proposal to allocate
land to the men who lived in these stations may suggest that the *Epystle's*
author had observed evidence for former agriculture around some of the
Roman forts along the line of the Wall.

---

[64] Quoted by Merriman (1984), 26.   [65] ibid., 27.
[66] Hingley (2008a), 59–66.   [67] Quinn (1966), 107–8; Canny (2000), 198–9.
[68] E. Birley (1961), 24.   [69] Hingley (2008a), 92.   [70] Shannon (2007), 1.

SUMMARY: A GENEALOGICAL FRONTIER

The imagining of continuity on the frontier and the linking of the Romans to the contemporary population of England appears to be fundamental for the writer of the *Epystle*. This idea subsequently became widely adopted, projecting the Wall as the ancient boundary between England and Scotland. This is a concept that appears more prominent at times of political tension between the two countries, through an emphasis on either the rebuilding of the Wall or its ruination. Two examples from the late seventeenth and early eighteenth centuries elucidate this point. In his geographical dictionary of the world, Edmund Bohun wrote of the Picts' Wall as 'the most ancient Boundary between *England* and *Scotland*'.[71] In the immediate aftermath of the 1707 Act of Union, Daniel Defoe wrote of the wars between Scotland and England as ancient 'Quarrels, Wars and Devastations' that united the history of the Roman, medieval, and modern borders.[72] The accounts of Bohun and Defoe will be considered more fully in Chapter 6, but it is significant that this concept of the ancient genealogy of the frontier that they drew upon continued as a powerful theme for English authors.

This idea comes through to the present day. In a historical introduction to Gildas' volume, John Morris observed that 'the mid fourth century Roman frontier is still the border between England and Scotland'.[73] In one sentence, Morris brings the Roman northern frontier of the province of *Britannia* into a genealogical sequence 1,600 years long, an association that draws upon Hadrian's Wall, the medieval frontier of England, and the contemporary national boundary, while also adopting Gildas' dating scheme for the Roman Walls. Morris' comment reminds me of a fieldtrip to Housesteads Roman fort on Hadrian's Wall that I made with undergraduates from Durham University in 2001, when one student remarked to another that the land to the north was Scotland. This appears to be a common assumption today, exemplified by recent cartoons in a number of newspapers, including an example illustrated in Chapter 15. Bohun, Defoe, Morris, and this cartoonist have drawn a direct link between, on the one hand, the Romans and the English, and on the other, the Picts and the Scots. The Picts' Wall has been invested with a genealogical claim for the civility and order of the English in opposition to the barbarity and warlike nature of the people living to its north.

With the linking of the Roman Wall to the medieval and modern frontier, three problems are immediately apparent. First, this linear association appears to imply that there has been a continuous border history along the frontier. Uniting the Roman province of *Britannia* with the medieval kingdom and modern nation of England grossly oversimplifies the complex history of both this region and the modern countries to either side of the Wall. The frontier between the two kingdoms was not established until the tenth and eleventh

---

[71] Bohun (1693), 318.   [72] Defoe (1709), 3.   [73] Morris (1978), 4.

centuries. The physical presence of the Wall has, however, caused an eddy in time in the works reviewed here, relating Roman frontier affairs to the actions of medieval and modern England. The powerful nature of this divisive and hierarchical spatial measure is significant, since it places the English in a dominant position and explains the symbolic power of the Wall for those living to its south. We shall see that those living to the north of the Wall have often told rather different stories about the monument.

Second, such claims appear to suggest that the Wall is located on the border that developed between the two countries from the tenth to eleventh centuries, although the national border actually lies further to the north. The author of the *Epystle* proposed the building of a new fortification along the northern boundary of the kingdom; in the absence of such a construction, the Roman Wall has often been used as a conceptual dividing line that serves precisely this role despite its geographical misplacement. Whether the building of medieval castles, churches, bastles, and peel towers along the line of the Wall, together with its use as the base for the night watches in the frontier zone, illustrates any clear conception during the medieval period of its role in Roman times is unclear, but this possibility could be explored further through archaeological fieldwork.

The third problem with this genealogical conception is that it is debatable whether either the medieval or the modern English population is directly descended from those who inhabited Lowland Britain during the Roman period. As has been discussed above, an alternative origin myth for the English proposes Germanic or Teutonic ancestry. Although the idea of a continuity of population from Roman to modern times to the south of the Wall has been influential since the late sixteenth century, it is overtly simplistic. In comparable terms, any attempt to link the medieval and modern populations of Scotland to the Picts and Caledonians ignores the population movements that occurred in post-Roman times.

Deconstructing the association between Hadrian's Wall and the national frontier of England would, however, undermine a powerful historical conception of national mythology.[74] The fact that English writers *have* drawn deeply on the idea of historical continuity in conceptualizing the Wall indicates the power of this genealogical image and makes its categorical dismissal problematic, since this would be to ignore the significance of this concept of English identity that draws on the past in teleological terms.[75] The Wall's location, together with the idea that it was partly built for and by the ancient ancestors of the population of Lowland Britain to its south, are tied into the conceptual and genealogical space of English nationhood, a concept that remains current in some circles today.

---

[74] cf. Miller (1995), 35.   [75] cf. Colls (2002), 7.

5

Ellenborough (Maryport): Recognizing Roman Civility in the Border Landscape

[Camden's] northern tour of 1599...has...been recognized as the starting-date for systematic Roman Wall studies...

Leslie Hepple (1999, 1)

INTRODUCTION

The Picts' Wall was a focus of considerable interest during the late sixteenth century and the first decade of the seventeenth.[1] Late in the reign of Queen Elizabeth and during the succeeding reign of King James, playwrights, poets, historians, antiquaries, and mapmakers were intent on exploring the character and history of England and establishing an identity for the English.[2] In this context, William Camden's influential volume *Britannia* used classical texts to construct an ancestral geography for the kingdom.[3] Camden (1551–1623) had studied classics in Oxford and was a master at Westminster School.[4] *Britannia* was his most influential work; first published in Latin in 1586, it was republished on several occasions during the next twenty-five years, but the first English translation was not published until 1610. In these revised editions, the information was supplemented and improved and they also included many new illustrations. Camden's first volume covered England and Wales in detail and contained some information about Scotland and Ireland, which was expanded in the subsequent editions.

Camden's focus on the Roman past in *Britannia* placed the territorially marginal areas of Britain in a subservient position relative to the heartlands of England where he argued that Roman control had introduced civility to the

---

[1] E. Birley (1961), 1; Hepple (2003a), 159; Hingley (2008a), 93–4.
[2] See Helgerson (1992), 1; Marshall (2000); Ivic (2002).
[3] Hepple (2004), 148.
[4] Herendeen (2007); Levine (1987), 93.

ancient population.[5] Nevertheless, he also emphasized the significance of the Picts' Wall, drawing on the wealth of Roman culture then being discovered along its line. The first edition of *Britannia* included a short but important description of the remains. The publication of several revised editions from 1586 to 1610 attracted the interest of several antiquaries who lived close to the remains of the Wall.[6] These gentlemen began to collect Roman inscribed stones and their comments informed Camden's revised editions of *Britannia*.[7] In 1599, Camden visited the Wall and collected information to provide a more detailed description.[8] A new comprehension of the significance of the Wall was emerging as the result of the exploration of its remains and the collection of Roman inscribed stones from particular places along its course.

Interest in the Picts' Wall appears to have peaked in the first decade of James's reign (1603–25). Between 1604 and 1609, this king made a serious attempt to unify England and Scotland into Great Britain.[9] It has been argued that, as a result of James's efforts, certain people began to draw upon the concept of Great Britain at this time, while this idea was to be re-invented and re-projected in a more coherent form during the eighteenth century.[10] Chorographies, histories, and plays produced during this time projected images of ancient Britons and classical Romans and studied their interactions. These ancient figures were drawn upon to contemplate a unified Great Britain.[11] The references to the Picts' Wall in poems, political tracts, and antiquarian works of this date demonstrate the symbolic role played by this monument in imagining the relationship of the English to the peoples living further to the north and west.[12] This chapter will focus attention on Camden's image of the character of the Picts' Wall and will compare this with the creation of a living spirit for the monument in 'Song XXIX' of Michael Drayton's poetical work, *Poly-Olbion* (1622). The relationship of these works to the Wall's function in bounding contemporary England will be explored and some observations on the relationship between history and story in the writings of Camden and Drayton will be made.

WILLIAM CAMDEN'S ACCOUNT OF THE PICTS' WALL

The editions of *Britannia* produced from 1586 to 1722 had a major impact on English antiquarian and historical scholarship, raising the profile of the Roman Wall.[13] The 1586 edition included some detailed information on

---

[5] Hingley (2008a), 23.
[6] Collingwood (1921a), 48; Hepple (2004), 148.
[7] Hepple (2003a), 159.   [8] E. Birley (1961), 5–6.
[9] McEachern (1996), 138–60; Wormald (1994), 19–25.
[10] Marshall (2000), 4; cf. Canny (1998), 1–2.
[11] Hingley (2008a), 23.
[12] cf. H. Griffiths (2003); Hingley (2008a), 93–101.
[13] Hepple (2003a), 160; Hingley (2008a), 24, 98.

Roman sites in the English borderlands, together with a four-page description of the history of the '*Mvrus Picticus*'.[14] Camden's account provided a thorough and reasoned assessment of the knowledge available for the Wall, since little appears to have been studied or recorded before his time. Eric Birley observed that Camden drew on earlier manuscript sources for this account, including John Leland, Christopher Ridley, and another unidentified author.[15] The changing knowledge of the monument over the subsequent two decades is reflected in the later editions of *Britannia*. The visit of Camden and Robert Cotton to the Wall in 1599 was a highly significant event, since it led to the first detailed description of the remains.[16] Once a pupil of Camden, Cotton was a collector of manuscripts and antiquities who assisted him in the revisions of *Britannia*. Their visit to the monument resulted in a substantial enlargement of the materials on the Wall in the 1600 and 1607 editions.[17] This knowledge was also based on records, chronicles, and information provided by local informants.[18]

Camden and Cotton travelled along the Wall from summer until December 1599. The two friends toured the Roman frontier works looking for Roman inscriptions and remains, and meeting local landowners. They visited the Roman sites at Moresby, Maryport, Carlisle, and Bowness; they then travelled to Naworth, which is very close to Lanercost, and the Roman sites at Willowford and Carvoran (Figure 5.1).[19] They turned south, omitting the most impressive sections of the Wall and several Roman stations, including the fort at Housesteads. This detour was necessary because, as Camden reported, it appeared unwise to visit these places owing to the threat posed by robbers and thieves.[20] Despite the fact that the borderlands were more settled by the end of the sixteenth century than they had been before, the Armstrongs of Housesteads remained notorious for their lawless behaviour throughout the seventeenth century.[21] Reginald Bainbrigg also visited the Wall in 1599 and 1601 and appears to have explored some of the sites missed by Camden and Cotton, supplying information for inclusion in *Britannia*.[22] He did visit Housesteads, although this expedition may have been carried out in haste.[23]

---

[14] Camden (1586), 461–4.
[15] E. Birley (1961), 1–4; cf. Shannon (2007), 1.
[16] Hepple (1999).   [17] ibid., 2.
[18] E. Birley (1961), 1–7; Hepple (2003a), 160.
[19] Hepple (1999), 2–3.
[20] Camden (1610), 800; cf. Crow (2007), 324.
[21] Woodside and Crow (1999), 70–3.
[22] Edwards (2001); Hepple (1999), 5, 8.
[23] Haverfield (1911), 359.

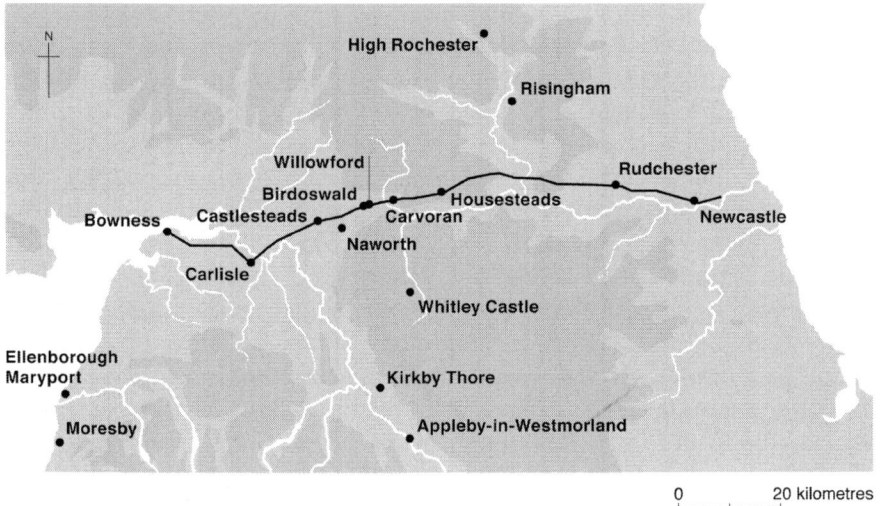

Fig. 5.1. Places mentioned in Chapter 5. Drawn by Christina Unwin.

After making this detour, Camden and Cotton returned to the line of the Wall, examining Rudchester and then following the remains to Newcastle.[24] There is no evidence that they travelled northwards to explore the Roman sites beyond the Wall at Risingham and High Rochester. The 1607 edition of *Britannia* includes twelve inscriptions from these two Roman sites but Bainbrigg may have provided these.[25] Leslie Hepple has suggested that Cotton probably returned to visit Risingham and High Rochester between 1601 and 1607 in order to record and collect the Roman stones taken to his house at Conington (Cambridgeshire).[26] The 1607 edition of *Britannia* also included details of new inscriptions recorded by Bainbrigg from other Roman sites.[27]

Camden's account of the Wall in the 1610 edition of *Britannia* combined the information from his own studies and material from his various informants and, importantly, was translated into English. The Wall is one of the few ancient features indicated on the map of Britain that forms the frontispiece of this volume. Camden's description names the monument in various ways: 'Picts Wall', 'Vallum', 'the Wall of *Severus*', and 'the Trench, or rampire of *Severus*';[28] but he gives primacy to 'Picts Wall'. Seven pages are devoted to a detailed description of the history of the Wall, while individual places along its

---

[24] Hepple (1999), 5.
[25] ibid., 8–9.   [26] ibid., 5.
[27] Hepple (2002), 89.   [28] Camden (1610), 778, 782, 789.

line are described in the sections of the book exploring Cumberland and Northumberland. This fairly detailed chorographical description of the Wall is accompanied by numerous engravings of Roman inscribed stones found along its line.

Camden's enthusiasm for the Picts' Wall is communicated by the style of his prose. He called it 'that most famous monument of all Britaine' and described its course and remains in detail.[29] He provided an analytical description, referring to the remains of the Wall between '*Tine-mouth*' and '*Solwey frith*':

> there are yet such expresse tokens of it in this place, that you may tracke it as it were all the way it went: and in the *Wasts*, as they tearme them, I my selfe have beheld with my owne eyes on either side, huge peeces thereof standing for a great way together, only wanting their battlements.
>
> Verily I have seene the tract of it over the high pitches and steep descents of hilles, wonderfully rising and falling: and where the fields lie more plaine and open, a broad and deep ditch without, just before it, which now in many places is grounded up: and within a banke or militarie highway, but in most places interrupted. It had many towres or fortresses about a mile distant from another, which they call *Castle steeds*; and more within, little fensed townes tearmed in these daies *Chesters*, the plots or ground workes whereof are to be seene in some places four square: also turrets standing between these, wherein soldiers being placed might discover the enemies.[30]

This description draws a distinction between three classes of structures: 'turrets', '*Castle steeds*' (i.e. milecastles), and '*Chesters*' (forts). Camden adopted some of the language and terminology of Gildas and Bede to conceptualize the remains associated with the Wall. He wrote of 'little fenced townes',[31] while the Roman fort at Risingham (Northumberland) is described as a 'towne . . . of ancient memorie'.[32] Camden also used the word 'city' to address post-Roman Carlisle.[33] These references to the surviving remains of Roman monuments in the landscape of the Wall suggested the former existence of a string of Roman urban places along the Wall's course.

Camden used classical texts and early medieval accounts to assess the evidence for the construction and sequence of the Wall.[34] Drawing on information from the *Life of Hadrian* by 'Spartianus' (one of the pseudonyms used by the author of the work now known as the *Historia Augusta*), Camden proposed that Hadrian had been the first to construct a wall of 'stakes or piles

---

[29] ibid., 782.   [30] ibid., 793.
[31] '*opidula*' in Camden (1607), 652.
[32] Camden (1610), 803. This is also likely to reflect the presence of the deserted medieval village on this site (Lindsay Allason-Jones pers. comm.).
[33] Camden (1610), 779.
[34] ibid., 789–95.

pitched deepe in the ground' along the line.[35] He also suggested, drawing in particular on Bede, that the Emperor Severus subsequently built a '*Vallum* or Rampier . . . of turffes'.[36] After a long and rather confusing discussion, Camden suggested that after the Picts and Scots broke through the northern turf wall (the monument now known as the Antonine Wall), the departing Romans built a stone wall along the line of Severus' turf wall.[37] Camden differed from Bede in his account of this sequence only by suggesting an initial phase of construction of the Wall under Hadrian. It is clear that Camden considered Severus' turf Wall to be the monument known today as the Vallum. His discussion of the late Roman history of the Wall repeats much of the texts of Gildas and Bede verbatim. As a result of Camden's reiteration, these early medieval writings continued to influence ideas about the Wall for a number of centuries. Despite Camden's argument that the stone Wall was built by the departing Romans, several broadly contemporary accounts reflect an alternative chronology by arguing that it was the work of the Emperor Severus.[38]

COLLECTING ROMAN STONES

The Roman frontier defences along the Cumbrian coast were not firmly tied in with Hadrian's Wall until the archaeological investigations of the 1920s.[39] Nevertheless, the collection of Roman inscribed stones at Ellenborough brought the site to the attention of Camden, who visited there before continuing to explore the Picts' Wall. To the north of the port and town of Maryport are the earthwork remains of a Roman fort that was called *Alauna* in Roman times.[40] Visitors to the site today can view the important collection of Roman inscribed stones housed in the on-site museum. In the 1580s John Senhouse began collecting carved Roman stonework from the extensive Roman site on his estate.[41] His collection may have included ten inscribed stones and appears to be the earliest assemblage of ancient antiquities in England.[42] These Roman stones have remained in the ownership of Senhouse's heirs and today form one of the most important collections of Roman inscribed stones in Britain.[43]

---

[35] Camden (1610), 790.   [36] ibid., 790–1.   [37] ibid., 793.
[38] Including Drayton (1622), 159; Gray (1649), 3.
[39] Collingwood (1931), 59–60.
[40] Breeze (2006a), 397–407; R. Wilson (ed. 1997).
[41] Hepple (2003a), 162.
[42] Haverfield (1914), 135; Hepple (2003a), 163; Lax and Blood (1997), 53.
[43] Breeze (2006a), 398.

The 1610 edition of *Britannia* includes Camden's visit to '*I. Sinhous*' at '*Ellenborough*'.[44] Ellenborough was the name of Senhouse's manor, close to the Roman site. Writing about the site from which the inscribed stones came, Camden records 'now, Corne growes where the town stood, neverthelesse many expresse footings thereof are evidently to be seene: The ancient vaults stand open, and many altars, stones with inscriptions, and Statues are heere gotten out of the ground.' He observed that Senhouse, who had died in 1604, was:

> a very honest man, in whose grounds they are digged up, keepeth [these objects] charily [carefully], and hath placed orderly about his house ... And I cannot chuse but with thankfull heart remember, that very good and worthy Gentleman not onely in this regard that most kindly hee gave vs right courteous and friendly entertainment, but also for that being himself well learned, he is a lover of ancient literature, and most diligently preserveth these inscriptions, which by others that are unskillfull and unlettered be streight waies defaced, broken, and converted to other vses to exceeding great prejudice and detriment of antiquity.

There is nothing else in Camden's *Britannia* that quite matches this enthusiastic tribute.[45] Camden's reference to Senhouse as a lover of ancient literature suggests that he was a learned man, but very little else is known about his life.

Camden's remark that these Roman stones were 'digged up' by Senhouse suggests that excavations were deliberately being made in order to uncover ancient deposits.[46] Planned excavations on Roman sites in Britain are rarely attested prior to the seventeenth century and this is the earliest record of the uncovering of ancient inscriptions in northern England.[47] Camden writes in detail about one particularly fine Roman stone, first noted in the 1587 edition of *Britannia* and reproduced as an engraving in the 1610 edition (Figure 5.2).[48]

Three other collections of inscribed stones from the Wall were formed at this time, at Naworth (Cumbria), Appleby-in-Westmorland (Cumbria), and, further afield, at Conington (Cambridgeshire). Leslie Hepple has discussed these in detail, observing that they are four out of five of the earliest collections of Roman antiquities in Britain; the fifth being a group of stones from *Caerleon* (Newport, Wales).[49] Smaller assemblages of Roman stones were also made at this time, such as those at Carlisle and Bath. The inspiration for collecting these stones was provided by the Italian Renaissance tradition of acquiring classical sculptures,[50] and the search for ancient inscriptions extended across much of Europe during the last two decades of the sixteenth century.[51] As relations

---

[44] Camden (1610), 769.   [45] Hepple (2003a), 162.
[46] ibid., 162–3; cf. Lax and Blood (1997), 53.
[47] Hingley (2008a), 164–9.   [48] RIB, n. 812.
[49] Hepple (2003a), 161.   [50] Brennan (2004), 9–19; J. Scott (2003), 15.
[51] McKitterick (1997), 108.

Fig. 5.2. Roman inscribed stone from Ellenborough, Maryport, Cumbria. From Camden (1610), 770. Reproduced by permission of Durham University Library, Cosins W.3.12.

with continental Europe improved towards the end of Elizabeth's reign, travel overseas became possible for English visitors.[52] The four gentlemen who collected stones from the Wall appear to have been copying a continental tradition in which classical objects were collected and displaying in garden settings.[53]

Lord William Howard (1563–1640) assembled a collection of Roman stones at his house at Naworth (Cumbria), just to the south of the Wall and close to Lanercost Priory.[54] Howard was an active member of antiquarian circles in London and was a friend of Camden and Cotton.[55] He was a Catholic and had

---

[52] Brennan (2004), 18–19.   [53] Hepple (2003a), 161.
[54] Hepple (2002).   [55] Ovenden and Handley (2004).

spent some time in the Tower of London, only gaining possession of Naworth Castle following a long lawsuit.[56] His family had a long association with this estate around which he had accompanied Camden and Cotton as a guide during their visit to the Wall here.[57] Camden described him as 'a singular lover of venerable antiquity and learned withall'.[58] Howard restored the building and estate, making Naworth his home until he died in 1640.[59] He also made an important contribution to the establishment of greater stability in the border region during the reign of James I.[60] Walter Scott described him as having been 'the terror of the moss troopers',[61] the disorderly elements within medieval and early modern border society.[62]

Like the neighbouring buildings at Lanercost, those at Naworth were largely built of stone derived from the Wall.[63] Howard commissioned a survey of his estate in 1603 and the resulting map marked the 'Pight Wall'.[64] While resident at Naworth, Howard provided Camden with some notes that he incorporated in the 1607 edition of *Britannia*.[65] Howard also assisted Cotton in obtaining some items for his collection of Roman inscriptions.[66] In displaying inscribed stones in his walled garden, Howard may have been drawing upon Senhouse's example at Ellenborough.[67] By 1608, he had acquired at least twelve stones and his entire collection appears to have included at least twenty items, mainly from the Roman site at Birdoswald close to Naworth. Howard also collected books and manuscripts throughout his time at Naworth, accumulating a renowned library.[68] His collection of stones was neglected after his death and later moved to Rokeby near Barnard Castle, probably during the 1730s, where it remains today.[69]

Reginald Bainbrigg (1544/5–1612/13) was the headmaster of Appleby Grammar School (Cumbria) and a member of the local gentry,[70] who made a collection of Roman stones. Like Howard, Bainbrigg assembled a library of scholarly books acquiring 295 volumes of which 158 survived and were deposited at the University of Newcastle in 1966.[71] That Bainbrigg was a provincial schoolmaster indicates that the collecting of Roman inscribed stones at this time was not merely an interest of the landed elite.[72] It is known that Bainbrigg travelled from Appleby to visit the remains of the Picts' Wall in 1599 and 1601, and took extensive notes that were used by Camden. Bainbrigg's two journeys took him along the western parts of the

---

[56] Hepple (2002), 87.   [57] Ovenden and Handley (2004).
[58] Camden (1610), 783.   [59] Hepple (2002), 87.
[60] McCord and Thompson (1998), 144; Ovenden and Handley (2004).
[61] W. Scott (1814), 85.   [62] Bosanquet (1904), 193.
[63] Hill (2000), 192, n. 3.   [64] Whitworth (2000), 38; Wilmott (2001), 147–8.
[65] Hepple (2002), 89.   [66] ibid., 90–1.   [67] ibid.
[68] Ovenden and Handley (2004).   [69] Hepple (2002), 93–9.
[70] Edwards (2001); Hepple (2003a), 167–8.
[71] Edwards (2001), 25; Winchester (2004).   [72] Hepple (2003a), 169.

Fig. 5.3. Some of the more impressive of Reginald Bainbrigg's stones, carved in the early seventeenth century. These are built into a modern wall in Appleby. Photograph by Richard Hingley, 2011.

Wall but he also travelled into the unsettled area of Redesdale and North Tynedale at considerable personal risk.[73] Camden writes of him as 'Reginald *Bainbrige*, a right learned man . . . who of his courtesie hath exemplified for me many antique inscriptions'.[74]

Bainbrigg began his collection of Roman items during the late sixteenth century and assembled a number of original inscriptions from sites close to Appleby, together with copies of original stones that are of variable quality (Figure 5.3).[75] In 1602, these were housed in a small building in his garden in Appleby. Most of his collection has since been lost,[76] but sixteen of these stones are now built into a wall in Chapel Street, opposite the site of the old Appleby Grammar School.[77] They include several original Roman inscriptions from Whitley Castle and Kirkby Thore. Bainbrigg commissioned some new inscriptions, including a stone commemorating the founding of Appleby School and another recording Bainbrigg's life.[78] The inscriptions noted that he had been teaching at Appleby for twenty-two years and was fifty-seven years old.[79] Another gives what Ben Edwards has titled 'a thumbnail sketch of the history of Appleby', suggesting that the town was a Roman station at the

---

[73] Haverfield (1911), 347.   [74] Camden (1610), 761.
[75] Edwards (2001); Winchester (2004).   [76] Haverfield (1911), 348.
[77] Hepple (2003a), 167–8.   [78] Edwards (2001), 26–8; Hepple (2003a), 168.
[79] Winchester (2004).

time of Marcus Aurelius.[80] Camden adopted this story, stating that 'Apelby' was formerly a Roman 'station' called 'ABALLABA'.[81] Appleby was the county town of the former county of Westmorland and the importance of Bainbrigg's claim for an ancient foundation is evident from Camden's observation that the town was 'so sclenderly inhabited, and the buildings so simple, that were it not that by reason of the antiquity it had deserved to be called the chiefe towne of the shire . . . it would be little better than a village.'[82]

Bainbrigg recorded the discovery of an inscription during his visit to the Roman site at Castlesteads (Cumbria). A Roman inscribed stone was dug up here in 1600 by a 'country man, that buylded a square howse neare unto that place; he sunke deape into the ruynes of this castle, where he found faire and strong walls of hewen stone, among whiche I saw the rarest worke that ever I saw in my liff . . . '.[83] Bainbrigg continues his account of the remains, which evidently were still uncovered, by describing the ruins of what he terms a *'hypocaustum Romanum'* (Roman hypocaust), comparing it to a hypocaust uncovered at 'Flint castle in flintshire' and previously described in *Britannia*. Many of the inscriptions described by Camden and his informants may have been found during comparable attempts to secure building materials for new houses, but information about the find spots of individual items were rarely recorded in any detail. Bainbrigg's account therefore provided the first detailed description of an excavated structure on Hadrian's Wall.[84]

Robert Cotton also took carved Roman stones from the Wall for a collection at his house at Conington, where he used them to line his octagonal summerhouse.[85] A wealthy Huntingdonshire landowner, Cotton collected stones from a number of sites during travels to northern England.[86] Fifteen of the twenty or so Roman inscriptions in his collection are now housed at Cambridge in the Museum of Archaeology and Anthropology.[87] Cotton's Roman stones were evidently a source of inspiration, since he commissioned a number of gravestones at the church in Conington that drew upon these Roman examples. These included the Cotton-Paris monument, which may have been designed with Inigo Jones and which commemorates Cotton's great-grandfather Thomas Cotton and his wife Joanna Paris or Parys.[88] This monument appears to have at least a passing resemblance to the most impressive of the Roman altars from Ellenborough (Figure 5.2), an object that Cotton had illustrated for the 1607 edition of Camden's *Britannia*.

---

[80] Edwards (2001), 27.   [81] Camden (1610), 761.
[82] Subsequent research has undermined the idea that Appleby was a Roman settlement and the name *Aballava* is now identified with the Roman Wall fort at Burgh-by-Sands (Cumbria); Breeze (2006a), 350.
[83] Bainbrigg (fo. 320); transcribed in Haverfield (1911), 354.
[84] E. Birley (1961), 204.   [85] Hepple (2003a), 164.
[86] Hepple (1999), 13–15.   [87] G. Davies (1997), 129; Hepple (2003a), 165.
[88] Howarth (1997), 44, 49.

MICHAEL DRAYTON'S PICTSWALL

These collections of stones illustrate the powerful attraction of the Picts' Wall to late Elizabethan and Jacobean antiquaries. Poetic and political writings of the period suggest that the monument was well known across England.[89] In a speech to Parliament in March 1603, James I reflected on the fact that only 'little small brookes, or demolished little walles' divided England and Scotland, presumably providing a reference to the Picts' Wall.[90] In the following month, the poet and historian Samuel Daniel presented a poem to James in which he observed that, 'No Wall of Adrian serves to separate/Our mutuall love, nor our obedience', referring to the attitude of the English and the Scots to their new king.[91] Daniel was following an earlier tradition of attributing the Wall to Hadrian rather than calling it the Picts' Wall,[92] but he also emphasized the Wall's ruination.[93] The most interesting reference to the Picts' Wall was included in the second volume of Michael Drayton's work, *Poly-Olbion* published in 1622.

Drayton (1563–1631) was a poet from Warwickshire who produced a number of influential works.[94] His two-volume work of thirty poems, *Poly-Olbion*, narrated the character of individual regions of England and Wales through their chorography. The penultimate poem, 'Song XXIX', addresses the northern borderlands, in which Drayton mused on the history of the conflicts on this frontier, giving voice to the spirit of 'aged *Pictswall*'. The work has not been studied in any great detail, despite the impact of some of Drayton's other works upon his contemporaries.[95] *Poly-Olbion* was not a significant success when it was first published, due to its old-fashioned style. It has been described as 'a fifteen-thousand line descriptive poem in pedestrian hexameters'.[96] The thirty individual poems that make up the two volumes provide something of a challenge to Stuart absolutism.[97] The first volume of poems about the South was published in 1612, but the second about the North was published almost ten years later.[98] Much of the entire work, however, may have been written some time before the last volume went to press.

The narrative structure and content of *Poly-Olbion* drew directly on Camden's *Britannia*.[99] Camden's book was in prose, while Drayton's poems

---

[89] cf. H. Griffiths (2003); Hingley (2008a), 96–101.
[90] James I (1603), 272; cf. H. Griffiths (2003), 89.
[91] Daniel (1603), section 2; cf. Wormald (1994), 18.
[92] cf. Shannon (2007), 10–11.
[93] H. Griffiths (2003), 89.   [94] Prescott (2004).
[95] Brink observes that it has appealed only to 'curious antiquaries' (1990, ix).
[96] Helgerson (1988), 356.
[97] ibid., 356–7; Helgerson (1992), 128–9.   [98] Brink (1990), ix.
[99] Brink (1990), 86; Herendeen (2007), 214; Klein (2001), 210.

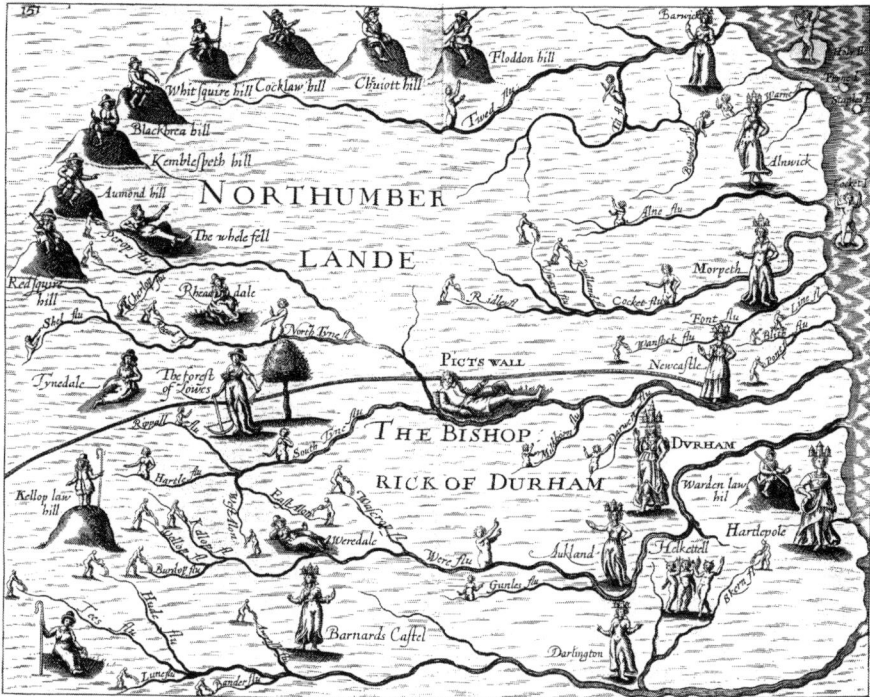

Fig. 5.4. William Hole's map of Northumberland, which was engraved to accompany the second volume of Michael Drayton's *Poly-Olbion* (1622). Reproduced by permission of the Bodleian Library, Bookstack Mal 13(2).

were more artistically inspired,[100] but both accounts explore the landscape of Britain and combine chorography with history. Much of the history incorporated in Drayton's poems, including many of the details provided about *Pictswall* himself, is derived from Camden's writing.[101] The order of the poems, for example, derives from the sequence of counties in *Britannia*.[102] A major difference in Drayton's text, when compared to *Britannia*, is that the landscape is addressed through the voices of a variety of spirits of place (Figure 5.4).[103] These spirits are figuratively represented on the maps of each county accompanying the poems.[104]

It has been noted that the human body is the 'governing image' in *Poly-Olbion*.[105] The frontispiece of volume one portrays Britain as a female figure, clothed with a map. The engraver William Hole produced the maps of all thirty counties featured in the poems. These were influenced by the earlier

---

[100] Ewell (1978), 311.
[101] cf. Moore (1968), 787; Brink (1990), 86; Herendeen (2007), 214.
[102] Klein (2001), 210.
[103] Moore (1968), 784; Helgerson (1992), 117–18.
[104] Ewell (1978), 300.   [105] ibid., 299.

cartography of Christopher Saxton, but are unusual in the Jacobean context because they include the mystical characters who narrate each song.[106] Hole was a prolific engraver who had produced many of the images for the 1607 and 1610 editions of *Britannia*.[107] Drayton's characters represented the spirits of features in the landscape, including mountains, forests, rivers, and valleys; they directly transform geography and landscape into human form.[108] The maps do not show very much evidence for the human occupation of the landscape, although towns and cities are often represented by a human figure. The ancient monuments of Stonehenge and the Picts' Wall are also marked on the relevant country map.

The physical line of the Picts' Wall runs across Hole's map of Northumberland (Figure 5.4), accompanying 'Song XXIX', Reclining immediately below the name 'PICTS WALL' and just above the River Tyne is a male figure, apparently the spirit who narrates part of the poem (Figure 1.3). He is placed above the course of the river, just downstream of the confluence of the North and South Tyne, in the vicinity of Heavenfield. *Pictswall* is one of many figures shown on this map; while female figures usually represent rivers, dales, and towns, male figures usually represent hills.[109] The female figures that represent 'Weredale' and 'The whele fell' are in a similar pose to that of *Pictswall*. The female spirits of cities and towns wear headgear of urban buildings and walls. The course of the Roman Wall springs out of *Pictswall*'s head, while his left hand is closed around it. *Pictswall* is evidently based on an image of a classical water god, and his position just above the River Tyne close to the point where the South and North Tyne meet may suggest that he represents the river itself. It is more probable, however, that this spirit represents aged *Pictswall*, as unclothed females invariably represent rivers and dales. It is also possible that this male figure represents a hybrid spirit, including the Wall and the Tyne, although this would be very much at odds with the spirit of Drayton's poem in which *Pictswall* argues vociferously with the local streams and rivers.

Pictswall appears to represent a man of indeterminate age dressed in a hybrid manner; Aileen Ribeiro suggests that 'he wears a contemporary (early 1620s) non-elite doublet and plain linen collar, with the lower half of his body in a short "skirt", possibly a long shirt, which *may* show the influence of early Gaelic' (Scottish/Irish) dress', while his bare legs may also reference the Highlands.[110] It is possible that this figure is intended to represent an ancient northern Briton, partly dressed in contemporary clothing to emphasize his continued vitality. Perhaps he is intended to represent the Jacobean conception of a Pict. The naming of the monument as the 'Picts' Wall' sometimes

---

[106] Klein (2001), 201; Moore (1968), 784.
[107] A. Griffiths (2004).
[108] Ewell (1978), 300; Helgerson (1992), 117–18.
[109] cf. Mikalachki (1998), 30–1.
[110] Aileen Ribeiro (pers. comm.).

appears to have caused some confusion, hinting at the idea that the Wall, or an element of it, was actually built by the Picts.[111]

'Song XXIX' of Drayton's poem focuses on the history of the conflicts along the English–Scottish border. The spirits of hills and rivers, including the Tyne and the Forth, narrate the long sequence of the medieval border wars between the English and the Scots. *Pictswall*'s speech occurs towards the end of the narrative:

> But *Pictswall* all this while, as though he had been lost,
> Not mention'd by the *Muse*, began to fret and fume,
> That every petty Brooke thus proudly should presume
> To talke; and he whom first the *Romans* did invent,
> And of their greatnesse yet, the longest-liv'd monument,
> Should thus be over-trod; wherefore his wrong to wreake,
> In their proud presence thus, doth aged *Pictswall* speake.
>
> Me thinks that *Offa's ditch* in *Cambria* should not dare
> To thinke himselfe my match, who with such cost and care
> The *Romans* did erect, and for my safeguard set
> Their Legions, from my spoyle the proling *Pict* to let,
> That often In roads made, our earth from them to win,
> By *Adrian* beaten back, so he to keep them in,
> To Sea from East to West, began me first a wall
> Of eightie myles in length, twixt *Tyne* and *Edens* fall:
> Long making mee they were, and long did me maintaine
> . . .
>
> And when I first decayd, *Severus* going on,
> What *Adrian* built of turfe, he builded new of stone;
> And after many a time, the *Britans* me repayr'd
> To keep me still in plight, nor cost they ever spar'd
> Townes stood upon my length, where Garrisons were laid,
> Their limits to defend; and for my greater ayd,
> With Turrets I was built, where Sentinels were plac'd,
> To watch upon the *Pict*; so me my Makers grac'd
> With hollow Pipes of Brasse, along which that went,
> By which they in one Fort still to another sent,
> By speaking in the same, to tell them what to doe,
> And so from Sea to Sea could I be whispered through.
>
> Upon my thicknesse, three march'd eas'ly breast to breast,
> Twelve foot was I in height, such glory I possest.[112]

Although *Pictswall* describes himself as 'the longest-liv'd monument', he appears no longer to fulfil a defensive function in the Jacobean borderlands due to his old age and the ruination of time. His survival as a vital spirit of

---

[111] Hutton (1802), 1; Bates (1895), 7–8.
[112] Drayton (1622), 158–9.

place reflects both the excellent physical survival of the Roman Wall in the landscape of early seventeenth-century northern England and in the Jacobean mind.[113] *Pictswall* may be aged and ruined, but he is still relevant to the definition of the border, especially as a result of his ancient genealogy. Nevertheless, he is clearly frustrated at being 'lost' as a result of prior claims made in the poem by 'petty Brooks' to roles of importance in protecting England's northern borders from invasion. In these terms, *Pictswall* is aged and outdated but, unlike Adrian's Wall in Samuel Daniel's poem, he is not irrelevant.

STORY AND HISTORY

Despite the considerable differences in their focus, it is important not to exaggerate the division between Camden's and Drayton's writings about the Wall. Drayton's aged *Pictswall* is a living and vital figure, while Camden's account of the monument appears rather more descriptive and analytical. William Moore has suggested, however, that the close relationship of poetry and scholarship was a natural one for some authors in Jacobean England.[114] At this time, scholars were often poets, while poets drew on scholarly approaches. The poetry and maps in *Poly-Olbion* do not aim to divide 'truth' from 'fiction', although it has been observed that the Renaissance saw the beginning of an estrangement, if not an entire separation, between the concepts of 'history' and 'story'.[115] Anne Lake Prescott has argued that, as a writer of chorography, Drayton 'feels the tug between history and story' and allows the landscape to narrate this concept.[116] After Drayton's time, prose histories tend to become increasingly critical of their sources, in contrast with their counterparts in verse.[117] At the same time, the final divorce between knowledge and tale has never entirely occurred; indeed, two decades ago Prescott suggested that 'a reconciliation may be in prospect'.[118]

Camden provides a fairly lengthy description of the history and structure of the Wall, an account that has long been considered to represent the start of the systematic study of the monument.[119] As Leslie Hepple has argued, 'The northern tour of 1599 enabled Camden to write at first hand of the Roman heritage of the border counties . . . It has also been recognized as the starting date for systematic Roman Wall studies'.[120] In late Tudor and early Stuart

---

[113] Hingley (2008a), 93–4.   [114] Moore (1968), 784.
[115] Prescott (1991), 308.   [116] ibid., 313.
[117] Hardin (1973), 33.   [118] Prescott (1991), 308.
[119] E. Birley (1961), 1; Breeze (2006a), 15; Hepple (2003a), 160.
[120] Hepple (1999), 1.

England, there was also a development towards greater accuracy in the recording of topographical information through the advances made in cartography,[121] as exemplified by the maps in *Britannia*. At the same time, antiquarian studies witnessed an increasing focus on the observation and recording of material objects alongside a more critical assessment of the available source material.[122] Camden's accounts of the Roman remains at particular places, including Ellenborough, have led to his work being called 'proto-archaeology', or even 'archaeological'.[123] His excellent scholarship in compiling and updating *Britannia* has been incorporated by later generations into the genealogy of the developing and improving study of the Wall.

To what extent is this reflection on the chorographical approach pursued by Camden valid? It has been argued that modern accounts of the history of archaeology often seek an origin for the discipline by placing particular emphasis on the detailed descriptions of ancient monuments in the works of antiquaries such as Camden.[124] Camden's analysis of the construction phases of the Wall, explored in detail above, presents a broadly chronological narrative derived from a critical reading of the available materials. Camden also uses the material evidence derived from first-hand inspection to critically assess what had been written before. Anne Lake Prescott writes that at this time a new generation of antiquaries was trained 'to examine sources, compare authorities, calculate chronology, sniff out anachronism, and study coins, inscriptions, and statuary'.[125] Camden focuses upon the chronology of the construction and use of the Wall to create a historical and largely sequential narrative. In these terms, Camden's method has been compared to the verification of hypotheses, partly based on field studies along the Wall conducted at particular places.[126]

It is interesting, however, that Camden does not always follow these precepts. Indeed, some of his writing about the Wall does not appear to convey an entirely sequential concept of time, an issue that, in turn, informed Drayton's creation of aged *Pictswall*. Barbara Ewell suggests that Drayton's writings on the English landscape explored the spatial order of the land, emphasizing its unity in a manner that effectively contradicted the chronological principals of history, an approach prefigured by some of Camden's scholarship.[127] For example, Camden connects the activities of soldiers on the Roman Wall with the watches maintained along the frontier of the kingdom in medieval and early modern times, practices that had only just ceased. From a modern point of view, this bypasses the linear sequencing of time on which historical

---

[121] Marchitello (1997), 77.   [122] Hingley (2008a), 82–7.
[123] H. Griffiths (2003), 95; Kunst (1995), 123.
[124] Gazin-Schwartz and Holtorf (1999), 7.
[125] Prescott (1991), 308.
[126] cf. Kunst (1995), 123–4.   [127] Ewell (1978), 311.

reasoning was beginning to be based at this time,[128] since it directly connects two periods in the history of this landscape divided by over a millennium. In the terms explored above, an encounter with the material remains of the Wall caused an eddy in time for the late Elizabethan and Jacobean scholars who wrote about its contemporary significance.

Camden noted that at the Roman station called 'Seven shiel' on the Wall, 'the wing Sabiniana' kept 'watch and ward' over the Roman frontier.[129] Elsewhere he writes of the Roman army under the Emperor Theodosius, in the late fourth century, 'standing watch and ward in their severall Stations' on the Wall.[130] 'Watch and ward' was a term used in association with the sixteenth-century night watch along the border and Camden's adoption of this term conflated the watch of the Wall in both Roman and recent times.[131] This is a tradition that is also incorporated into the two late Elizabethan proposals, studied in Chapter 4, to build new fortifications along the border with Scotland. Another reference to the Wall in *Britannia* suggests that this idea of common Roman and English frontier defence was a widespread concept along the line of the Wall at the time of Camden and Drayton.

Camden records that the people who lived along the Wall:

> talke much of a brazen trunke (whereof they found peeces now and then) that set and fitted in the wall artificially, ranne between every Fortress, and Towre, so, as that if any one in that towre so ever conceived the wathword [watchword] into it, the sound would have been carried streightwaies without any stay to the next, then to the third, and so then all one after another, and all to signifie at what place the assault of the enemie was feared . . . But since the wall now lies along, & no pipe remaineth there, many tenants hold farmes and lands of our Kings here round about, in *Cornage*, as our Lawers speake, that is, that they should give knowledge unto their neighbours of the enemies approaching by winding of a horne: which some thinke had the first originall, from an ancient custome of the Romans.[132]

Camden derived some of this information from a local tradition that described a brass speaking-tube embedded in the fabric of the Roman Wall, first recorded by Christopher Ridley.[133] To create a historical context for the significance of this tale, Camden added the information about the medieval practice of cornage and connected this with the speaking-tubes to construct a permanent condition of border warfare. In Drayton's poem, *Pictswall* draws on the same idea, claiming that 'from Sea to Sea could I be whispered through'. Other seventeenth-century writers have also written about the speaking-tubes of the Roman Wall.[134]

---

[128] cf. Prescott (1990), 130.   [129] Camden (1610), 801; cf. Breeze (2006a), 178.
[130] Camden (1610), 792–3.   [131] cf. Abbatt (1849), 78.
[132] Camden (1610), 787.   [133] E. Birley (1961), 3.   [134] cf. Gray (1649), 3.

This story survived for centuries along the Wall, but was dismissed and explained away by nineteenth-century antiquaries. The influential Victorian antiquary John Collingwood Bruce argued that the tradition of speaking-tubes arose because of the discovery of lead and ceramic water pipes among the remains of the Roman Wall.[135] He emphasized that there was no evidence to indicate the discovery of such items within the curtain Wall itself. One of Bruce's contemporaries, J. T. Fowler noted that:

> When I made a pilgrimage along the whole length of Hadrian's Wall in the summer of 1877, I saw the very aged landlady of a little thatched public-house in the village of Beaumont, between Carlisle and Bowness. She seemed to think that all 'the ancients', including the Romans, Belted Will, and the Dacres, were great people in those parts, but especially the Romans, who built that great wall, the greatest wonder of which was its pipes, through which they 'shotot' (shouted) from Newcastle to Carlisle. I should have thought she meant some shooting of projectiles had I not been acquainted with the speaking-tube tradition, which doubtless was purely 'oral' in her case.[136]

J. Wilson undermined the earlier accounts that had connected the Roman signalling activities with the medieval practice of cornage by addressing the evidence for the origin of the latter in medieval times.[137] Cornage may have represented a medieval practice through which people held land from the king in exchange for keeping watch and alerting the locality by sounding a horn when there was a threat of invasion or disruption. Bruce considered that myths such as that of the speaking-tubes 'will not long outlive the electric telegraph'.[138] These writers were trying to separate facts about the Wall from fiction, but for Camden the correspondence of the Roman and the medieval signalling practices was highly significant, since he also tells his readers that 'The fabulous tales of the common people concerning this wall I doe wittingly and willingly overpasse'.[139]

Camden's account did not always follow this rule.[140] In discussing the remains of the Roman outpost fort at Risingham (Northumberland), Camden relates a remarkable local tale of local giants: 'The inhabitants report, that the *God Magon* defended and made good this place a great while against a certain *Soldan*, that is, an *Heathenish Prince*; Neither is this altogether a vaine taile. For that such a God was heere honoured & worshipped, is plainly proved by these two altar stones lately drawn out of the river there . . . .'[141] This tale related the contemporary inhabitants of Risingham to the ancient past, drawing on two Roman inscribed stones that had recently been found in the river that runs alongside the site.[142] Soldan appears to have been a second giant and

---

[135] J. C. Bruce (1851), 76–7.   [136] Fowler (1878).
[137] J. Wilson (1901), 314.   [138] J. C. Bruce (1851), 76.
[139] Camden (1610), 795.   [140] cf. Glazier (2007), 43.
[141] Camden (1610), 803.   [142] in particular, RIB, n. 1225.

D<small>URHAM</small>

This Antick Figure I find cut out on a
Rock near Rifingham in Reads-Dale
called the Soldans Stone.

Fig. 5.5. An excerpt from John Warburton, *A Map of the County of Northumberland* (1716) showing 'Antick Figure . . . on a Rock near Risingham'. Reproduced by permission of the British Library, Maps 183.n.5.

a later record on John Warburton's map of Northumberland (1716) suggests that the story of this giant references an inscribed figure carved on another stone discovered close to Risingham (Figure 5.5). Mythical stories of giants and spirits were often used by local people to account for ancient monuments where little was known about the history of the structures,[143] such as Drayton's giant who narrates the history of the Picts' Wall. The information from Risingham indicates that these tales of giants connected with Roman remains in Britain may sometimes have been created as a result of the discovery of inscribed stones.

---

[143] Voss (1987), 81. For example, the eighth- or ninth-century elegyic, *The Ruin*, referred to Roman ruins as the works of giants (Eaton 2000, 126–7).

It is quite possible that Camden decided to omit other tales of giants and spirits along the Wall, judging them as irrelevant to his account of the monument, which aimed to emphasize its structure and history. The Victorian antiquary Charles Roach Smith, who visited the Wall on a number of occasions, wrote of the 'unlimited beliefs in local divinities along the Wall'.[144] Unfortunately, Camden's decision not to record such tales has meant that knowledge of the folklore of the Wall is far from complete; but some further information will be considered in Chapter 10.

SUMMARY: A CIVIL FRONTIER

Histories of archaeology often emphasize that Camden and his informants helped to create an orderly approach to the description of the Wall's remains and the associated Roman artefacts. There is certainly a great deal of truth in this argument, but Camden's motivation in describing the Wall was not entirely to uncover and relate archaeological and historical evidence. Antiquarian research and publication at this time was also a means for constructing identities and territorial claims for aristocratic landowners across England, reflecting changes in concepts of land ownership during the sixteenth century.[145] *Britannia* contended that Elizabethan and Jacobean England had inherited its civil and political identity from the Roman province of *Britannia*,[146] which explains the importance of the Picts' Wall as the boundary of this civil area. The common practice of the border watch on the Roman and the medieval frontiers explains Camden's belief in the living significance of this ancient monument. In comparable terms, Drayton's aged *Pictswall* enunciates the claim of English superiority over the Scots, a theme that was being challenged by James I's attempts to unite the two kingdoms.

Camden's emphasis on bringing the Roman past to life along the line of the Wall focused attention on the identity of the places he addressed. In this context, he linked contemporary individuals to the ancient past of the places in which they lived, making claims to the inheritance of civilization and landed rights.[147] John Senhouse at Ellenborough is linked to the idea of the civil present by the Roman remains that he recovered and displayed on his estate. Senhouse's 'courteous and friendly' reception of Camden and Cotton brings to mind the idea of the ancient introduction of civil behaviour to Britain by the Romans, contrasting it with the politically unstable and dangerous nature of the contemporary border landscape close to Housesteads. The preservation of Roman antiquities—at places such as Ellenborough, Naworth,

---

[144] C. R. Smith (1883), 181.   [145] cf. Swann (2001), 99–103.
[146] Kunst (1995), 125; cf. Hingley (2008a), 25–6.   [147] Hepple (2003a), 170.

and Conington—linked each landowner to the classical and civil past of his own estate. In a comparable manner, the claim for Appleby's Roman origin established the ancient ancestry and genealogical importance of this depopulated Jacobean county town.

The account of the Roman Wall in Camden's *Britannia* was highly significant, since the rediscovery of Roman antiquities from the remains of the frontier works enabled a handful of late Elizabethan and Jacobean gentlemen to recover an idea of the Roman occupation of the English border. This enabled them to imagine a spatial connection with classical antiquity for particular places with visible and buried Roman remains. The discovery of material objects derived from classical antiquity in these marginal lands had a particular relevance for those who were intent on creating political stability across the frontier by imposing metropolitan order.[148] The significance of these Roman materials was conveyed through antiquarian scholarship, but also through the production of Drayton's poems.

This development of an interest in Roman civility across the English borderlands appears, however, to have ceased in the troubled early decades of the seventeenth century. Eric Birley observed that the period from 1610 to the 1690s was an almost complete blank in the antiquarian study of the Wall.[149] The monument also ceased to play a political role, although one exception is provided by Edmund Waller, in a poem entitled *A Panegyric to My Lord Protector*, in which the author makes a reference to Oliver Cromwell's actions in Scotland, observing:

> A Race unconquer'd, by their Clyme made bold,
> The Calidonians arm'd with want and cold,
> Have, by a fate indulgent to your Fame,
> Bin, from all Ages, kept, for you to tame,
> Whom the old Roman wall so ill confin'd,
> With a new chain of Garisons you bind.[150]

The Roman Wall, which is presumably the monument that we know as Hadrian's Wall, is seen as having failed to separate the Caledonians living to its north from the richer lands to the south. In this context, Cromwell's military activities in Scotland are considered to have created greater security and order for those living in England.[151] Waller's reference to the ineffective nature of the Roman Wall reflected continuing English concerns regarding the threat from the north, but a strong interest in the physical remains of the

[148] Newton (2006), 96–7.
[149] E. Birley (1961), 8–9. Birley notes some activities on the Wall at Carlisle, South Shields, and elsewhere, and an early account of Newcastle that was published at this time also included a consideration of the Wall (Gray 1649, 3–6).
[150] Waller (1655), 5.
[151] cf. W. Ferguson (1977), 136–7; Mack (2006), 95–6.

monument was revived in the new political climate during the final years of the seventeenth century. This renewed interest appears to have been encouraged by the revisions of Camden's *Britannia* published in 1695 and 1722. *Britannia* remained the most authoritative account of the Wall throughout the seventeenth century and into the eighteenth and only ceased to play such a pivotal role after the publication of John Horsley's *Britannia Romana* (1732). Drayton's image of aged *Pictswall* was, however, largely forgotten and only rediscovered in the late nineteenth century.

PART II

The Roman Wall

This section of the book explores the continuing life of the Roman Wall during the eighteenth and nineteenth centuries. Rosemary Sweet has noted a semantic shift in the cultural significance of the monument from the 'Picts' Wall' of the seventeenth century to the 'Roman Wall' of the eighteenth.[1] Immediately following the Union debates of the first decade of the eighteenth century, several political tracts referred to the ruined nature of the 'Picts' Wall' in order to reflect upon the contemporary relationship between England and Scotland. In this context, the descriptions of the Wall in the revised editions of Camden's *Britannia* published in 1695 and 1722 continued to use this name. After the second decade of the eighteenth century, the monument is often called the 'Roman Wall', a change that reflects the effect of the 1707 Act of Union. The old name was, however, revived at particularly stressful periods, such as after the invasion of northern England by the Jacobite army in 1745 and during the early nineteenth century when it was drawn upon in the context of Irish and Scottish immigration into England. In the later nineteenth century, the name 'Hadrian's Wall' began to be adopted, reflecting the increasingly powerful argument that this emperor had commanded the monument's construction.

[1] Sweet (2004), 162.

6

Castlesteads: Reviving Interest in the Wall

Such Care have that warlike People taken to render a Climate of these
Northern Regions agreeable to their Constitutions.

George Smith (1742b), 76

INTRODUCTION

In 1695, a new edition of Camden's *Britannia* was published. Although there
was little additional information on the Picts' Wall,[1] antiquarian interest in the
monument increased significantly during the early decades of the eighteenth
century. This chapter will explore the new interpretations of the Wall that
developed during the first half of the eighteenth century, up to the Jacobite
uprising of 1745–6, an event that forms the focus for the following chapter.
The conceptual role of the Wall with regard to the unity and disunity of
England and Scotland will be examined, the results of the Act of Union of
1707, and the concomitant revival of interest. George Smith's particular
interest in the Roman fort at Castlesteads (Cumbria), exemplifies a new

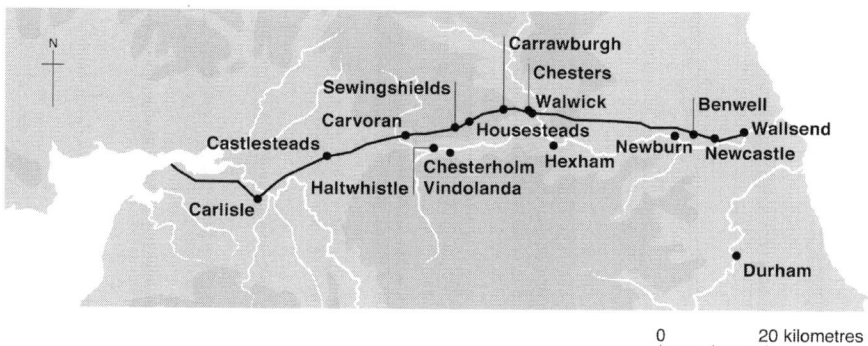

Fig. 6.1. Places mentioned in Chapters 6 and 7. Drawn by Christina Unwin.

---

[1] Camden (1695), 870.

The Roman *Altar lately found at* Cast Steeds *in* Cumberland, *with other Curiosities there; communicated by* G. Smith, *Esq;*

Little Pedestals, like Portable Altars, found also at Cast Steeds,

N. B. We hope to be able to oblige the Publick, in our *Supplement*, with the learned Mr *Ward*'s Opinion of these Curiosities and his Explanation of the *Inscription*,

Fig. 6.2. The altar (top) and hypocaust (bottom) at Castlesteads. From G. Smith (1741). Reproduced by permission of the Bodleian Library, Bookstack, M09.F07416.

approach to the Wall's remains. In 1741 a Roman building uncovered here was the first excavated Roman structure on the Wall to be illustrated in print (Figure 6.2). Since this time, the site has deteriorated and little of the fort remains visible.[2] George Smith reflected on the excavation of the foundations of this Roman building.[3] He argued that the heat from the hypocaust helped the soldiers to deal with the inclement climate of northern England. The excavation and planning of this building represented a new way to display antiquarian knowledge of the Wall. It supplemented the detailed maps and descriptions of the surviving remains of the monument produced earlier in the century by John Warburton, Alexander Gordon, and John Horsley. This chapter will assess the developing knowledge of the Wall and, particularly, the contribution of the mapping and the recording of inscriptions. Before turning to the antiquarian work, reflections upon the Wall by novelists, satirists, and an engraver will be addressed in order to illustrate its growing fame.

TIMOROUS TALK OF THE PICTS' WALL

Political developments in Britain at the beginning of the eighteenth century may help to explain the revival of interest in the Wall. There was almost constant political turmoil in Scotland following James VII's flight into exile in 1688.[4] These political problems intensified from 1701 in the context of William III of England's heir, the future Queen Anne, having no living heirs.[5] Concerns in England focused on the succession to the Scottish Crown.[6] The Act of Union in 1707, uniting the Crowns of England and Scotland, swiftly settled this debate.

During these problematic times, some Scottish and English intellectuals felt a need to define clear historical identities for themselves, and the physical remains of the Picts' Wall were used as a means to contemplate the ancient ancestry of the border between their two countries. An English writer from Suffolk, Edmund Bohun wrote that '*The Picts Wall* [. . .] was the most ancient Boundary between *England* and *Scotland*; begun by *Hadrian* the Emperour to separate the *Picts* (or Barbarous Northern Nations) from the Civilized

---

[2] Breeze (2006a), 330–3; see E. Birley (1961), 204.
[3] G. Smith (1742b), 76.
[4] Devine (1999), 4–5; Robertson (1995), 198.
[5] Robertson (1995), 201; W. Ferguson (1977), 197–203.
[6] Robertson (1995), 202; Devine (1999), 3.

Roman-Britains, in 123.'[7] Bohun observed that an initial frontier had been constructed of turf, stakes, and palisades and was later made into a 'solid Wall of Stone' by Severus and subsequently rebuilt several times. His comments created a direct link between, on the one hand, Hadrian and the English and, on the other, the Picts and the Scots—an idea that was already familiar from Bede. He drew on one of the few classical texts that referred to the building and use of the Wall (*HA* XI, 6), which had emphasized that it was built to separate the barbarians from the Romans. The view that Hadrian's Wall is the border between Roman/English civilization and Pictish/Caledonian/Scottish barbarism was drawn from classical texts and has remained influential ever since. It is a spatial measure that, whether it is used literally or ironically, establishes a hierarchy of relative civilization, placing the English in a dominant position.[8]

The textural and illustrative representations of the Picts' Wall from 1705 to 1710 explored the relationships between Scotland and England through the metaphor of the monument. Several of these accounts play down the significance of the Picts' Wall, reflecting the current political climate in a comparable manner to the Jacobean writings that have been considered in Chapter 5. Two political tracts written in the immediate aftermath of the Act of Union of 1707 reflect the new political alignment. In 1708, an anonymous pamphlet was published, entitled *The Union-Proverb: viz. If Skiddaw has a Cap, Scruffell wots full well of That* was published, which has been attributed, probably erroneously, to Daniel Defoe. A note in preface explains this proverb: 'To the TRUE British Reader . . . *Skiddaw* and *Scruffell*, are two Neighbour-Hills, or *high Mountains*; the one in *Cumberland* in *England*, the other in *Anandale* in *Scotland*: And if the *former* happens at any Time to be capp'd with *Clouds*, or foggy *Mists*, it will not be long ere *Rain*, or the *like*, falls on the *latter*'.[9] The pamphlet continues by emphasizing the threat of French invasion and emphasizes the '*Joint-happieness* of *England* and *Scotland*, lately united under the Name of *Great Britain*'.[10] At the end of the pamphlet, the author concludes:

> there can be no Necessity now for any more idle timorous *Talk* of the Picts-Wall, or irritating *Tattle* about BOTHWELL BRIDGE. Those things, as well as the bloody *Murder* of the Bishop of *St. Andrews*, must be quite obliterated; in order that GREAT BRITAIN may enjoy an *undisturb'd* UNION, and continue in a *profound Peace*, for fear of the *Proverb*.[11]

A second pamphlet, *The Story of the Injured Lady*, was the work of Jonathan Swift (1667–1745), the Dean of St Patrick's Cathedral (Dublin). Swift was an Anglo-Irish Protestant who was born in Dublin and had family connections in

---

[7] Bohun (1693), 318.   [8] Hingley (2008a), 132.
[9] Anon (1708), pages 1–3.   [10] ibid., 4–5.   [11] ibid., 19.

England.[12] He wrote several political pamphlets on Irish affairs; this particular text was probably written in 1710, but not published until 1746 in the eleventh volume of Swift's *Miscellanies*. It explored the political relationships between England, Scotland, and Ireland.[13] Swift personalized England as a man, who has a relationship with two women, Scotland and Ireland. This *Story* is written from the perspective of Ireland, who observes at the beginning that 'Being ruined by the Inconstancy and Unkindness of a Lover, I hope, a true and plain Relation of my Misfortune may be of Use and warning to credulous Maids, never to put too much Trust in deceitful Men'.[14] She explains: 'A GENTLEMAN in the Neighbourhood had two Mistresses, another and myself; and he pretended honourable Love to us both. Our three Houses stood pretty near one another; his was parted from mine by a River, and from my Rival's by an old broken Wall'.[15] This 'broken Wall' must represent the Picts' Wall, which is played down to emphasize the growing significance of the Union. The wide Irish Sea is interpreted as a river to emphasize England's close connection with the Protestant population of Ireland. Ireland presents an 'impartial' account of the character of her rival, Scotland, referencing a lack of cleanliness, apparent in many of Swift's other writings about women.[16] Swift's view of Ireland is far more positive: 'I was reckoned to be as handsome as any in our Neighbourhood, until I became pale and thin with Grief and ill Usage'.[17] The ruination of the Wall was to become a common motif during the eighteenth and nineteenth centuries in criticizing both the English and the Scots.[18]

When Daniel Defoe wrote of the Union of Great Britain, he recalled the 'very Origin' of the border issue, mentioning 'The Famous *Picts* Wall built in the Time of the *Romans*, the remains whereof are visible to this day, are sad Tokens of the Ancient Quarrels, Wars and Devastations that were carried on between the two Kingdoms, even beyond our Accounts of Time.'[19] Defoe (1660?–1731) was a writer and businessman from London who had been sent to Edinburgh in 1706 as an agent of the English Parliament.[20] His view is comparable to the two accounts discussed above, since the Wall has effectively become almost an embarrassment in the context of contemporary political Union. A decade later, in *The Farther Adventures of Robinson Crusoe* (1719), Defoe wrote again about the Picts' Wall, comparing it to the Great Wall of China.[21] During his travels, Crusoe comes across the remains of the Great Wall of China: 'we had pass'd this mighty Nothing, call'd a Wall, something

---

[12] Kumar (2003), 143; Probyn (2004).
[13] Swift (1746); cf. Hingley (2010a), 30–1.   [14] Swift (1746), 103.
[15] ibid., 104.   [16] Barnett (2007), 4–5.   [17] Swift (1746), 105.
[18] Hingley (2010a), 31.   [19] Defoe (1709), 3.   [20] Robertson (1995), 222–4.
[21] Defoe (1719), 292. Defoe may have been drawing here on the Scottish antiquary Robert Sibbald (1707), 3.

like the *Picts* Wall, and so famous in *Northumberland*, and built by the *Romans*'.[22] Crusoe asks his companion:

> do you think it would stand out an Army of our Country People, with a good Train of Artillery; or our Engineers, with two companies of Miners; would they not batter it down in ten Days, that an Army might enter in Batallia, or blow it up in the Air, Foundations and all, that there should be no Sign of it left?

EMPHASIZING THE WALL

A very different picture of the scale and significance of the Wall is presented by an engraving of 1707, which reconstructs the monument in a graphic manner (Figure 6.3).[23] The name 'THE PICTS WALL' is inscribed on the stone curtain Wall, just below the battlements (at the top left-hand corner of the image). This striking composition, designed and engraved by Jan Goeree, was published as the frontispiece to Volume Six of James Beeverell's *Les Delices de la Grand' Bretagne*,[24] an account of Great Britain and Ireland published in Leiden.[25] This particular volume addressed southern Scotland, and the engraving represents this geographical focus since the Roman Wall had often been taken to be the border between England and Scotland. This image appears to provide a political comment on the Union of Scotland with England.[26] The text on the engraving relates to the Scottish Royal House: '*Nemo me impune lacessit*' on the banner at the lower left translates as 'No one provokes me with impunity', a motto that first appeared on the Order of the Thistle, which had been established in 1687 and had been added to the Scottish Royal Coat of Arms at some point during the 1680s. The knight has a saltire cross over his breastplate and the gentleman next to him also wears a saltire pendant. The Scottish arms are shown crowned, a reference to the marriage of Mary, Queen of Scots and Francis, Dauphin of France, in 1558. The second part of the banner reads '*pour ma defence*', a French translation of the Scottish Royal Arms' original medieval motto, '*In defens*'. This heraldic history suggests that the image shows a point of view from the north of the Picts' Wall.

It is not, however, entirely clear from the image whether the scene portrayed is set to the north or to the south of the Wall and this may be deliberate. The

---

[22] Defoe (1719), 292.

[23] I am very grateful to Christina Unwin for bringing this image to my attention.

[24] Beeverell (1707a).

[25] Volume One of *Les Delices* contains a section on '*La Muraille de Sévère*' in which the author notes that '*Les Anglois* l'apelent The Picts Wale' (Beeverell 1707b, 241–2).

[26] I am grateful to Sam Smiles and John Bonehill for comments on this image.

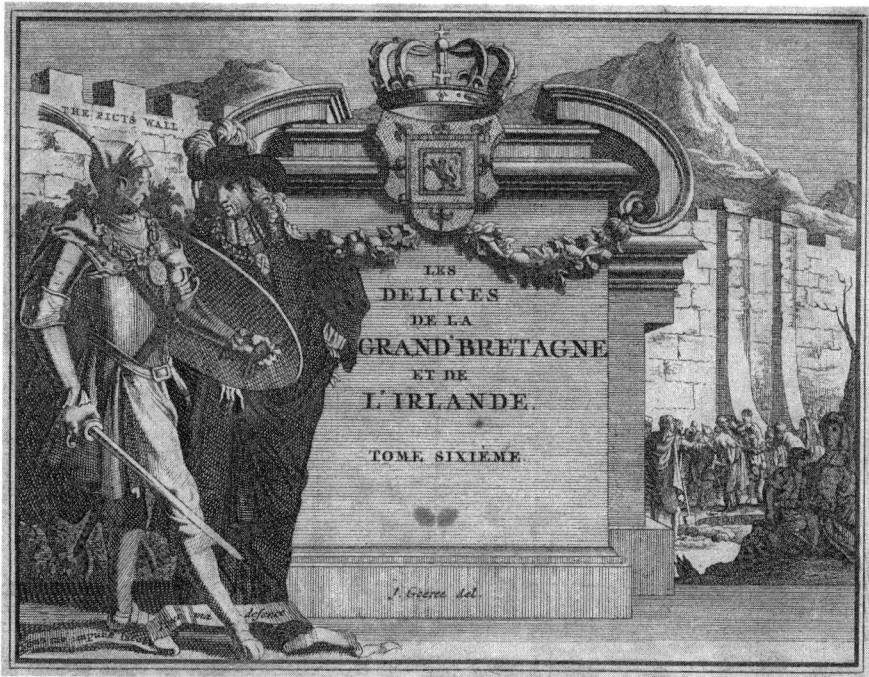

Fig. 6.3. J. Goeree's engraving showing the Picts' Wall. From Beeverell (1707a). Engraving in the possession of Richard Hingley.

figures in the middle ground may be shown in the act of digging the ditch to the north of the Wall. If this was so, they would be beyond the Picts' Wall and this raises the question of why the Picts' Wall is so closely associated with the Scottish Royal House. Perhaps the artist is representing the Jacobite claim to the throne of England and Scotland by turning the Wall around. There was a good deal of speculation about Pictish society in early seventeenth-century antiquarian studies that connected these people with the Stuarts and perhaps this image is drawing upon such association.[27]

Goeree has represented the Wall as truly massive, complete, and in use, but the structural details suggest that the artist had little comprehension of the form or structure of Hadrian's Wall and it is possible that the reconstruction is based on an engraving of the medieval walls of a Western European city. By contrast, the accounts of Swift, Defoe, and the anonymous author of *The Union-Proverb* all stress the comparative insignificance of the Picts' Wall.

Despite its apparent political irrelevance to some commentators, antiquaries were developing a more sustained interest in the physical remains of the monument at this time. During the early eighteenth century, visitors to the Roman Wall included travellers from southern England and from Scotland,

[27] John Bonehill (pers. comm.).

reflecting improved security in the border region. The area around House-steads was still troubled by the Armstrongs until about 1704, when Nicholas Armstrong was hung for his crimes and his brothers left to seek their fortunes in America.[28] R. C. Bosanquet has suggested that these changes brought House-steads 'within the pale of civilization'.[29] Following the suppression of robbery in the region, travel to visit the most impressive sections of the Wall became a rather less challenging activity.

The earliest eighteenth-century antiquary to develop a detailed interest in the Wall was Christopher Hunter of Durham, who visited Roman sites, including Chesterholm (Vindolanda) and Housesteads, in April and May 1702.[30] Hunter also travelled to Ebchester and sites to the north of the Wall at High Rochester and Risingham.[31] Hunter's early accounts of the Roman remains have provided important information to archaeologists studying the Wall.[32] He may have been able to gain access to Housesteads, in lands where others had long feared to tread, because of his apparent Jacobite sympathies and because he was a doctor.[33] Hunter also built up a collection of Roman inscribed stones, which were later acquired by the Dean and Chapter of Durham Cathedral, now part of the collection at the Old Fulling Mill Museum in Durham.[34] Hunter's observa-tions are of particular interest here, since he recorded the rebuilding of a substantial section of the curtain Wall. He notes that he travelled from High Rochester to '*Carron*' and that, 'between which and *Walwich*', which is Walwick near to Chollerford, 'the Wall has been repair'd and fronted with its old Stones again'.[35] In his original notes, on which his letter appears to have been based, he uses the name 'Carrow' rather than 'Carron',[36] probably Carraw just to the west of Carrawburgh fort. Hunter also noted that some of the Roman inscriptions that he illustrates were 'upon' this repaired Wall.[37] This suggests that a section of the curtain Wall had been refaced at this time for as much as four kilometres, but Hunter does not indicate why this had been carried out.

Hunter's description of this section of curtain Wall is supported by Robert Smith's account of an inspection of the remains in 1708. From County Durham, Smith made two journeys to the Wall in 1708 and 1709.[38] His visits appear to have formed the basis for the revised information on the Wall that was included in the 1722 edition of *Britannia*.[39] Eric Birley has observed that Smith produced the first 'reasoned description' of the course of the Wall from

---

[28] E. Birley (1961), 179; Bosanquet (1956), 168–9; Crow (2004a), 127; Rushworth (2009), 330.
[29] Bosanquet (1904), 193.
[30] Rogan (1954); Rushworth (2009), 3.
[31] C. Hunter (1702a); C. Hunter (1702b).
[32] cf. E. Birley (1961), 12, 184–5.   [33] Bosanquet (1956), 168–9.
[34] Haverfield (1899b), 3; Goodwin revised by Horsman (2004).
[35] C. Hunter (1702a), 1132.   [36] C. Hunter (1702b).
[37] C. Hunter (1702a), 1132.   [38] E. Birley (1961), 13–14, 50–1; Bosanquet (1956).
[39] Camden (1722), 1051–9.

Carlisle to Wallsend, including original observations about the structure of the monument.[40] Smith examined the section of the Wall between Newcastle and Carlisle in 1708, making a short topographic description of sites such as Chesters, Housesteads, and Carvoran, which he described as 'cities'.[41] In addition to the 'greater Forts and fortified Cities', he described the different features of the monument, including 'great numbers of little Forts or Castles, which the Inhabitants thereabouts generally call Mile-Castles', since they occurred every mile.[42] Smith notes that, for two and half miles to the east of Carrawburgh, 'the true Wall is to be seen standing, with a front of Ashler both inside and outside. It is in many places here, about two yards high'.[43] During his second journey of 1709, Smith explored the remains of the Wall between Newcastle and Wallsend.

A few years later, John Warburton produced a detailed and significant record of the course and structure of the 'Roman Wall' in his map of Northumberland (1716; Figure 6.4).[44] Originally from Lancashire, Warburton (1682–1759) was a herald and antiquary,[45] who worked as an excise officer and also complied maps. His Northumberland map has been widely admired as the first relatively accurate representation of the course of the Wall.[46] It was dedicated to the Prince Regent, 'His Royal Highness GEORGE AUGUSTUS Prince of Wales' (Figure 6.5), drawing a direct connection between the Roman imperial past and the royal family. The inset at the top left of this map shows an image of George Augustus and other members of the royal family, supported by Roman inscribed stones derived from Hadrian's Wall and other sites across northern England. This image depicts Apollo and the nine Muses on Mount Helicon, presumably intended to associate the dedicatee with cultural renewal and enlightened patronage.[47] As such, the map draws upon the associations made at this time between Augustan Rome and contemporary England.

This map included illustrations of Roman objects derived from sites in northern England, including twenty-two inscribed stones, thirteen coins 'found in ye foundations of ye Roman Wall', and a pair of Roman leather shoes. The full course of the Wall in Northumberland is shown on the map, while a foreshortened version of the Cumbrian section is also included and this appears to be the first attempt to mark individual forts and turrets, in addition to the line of the fortification and the main outlines of the Roman road-system.[48] Eric Birley has reviewed Warburton's 'intelligent use' of some

[40] E. Birley (1961), 14.
[41] Camden (1722), 1051–8.   [42] ibid., 1055.   [43] ibid., 1054.
[44] Hunter Blair (1956).   [45] Woodcock (2004).   [46] Whitaker (1949), 53.
[47] Sam Smiles (pers. comm.).   [48] Macdonald (1933), 47.

Fig. 6.4. An excerpt from John Warburton's *A Map of the County of Northumberland* (1716) showing the Roman Wall between Wallick (Walwick) and Newcastle. Reproduced by permission of The British Library, Maps 183.n.5.

of the Roman inscriptions to identify the names of the Roman sites shown on the map.[49]

Warburton evidently undertook extensive surveying to produce this map and also conducted some limited uncovering of ancient remains at Chester-holm, probably during 1715 or 1716.[50] Warburton discovered a Roman altar and the leather shoes, both used in the illustration of the map.[51] He was later to argue that the controversies provoked in London by the publication of his map had revived the study of Roman learning in Britain, resulting directly in

[49] E. Birley (1961), 12.   [50] ibid., 185; R. Birley (2009), 17–18.
[51] R. Birley (2009), 17, 157; the altar is RIB, n. 1648.

Fig. 6.5. The inset from the upper left corner of John Warburton's *A Map of the County of Northumberland* (1716), which dedicates it to George Augustus, Prince of Wales. Reproduced by permission of The British Library, Maps 183.n.5.

the refounding of the Society of Antiquaries.[52] At the time he wrote these comments, Warburton had recently been ejected from this Society.[53]

The activities of Hunter, Smith, and Warburton on the Roman Wall represent a broader awakening of interest in the monument, indicated by the succession of English and Scottish antiquaries who visited during the 1710s and 1720s.[54] Local men who are known to have visited the Wall include James Jurin, who was Headmaster of Newcastle School when he explored the Wall in 1714, making drawings of at least twenty Roman inscriptions.[55] He was also one of the natural philosophers resident in the north of England at this time, and his friends and associates included William Nicolson and John Horsley.[56] Jurin, who later became famous for his efforts to establish smallpox inoculations, gave public lectures in the north on experimental philosophy and Newtonism.[57] He left Newcastle in 1715, but retained an interest in Roman inscriptions after he had moved to London. Nicolson, who was Bishop of Carlisle, took a great interest in the Wall and provided information for the 1722 edition of *Britannia*.[58] The work of John Horsley will be considered below.

The Scottish antiquary Sir John Clerk of Penicuik (1676–1755) and Alexander Gordon toured the Tyneside section of the Roman Wall in 1724 during Clerk's review of the latest developments in English colliery management.[59] Clerk was an Augustan aristocrat who had been educated at Glasgow and Leiden where he had studied Roman history, after which he toured Italy.[60] He had been a prominent figure on the Scottish side in the negotiations leading to the Act of Union of 1707.[61] Modelling his lifestyle on a Roman pattern, Clerk developed an interest in the Roman remains of Scotland, amassing a significant collection of stones.[62] His visit to England's Roman Wall was a natural outcome of his developing interests in Roman culture.

AUGUSTAN GRANDEUR AND SCOTTISH REACTIONS

In 1725, two influential English antiquaries, William Stukeley and Roger Gale, toured the Wall together. Stukeley's exploration of the remains of the Wall was not published until eleven years after his death in 1776. He recorded that he had transcribed the notes written daily during this journey in 1725,[63] but it is not clear whether he updated his account at a later date. His omission of any

---

[52] Warburton (1753), vi–vii; see Pearce (2007), 5.
[53] Woodcock (2004).
[54] E. Birley (1961), 14.
[55] Jurin (1718); cf. Rusnock (1996), 64–5.
[56] Rusnock (1996), 11; Hepple (2003b), 154–7.
[57] Rusnock (1996), 11.   [58] E. Birley (1961), 10–13.
[59] Ibid., 14–15; Whitworth (2000), 48. Gordon's important study of the remains of the Wall is considered below.
[60] Brown (1987), 34–5; Brown (2004); Mitchison (2004).
[61] Duncan (1993), 3–4.   [62] Keppie (1998), 14–15.   [63] Stukeley (1776), 17.

discussion of the destruction of the remains of the Wall caused by the construction of a new military road during the early 1750s may suggest that he published his original observations without making too many changes. Stukeley uses the term 'The Vallum' to address the Wall, but also mentions that the local people called it the 'Pights wall', noting that 'they do this with a guttural pronunciation which we of the south cannot imitate'.[64] He compares it to the Great Wall of China, arguing that:

> The Romans, tired out with the untractable disposition of these people, whose country they judged not worth while wholly to conquer, resolved to quit their strength northwards, and content themselves with the desirable part of Britain, and, by one of the greatest works they ever did, seclude the Caledonians, and immortalise their own name by an inexhaustable fund of monuments, for posterity to admire.[65]

He contends of the area of the Wall:

> in the times of the perfection of this work it must be looked upon as the best planted spot of ground in the island: and we may imagine the glorious show of towns, cities, castles, temples, and the like, on the south side of this Wall, by contemplating the prodigious quantities of their ruins and memorials beyond that of any other part of Europe, scarce excepting imperial Rome.[66]

Stukeley described 'The amazing scene of Roman grandeur in Britain which I beheld [on] this journey', and sought to preserve through his description 'the memory of such things as I saw; which, added to what future times will discover, will revive the Roman glory among us'.[67] Finally, he argued, 'This tribute at least we owe them, and they deserve it at our hands, to preserve their remains'. Perhaps this last comment *was* written after the destruction that occurred during the early 1750s.[68] Stukeley produced some descriptions of the monument and a number of images of places along its line (Figure 6.6).

Stukeley had never crossed the English Channel and had no first-hand experience by which to compare the Roman Wall with the classical remains of the city of Rome.[69] Nevertheless, the study of the Roman remains of Britain inspired him to reflect on those aspects of Roman civilization felt to be appropriate for a country that was acquiring an increasingly extensive empire.[70] By exploring the monumentality of this impressive Roman structure, Stukeley was effectively seeking to project the surviving remains of the Romans in Britain into the context of England's neo-classical present,[71] a connection upon which Warburton's map had also drawn. The 'grandeur' of these remains was taken as a reflection of the contemporary imperial greatness of early eighteenth-century, 'Augustan' England, a united country that was seen as improving on the example of imperial Rome. Augustan society drew

---

[64] ibid., 55–66.
[65] ibid., 56.   [66] ibid., 67.   [67] ibid., 76–7.
[68] cf. Stukeley (1754a), 139.   [69] cf. Stukeley (1754b), 140.
[70] Haycock (2002), 119.   [71] Ayres (1997), 96–7.

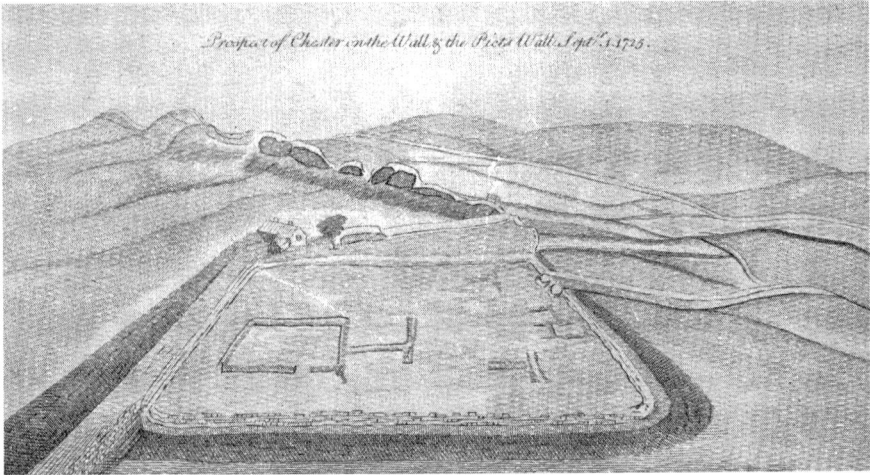

Fig. 6.6. An engraving showing the Roman fort at Greatchesters, entitled *Prospect of Chesters on the Wall & the Picts Wall, Septr 1725*. From Stukeley (1776). Reproduced by permission of the Bodleian Library, Oxford, Bookstack D 3.9 ART.

upon Rome in order to reflect upon the compromise reached between monarchy and Parliament following the Revolution of 1688.[72]

During the eighteenth century, educated sons of the English gentry often travelled to visit the ancient ruins of Rome as part of the 'Grand Tour', the travels of classically educated wealthy young men to visit the ancient remains of Rome and Italy.[73] Classical texts and architecture were prime aristocratic interests at this time, but Philip Ayres has argued that the Roman remains of Britain created an attachment to the classical past through which the new Roman culture of eighteenth-century Britain was conceived.[74] With regard to the Wall, Stukeley suggested, 'Hither let the young noblemen and gentry travel, to admire the wonders of their native country, thick sown by that great, wise and industrious people, and learn with them how to value it.'[75] The particular significance of classical Rome in Augustan England helps to explain the direct political value of the remains of the Roman Wall during the early eighteenth century.[76] Exploring, describing, mapping, and publishing accounts of the surviving remains of the Wall were intended to encourage future high-profile visitors.

The writings of the Scottish antiquary Alexander Gordon suggest that views on the significance of the Roman Wall differed either side of its line. As this

---

[72] Ayres (1997), 1–15; Sachs (2010), 31–2; Stray (1998), 17.
[73] cf. Arnold (1998); Buzard (2002); J. Scott (2003), 53.
[74] Ayres (1997), xv; cf. Hingley (2008a), 116–18.   [75] Stukeley (1776), 67.
[76] Ayres (1997), 96–7.

topic has been explored in some detail in a recent article,[77] a summary will be provided here. Gordon (*c.*1692–1745?), who probably originated from well to the north of the Antonine Wall at Aberdeen, had travelled to Italy and lived in London, working as an opera singer.[78] In 1726 he published *Itinerarium Septentrionale*, an account of the Roman military remains of southern Scotland and northern England, including the two Roman Walls. This was one of the most original antiquarian works to be produced in eighteenth-century Britain.[79] Gordon had conducted extensive surveys of the Roman monuments across a substantial area to produce this account. He described the Roman Wall in England, noting that '*Severus* built his Wall originally upon the very same Ground where Hadrian made his *Vallum*',[80] providing an account of the course of '*Hadrian's Vallum*' and '*Severus's* Wall'. Gordon states that he had produced a 14-foot map of the Wall of Hadrian and Severus that was about to be published, but unfortunately it does not survive.[81] Despite this, he produced the fullest description yet of the Roman Wall and his account of the Antonine Wall was even more detailed.[82]

Gordon recorded and mapped the Roman stations and Walls across central Britain, using their substantial surviving remains to conclude:

> If *Scotland* boasts of being numbered among the Nations which never bowed their Necks to the Yoak of *Roman* Bondage, I think, from the foregoing Sheets, it appears plain, that their Pretence is not built upon a wrong Foundation: For, from the Tenor of the whole *Roman* History in *Britain*, it cannot be shewn, that the *Scots* and *Picts* ever suffered the least Part of their Country to lie under Subjection, any considerable Time, without re-possessing themselves thereof, and taking a just Revenge upon their Enemies and Invaders.[83]

The remains of Roman military operations across Lowland Scotland and northern England were evidently of deep significance for this account. Their scale and permanence provided proof of Scottish valour and nobility, ideas that drew, in turn, upon classical texts.[84] Gordon's account was written just under twenty years after the Act of Union and his work exhibits anxiety over the English cultural domination of Scotland.[85] He drew directly on Bede to argue the role of the provincial Britons to the south of the Wall in the failure to subdue those to its north. Gordon was drawing a direct parallel between, on the one hand, the ancient Caledonians and Scots of his own day and, on the other, between the Romans and contemporary Englishmen, the latter observation also reflecting the absorption of Roman imperial culture by Augustan society across the Lowlands of Britain.

---

[77] Hingley (2010a), 32–4.   [78] Brown (2004).
[79] Hingley (2008a), 122–33.   [80] Gordon (1726), 71.
[81] ibid., 188.   [82] Hingley (2008a), 129–31.
[83] Gordon (1726), 135.   [84] ibid., 136.   [85] Hingley (2008a), 123.

The influential English antiquary, Roger Gale (1672–1744) disagreed directly with Gordon's conclusions in a letter to Sir John Clerk.[86] Gale was particularly interested in the Roman occupation of Britain, having visited the Roman Wall with William Stukeley in 1725. In a letter to Sir John Clerk, Gale reacted to Gordon's claims for the valour of the ancient Scots:

> I cannot think it not a scandall for any nation to have been conquered by the Romans, but a great misfortune not to have submitted to their arms, since their conquests were so far from enslaving those they vanquisht, that they tended onely to the civilizing and improving their manners, reducing them under Roman laws and government from their wild and savage way of life, instructing them in arts and sciences . . .[87]

These contrasting views on the Roman conquest articulate what can be interpreted as opposing Scottish and English views of the Roman legacy, but Clerk's view of the Roman invasion combines both ideas. Some of Clerk's observations effectively synthesize the claims of both Gordon and Gale,[88] demonstrating that the significance of the Wall cannot be defined simply in terms of a dichotomy between English and Scottish interpretations.[89]

Modern scholars have usually followed Gale in criticizing Gordon's political motivation and have also ignored the significance of his innovative surveying and recording work. Eric Birley has suggested that Stukeley and Gale had a far more significant impact than Gordon on the study of the Wall, although he does concede that Horsley's work owed a great deal to Gordon.[90] It should be noted, however, that Gordon's plans of Roman sites and landscapes were based on methodical and thorough surveying work and accompanied by lengthy and detailed descriptions.[91] If Horsley had not been conducting an even more detailed study of the same relics, which was published in 1732, the value of Gordon's surveying would doubtlessly have been far more fully acknowledged.[92]

Gordon was evidently motivated by the contemporary political situation, but so were his English contemporaries. Gale's comments on the value of a Roman cultural inheritance for the English reflects the context of early eighteenth-century England, a society that claimed to be building upon and improving upon the example of Augustan Rome.[93] This attitude to culture claimed the Roman Wall for the English and used the monument, despite its

---

[86] Gale (1726); cf. Haycock (2002), 119.

[87] Gale (1726), 87–8; partly quoted by Ayres (1997), 100.

[88] For a detailed discussion of Clark's attitudes to the relevance of classical Rome to contemporary Scotland, see Brown (1987).

[89] e.g. Clerk (1742), 96; cf. Smiles (1994), 42–3; Hingley (2010a), 33.

[90] E. Birley (1961), 15; cf. Haycock (2004).

[91] Hingley (2008a), 124.   [92] Sweet (2004), 167.   [93] Ayres (1997), 96–7.

ruined state, to provide a degree of seclusion from the Scots.[94] During the later sixteenth century, Camden had communicated the idea that the English to the south of the Wall had been made civil, while many of the Scots and Irish were excluded from civility by their continuing barbarity, a concept that has had considerable power ever since. This myth for the origins of English civilization links the people south of the Wall directly to the imperial Romans and determines a genetic origin for the Scots among the barbarian Irish, Caledonians, and Picts. It has proved to be a far more influential concept in England than Gordon's counter-claim of Scottish vitality and resistance. Indeed, we shall see that the English myth of a direct inheritance of empire from the Romans has informed many popular images of the Wall and the work of scholars of Roman Britain, right down to the present day.

Inspired by such ideas, visitors continued to visit the Wall in the following decade. Daniel Defoe visited some parts of the monument in the 1720s, writing about it in his *A Tour thro' the Whole Island of Great Britain*.[95] He mentioned that, while in Newcastle:

> I was tempted greatly here to trace the famous *Picts* Wall, built by the *Romans*, or rather rebuilt by them, from hence to *Carlisle*; of the Particulars of which, and the Remains of Antiquity seen upon it, all our Histories are so full; and I did go to several Places in the Fields thro' which it passed, where I saw the Remains of it, some almost lost, some plain to be seen. But Antiquity not being my Business in this Work, I omitted the Journey, and went on for the North.

Defoe's comment about the rebuilding of the Wall by the Romans is difficult to understand and he was presumably referring to the idea that the curtain Wall was not the first line of fortification and that the ancient Britons built the earlier earthworks along this line. Later on at Carlisle he noted that the castle had been strongly garrisoned to check the invading Scots and remarked that 'from below this Town the famous *Picts* Wall began'.[96]

John Loveday of Caversham in Berkshire travelled widely in Britain during the 1730s and his records provide details about the challenges faced by potential visitors to the Wall.[97] Loveday was planning to visit the monument but was concerned about his personal security and asked a friend about the local conditions. Dr Richard Richardson, a botanist and antiquary, wrote to a mutual acquaintance of Loveday's, 'If your friend designes to trace the Picts Wall from New Castle to Carlile, he must hier a Guide, for a great part of that Country is very thinly inhabited as wel as in Scotland and places of good accomodation not very frequently met with.'[98] Mr Baker of Cambridge,

---

[94] Hingley (2008a), 132–3.   [95] Defoe (1726), 195.
[96] ibid., 228.
[97] Markham (1984), 16–17, 127. I am grateful to Paul Bidwell for this reference.
[98] Loveday Family Papers, June 7, 1753, quoted in Markham (1984), 127, 458 n. 6.

however, remarked that, 'If Mr Loveday designs to visit the Picts Wall, I think he may do it very safely. I have been there many years ago, and found it as safe travelling there as in any other part of England.'[99] Loveday was not able to inspect the Wall in any detail during his visit of 1732, noting that 'besides want of time to see that also, moreover upon view of it and farther Consideration, I found it impracticable to think of tracing it on horseback, it runs so through Inclosures, far sometimes from public Roads. If God gives me Life 'tis my full Intention to walk it on foot another Summer or two'.[100] This suggests that in its western sections, the line of the Wall was difficult to access.

JOHN HORSLEY'S ROMAN WALL

In contrast with many of his contemporaries, the antiquary and natural philosopher John Horsley was interested in the remains of the Roman Wall primarily as a source of detailed knowledge about the Romans in Britain. Horsley (1685/6–1732) was a dissenting minister and natural scientist.[101] He had been educated at Newcastle Grammar School, very close to the line of the Roman Wall, and undertook an MA at the University of Edinburgh.[102] His volume, *Britannia Romana, or the Roman Antiquities of Britain* (1732), made a fundamental contribution to knowledge of the Wall, but Horsley modestly states that the subjects addressed in the volume 'by many will be thought of no great importance'.[103] This book described and illustrated the 'Roman Wall', its 'stations', and the inscriptions found among its ruins (Figure 6.7).[104] This includes detailed maps based on surveys made by George Mack of particular lengths of the Wall and included plans of the major Roman sites and objects derived from these sites (Figure 6.8).[105]

Horsley's writings are more analytical and descriptive than those of his contemporaries and, indeed, the author addressed the importance of the material and of the analysis of detailed information in the preface. He compared his approach to the Roman remains with the studies of mathematics and natural philosophy undertaken by both himself and his contemporaries.[106] Michael Hunter has discussed the development of a greater focus on archaeological materials during the late seventeenth and early eighteenth centuries and Horsley's work is to be seen in this context.[107] Referring to his contemporaries'

---

[99] Loveday Family Papers, June 7, 1753, quoted in Markham (1984), 127, 458 n. 6.
[100] Loveday Family Papers, August 30, 1732, quoted in Markham (1984), 132, 458 n. 10. Loveday also visited St Nicholas' Church in Newcastle in 1735, commenting on the proximity to the building to the Picts' Wall (ibid.), 186.
[101] Sweet (2004), 167; Haycock (2004).   [102] Haycock (2004).
[103] Horsley (1732), i.   [104] ibid., 98–158, 207–86.   [105] E. Birley (1974), iv.
[106] Horsley (1732), ii.   [107] M. Hunter (1995), 183–200.

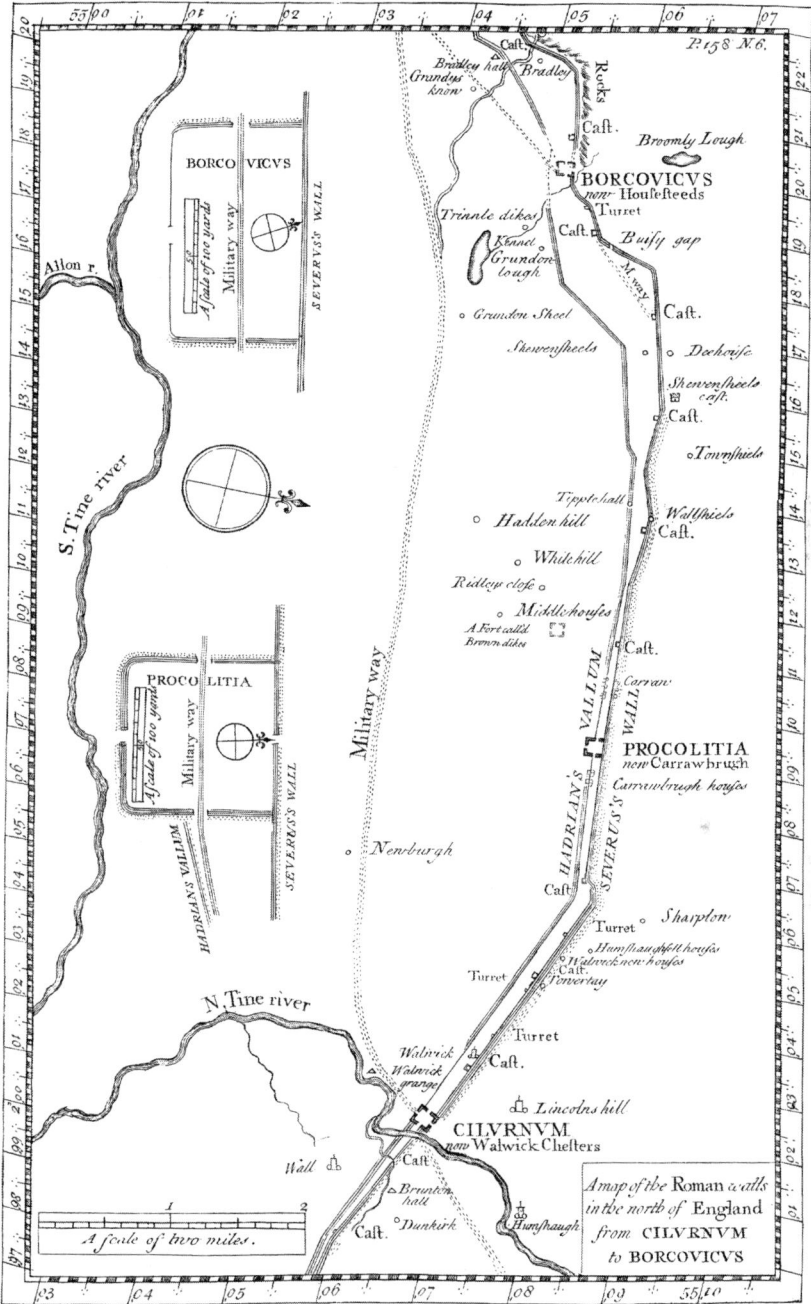

Fig. 6.7. George Mack's map of the Roman Wall from Chesters to Housesteads, taken from Horsley (1732). Reproduced by permission of Durham University Library, Routh 59.A.12.

Hadrian's Wall: A Life

CUMBERLAND

LXVIII

GENIO LOCI
FORTVNÆ RED
ROMÆ ÆTERNÆ
ETFATO BONO
GCORNELIVS
PEREGRÍNVS
TRIBCOHORTI
EXPROVINC
MAVRCÆSA
DOMOSEÆD
DECVR

LXVIII

VOLANTI
VIVAS

Genio loci Fortunae reduci Romae aeternae et Fato bono
Gaius Cornelius Peregrinus tribunus cohortis ex provin
cia Mauritaniae Caesariensis domos et aede decuriom *retulit*

Volanti vivas

Fig. 6.8. George Mack's illustration of the Roman altar from Maryport, taken from Horsley (1732, Cumberland LXVIII). Reproduced by permission of Durham University Library, Routh 59.A.12.

attempts to communicate the importance of the topic to their audiences, their 'large commendations of the subjects', Horsley expressed his particular wish to disseminate knowledge which 'not only pleases, but enriches and cultivates' the mind.[108] In justifying 'knowledge, some say, which brings no real advantage to mankind', he argues the importance of antiquarian scholarship, including information on the lines of the Roman Walls and the importance of the exact reading of inscriptions. Horsley does, however, reflect on the broader context for his studies, observing that:

Such vast works, suitable to so powerful and extensive an empire, all laid in desolation!...What surprising revolutions and catastrophes may we read not only in history, but in these very monuments! How men rais'd on a sudden, and then more suddenly cast down again, disgrac'd, and murder'd! At least all those great men, as well as most of their great works, are now reduced to ashes.[109]

The desolated condition of the memorials of Roman rule in Britain caused Horsley to reflect briefly on human life and death, but this is a rare contemplation of the meaning of the memorials of Roman rule in Britain.

[108] Horsley (1732), ii.   [109] ibid., iv.

Horsley did not use the name 'Picts' Wall' but followed the example set by Warburton's map by calling the monument 'the Roman Wall'. He also broke down the sequence of the Wall, building on earlier suggestions and proposing that:

> It is evident that there have been three different *praetenturae* erected here at different times, and by different persons; the first of which was a series of stations or forts, placed quite cross the country. And this I apprehend was done chiefly by *Julius Agricola*, and so is the most ancient of the three. Next to this was erected *Hadrian's vallum* and its appurtenances . . . The last and strongest fence of all was built by *Severus*, which is the stone wall with its appurtenances that lies north from the others.[110]

Horsley's account gave credence to a number of earlier writers, including Drayton, Gray, and Gordon, who had suggested that the curtain Wall was built by Septimius Severus.[111] This undermined the earlier suggestions of Gildas, Bede, and Camden that this structure had been built during the collapse of Roman power during the late fourth and early fifth centuries. Horsley discussed the possibility that the stone Wall had been built by either Hadrian or Antoninus Pius, eventually attributing the Vallum directly to Hadrian.[112] Therefore, Horsley proposed a three-stage programme for the construction of the Wall, which Eric Birley calls the 'general theory of Agricola, Hadrian, and Severus'.[113] This theory of three phases was only conclusively replaced during the early twentieth century, when the idea that Hadrian had built the stone curtain Wall was finally accepted.

Horsley provided a detailed account of the '*vallum* or *turf wall* (as it is frequently called by the country people)'.[114] He observed 'the principal *agger* or *vallum*' had a ditch to its north and suggested that a further *agger* occurred further to the north. This northern *agger*, he supposed, 'has either been made for an inner defense in the case the enemy might beat them [the Romans] from any part of the principal *vallum*, or to protect the soldiers against a sudden attack from the provincial *Britons*.' He noted that this *agger* 'is generally somewhat smaller than the principal *vallum*, but in some places is larger'. This suggests that Horsley was attempting to define a structure that faced north and to find in the Vallum a parallel to the Antonine Wall; this provided a justification for identifying this earthwork as Hadrian's frontier line. His two illustrations of the Vallum in cross-section emphasize its potentially defensive nature, with a turf rampart ('Hadrian's Principal Agger') to the south of a substantial ditch (Figure 6.9).[115] In both these cross-sections the structure identified by Horsley as the turf rampart represents a bank that is now called

---

[110] ibid., 98.
[111] cf. Maxfield (1982), 65–6.   [112] Horsley (1732), 117–18.
[113] E. Birley (1961), 58–9.   [114] Horsley (1732), 116–17.
[115] E. Birley (1961), 117.

The profile of the Roman walls in Northumberland about half a mile west from Carraw.

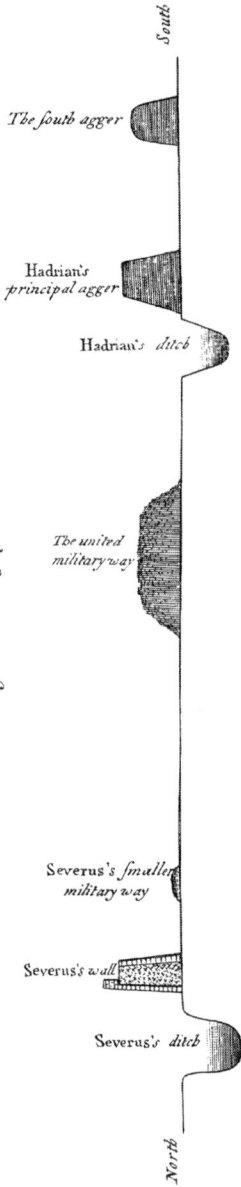

South

The south agger

Hadrian's principal agger

Hadrian's ditch

The united military way

Severus's smaller military way

Severus's wall

Severus's ditch

North

The profile of the walls about a mile west from Carraw, where Severus's military way is separated from Hadrian's north agger.

The south agger

Hadrian's principal agger

Hadrian's dit[ch]

The old military way or north agger of Hadrian

Severus's greater military way

Severus's smaller military way

Severus's wall

Severus's ditch

A scale of 9 paces or 15 yards

Fig. 6.9. Two cross-sections of the Roman frontier, taken from Horsley (1732), between pages 158–9. Reproduced by permission of Durham University Library, Routh 59.A.12.

the 'marginal mound'. It has been suggested that this bank may have been derived from the repeated cleaning of the Vallum's ditch and, although this is uncertain, this bank was certainly not a well-defined turf rampart of the type illustrated by Horsley.[116] Later cross-sections of the Vallum usually show the earthworks with a more regular bank on each side of the ditch (Figure 2.4). Such an arrangement does not support the idea of a defensive function for the Vallum.[117]

Horsley also discussed the 'stations *per lineam valli*' (on the line of the Wall) in the context of 'lasting summer encampments as well as winter quarters' by drawing on the classical writer Vegetius.[118] He remarked that the term '*statio*', as used by Caesar, Tacitus, and 'other good writers', was pertinent for the Roman places along the Wall. He presented a clear military purpose for the function of the regular Roman encampments along the Wall, contrasting with earlier references to these sites as towns and cities. Horsley was also drawing on the Roman inscriptions that had been found along the Wall, which often named Roman legions and auxiliary units.

The author's stated intention, to focus on the detailed analysis of the materials derived from the Wall, contrasted clearly with the motivations of many of his contemporaries, since this required no broader justification. Horsley articulated a powerful idea explored by later antiquaries and archaeologists—that scholarship is valuable in its own terms without any detailed recourse to the social context in which it takes place. Horsley produced a substantial, useful, and, in modern terms, a remarkably accurate record of the Wall and its inscriptions, an approach that appears to have foreshadowed the archaeological works of the late nineteenth to early twenty first centuries. As a result, Horsley's volume has been eulogized. John Collingwood Bruce asked, 'is it too much to say that he was the father of the science of Archæology?'[119] Seeking to define a scientific approach to questions and answers about the Wall, R. G. Collingwood argued that, with regard to Horsley's work, 'we feel that we have emerged from a tentative and amateurish, a pre-scientific, study of the subject, in which grave oversights and fundamental errors are expected and pardoned, into an age of clear thinking, where problems are faced and evidence mustered in a scientific spirit.'[120] Eric Birley wrote that students of Hadrian's Wall have long found in 'Horsley's methodological analysis and interpretation of [the Wall's] component parts an essential starting-point for further research.'[121] Indeed, *Britannia Romana* also constitutes a fundamental text for interpreting the condition of the Wall during the early eighteenth century.[122]

---

[116] RFa, 52–3.
[117] Simpson and Shaw (1922).   [118] Horsley (1732), 100.
[119] J. C. Bruce (1851), 104–5 n. a.   [120] Collingwood (1921a), 52.
[121] E. Birley (1974), iii.   [122] ibid., iv.

Despite this, Horsley's field observations have been called 'erratic', reflecting his interpretation of the Vallum as a defensive structure.[123]

GEORGE SMITH AT CASTLESTEADS

George Smith (1700–1773) of Wigtown (Cumbria) also undertook very important antiquarian research although his contribution has not been as thoroughly studied. Smith was a true polymath, who combined a deep interest in the Cumbrian landscape with antiquarian scholarship, work on natural features, research on astronomy, and the production of maps. Born in Scotland, he was a schoolmaster at Boothby near Carlisle, supplementing his income as a collector of excise taxes.[124] He is best known for what Emily Lorraine de Montluzin has termed his 'astonishing series of articles and letters' published in *The Gentleman's Magazine*, which amounted to over one hundred pieces on a wide variety of topics.[125] De Montluzin argues that Smith's contribution to the early Romanticism of the sublime has been seriously underplayed.[126] His letters in *The Gentleman's Magazine* included detailed images of ancient monuments and artefacts, his observations about the Roman site at Castlesteads, other inscriptions from the Wall, the Bewcastle Cross, and the stone circle of Long Meg and Her Daughters.

Reginald Bainbrigg had been the first to provide an account of the Roman site at Castlesteads, which he visited in the early seventeenth century. During the early eighteenth century the remains of the Roman buildings were quarried to provide ready-dressed stone.[127] John Horsley noted that the local landowner, Joseph Dacres Appleby, had employed people to dig stone close to Castlesteads and two Roman inscriptions were recovered, 'for which considerable generosity he must merit the thanks of all curious antiquaries'.[128] In 1741, Appleby's widow, Susana Maria, excavated a bath-house close to the fort.[129] Smith visited Castlesteads the same year and published innovative visual representations of the remains of this building and an altar (Figure 6.2).[130] These formed part of a series of images of Roman stones derived from the western part of the Wall produced by Smith as drawings and made into engravings for *The Gentleman's Magazine*.[131] Smith's image of the altar gives its ornamentation an almost vegetational character.

---

[123] Maxfield (1982), 67.
[124] de Montluzin (2004), 69.   [125] ibid., 67.   [126] ibid., 67–72.
[127] E. Birley (1961), 204.   [128] Horsley (1732), 261.
[129] E. Birley (1961), 204.   [130] G. Smith (1741); this inscription is RIB, n. 1983.
[131] de Montluzin (2004), 87 n 12.

Smith described the remains of a Roman building at Castlesteads in two letters published in the *Magazine*. In the first Smith recorded that 'In the Wood where the Fort has been, that Lady found some time ago, buried in the Rubbish, a regular Clay floor with several Pedestals upon it'.[132] Smith's caption for his engraving of this Roman building, 'Little Pedestals, like portable Altars', indicates that he had little idea of its purpose.[133] John Ward, Professor of Rhetoric in Gresham College (London), replied to Smith's letter, stating that he wished that 'a more accurate description' had been given of the building, but he suggested that the 'pillars [were] erected for the support of a hot bath', and compared these remains to a 'hypocaustum' recently uncovered at Lincoln.[134] Knowledge of hypocausts was increasing at this time and in 1706 an illustration of an example at Wroxeter (Shropshire) had been published in the *Philosophical Transactions*.[135]

In the second letter, Smith provided a further representation of the building, which he called 'an ichnographical Plan'.[136] Drawing on Ward's suggestion that the Castlesteads discovery was a hypocaust, Smith observed, 'Such Care have that warlike People taken to render a Climate of these Northern Regions agreeable to their Constitutions'. In recent times, visitors to the Wall have often made observations about the inclement climate and its likely impact on the Roman soldiers settled along the Wall, but Smith appears to have been the first to do so. He also mentioned that 'Mrs *Appleby*, who deserves to be gratefully remember'd by all Lovers of Antiquity, took great Pains to preserve what she cou'd of those valuable Remains of the Antients'. Eric Birley has noted that this is the first female antiquary recorded in the history of the Wall.[137]

The Gentleman's Magazine and the *Philosophical Transactions* constituted significant communicators of antiquarian discoveries at this time. The publication and circulation of representations of Roman remains enabled antiquaries to recognize and categorize some recurring types of Roman structures, including hypocausts and also the mosaics that had been uncovered across the southern parts of Britain.[138] The discovery of the Castlesteads hypocaust occurred towards the end of a frenetic period of research that had led to the detailed mapping and description of the Roman Wall. During the first half of the eighteenth century, these two journals published several articles on the discovery of Roman inscriptions along the line of the Wall. Together with the volumes produced by Gordon and Horsley, these drew the attention of many across Britain to the discoveries that were being made in the North.

---

[132] Smith (1742a).
[133] G. Smith (1741).   [134] Ward (1742), 31.
[135] cf. M. Hunter (1995), 186.   [136] G. Smith (1742b), 76.
[137] E. Birley (1961), 204.   [138] Hingley (2008a), 164–9.

SUMMARY: REASSERTING THE WALL

There is little to link Horsley's analytical approach to the Wall with the satirical and literary associations drawn upon by Swift and Defoe. Horsley's detailed account of the Roman remains of Britain largely excludes the contemplation of contemporary culture and politics. Swift and Defoe utilized the Picts' Wall to provide historical depth for their observations on the political relations of England, Scotland, and Ireland. The antiquarian works produced by Warburton, Stukeley, and Gordon incorporated political assessments of the contemporary significance of Roman rule, developing contrasting English and Scottish perspectives.

When viewed in the context of twentieth-century Wall scholarship, Horsley's contribution seems to be the most contemporary of the accounts studied in this chapter. George Smith's musings about the hypocaust at Castlesteads demonstrates, however, that in Stukeley's time the analytical techniques of stratigraphic excavation were still to be invented and applied to the Wall. The excavated structures along its line could only be dated to the Roman period either because they produced datable inscriptions and coins, or because they could be recognized as types of structures that appeared to be of Roman date. Antiquarian knowledge of the Roman Wall at this time was mainly restricted to the mapping of its physical remains, the classification of the various types of sites along its line, and the study of the Latin inscriptions. Although detailed knowledge of the structure of the Wall was emerging, little of the monument had been uncovered or studied to any great degree.

From an imaginative perspective, the amassing of detailed information about the monument may be uninspiring for general readers.[139] Horsley had sought to create a detailed knowledge of the Wall that excluded a broader attempt to justify antiquarian studies, but the military events of 1745 in the frontier lands were to lead to the re-evaluation of the contemporary significance of this monument.

---

[139] Hutton (1802), v–vi.

7

Newcastle and Carlisle: Reconstructing the Roman Wall

> In the present situation of affairs, a plan of the method antiently practis'd by the vigilant *Romans* for securing the isthmus of *Britain* with some remarks on it, will not I believe be unacceptable to the public.
>
> George Smith (1746c), 357

INTRODUCTION

The increased security created across the border landscape during the early eighteenth century made it safer for visitors travelling to view the Wall, leading to an increase in knowledge and interest in its remains. This sense of security was, however, periodically disturbed by concerns about possible invasion from the north, exemplified particularly in the Jacobite uprisings of 1715 and 1745–6.[1] The Jacobites were committed to the return of the dynasty of James VII of Scotland and II of England, a family that had lost the thrones of England, Scotland, and Ireland in the Revolution of 1688.[2] Jacobitism was also linked directly with the idea of the potential reintroduction of the Catholic faith. Although some early eighteenth-century political pamphlets had emphasized the ruination of the Picts' Wall, the conceptual significance of this Roman frontier was emphasized at times of political tension and insecurity. In particular, during 1745–6, Charles Edward Stuart's army overran Carlisle, penetrated the line of the Roman Wall, and advanced southwards into England. In the context of this uprising and also of the earlier events of 1715, the physical remains of the Wall took on a particular significance.

The practical reaction to these two events included three surveys of the Roman remains of the Wall, each of which appears to have been motivated by the desire to map and define the character of this ancient military

---

[1] Devine (1999), 37–8, 37–44; Pittock (1997), 114–18.
[2] Devine (1999), 31.

frontier. These surveys—which were undertaken by John Warburton (1716), George Smith (1746a), and Dugal Campbell and Hugh Debbieg (1750)—located and recorded the Roman remains. There is some evidence to indicate that all three mapping projects were motivated by a desire to supplement contemporary military endeavours on the frontier. In the aftermath of the Jacobite uprisings, it was proposed to reconstitute certain elements of the Roman frontier to impose a new order across a still unsettled border landscape as part of a broader programme of the surveying and construction of military landscapes across northern Britain. Political events and cultural attitudes during the early eighteenth century promoted the practical value of the monuments derived from the Roman military occupation of lowland Scotland and northern England, since they were perceived as physical examples of military strategy for the commanders and soldiers appointed to manage the threat from the Scottish Highlands and Islands.[3]

After the 1715 uprising, the government constructed a series of new garrisons in the Highlands, and between 1725 and 1737 a significant programme of road and bridge building was undertaken across northern Britain under the influence of General George Wade. This involved the mapping of the landscape and the building of military roads and stations, and these actions affected a 'neo-Roman' ordering of the landscape, drawing inspiration from the surviving remains of the Roman infrastructure.[4] The development of the study of Roman forts, marching camps, roads, and frontiers across southern and eastern Scotland has been considered elsewhere, including the important work of William Roy.[5] This will be developed by exploring the role given to the Roman Wall as a genealogical frontier, drawing in particular on the actions and writings of Matthew Ridley, George Smith, William Stukeley, and John Warburton.

REBELLION AND THE FALL OF CARLISLE

The map-maker and antiquary George Smith lived close to the west end of the Wall, which provided him with an ideal base for exploring Roman sites and brought him into close contact with the events of the final two months of 1745. Charles Edward Stuart had landed in Scotland in July of that year and, between September and November, marched south from Edinburgh, taking

---

[3] Hingley (2008a), 101–2.
[4] Harris (2002), 169; Hingley (2008a), 134.
[5] ibid., 133–48.

Carlisle with around 5,500 infantry and cavalry.[6] Smith directly experienced the action in and around Carlisle in November and December and wrote a lengthy letter to *The Gentleman's Magazine* during the following year in which he described his involvement and drew a remarkable message for contemporary times from the Roman history of the frontier. This letter was published in three parts between May and July 1746, a few months after the rebels had been defeated.

In the initial section, Smith addressed the troubles leading up to the fall of Carlisle in November 1745.[7] The map that accompanies his article (Figure 7.1) marks particular events that occurred in and around Carlisle during what Smith calls the 'pretended siege' of the city by Charles Edward's army.[8] This document was published in the *Magazine* as an ambitious engraved fold-out map.[9] Smith had met some of Charles Edward's troops, 'the prince's lifeguard', at Naworth Castle on 11 November, immediately prior to the surrender of the city.[10] He noted that they 'were very solicitous to see a map of England' and mentioned that he provided this as part of an attempt 'to try if I could penetrate their intentions'. Smith also described the difficult situation in which the local population were placed by the Jacobite army, giving an account of the events of 12 November, when 'About noon several hundreds of a wretched, ill-looking, shabby crew pass'd by armed with targets, broad swords, muskets, & c. and seemed very angry if no deference was paid to their flag: that afternoon and all the next day they spent in shooting sheep, geese, & c. and robbing on the highway.'

On the orders of King George II, General George Wade marched northwards to arrive in Newcastle at the end of October. By 15 November, Wade had realized that the rebels were moving towards Carlisle and advanced westwards to meet them.[11] Wade's army was only able to reach Hexham before being forced back to Newcastle by bad weather and the poor condition of the roads.[12] In November, Smith had travelled to 'Halt-wesel' (Haltwhistle) in an attempt to join Wade's army at Newcastle.[13] He records that, in the aftermath of the loss of Carlisle to the Jacobite army, 'the intercourse' with Newcastle was 'suspended' which made it difficult for him to follow the course of events as the rebels travelled further south into England. The Jacobite army moved southwards as far as Derby during December, but faced with serious armed resistance, were forced to retreat back north.

---

[6] Devine (1999), 43–4; K. Wilson (1998), 168.   [7] G. Smith (1746a).
[8] ibid., 234.   [9] Reitan (1985), 55; 60 n. 22.
[10] G. Smith (1746a), 233.   [11] Oates (2003), 147.
[12] Lawson (1966), 185–8; Oates (2003), 147–8.
[13] G. Smith (1746a), 234.

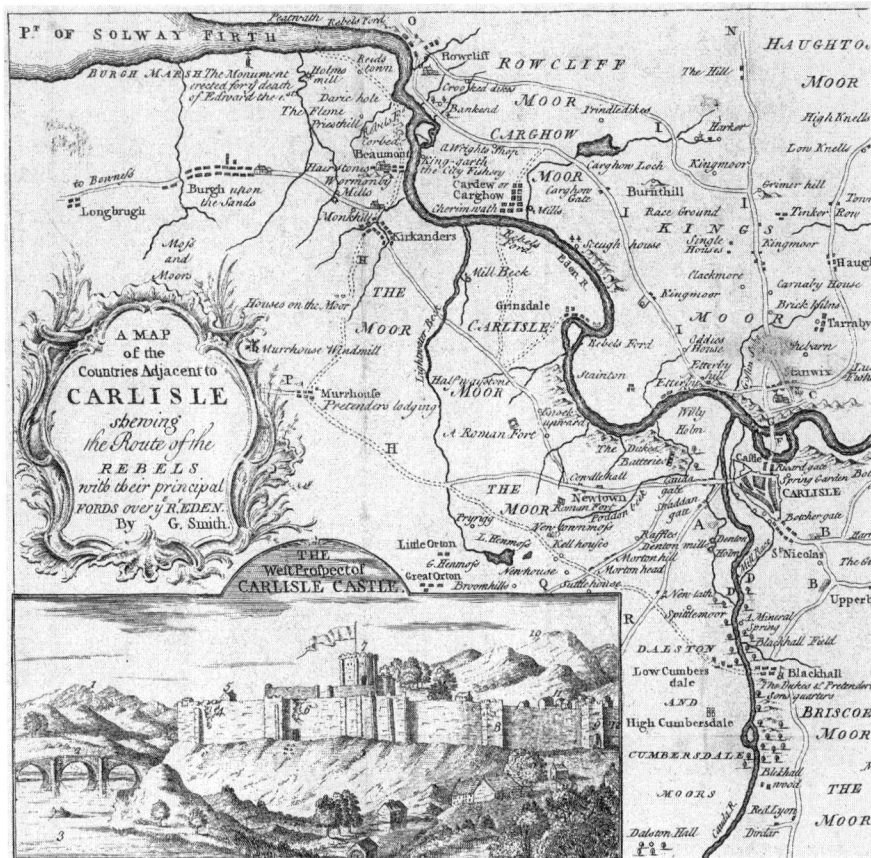

Fig. 7.1. An extract from a map produced by George Smith in 1746 entitled *A Map of the Countries Adjacent to Carlisle showing the Route of the Rebels with their principal fords over ye rr Eden*. The right part of the map has been cropped to show the detailed surveying and recording. Two sites just to the west of Carlisle are marked as 'Roman fort', but the map was intended primarily to show the military activities around Carlisle that occurred in the autumn and winter of 1745. Reproduced by permission of the Bodleian Library, Bookstack, M09.F07416.

The second part of Smith's letter discusses the recovery of the city and castle of Carlisle by the Duke of Cumberland, Prince William Augustus, King George II's second son.[14] The Duke had taken overall command of the army from Wade and pursued the rebels, arriving at Carlisle on Saturday 21 December.[15] Smith sent 'his royal highness a plan of the city and castle of

---

[14] G. Smith (1746b).   [15] Speck (2004); K. Wilson (1998), 174.

Carlisle', which included his own 'humble opinion [about] where the batteries might be commodiously rias'd, to distress the town least, and the enemy most.'[16] He also provided a description of the castle, noting that it was built on rising ground, 'close to the North-side of *Hadrian's* vallum' and speculating that it was 'at first probably one of Agricola's stations' and later became 'a place of note'.[17] The Jacobite army had left 400 soldiers at Carlisle and it took Cumberland's men ten days to force their surrender.[18] After being forced to abandon Carlisle, the rebels were driven back north, where they were finally defeated at Culloden, close to Inverness, in April 1746.[19]

The third part of Smith's letter contained *A Dissertation on the Roman Wall*, relating the recent military crisis to the rather more successful policy pursued by the Romans on the same frontier.[20] Smith stated his belief that, 'In the present situation of affairs, a plan of the method antiently practis'd by the vigilant *Romans* for securing the isthmus of *Britain* with some remarks on it, will not I believe be unacceptable to the public'.[21] He provided some information about the sequence of events on the Roman northern frontier from the late first century until the final departure of the Romans from Britain, and also described some of the main Roman sites around Carlisle and to the north of the Wall. Smith's map is marked with two 'Roman forts' to the west of Carlisle, although it does not show the course of the Wall itself.[22] He concluded his three-part letter by writing on the contemporary relevance of the Wall, suggesting that:

> I am none of those speculative visionaries that would call the wall from its ruins, tho' in imagination only; I am sensible it would ev'n be in a manner useless in the present practice of war. But had 6 or 7000 regular forces been plac'd in the line of the wall, from *Hexham* to *Brampton*, these, with the additional garrisons of *Carlisle* and *Newcastle*, and the rivers *Tyne* and *Eden*, woul'd have effectually prevented the incurtion of the rebel's into *England*.[23]

Smith recognized that it would have been impractical to rebuild the Roman Wall since it was outdated in military terms, but that a series of military units stationed along its western course would have prevented the Jacobite army from invading England and taking Carlisle, by presenting a united opposition to the army of Charles Edward Stuart.

---

[16] G. Smith (1746b), 301.   [17] ibid., 302.   [18] Speck (2004).
[19] Devine (1999), 44.   [20] G. Smith (1746c).   [21] ibid., 357.
[22] Interestingly, neither site labelled on the map as 'Roman fort' is located in the vicinity of the forts that are now recorded as having occurred along the Wall.
[23] G. Smith (1746c), 357–8.

LOYAL RESISTANCE AT NEWCASTLE

The population of Newcastle had a very different experience during October to December 1745. On the outbreak of the uprising and the surrender of Edinburgh in August 1745, panic had caused large numbers of people to leave the town,[24] although a loyal address was sent to King George.[25] The Mayor, Matthew Ridley, summoned all the householders to a meeting at the Guildhall and it is reported that over 3,000 entered into an association to defend Newcastle.[26] The walls were refortified and cannons were mounted on the towers, which effectively deflected a party of rebels advancing on the town in October. While the Jacobite army overwhelmed Carlisle and crossed the line of the Roman Wall, to move further into England, Newcastle stood firm, remaining in English hands and acting as the base for military reprisals.[27] After defeating the Jacobite rebels at Culloden, the victorious Duke of Cumberland was greeted in Newcastle with a pageant that included the burning of effigies of the Pretender.[28]

Matthew Ridley, whose family had been prominent in the northeast since the sixteenth century, was a member of Newcastle's eighteenth-century urban oligarchy, serving as Mayor and Member of Parliament for Newcastle.[29] He died in 1778 and his burial monument, one of several in Newcastle Cathedral to the urban elite of the town, portrays him dressed in a toga in the guise of a Roman senator (Figure 7.2).[30] Drawing on Newcastle's Roman myth of origin, Ridley is depicted on his monument in the guise of a Roman gentleman. Matthew Ridley's memorial was carved by a well-known London sculptor, John Bacon, and transported to Newcastle by sea.[31] The inscription recalls Ridley's role during the rebellion, noting that:

> He four times served the Office of Mayor, in which Station in the Year 1745, he rendered essential Service to his Country
> averting by his Prudence and Activity the Attack meditated against this Town by the Enemies of the House of *Brunswick*
> and thereby materially checking the Progress of their Arms.

This testimonial emphasizes the key importance of Newcastle, but it also draws upon Newcastle's Roman myth of origin.

Newcastle upon Tyne was one of the most important towns of England in the eighteenth century with an origin myth that drew upon the Roman Wall.[32] Ridley and his colleagues at Newcastle will have been well aware of the former

---

[24] K. Wilson (1998), 333.   [25] Oates (2003), 143.   [26] K. Wilson (1998), 334.
[27] Oates (2003).   [28] Speck (2004); K. Wilson (1998), 335.
[29] Pears (2008), 1.
[30] ibid., 3–4. Ridley's tombstone was erected in the parish church of St Nicholas, which then became the cathedral of the new diocese of Newcastle in 1883 (Paul Bidwell pers. comm.).
[31] Pears (2008), 5.   [32] Sweet (1997), 159.

Fig. 7.2. The burial memorial of Matthew Ridley at Newcastle Cathedral. Photography by Richard Hingley, 2011.

role of the Roman Wall as a military frontier that had provided a defense against invasion from the north and this probably helped to inspire this choice of Roman imagery. Although there were few traces of the Wall visible in and around Newcastle at Ridley's time, antiquaries had long emphasized the town's Roman origins.[33] Indeed, John Horsley had recorded a tradition that

---

[33] Camden (1610), 809; Gray (1649), 2–3.

the Roman Wall ran directly under St George's porch, near the north-west corner of St Nicholas' Church.[34] Matthew Ridley's representation in Roman terms emphasized his role as a member of the hereditary oligarchy of Newcastle,[35] but it also played on an international association with the culture of classical Rome that was widely admired in eighteenth-century England.[36] It is notable that the Ridley family home at Blagdon Hall was refurbished in Palladian style between 1752 and 1757, and that Matthew Ridley's son, Sir Matthew White Ridley, is portrayed in a toga on his own burial monument, also in Newcastle Cathedral.[37]

RE-ESTABLISHING THE ROMAN FRONTIER

By the time of the Duke of Cumberland's visit to Newcastle in July 1746, the military troubles in northern England had been settled and violent government reprisals were taking place across the Highlands and Islands of Scotland. The disruption caused by the invasion of England, however, required further attention. The problematic events of October to December 1745 required that military communications between Newcastle and Carlisle be improved, since Wade and his army had faced considerable problems manoeuvring through this terrain, which had contributed to the crisis. During the early 1750s, the physical remains of the Roman curtain Wall were used to provide the footings for the new military road that was intended to ensure that such a state of affairs would never again occur.

In his 1753 monograph on the Wall, *Vallum Romanum*, John Warburton drew a parallel between the Roman army in Britain and the Hanoverians in the border region. In particular, he directly connected the Roman Wall with the new military road, then undergoing completion.[38] This road, he claimed, fulfilled a comparable purpose to that of the Roman Wall.[39] Warburton stated that he had been interested in the military parallel between the Roman and contemporary frontiers since the first Jacobite uprising in 1715, when he had been living in Hexham and working as a government informer.[40] He added that he had undertaken his initial survey of the Roman Wall that year in order to demonstrate to the government the need to repair the Roman road to allow the passage of troops and artillery, but his advice had been ignored until the second uprising of 1745 raised the political stakes.[41]

---

[34] Horsley (1732), 133. Archaeological work during the twentieth century was to indicate that the Wall's course lies some way further to the south (Paul Bidwell pers. comm.).

[35] cf. K. Wilson (1998), 315. Lindsay Allason-Jones (pers. comm.) has pointed out that the tombstone also includes a representation of the *Magna Carta*.

[36] Pears (2008), 1–2.   [37] ibid., 1, 7.   [38] Hingley (2008a), 133–9.

[39] Warburton (1753), iv.   [40] Woodcock (2004).   [41] Warburton (1753), iii.

Warburton used the increased political prominence of the Roman Wall to emphasize its significance to his prospective readership. His volume drew upon a royal connection through its dedication to the Duke of Cumberland, 'Captain General of all His Majesty's forces'. Warburton stated that the second of the three sections of the book contained 'a large Account of the present State of the Walls, and Military Roads, more particularly that now re-edifying at National Expense, for the Passage of Troops and Carriages from *Carlisle* to *Newcastle upon Tyne*.'[42] An Act of Parliament had been passed for this construction scheme a few years before.[43] Warburton observed that, 'Thus after an application of thirty-eight years I at length obtained my desire, and have now the pleasure of being a coadjutor in the re-edification of this *truly royal military road*, which will infallible prevent all future invasions from *Scotland*, and consequently prove an everlasting benefit to *Great-Britain* in general'.[44] The context for Warburton's claim to authority over the idea of a new military road is unclear, but he is well known to have made a number of rather grandiloquent claims to fame.

Warburton drew on the evidence for the Roman infrastructure to support his claim that the military road had re-established the Roman order in this border landscape. Observing that Camden and Cotton had not been able to visit certain sections of the Wall, he noted:

> Such was the wild and baron state of this country, even at the time I made my survey, that in those parts now called the *Wastes*, and heretofore the *Debatable Grounds*, I have frequently discovered the vestiges of *cities, towns* and *camps*, that seem never to have been trod upon by any other human creature than myself, since the *Romans* abandoned them.[45]

This exaggerated reflection drew upon the old concept that the border area of northern England and southern Scotland were 'Debatable lands' or contested grounds.[46] To Warburton, the ancient remains demonstrated Roman control over this area, which the establishment of the new military road was intended to recreate in the contemporary age. For Warburton and Smith, the significance of the Roman Wall lay in its role as a physical marker of former civility in this frontier context. By constructing the new road, the government was re-establishing a system of control across the landscape for the first time since the Roman period. This created a context in which civil life could, once again, prosper in the new Augustan age.

Warburton accompanied his account with an authoritative map of the Wall, which showed the course of the Wall and detailed a number of forts along its line. Although he claimed the map as his own, he actually copied much of the detail from an official survey undertaken for the Board of Ordnance in 1749 by the military surveyors, Dugal Campbell and Hugh Debbieg (Figure 7.3).[47]

---

[42] ibid., ii.   [43] Act of Parliament (1750).   [44] Warburton (1753), iv.
[45] ibid., v.   [46] cf. Lamont and Rossington (2007), 1.
[47] Lawson (1966), 194–8; Macdonald (1933), 54.

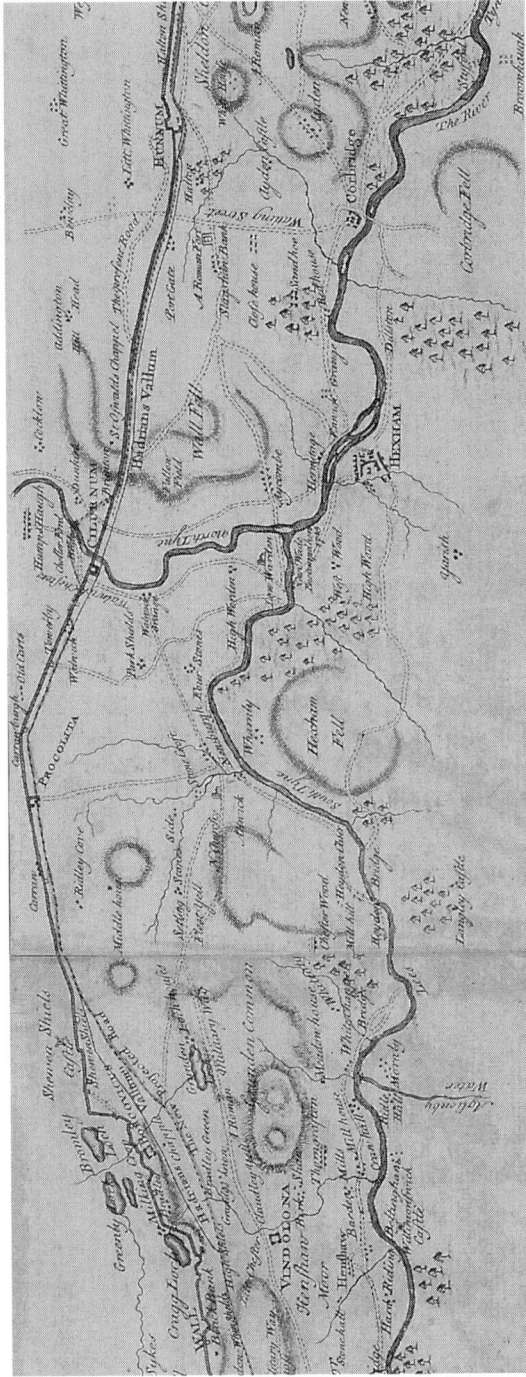

Fig. 7.3. An excerpt from Campbell and Debbieg's *A Survey of the Country between Newcastle and Carlisle* (1750). This shows the details of the Roman Wall between Steel Rigg and Halton Chesters. Reproduced by permission of The British Library, Map K.Top.5.103.

Campbell and Debbieg's map marked the Roman remains in the landscape through which the new road was to be built and also included insets showing plans, elevations, and cross-sections of the monument. These provided detailed information about the monument, including two cross-sections of the frontier works at Port Gate and Bradley, a profile of 'Severus's Wall' where it was cleared of rubbish close to St Oswald's, and a section of the face of the Wall half a mile west of Harlow Hill (Figure 7.4). These details provided an indication of the state of the Wall prior to the construction of the new road.

Why did these two military surveyors record so much of this information? The planning for the construction of the new road was based on the idea of using the available Roman stone remains as bottoming, but it appears unlikely that such an extensive survey of the Wall's remains would have been conducted purely for this purpose. Campbell and Debbieg appear to have been motivated by the desire to record the physical measures by which the Romans had imposed peace on this unsettled frontier territory. Debbieg (1731/2–1810) was also involved in the survey of Scotland, where he probably worked with William Roy.[48] During the late 1740s and 1750s, Roy became deeply interested in the remains of Roman military monuments, eventually producing a very detailed record of the Roman landscapes of Scotland.[49] Debbieg and Campbell were evidently motivated by comparable interests, since one of the insets on their published survey records '*A Plan of Cilurnum the Roman Station at Walwick Chesters with part of the Plan of Severus Wall & Hadrians Vallum Shewing how they are connected at the Stations and by their mutual Relation to one another*' (Figure 7.5). This illustrates in some detail the fort at Chesters, a number of 'towers' (turrets), and a 'castellum' (milecastle). It is clear that a number of the men involved with work along the Roman Wall during the 1740s and 50s—including Debbieg, Campbell, George Smith, and Warburton—considered the Roman military infrastructure to be a relevant model for contemporary activities.

The new road used the foundation of the Roman curtain Wall as its base for much of its eastern section, from Newcastle to Sewingshields. This has usually been seen in pragmatic terms, drawing on the idea that the Wall provided well-built and dry foundations and also a ready source of stone. This close relationship between the new road and the curtain Wall suggests, however, that the road planners sought to use the Roman structure as both the physical and conceptual foundation for the re-establishment of a Roman-style

---

[48] Kopperman (2004); Lawson (1966), 195–6; Seymour (ed. 1980), 5.
[49] Hingley (2008a), 139–48.

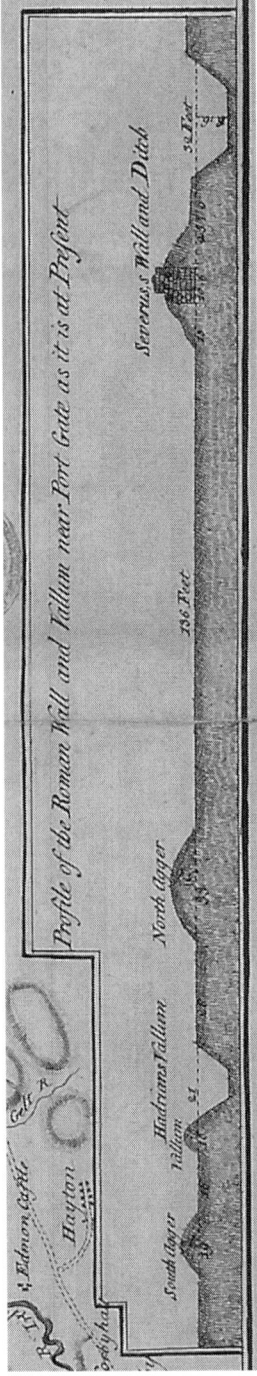

Fig. 7.4. An excerpt from Campbell and Debbieg's map showing a cross-section of the Roman Works near to Port Gate. Reproduced by permission of The British Library, Map K.Top.5.103.

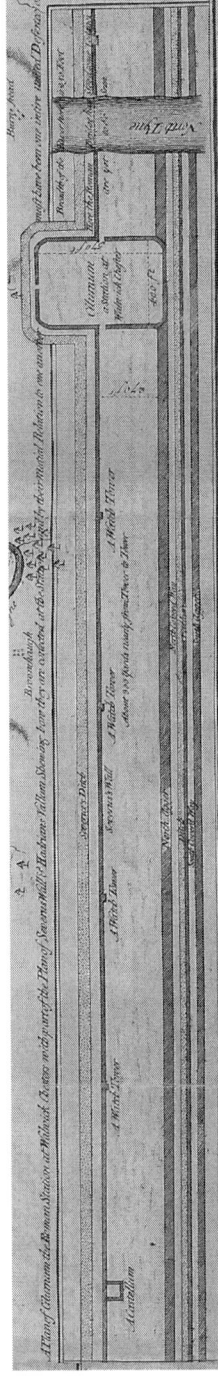

Fig. 7.5. An excerpt from Campbell and Debbieg's map showing the Roman works close to Walwick Chesters. Reproduced by permission of The British Library, Map K.Top.5.103.

order in this border landscape. The pragmatic solution of building the new road upon the foundations of the old Wall created a link between Roman and Hanoverian frontier order. The 1750 Act of Parliament specified that the road would be turned into a turnpike in order to enable the collection of tolls from travellers,[50] establishing a civil measure for the creation of stability and order in this frontier region.

WILLIAM STUKELEY AND PRINCESS AUGUSTA

The construction of the turnpike road has been judged as an act of pure vandalism that severely damaged the remains of the Roman Wall. While it was being built, William Stukeley made strenuous efforts to have the new road moved to another line. Stukeley noted in his diary that, on 15 July 1754, he dined with the Reverend Mr Wastal of Yorkshire who had told him that 'they have destroyed the Roman wall intirely for many miles. They take all the stones of the wall, beat them to pieces, to make the foundation for their new road'.[51] Stukeley notes that Wastal had asked a shepherd to look 'diligently' for inscriptions some years before and that 'he presently found a dozen.' Wastal currently had 'many' of them at his home at Simonburn, on the Wall close to Hexham, which Stukeley advised him to donate to the Cathedral Library in Durham. In October 1754, Stukeley recorded that he visited the Princess of Wales, Augusta of Saxe-Gotha (1719–1772), who had become Princess Dowager of Wales, after her husband's recent death.[52] Stukeley conversed with the Princess, chiefly about the Roman Wall and Herculaneum,[53] taking the opportunity to inform her about the damage then being caused by the building of the road.

Stukeley went to some lengths to justify his claims for the importance of the Wall. He observed to the Princess that, 'I loved my own country', and also that 'the Northumbrian wall was the greatest work the Romans ever did anywhere'. Stukeley mentioned that he had travelled the whole length of the Wall, recording 'innumerable' relics that were 'now lying neglected' and noting that:

> I took occasion likewise to express my concern at the havoc now making of this most noble antiquity by the surveyors of the new road carrying on by act of Parliament, who pull the cut and squared stones of the wall down, and beat

---

[50] Act of Parliament (1750), 1–3.   [51] Stukeley (1754a), 139.
[52] Bullion (2004).   [53] Stukeley (1754b), 140.

'em to pieces with sledg hammers to lay the foundation of the road with 'em, and in a country abounding with stones, and where the Roman road still remains, if they take the pains to seek for it, which would much shorten their labour.[54]

He noted that the Princess asked him why he had never travelled abroad,[55] which could, perhaps, suggest a certain cynicism in her mind with regard to Stukeley's claims about the Wall's cultural significance.

Stukeley drew upon a religious message in his debate with the Princess to stress the importance of his argument for the significance of the Roman remains of Britain. In his diary, immediately after his comments on the destruction of the Wall, he noted that they:

> discoursed on the first preaching of the gospel in Brittain, by S. Paul, at Chichester, where resided Pudens and Claudia, his disciples, mentioned in his Epistle; of Constantine the Great and his mother, both natives of Brittain. Empress Helena built those magnificent temples at Nazareth, Bethlehem, Jerusalem, and other places in the Holy land where our Saviour's nativity, crucification, &c.

The tale about St Paul preaching at Chichester arose from the discovery of a Roman inscribed stone in the town in 1723 that named Togidbnus and this is discussed at length elsewhere.[56] This story emphasized the importance of the Roman remains of Britain through their association with the introduction of Christianity, an observation that drew on the accounts of Gildas and Bede.

Stukeley was not at all confident that his efforts to champion the Wall had persuaded the Princess to take action. Four days after his interview he wrote a letter in which he asked for the Princess' 'powerful patronage to protect this most noble, most magnificent work, from further ruin, not from enemys, but from more than Gothic workmen, quite thoughtless and regardless of this greatest wonder, not of Brittain only, but of Europe'.[57] He requested a change in the course of the new road, noting 'there is a road made the whole length of the wall by the Romans. It was the business of the surveyors of the work to trace out this road. They would have found it pretty strait, well laid out in regard to the ground, and it would have been a foundation sufficient for their new road.' Proposing that the remains of the Wall should be protected, he argued that:

> Surely it well became the wisdom of the legislature to act with great deliberation in so important an affair, especially in regard to the preservation of this greatest wonder of Roman magnificence, not only what is now left whole or in ruins, but

---

[54] ibid., 140–1.   [55] ibid., 140.
[56] Hingley (2008a), 184–91.   [57] Stukeley (1754c), 141.

that ever was. . . . This mighty wall of four score miles in length is only exceeded by the Chinese wall, which makes a considerable figure on the terrestrial globe, and may be discerned at the moon.[58]

Finally, he argued that the Princess should visit the remains, asking, 'Would it be unbecoming a monarch to visit it where so many great emperors have been in person . . . ? How carefully do the Popes support and repair the ruins of Roman magnificence, well aware of the benefits accruing from the resort of travellers to see them?'[59]

In November, Stukeley visited the Princess once again, presenting her with a copy of Warburton's book and a letter 'magnificently bound in gilt paper' in which he acquainted her with the 'havoc' made of the Wall by the military builders.[60] He recorded in his diary that the Princess promised once again to have the construction of the road brought to a halt. Nevertheless, the building work went ahead unhindered and although some attempts were made by local people to protect the remains of the Wall along certain parts of its course, large sections of the curtain Wall were damaged and covered up during the 1750s.[61]

Archaeologists have usually condemned the construction of the military road. Charles Roach Smith argued that: 'The injury this sweeping and monstrous act of Vandalism inflicted on the dependant stations, as well as on the earthworks, can hardly be imagined.'[62] R. G. Collingwood observed, perhaps rather unfairly, that Warburton:

enjoys an immortality like that of the person who burnt down the temple at Ephesus: for he was the man by whose advice the Wall was destroyed, in order to build General Wade's Military Road along its foundations. Happily, the lie of the land westward from Sewingshields made it necessary for the road to diverge from the Wall, and to that we owe the preservation of what is left . . .[63]

These comments are particularly unfair to Wade, since he had died some time before the road was constructed. Sir George Macdonald followed Collingwood and condemned Warburton as 'the Vandal who openly boasts' of having prompted the scheme under which Hadrian's Wall was destroyed in order to facilitate the building of this new road.[64] Stukeley, Collingwood, and Macdonald all viewed the construction of the Hanoverian road as a desecration of the remains of the Roman monument, but other views have been expressed.

---

[58] Stukeley (1754c), 142.   [59] ibid., 143.   [60] Stukeley (1754d), 143.
[61] Lawson (1966), 198–9; Whitworth (2000), 50–1.
[62] C. R. Smith (1852), 18.   [63] Collingwood (1921a), 53.
[64] Macdonald (1933), 40.

William Hutton and Robert Forster followed Warburton in viewing the turnpike road effectively as a reconstitution of the Roman Wall.[65] R. C. Bosanquet noted that much of the curtain Wall and connected structures survived below the level of the metalling, as had been shown by the remains uncovered at Walbottle in the 1860s.[66] In fact, the building of the turnpike road may have served to protect the remains of the curtain Wall in some places from destruction by agricultural activities.[67] New discoveries were made as a result of the construction programme. As has been discussed above, the Reverend Wastal had collected many inscribed stones that had been disturbed during the work and other local men also observed Roman remains during the road construction. Robert Shafto surveyed the Roman site close to his house at Benwell during road construction in 1751 to 1752 and produced a colour pen and ink wash illustration of the bath-house at this site (Figure 7.6).[68] A number of Roman altars were also discovered, several of which were donated to the Society of Antiquaries of London and are now in the collection of the British Museum. A stone with an inscription recording construction work on the curtain Wall in AD 158 was found during the building of the military road close to Newburn.[69]

Warburton saw the opening up of the landscape in entirely positive terms as the creation of security and civil society on the frontier. There was also, however, an unforeseen impact on the well-preserved remains of the forts and *vici* along much of the Wall. Bosanquet argued that the secondary results of the road's construction were disastrous, since the government's example encouraged landowners along the Wall to improve their property by levelling the Roman remains that lay along its line.[70] As a result, the Roman remains at Rudchester, Haltonchesters, Carrawburgh, and Carvoran were systematically cleared over the next one hundred years.

POPULARIZING THE WALL

Warburton's book was intended as a 'pocket companion' to the Wall. Most of its material was copied from the accounts of earlier antiquaries,[71] but a coherent and conveniently sized account of the Wall was something entirely new. Warburton justified the publication of the book in the following terms:

---

[65] Hutton (1802), 172; Forster (1899), 202–3.
[66] Bosanquet (1926), 18; cf. J. C. Bruce (1865), 223; N. Hodgson (2011), 7 n. 11.
[67] Bosanquet (1926), 18.
[68] E. Birley (1961), 17, 163; E. Lewis (2007), 109.
[69] N. Hodgson (2011), 4; updating the information in *RIB* 1389.
[70] Bosanquet (1926), 18–19.
[71] E. Birley (1961), 18.

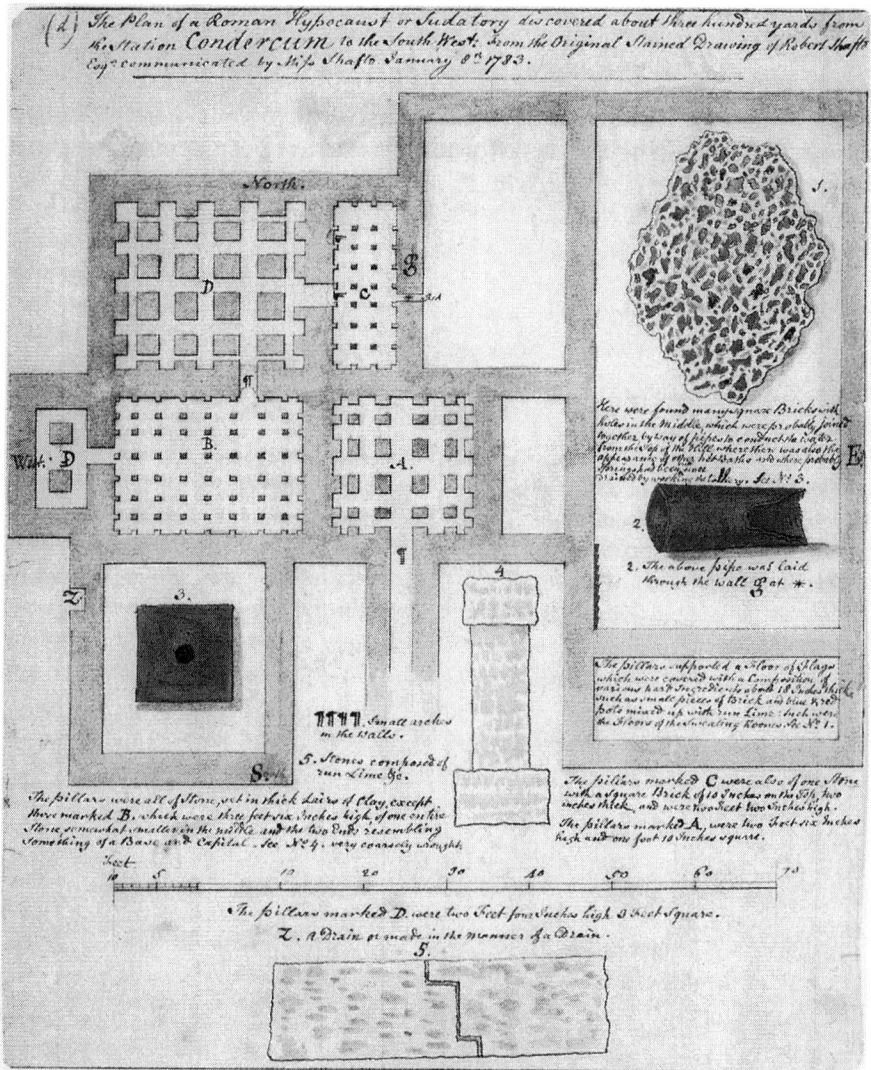

Fig. 7.6. Sketch of the Roman bath-house at Benwell by Robert Shafto, *c.*1751. Reproduced by permission of the Society of Antiquaries of London, *Britannia Romana* 89.4.

all books hitherto published, relating to the *Picts Wall*, are in large unwieldy folio volumes, and intermixed with other matters quite foreign to my purpose, or intention, which is no more than to provide a pocket companion for such learned travellers and others, whose curiosity may lead them to visit the superb remains of the famous *Picts Wall*, now justly esteemed the honour of *Great Britain*.[72]

[72] Warburton (1753), vii.

He noted that 'By this portable publication the sculptures, and inscriptions, with the readings and remarks on them, may be compared with the original altars and other stones on the spot.' Warburton stated that, 'All antiquaries that I have conversed with, who have made the accustomed tour of *Europe*, allow the *Picts Wall* to be the most superb remains of *Roman* grandeur that is now to be seen on this side of the Alps'. It is notable that this claim is rather less extreme than Stukeley's in his discussions with the Princess of Wales.

Warburton suggested that, as a result of visiting the Wall, 'both pleasure and instruction will accrue to such of our young nobility and gentry who shall travel to see them: An emulation will be raised among our youths of fine genius: *Roman* learning will become their favourite study, and old *Rome* in time be rivalled by *Britain*'. Warburton noted that he had written the book, 'as an Inducement to the young Nobility and Gentry of *Great Britain*, to make the *Tour* of their native Country, before they visit foreign parts'.[73] This is a reference to the 'Grand Tour'. Warburton wrote this book partly to raise money,[74] but also to encourage the English gentry to travel to and explore the Wall as an alternative to visiting Italy and the Mediterranean. Stukeley also glorified the remains of the Wall: 'Hither let the young noblemen and gentry travel, to admire the wonders of their native country, thick sown by that great, wise and industrious people, and learn with them how to value it'.[75] Although Stukeley's account of his travels to the Wall may have inspired people to visit the monument, his volume was far too large to be easily portable. Warburton's book was the first to contain a study of the remains of the Wall in a single relatively small volume and its example has been widely imitated.[76]

SUMMARY: REBUILDING THE ROMAN WALL

Stukeley and Warburton considered the Roman Wall to represent a physical marker of Roman civility in a frontier context, an issue that was brought into sharp focus by the troubled events of 1745. Warburton's argument for the restoration of the civil frontier is reminiscent of the proposal in the Elizabethan *Epystle* to build a new frontier work, an idea that arose from an earlier threat of invasion from the north. The drawing of political and military lessons from the Roman Wall provides one explanation for the quantity of antiquarian research that was conducted during the first half of the eighteenth century and the number of consequent publications. At this time, the first detailed surveys of individual forts on the Wall were produced, along with representational maps of the course of the Wall and the provision of more accurate depictions of some of the altars and other carved stones. The first excavations on the Wall were conduced that produced drawings of Roman buildings at Castlesteads and Benwell.

---

[73] Warburton (1753), cover page.   [74] Woodcock (2004).   [75] Stukeley (1776), 67.
[76] Including, Hutton (1802); J. C. Bruce (1851); H. Davies (1974); Burton (2003); Breeze (2006a).

The encouraging of visitors to the Roman Wall by Warburton and Stukeley was part of a broader later eighteenth-century movement to promote the exploration of the British countryside as an alternative or supplement to the 'Grand Tour'.[77] Despite Warburton's guide and the construction of the new road from Newcastle to Carlisle, however, fewer antiquarian visitors produced accounts of their travels to the Wall during the final forty years of the century. As Scotland became more fully united in the British imperial project, the Roman Wall appears to have ceased to play such a significant role.

Rosemary Sweet has suggested that at this time the 'coherence' of the Roman vision of antiquity was 'fractured and complicated' by competing histories of origins.[78] The half-century following 1745 witnessed a greater emphasis on the culture of the Scottish Highlands and the Lake District, resulting in a great increase to the number of visitors to these regions.[79] This appears to have coincided with a shift away from the contemplation of Roman antiquities, both in Britain and abroad, together with the refocusing of attention on classical Greek and Gothic antiquity.[80] In Britain, there was a growing interest in the remains of a variety of ancient monuments, including castles, abbeys, and megaliths, together with a focus on the sublime qualities of certain landscapes. Interest in the pre-Roman people of Britain increased in the century following the 1730s,[81] as some antiquaries began to explore and study megaliths, ancient houses, and artefacts.[82] Images of antiquity produced at this time often featured druids and megalithic monuments.[83]

Later eighteenth-century accounts of Roman finds from Britain often reflected upon the inferiority of these remains compared to those of Italy and the Mediterranean. The discoveries of impressive classical remains at Pompeii and Herculaneum during the middle of the eighteenth century resulted in a more critical reflection on the Roman antiquities of Britain.[84] Horace Walpole, for example, described them as 'very indifferent', noting that they 'inspire me with little curiosity'.[85] Nevertheless, Roman Britain was a popular theme for painters at this time. The main values derived from the Roman past at this time related to the ancient Britons' opposition to the invading Romans and also to the introduction of Christianity.[86] Peter Mortimer has considered why the Wall does not have a great literary history, noting

---

[77] Glendening (1997), 3; Haycock (2002), 110–11.
[78] Sweet (2004), 187.   [79] Buzard (2002), 43–5; Hooper (2002), 176–7.
[80] Smiles (1994), 46–74; Witcher (2010a), 131.
[81] Piggott (1976), 121–2; Smiles (1994), 16–18, 48–74.
[82] Hingley (2008a), 215–18; Morse (2005), 83–94.
[83] Smiles (1994), 165–93; Sweet (2004), 135–6.
[84] Hingley (2008a), 233–4; cf. Bowersock (2009), 70–5.
[85] Walpole (1780), 204; cf. Levine (1987), 104–5.
[86] Smiles (1994), 44–5.

that 'I have no idea why this is, given its sense of grandeur and often lonely romanticism.'[87] It would appear that during the late eighteenth century, the physical remains left by an oppressive imperial occupying power lost much of the attraction they had possessed during the earlier part of the century.

Further descriptions of the Wall were periodically published by local people. A local militia officer, John Dawson of Brunton, kept notes in his diary of visits to the Wall during the summer of 1769.[88] On 20 June, Dawson visited Chesters to view the remains of the fort and bridge, travelling west of Walwick to examine the remains of the Wall on 1 July, and to 'Sewen Shields' castle on the 10 July.[89] John Brand explored the course of the Wall during the 1770s and included some detailed information in his book *The History and Antiquities of the Town and County of the Town of Newcastle upon Tyne*.[90] William Hutchinson also included a lengthy description of the 'Picts Wall' in his book, *A View of Northumberland*,[91] mainly derived from the earlier writings of Horsley, Gordon, and Warburton. In general, however, antiquarian interest in the Wall declined and most visitors came from the region through which the course of the Wall runs.

[87] Mortimer (2007), 8.
[88] I am grateful to Paul Bidwell for this reference.
[89] Dawson (1769), 51.
[90] Brand (1789), 137–42; 601–18.
[91] Hutchinson (1778), 19–41.

8

The Mithraeum at *Borcovicium* (Housesteads): Reasons to be Cheerful?

This shapeless mound thou know'st not what to call,
Was a world's wonder once—This is the Roman Wall.
Thomas Doubleday (1822), lines 28–36

INTRODUCTION

John Collingwood Bruce was one of the most significant Wall experts of the nineteenth century. In 1849, Bruce organized a tour for a group of interested individuals, the first of the Hadrian's Wall Pilgrimages that have visited the Wall on regular occasions since.[1] This first Pilgrimage explored the entire length of the Wall and included a visit to the Roman remains at *Borcovicium* and the temple dedicated to Mithras just to the south.[2] Housesteads, an iconic fort of the Roman empire, is the most impressive of all the Roman stations along the line of the Wall,[3] which has been attracting visitors since the eighteenth century.[4] Since Bruce's time, extensive excavations have been undertaken, during the late nineteenth century, in the 1930s, and from 1959 to the 1980s, uncovering the very substantial remains of the fort and its associated *vicus* located on an exposed south-facing hill but protected by the well-preserved curtain Wall.[5]

Little of the temple of Mithras at Housesteads was visible at the time of the first Pilgrimage. Despite this, Bruce drew religious and imperial messages from this place of pagan worship. The impressive features that were just beginning to be uncovered at the fort inspired Bruce to draw a comparison between the fallen empire of Rome and the glorious contemporary domestic, religious, and imperial condition of Britain. He assessed the significance of the Wall's

---

[1] E. Birley (1961), 25; N. Hodgson (2009a).
[2] Subsequent research has indicated that the correct name for this place was probably *Vercovicium* (Rivet and Smith 1979), 493.
[3] Breeze (2006a), 234.   [4] Crow (2004a), 10.   [5] Rushworth (2009).

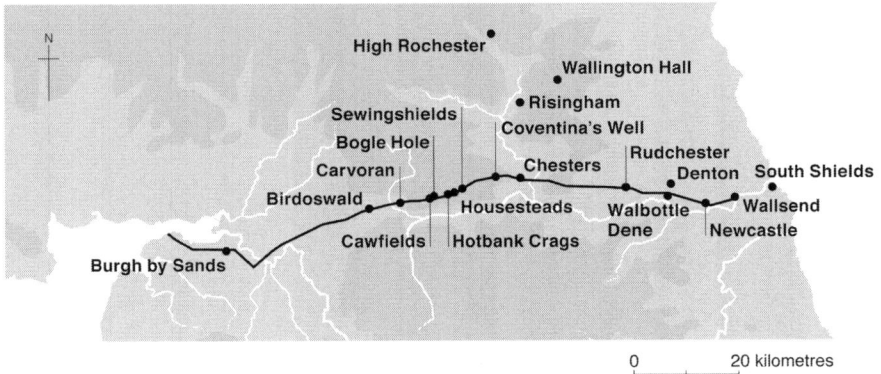

Fig. 8.1. Places mentioned in Chapters 8, 9, and 10. Drawn by Christina Unwin.

remains by emphasizing its contemporary political and cultural importance—metaphorically rebuilding its remains as a topic of current political, religious, and cultural concern. In this context, Bruce was reacting to almost a century of comparative disregard for the Wall, a situation that will be explored here before focusing on Bruce's *Borcovicium* lecture.

REASONS TO BE CHEERFUL?

Detailed antiquarian descriptions of the physical remains of the Wall had ceased for a while after the works of Warburton and Stukeley, but two visitors from the South may have been the first to walk the entire length of the Roman Wall in 1801.[6] William Hutton from Birmingham and the Reverend John Skinner from Somerset recorded their visits and encounters with people living along the line of the Wall. Hutton (1723–1815), who toured the Wall on foot in 1801 at the age of 78, described his successful published book, *The History of the Roman Wall* (1802), as 'my laborious, my romantic, and even my Quixote undertaking'.[7] A well-known historian,[8] Hutton was a dissenting bookseller who had worked himself up from a position of poverty to a comfortable financial situation and, as Rosemary Sweet has observed, was 'the antithesis' of those qualities that are usually associated with antiquaries—social status, land, Anglicanism, and Tory politics.[9]

---

[6] Another visitor at this time was the Roman Catholic priest John Lingard from Lanchester, who left notes of visits to the Wall in 1800 and 1807 (Bosanquet 1929).

[7] Hutton (1802), 313.   [8] Elrington (2004).   [9] Sweet (2004), 314.

Hutton drew much of his knowledge of the Wall from the writings of Camden, Horsley, and Warburton.[10] He took with him on his tour maps from the Gibson edition of *Britannia* (1695 or 1722) and Warburton's volume.[11] He walked 600 miles between 4 July and 7 August 1601 and examined what he described as 'a shattered Wall'.[12] It is hardly surprising that he was extremely grateful for the eighteenth-century military road, writing of 'the great, beautiful, and the famous Roman military way, first formed, I believe, by Agricola, improved by Severus, and brought into its present state by George the Second'.[13] Eric Birley has observed that Hutton's book is 'very readable' because of the light it sheds on contemporary life and manners, but that it has less value as a description of the physical remains of the Wall.[14] Hutton sought to communicate his emotional experience of the Wall to his audience in order to bring its remains to life.[15]

At the beginning of his book, Hutton remarked on his experience of 'a few mutilated Ditches and a broken Wall',[16] intentionally downplaying the significance of the extensive remains he described. In his preface he disparages the efforts of earlier antiquaries:

There are few pursuits, in the compass of letters, more dry than that of Antiquity. The Antiquary feeds upon withered husks, which none can relish but himself; nor does he seem to possess the art of dressing up his dried morsel to suit the palate of a reader, for his language is often as dry as his subject; as if the smile was an enemy to Truth. Mere dull description, like a burnt cinder, is dead matter. If he designs a *treat*, why not infuse a little spice to suit the taste of his guest?[17]

Hutton's observation about 'dry husks' reflects critically upon the detailed attention that earlier antiquaries had focused upon the Roman inscriptions derived from the Wall.[18] Indeed, Hutton, who knew no Latin, could make little out of these objects.

The Wall's significance to Hutton is more immediate, general, and less pedantic. He observes that 'I would enliven truth with the smile, with the anecdote; and, while I travel the long and dreary Wall, would have you travel with me, though by your own fire-side; would have you see, and feel, as I do; and make the journey influence your passions, as mine are influenced'.[19] He wrote of the Wall as:

one of the grandest works of human labour, performed by the greatest nation upon earth. What shall we say of that production, which was the utmost extent of Roman effort, and which stands unrivalled in Europe! How much delight would it

[10] Hutton (1802), x.   [11] ibid., 108.   [12] ibid., xiii.
[13] ibid., 172.   [14] E. Birley (1961), 19.
[15] Nesbitt and Tolia Kelly (2009), 378–9; Sweet (2004), 313–14.
[16] Hutton (1802), iii.   [17] ibid., v-vi.   [18] Sweet (2004), 313.
[19] Hutton (1802), vi-vii.

afford the modern antiquarian eye, could he survey the works of Agricola, Hadrian, and Severus, as they then appeared! the noblest sight ever beheld in the Island! the work of strength, of genius, and of years! Men have been defied for trifles compared to this admirable structure; a Wall seventy miles in length, furnished with eighteen Cities, eighty-one Castles, and three hundred and thirty Turrets, with all their mounds, roads, ramparts and astonishing apparatus! One sight would raise the mind to a rapturous sublimity.[20]

Echoing the comments of Stukeley and Warburton, he described the Wall as 'the grandest work ever produced by European hands'.[21]

Hutton had a negative view of the monument's builders and those who, over the ages, attacked each other across its line: 'That *man* is born a savage, there needs no other proof than Severus's Wall. It characterizes two nations as robbers, and murderers'.[22] He observed that 'During four hundred years, while the Wall continued as a barrier, this was the grand theatre of war, as well as during ages after its destruction'.[23] He characterizes the barbaric actions of both the Scots and Romans:

> Our old historians always term the Scots *Barbarians*: to this I assent. They surprised the innocent, murdered them, laid waste their country, took the property, and *left the place*. Allow me, without the aid of Dr. Johnson, to illustrate the word *Barbarian*. Julius Caesar, Agricola, Antonine, Severus, &c. went one step farther than the Scots; they surprised, murdered, plundered, and *kept possessions*. Our venerable ancestors too, the Saxons, Danes, and Normans, who came over in swarms, butchered, robbed, and possessed; although they had no more right than I have to your coat.[24]

Camden, Drayton, Warburton, and Hutton all collapsed medieval border warfare into the Roman history of the Wall, imagining a period of violence that started in the first century and ended in 1707.[25] Hutton argued that 'The line of destruction' resulting from the lawless condition in this frontier territory 'extended twenty miles or more, on each side of the Wall' and included a long list of 'dreadful murders, robberies, and burnings...practised in the vicinity of the Wall' during the period prior to the Unification of England and Scotland.[26]

Hutton's attitude to the landscape of the central section of the Wall reflected these melancholy ideas. Housesteads, a marginal and unruly landscape until the eighteenth century, had continued to inspire feelings of awe in visitors.[27] Hutton was impressed by the view from close by, writing 'A more dreary county than this...can scarcely be conceived. I do not wonder it shocked Camden'.[28] He wrote that, Housesteads is 'the grandest station in the whole

---

[20] Hutton (1802), 27–8.   [21] ibid., 104.   [22] ibid., 2.
[23] ibid. 5.   [24] ibid., 7–8.   [25] cf. Abbatt (1849), 78.
[26] Hutton (1802), 90–1.   [27] Crow (2004a), 9–10.   [28] Hutton (1802), 229.

line', but it is also a place of 'melancholy relicks', a site which was once 'one of the greatest activity, but now a solitary desert, instead of the human voice, is heard nothing but wind'.[29] From a high point opposite Crag Lough, he observed that the 'prospects are not grand, but extensive and rather awful'.[30]

For Hutton, the Roman Wall had been built to counter the same problems that bedevilled the frontier until the early eighteenth century. He partly rejects Warburton's suggestion that the Romans provided a model for the establishment of settled conditions in this landscape, since he argues that peace was only finally established when the region was settled through the Union in 1707. In these terms, the eighteenth-century condition of peace on the border surpassed the achievements of the Romans. Hutton suggested that:

> From this happy period hostilities gradually subsided; and that generation, bred to rapine, dying away, posterity became humanized, the laws of protection and civil life assumed an energy, and property was secure on both sides of the Wall…Thus we have wandered through the long series of fifteen hundred years; have seen the rise, meridian, and fall, of the grandest work ever produced by European hands; have observed, with a melancholy eye, the depraved state of human nature, defection of law, of the power to protect, and the instability of property; but, with a smile, have seen the termination of a quarrel, which has continued fifty generations. This short inference may be drawn from the whole: that protection on one side, and liberty and obedience on the other, are the foundations of all just government.[31]

Hutton saw the unsettled history of the Wall in Roman and medieval times as fundamental to the historical identity of this landscape, but the creation of order during the early eighteenth century provided a reason for optimism. He dedicated his book to John Nichols, who printed the volume, adding that, 'Through your humanity [you] will feel, for the antient animosity, the plunder, and murder, upon the borders of the two respectable Nations; yet you will rejoice, that concord is established along the line of the Wall; and that, instead of rancour, robbery, burning, and blood, civilization has not only taken place, but even generosity.'[32] Union and peace enabled Hutton to overcome the melancholy of his gloomy reflections while exploring these ruined remains. In this context, the ruination of the Wall was to be celebrated since a defensive demarcation was no longer required. That Hutton was keen to make money from the sale of his book presumably helps to explain his upbeat message.

A further insight into the fruits of peace is provided by John Baillie's account of the Roman Wall that is contained in his volume *An Impartial History of the Town and County of Newcastle Upon Tyne* (1801). A minister of the Secession Church, Baillie had spent much of his life in Newcastle.[33] At the beginning of his

---

[29] ibid., 234–7.   [30] ibid., 240.   [31] ibid., 103–4.
[32] ibid., iii-iv.   [33] Cooper revised by Mercer (2004).

book, the author emphasized the importance of the Roman Wall's remains as highlighting the contemporary significance of Newcastle. In keeping with Hutton, Baillie is rather more critical of the actions of the Romans than many of his predecessors, explaining that 'It was from this love of conquest, fatal to the repose and independence of nations who had not before heard of the Roman name, that a large proportion of the human kind were subjugated or destroyed'.[34] He emphasized that, following the conquest, the Romans did seek to introduce civilization to their subjects and, as a consequence 'made some atonement for the sanguinary excesses to which their insatiable ambitions had impelled them'.[35] In addition, he noted that this:

> warlike people, intending their empire should run on in the long line of ages coeval with time itself, have accordingly left, to the admiration of mankind, the most stupendous monuments of their unrivalled power and profound policy. And in no country, in the extensive bounds of their once mighty empire, are left, to the investigation of the antiquary and the historian, more striking remains of their pristine greatness than in Britain; not in any part of the country, greater or more noble than those in Newcastle and its vicinity.

The rather confused description of elements of the Wall that follows draws upon John Brand's earlier account.[36] Baillie's particular interests, however, lay in providing a history of Northumberland that drew upon the former grandeur of the Wall. Having described the history of the Roman remains, Baillie observed: 'our sensations are relieved, when we see beautiful and fertile fields, covered with golden harvests, where once stood the ramparts of huge stones cramped with iron; and where fierce warriors conflicted in mortal combat, now the scene of harmless bleating flocks, and of sportive lambs, gamboling in wanton play, along the venerable ruins of camps and entrenchments.'[37] Baillie acknowledged his source for these sentiments in James Thomson's evocation of military ruins in a peaceful pastoral landscape, *The Seasons*, written in 1728.[38] Baillie portrays the Roman remains as an embarrassing reminder of the oppressive and dictatorial nature of former Roman imperial rule over the Britons, emphasizing the contemporary peaceful rural scenery now in British hands that had replaced these formerly martial landscapes.

The second man to walk the entire Wall in 1801 was John Skinner, curate of Camerton in Somerset who in later life undertook some important antiquarian research.[39] He travelled along the Wall from 11 to 27 September 1801, his journal providing a detailed, descriptive account of the condition of the monument, the inscriptions scattered along its course, and his experiences along the way,[40] although this was not published in full until 1973.[41] Eric

---

[34] Baillie (1801), 9–10.   [35] ibid., 10.
[36] ibid., 13–25; cf. Brand (1789), 137–42, 601–18.   [37] Baillie (1801), 26.
[38] cf. Sweet (2004), 162.   [39] Mitchell (2004); Painter (1973), 18.
[40] Skinner (1801).   [41] Painter (1973).

Birley has suggested that Skinner was an 'acute observer' who provided relevant information on the remains and the inscriptions.[42] Skinner rarely focused upon the contemporary significance of the Wall, although on one occasion he was inspired by the ruined remains at 'Rochester' (Rudchester) to comment on the life cycles of empires and individuals.[43] The use of the remains of the Roman Wall to reflect upon decline was to become an influential conceptual model during the following century.

REASONS TO BE GLOOMY?

The most influential Romantic antiquary to explore the remains of the Wall was Sir Walter Scott. A prolific novelist, Scott had an immense impact upon nineteenth-century historical studies, promoting an interest in the pre-Roman peoples of Scotland.[44] Several of his novels are set in the area of the Wall, but he was not particularly drawn to these Roman remains,[45] preferring Gothic antiquities and Border Ballads.[46] Scott was the first northern poet to reflect on the Wall in 'To a Lady, With Flowers from a Roman Wall':

> Take these flowers which, purple waving,
>   On the ruin'd rampart grew,
> Where, the sons of freedom braving,
>   Rome's imperial standards flew.
> Warriors from the breach of danger
>   Pluck no longer laurels there;
> They but yield the passing stranger
>   Wild-flower wreaths for Beauty's hair.[47]

Here Scott combines the Scottish 'sons of freedom' with flowers that reflect imperial purple. This reference to the resistance to the Roman conquest of Scottish territory, reflected contemporary views of the valour of the ancient Britons who resisted Rome, while also pondering on the fleeting nature of human life.

Scott referred to the Roman remains of central and northern Britain in three other works. In 1814, he published two volumes on *The Border Antiquities of England and Scotland*, containing a detailed account of the ruined abbeys, castles, and bridges of the Borders. The remains of the two Roman Walls are addressed in the introduction to the first volume, where Scott noted that the

---

[42] E. Birley (1961), 19.
[43] Skinner (1801), 115.   [44] Ash (1983), 432.   [45] Piggott (1976), 150.
[46] Piggott (1976), 150; Stafford (2007); Sweet (2004), 272. The imperial and military character of the Wall is presumably one reason for its limited history in literature (cf. Mortimer 2007), 8.
[47] W. Scott (1797).

'wall of Severus', by which he means the curtain Wall, was 'constructed with the greatest solidarity and strength'.[48] Scott argued that 'It is impossible, while tracing these gigantic labours, to refrain from admiring, on the one hand, the pains and skill which is bestowed in constructing them, and, on the other, the extravagant ambition which stimulated the conquerors of the world to bestow so much pain for the preservation of such a rude country'.[49] Drawing upon the earlier associations made between the Roman and medieval frontier, Scott's account of the origins of Border troubles suggested that the disputes between England and Scotland commenced in Roman times.[50] He did not discuss the Roman remains in any great detail, effectively downplaying these structures at the expense of the ruined medieval structures that he so admired.

Scott also addressed Roman remains in two of his novels. In *The Antiquary* (1816), a fictitious antiquary called Jonathan Oldbuck searched for the site of the first-century battle between Romans and Caledonians at *Mons Graupius* in eastern Scotland.[51] In Chapter 22 of his novel *Guy Mannering*, Scott discussed a journey made by one of his characters to the 'eastern wilds' of Cumberland to visit the remains of 'the celebrated Roman Wall'.[52] The narrator observes that the Roman remains indicate that 'our modern labours, like our modern tongues, seem but constructed out of their [the Roman's] fragments',[53] an observation reflecting the author's classical education in Edinburgh.[54] He saw this inheritance as linguistic and cultural rather than as entirely spiritual. The narrator in *Guy Mannering* referred to the 'public works' of the Romans as 'grave, solid and majestic'. Together with the reference in *The Border Antiquities* to the solidarity and strength of the Roman frontier works, this placed an emphasis on the utilitarian and military function of these Roman works.

The sense of fragmentation and partial continuity evident in Walter Scott's musings on the Wall is repeated in Thomas Doubleday's poem, 'The Roman Wall' (1822). Doubleday (1790–1870), a politician and author, was born and lived in Newcastle and wrote on a wide variety of subjects. His poetic work was enthusiastically received in his home region, although he does not appear to have been recognized by a wider public.[55] Exploring a valley close to his viewpoint on the Roman Wall, Doubleday wrote:

> Here plant thy foot, where many a foot hath trod,
> Whose scarce-known home was o'er the southern wave,
> And sit thee down; on no ignoble sod,
> Green from the ashes of the great and brave;
> Here strethc'd that chain which nations could enslave,

---

[48] W. Scott (1814), xviii.   [49] ibid., xx–xxi.   [50] ibid., iv.
[51] See Piggott (1976), 133–60.   [52] W. Scott (1815), 6.   [53] ibid., 7.
[54] Stafford (2007), 15.   [55] McCord (2004).

The least injurious token of their thrall,
Which, if it help'd to humble, help'd to save;
This shapeless mound thou know'st not what to call,
Was a world's wonder once—This is the Roman Wall.[56]

The poet wrote of the history of the Wall, a 'bound-stone' of the 'restless Pict',[57] drawing upon Bede to narrate its later contested history. This poem is a musing on life and death as much as it is an account of the decline and fall of empires. It emphasizes the former significance of the Wall; but, perhaps, the relevance of the Wall's decline in status as a wonder of the world is just a literary flourish, since the poet apparently intended to highlight the monument's significance. Doubleday's poem also drew on the spirit of Byron's evocation of the ruins of Rome in *Childe Harold*.[58]

Three contemporary accounts emphasized the ruination of the Wall to make political points about the bounding of England, ideas that drew upon a name for the monument that had been abandoned by most antiquaries.[59] In a commentary on the current political situation and the Poor Law in the *Cobbett Weekly Political Register*, the author stated that 'The Pict's wall is surely not standing? No: that cannot be, because the Scottish emigrate in great numbers to England'.[60] Catherine Gore's popular novel, *Pin Money* (1831), included a comparable attitude to the ruination of the Picts' Wall in which the disdainful 'Duchess of Trimblestown' comments on traders in London and concludes: 'There ought to be a Pict's-wall built up to defend us against the incursions of such hordes of barbarians'.[61] In *Bell's Life in London and Sporting Chronicle* of Sunday 21 October 1838, 'Rory O'More' published a reply to recent comments by the Scot, Sir Peter Laurie. 'Rory O'More' is a pseudonym, derived from the well-known sixteenth-century Catholic Irish rebel leader who had campaigned against the English,[62] while Laurie, who had been Lord Mayor of London, was a magistrate in Westminster and had been born in Scotland, moving to London around the turn of the century.[63] 'O'More' noted that Laurie had expressed an opinion that 'an impassable wall' could be raised around Ireland to prevent immigration to England.[64] 'O'More' replies to this by saying, 'suppose somebody had proposed to repair the *Roman Wall*, some forty years ago, and treat Scotland as you now propose to treat Ireland, who, think you, would be at this present writing, the Alderman of Aldersgate-ward? Live and let live, good Sir Peter: there is room enough in Babylon for both of you.' The idea of the Wall around Ireland is a reference to the Pale, the boundary between English and Irish territory that had been established in the fifteenth century.[65]

---

[56] Doubleday (1822), lines 28–36.   [57] ibid., lines 41–2.
[58] cf. Sachs (2010), 131–45.   [59] For addition detail, see Hingley (2010a), 34–5.
[60] Cobbett (1807), 490.   [61] Gore (1831), 303; cf. Copeland (2001), 125.
[62] Lenihan (2004).   [63] McConnell (2004).   [64] 'O'More' (1838).
[65] cf. Ellis (1988).

Irish immigration at this time was perceived by many of the educated middle classes of London as a threat to English society.[66] The satirical comments of Gore and 'O'More' indicate, however, that this idea was by no means universal.[67] Indeed, for those born outside England, the barbarian populations beyond the Wall could be assigned a particular role as valiant defenders of British liberty against Roman oppression. In 1843 the Scottish painter William Bell Scott produced a cartoon for a major composition, his entry in a fresco competition for the Houses of Parliament, entitled *A Battle Between Ancient Britons and Romans* (Figure 8.2).[68] John Batchelor has argued that the 'politics' of this image was 'against progress' and that it supported 'conservative nationalism'.[69] The Roman enslavers of British liberty are shown being overwhelmed by naked but valiant ancient Britons who are attacking and destroying the Wall. In the foreground a woman is supporting a Roman soldier's head in her right hand while taking his sword with her left. Her clothes indicate that she is Roman and she is evidently about to defend her fallen countryman from the oncoming Britons. In the background, Roman fortifications are visible and Britons are shown scaling the Wall. The original cartoon is now in the National Gallery of Scotland. The image was brought to the attention of the London public by the *Illustrated London News* which published an engraving taken from the cartoon and entitled *The Free Northern Britons Surprising the Roman Wall between the Tyne and the Solway*.[70] The *News* noted that the exhibition for the fresco competition was 'open gratis', and was being attended by 'vast multitudes of people'. The idea of British resistance to Rome was a popular topic for writers prior to the 1850s,[71] but paintings showing Britons overwhelming Romans are rare, presumably because of the difficult parallels drawn with Britain's contemporary imperial situation.

The three accounts of contemporary immigration, together with the images and writings reviewed above, demonstrate that people drew upon the Wall in a variety of different ways. Reflecting on its supposed former role in preventing immigration is very different from considering its overthrow by bands of valiant northern Britons. Much of the emphasis of these images and writings appears, however, to have been on the ruination of the Wall and these accounts show little appreciation of the monument's surviving physicality. During the mid nineteenth century, a new focus on the Roman Wall developed as the result of the work of John Collingwood Bruce who, with his co-workers sought to build knowledge of the Wall in order to reflect upon its contemporary significance as a national and imperial monument.

---

[66] Davis (2000), 24.   [67] Hingley (2010a), 35.
[68] Smiles (1994), 143–4; Usherwood (1996), 153.   [69] Batchelor (2006), 135.
[70] *Illustrated London News* (1843).   [71] Smiles (1994), 45.

Fig. 8.2. A pen and ink drawing by William Bell Scott entitled *A Battle Between Ancient Britons and Romans*. This was exhibited as part of the Houses of Parliament fresco competition in 1843. Reproduced by permission of the National Gallery of Scotland, Permanent collection, D 4713.9 C.

REASONS TO BE CHEERFUL, PART TWO

Newcastle had established itself during the early nineteenth century as one of England's major industrial cities with an intellectual life led by its architects, lawyers, and businessmen.[72] The Society of Antiquaries of Newcastle upon Tyne, founded in 1813, came to have a sustained impact upon the study of Hadrian's Wall.[73] Its predominantly middle-class membership worked to confirm the Society's newly found prominence through scholarly activity focused upon the Wall, with significant contributions from John Hodgson, John Collingwood Bruce, and John Clayton.[74] The pride such individuals possessed in the contemporary commercial success of Newcastle encouraged a focus on the considerable significance of the Roman Wall, and the concerns of earlier authors about Roman despotism and the military force were put aside.

John Hodgson's contribution, based on the research he had undertaken from 1810, was a very lengthy and well-observed account of the Wall in the *History of Northumberland*.[75] This publication led to a revival of public

---

[72] Usherwood (1996), 151.   [73] E. Birley (1961), 22.
[74] Usherwood (1996), 151–6.   [75] J. Hodgson (1840), 149–322.

interest in the Roman Wall, emphasized by the number of articles published in the early volumes of *Archaeologia Aeliana*.[76] Inspired by the work of Hodgson, John Collingwood Bruce began his attempt to promote the importance of the Wall during the spring of 1848. Bruce (1805–1892) was born and lived most of his life in Newcastle, where he was a teacher and worked as a non-conformist preacher in the Borders during the 1830s (Figure 8.3).[77] His experience of the Wall had started early, as when a boy, he had been taken one Christmas to look at Roman remains close to Denton.[78] He remarked that he had chipped a piece of one of the Wall stones and kept it in a drawer as a curiosity. He also noted that in 1823 he had observed some of the remains of the Wall while travelling to the University of Glasgow, writing to a friend that he intended to explore the Wall's remains more fully.[79] In 1830, Bruce examined the remains of the Roman Wall at its west end,[80] but he appears to have paid little further attention to the monument until the late 1840s.[81] In the spirit of the time, he had first developed an interest in the Saxon and Norman Gothic monuments of the North, before turning his attention to the Roman Wall.[82]

Bruce had a highly significant role in publicizing and promoting the Wall between 1849 and his death in 1892,[83] effectively raising the monument's profile in northern England, Britain, and overseas. He had intended to travel to Rome, but revolution in Europe forced him to abandon his plans and he decided to visit the Wall instead. He took two local artists, H. B. and T. M. Richardson, on his journey along the Wall (Figure 8.4).[84] When Bruce returned, he gave a lecture to the Newcastle Literary and Philosophical Society, using the Richardson brothers' watercolours as teaching aids. The members expressed doubt that the remains survived as depicted and this led to the first Pilgrimage to Hadrian's Wall in June 1849, with Bruce as a knowledgeable guide.[85] The group, which included three ladies, visited the ruins along the Wall line, while others joined these Pilgrims at particular sites.[86] Female involvement in the mainly male pursuit of antiquarianism was beginning to increase in Britain at this time and Bruce, following his non-conformist religious beliefs, was keen to encourage this.[87] He continued to study the remains of Hadrian's Wall and quickly developed a deep interest that was to influence the rest of his life.[88]

---

[76] E. Birley (1961), 22–3, 59–61.   [77] Bidwell (1999a), 2; Wroth revised by Fraser (2004).
[78] J. C. Bruce (1887), 265.   [79] Ibid.
[80] G. Bruce (1905), 40.   [81] J. C. Bruce (1887), 266.
[82] ibid; G. Bruce (1905), 97–109.
[83] Bidwell (1999a), 2–4; Breeze (2003); Miket (1984), 243.   [84] Ewin (2000), 54.
[85] Bidwell (1999a), 2; E. Birley (1961), 25.
[86] G. Bruce (1905), 114–21; E. Birley (1961), 25–7; Ewin (2000), 15–16.
[87] cf. Ebbatson (1994), 34; Hingley (2007a), 178.
[88] E. Birley (1961), 26; G. Bruce (1905), 110–14.

Fig. 8.3. A portrait of John Collingwood Bruce. Reproduced by permission of the Great North Museum and Society of Antiquaries of Newcastle upon Tyne.

Since 1849, the Pilgrimage has visited the Wall on twelve occasions, most recently in August 2009.[89] Paul Bidwell has written that the Pilgrimages have all served the same purposes: 'First, all have been acts of veneration for the best-known Roman monument in Britain... They have also been tours of inspection, examining the condition of the remains. Finally, they have been convivial, allowing a large group of people sharing a common interest to spend a pleasant and instructive week together.'[90] As such, each Pilgrimage has been a significant social event (Figure 8.5).

The initial Pilgrimage was one of the means through which Bruce sought to publicize the Wall. He also lectured on the remains in Newcastle and elsewhere and published a number of influential accounts. His impressive volume, *The Roman Wall*, was first published in 1851 and republished on two occasions. It

[89] N. Hodgson (2009a).   [90] Bidwell (1999a), 4.

Fig. 8.4. The Roman site at Housesteads in the mid-nineteenth century. From a drawing by H. B. Richardson reproduced in Bruce (1851), opposite 220.

provided a scholarly account based on the earlier researches of Horsley and Hodgson, and also some first-hand field experience.[91] Bruce presented many lectures and produced a second significant volume, *The Wallet-Book of the Roman Wall* (1863). This drew on Warburton's example in that it provided a conveniently sized guide that a visitor could carry along the Wall. The *Handbook* that subsequently emerged from this initiative has been republished on thirteen occasions.[92] Bruce became a widely acknowledged expert on Hadrian's Wall and published some accounts of excavations undertaken along its line, but he was primarily an effective publicist rather than an excavator or surveyor.[93]

Bruce's speech at the temple of Mithras in 1849 was significant since it helps to explain the particular interest that he developed through his work. The remains of this temple had been found to the south of the well-known Roman site at Housesteads in June 1821 and excavated the following year.[94] The Reverend John Hodgson had been fascinated by these remains and provided a detailed account in *Archaeologia Aeliana*, including a lengthy discussion of the worship of the pagan god Mithras.[95] Bruce built on this in his lecture, one of several impromptu talks that he presented during the first Pilgrimage.[96] Bruce used the occasion to draw a direct comparison between the fallen empires of Rome and the contemporary domestic and imperial condition of Great Britain. A number of published accounts help to give an impression of Bruce's comments.

[91] E. Birley (1961), 27.   [92] Breeze (2006a).

[93] Hodgkin (1892), 367; Breeze (2003), 3.

[94] E. Birley (1961), 180; Rushworth (2009), 4.   [95] J. Hodgson (1822), 273–9.

[96] E. Birley (1961), 26.

162   PUNCH, OR THE LONDON CHARIVARI.   [OCTOBER 23, 1869.

MEMBERS OF A LEARNED SOCIETY ON AN EXCURSION.

Learned Gentleman. "WE ARE NOW NEAR THE REMAINS OF A ROMAN WALL, AND ON EXAMINING THE GROUND LAST YEAR, IT WAS FOUND TO BE——"

Appreciative Native cuts in—"BARLEY, SIR; AND BEANS THE YEAR AFORE."

THE TORMENTS OF TIGHT-LACING.

DEAR MR. PUNCH,

BEING a young lady, of course, you know, I *must* dress in the fashion, and now that small waists have come in I am obliged to lace myself as tightly as I can, so as not to look *ridiculous*. My stays hurt terribly at first, they *are* so stiff and bony. Even now it is as much as I can do to sit through dinner without fainting. But I mean to persevere, and hope in a few days to measure an inch less, though I sadly fear I *never shall* be able to wear a waist of sixteen inches and a half, which my *modiste* says is now considered *fashionable*. And I am terribly afraid that what the doctors say is true, for since my dresses were made tight I have felt wretchedly unwell and sadly out of spirits. My head aches so, you can't think, and my cheeks are, O so pale, and getting actually *yellow*. Indeed, my sister tells me that I look a *perfect fright*, but then, you know, she's envious of my having a *fine figure*.

But the worst is that I feel so cramped and stiffened that I can hardly stir, and am really quite fatigued with the least possible exertion. I used to love a dance and was immensely fond of croquet. But I find with a pinched waist it's quite *impossible* to waltz, you get so out of breath and feel so sick and giddy. And as for playing croquet, why, you can't hit a hard knock, or stoop to pick a ball up, and your dress is made so tight you feel afraid of something cracking.

Another of my *miseries* is that my maid has the impertinence to follow the new fashion, and is getting quite unfit for work through her tight-lacing. When I tell her to run up-stairs to fetch a pocket-handkerchief, she moves as slow and stilly as I do myself, and comes down panting so that she can hardly gasp an answer to my questions. Then she constantly is getting nasty stitches in her side, and while she stands to do my hair she often feels so faint I have to give her sal volatile. The chance is too that when I come home from a party, I find that she has gone to bed with a sick headache, leaving poor me to retire to rest without the least assistance. Of course, you know, I'm bound to give her my old dresses, and she says they'd be of no use if she hadn't got a waist as small as mine, and so this is her excuse for her *imitative impudence*.

Of course it's very nice to be admired for one's good figure, and of course I'd rather *die* than dress out of the fashion. But stays are a great torture, and deprive one of a number of small comforts and enjoyments, not to mention one so vulgar as enjoying a nice dinner, which one has no room to swallow when one's squeezed to sixteen inches. I know our great great grandmothers were tortured like ourselves, but croquet wasn't known then, any more than waltzing. And as I dearly love all feminine *athletic sports* like these, I certainly *do* hope the fashion will soon change, and that one may wear one's waist as wide as nature made it.

Until then, believe me, yours, in *misery*,

A VICTIM.

To Mr. Layard.

" And the womanly soul, turning sick with disgust,
    Tried to force her way out from her Serpentine crust."
            Thomas Hood.

MAKE the Serpentine wholesome for roach, dace, carp, barbel,
And merit a statue of Serpentine marble;
But if you can't do it, pour back the old flood,
Nor poison my children with Serpentine mud.
            " *A Panic Struck Mother.*" (*Versified.*)

An Ultrahumane Idea.

As the wise suggestion season has yet some time to run, a question of which the discussion will perhaps be pursued is, whether it is not cruel to open living oysters, and whether they could not be previously steeped in some anæsthetic, which would not render them unpalatable or injurious, and so make them disagree with those partaking of them, as they would if they were eaten with chloroform.

Fig. 8.5. A cartoon showing 'Members of a learned society on an excursion'. This may well be designed to show a tour along Hadrian's Wall. A number of ladies are illustrated in a way that recalls the three women who accompanied the first Pilgrimage along the Wall in 1849. This cartoon is derived from *Punch*, for 23 October, 1869, 162. Reproduced by permission of Punch Ltd.

At the temple, Bruce was asked to explain to his audience the mysteries of Mithras.[97] He recalled, presumably with reference to both the pagan religion that had been practised at this place and also to the decline and fall of the Roman empire, that: 'I ... referred to the down-trodden condition of Britain at the time these walls were reared, but stated that now in Windsor's princely halls was seated a lady who ruled over "regions Caesar never knew," and who wielded a sceptre which was lovingly obeyed by four times the number of subjects great Julius ever swayed.'[98] At this point, Mr Falconar 'proposed three cheers for Queen Victoria, which were given with thrilling effect'. The reference to 'regions Caesar never knew' was taken from William Cowper's influential poem 'Boadicea—an Ode' (1782), which drew on the idea that Britain had supplanted Rome as the dominant world power and taken on its imperial mantle.[99] Richard Abbatt witnessed this lecture and noted that Bruce had 'compared the debasing worship of the Romans with the pure religion of Our Holy Redeemer'.[100] Many of those present evidently felt that the Christian religion was a reason for contemporary Britons to be grateful.

A revised version of the same lecture is included in Bruce's monograph, *The Roman Wall*, where he refers to the fate of Rome and the contemporary situation of Britain.[101] Reflecting on the ruination of the remains at Housesteads, the 'broken column and prostrate altar', Bruce observes:

> Another empire has sprung into being of which Rome dreamt not ... In that island, where, in Roman days, the painted savage shared the forest with the beast of prey—a lady sits upon her throne of state, wielding a sceptre more potent than Julius or Hadrian ever grasped! Her empire is threefold that of Rome in the hour of its prime. But power is not her brightest diadem. The holiness of the domestic circle irradiates her. Literature, and all the arts of peace, flourish under her sway. Her people bless her.[102]

Bruce contrasts Britain's present Christian greatness with its barbaric past, a theme that drew deeply on the pagan temple where he had delivered his lecture. In making these comments, Bruce appears to draw upon the preface to John Mitchell Kemble's influential book, *The Saxons in England*:

> On every side of us thrones totter, and the deep foundations of society are convulsed. Shot and shell sweep the streets of capitals which have long been pointed out as the chosen abodes of order: cavalry and bayonets cannot control populations whose loyalty has become a proverb here, whose peace has been made a reproach to our own miscalled disquiet. Yet the exalted Lady who wields

---

[97] G. Bruce (1905), 120.
[98] quoted in ibid, 121.   [99] Hingley and Unwin (2005), 151.
[100] Abbatt (1849), 29.
[101] See Hingley (2000), 21; Parchami (2009), 67; Smiles (1994), 144.
[102] J. C. Bruce (1851), 40–1.

the sceptre of these realms, sits safe upon her throne, and fearless in the holy circle of her domestic happiness, secure in the affections of a people whose institutions have given them all the blessings of an equal law.[103]

Kemble's volume had championed the supposedly Anglo-Saxon roots of British freedom and valour—a significant Victorian image.[104] Bruce drew on a different myth of origin, arguing that Victorian Britain had inherited Rome's imperial sceptre. This is not necessarily a denial of the supposed Anglo-Saxon racial origins for the Victorian English, but a reinvestigation of an issue that had been raised by Cowper's poem—an idea that created a direct link between Boudica's heirs and the imperial British.[105]

In David Lowenthal's terms,[106] Bruce's lecture at *Borcovicium* aimed to reconstruct ancient glories in the service of modern progress rather than reflecting on human and cultural decline in melancholy terms.[107] The reference to the idea that Great Britain currently possessed an empire far greater in extent than that of the classical Romans is set against the idea of the naked, savage, ancient Britons, demonstrating the dramatic progress in native manners and religion. As in Hutton's account of the Wall, these were reasons for nineteenth-century Britons to be cheerful. In his final comments in *The Roman Wall*, however, Bruce reflects further on this imperial parallel and raises some rather more problematic issues:

> We can hardly tarry, even for an hour, in association with the palmy days of the Great Empire, without learning, on the one hand, to emulate the virtues that adorned her prosperity, and on the other, to shun the vices that were punished by her downfall. The sceptre which Rome relinquished, we have taken up. Great is our Honour—great our Responsibility.[108]

These comments drew directly on the writings of Walter Scott, but also upon the sentiments penned by Edward Gibbon in the first volume of his highly influential series of books, *The Decline and Fall of the Roman Empire* (1776).[109]

Gibbon's monumental work, written and published in seven volumes between 1776 and 1778, had been inspired by a visit to the Capitol in the city of Rome.[110] It provided a survey of the collapse of Roman rule after AD 180, a 'revolution which will ever be remembered, and is still felt by the nations of the earth'.[111] With regard to the period of stability in the first two centuries AD, Gibbon noted at the start of his first volume that, 'The frontiers of that extensive monarchy were guarded by ancient renown and disciplined valour.

---

[103] Kemble (1849), vi. [104] cf. Smiles (1994), 113; Williams (2008).
[105] Hingley and Unwin (2005), 151. [106] Lowenthal (1985), 181.
[107] cf. Smiles (1994), 144–5. [108] J. C. Bruce (1851), 449–50.
[109] W. Scott (1814), xx–xxi; Gibbon (1776).
[110] Levine (1987), 73; Porter (1988), 60; Rogers (2011), 20.
[111] Gibbon (1776), 31.

The gentle but powerful influence of laws and manners gradually cemented the union of the provinces'. Political and military problems in the overseas territories during the early 1780s—including America—had ensured that this use of the idea of imperial decline and fall had a considerable impact in contemporary Britain.[112] Gibbon's work continued to have a significant influence for over two centuries.[113] Bruce's description of Hadrian's Wall reflects Gibbon's comments on his first encounter with the ancient ruins of Rome.[114] His lecture was, effectively, anticipating the need for the British to reflect on their current imperial greatness in the context of the contemporary crisis across Europe. The conclusion drawn by Bruce, however, differed fundamentally from the sentiments expressed by Gibbon, since he places a particularly religious emphasis on Britain's current responsibilities. As was to be expected of a non-conformist minister, he emphasized the need to follow the 'inspired word' of the Bible in managing the affairs of empire.[115] Bruce continued to muse on the imperial and national significance of the ruination of the Wall in later works and in a lecture that addressed the Antonine Wall.[116]

Contemporaries of Bruce in Newcastle also used the remains of the Wall to reflect upon current affairs. In his poem, 'To a Friend: on visiting the Roman Wall', published in 1867, Robert White drew the remains of the Wall into a consideration of decline and fall. White (1802–74), who was born in Roxburghshire, had moved to Newcastle in 1825. He began to write poems in 1829 and became a member of the Newcastle Antiquaries in 1852.[117] Describing the grand but ruined state of the monument, White commented on the Roman empire:

> It lasted not:—a heavy doom
> Impended o'er imperial Rome.
> She who had seen her flag unfurl'd
> O'er every region of the world,
> Beheld, at last, her power decay,
> And felt her sceptre pass away.
>   What were her crimes, and how she fell,
> Gibbon's historic pages will tell:
> Enough for us if soon or late
> Ourselves may shun such hapless fate.
> But while her errors we disown,
> Her virtues let us make our own...[118]

A cartoon published in *Punch* in 1869 reflected in a more satirical manner on the Roman Wall (Figure 8.5). One of a number of antiquarian-inspired cartoons that appeared in *Punch* during the nineteenth century, it is not

[112] Hingley (2008a), 227–9; Rogers and Hingley (2010).
[113] Bowersock (2009), 4–7.   [114] Rogers (2011), 16.
[115] J. C. Bruce (1851), 42; cf. Dowling (1985), 580–1.
[116] J. C. Bruce (1885), iii–iv; J. C. Bruce (1888), 144.
[117] Carlyle revised by Fraser (2004).   [118] White (1867), 221.

clear if the particular Roman Wall referenced in the illustration is actually Hadrian's. Although the main figure in the cartoon does not appear to be directly modeled on John Collingwood Bruce, it features ladies among the group searching for the remains of the Wall, which perhaps reflects the three women who had attended the first Pilgrimage almost twenty years before. As in the case of several other works studied in this chapter, this cartoon celebrates the overthrowing of the Wall through its contemporary invisibility, an image that Hodgson, Bruce, and Clayton were seeking to critique through their detailed antiquarian works.

SUMMARY: AN IMPERIAL WALL

During the first half of the nineteenth century, the Roman Wall appears to have enabled antiquaries, poets, and historians to reflect on the former grandeur of Rome while keeping in mind the political oppression of the ancient Britons and the inevitable fall of all empires. Ali Parchami has observed that Bruce's comments in *The Roman Wall* foreshadow the imperial rhetoric of the late Victorians.[119] By the 1880s, Roman parallels were drawn upon directly to help justify and support British imperial endeavour, leading to an increased interest in the associations between the Roman and the British empires.[120] The geographical proximity of the Roman Wall to Newcastle appears to have led a few local men to draw upon this imperial comparison during the middle of the century at a time when others were using the same analogy to praise the triumphs of British expansionism.[121] The national role of the Wall as the perceived boundary of England helped to reinforce its significance as an imperial analogy. Richard Abbatt, who attended the first Pilgrimage, wrote an account of the monument in which he considered the idea that the physical remains of the Wall had acted as a barrier to potential marauders for centuries after the end of the Roman period, impeding the 'motion of plunderers on both sides'.[122] He drew a direct connection between the Roman and medieval uses of the Wall, stating:

> The contribution for 'watch and ward upon the wall,' which, to a comparatively late period, was so heavy upon the villages of the border counties, was a substitution for the harassing personal services of watching and guarding the wall, before this duty was transferred to the castles. Although no longer a complete defence,

---

[119] Parchami (2009), 67.
[120] Betts (1971); Hingley (2000), 22–3; Parchami (2009), 74; Vance (1997), 233–5.
[121] cf. Larson (1999), 213–16.
[122] Abbatt (1849), 78.

the wall was probably a considerable barrier previous to the fifteenth century, when numerous beacons, erected about that time over the country, proclaimed the necessity of alarming, in times of danger, a great breadth of country.

Perhaps the ruined state of the Roman Wall explains the relative introspection of some of the ideas explored in this chapter at a time of general imperial confidence. It appears, however, that William Hutton and John Collingwood Bruce primarily emphasized the positive message of the Roman Wall. The ruination of the monument was used to reflect upon peace in the border lands and upon the contemporary power of Britain as an imperial nation and the idea of the cultural and religious progress that had been made since the time of Roman oppression during the second century. An impressive painting in a Northumbrian country house provides one further useful reflection upon these issues.

9

Wallington Hall: Native Troops
on the Wall

As a piece of life and teeming invention it is altogether
glorious, and could only be produced by a true poet.
Dante Gabriel Rossetti (quoted in R. Trevelyan 1978), 123.[1]

INTRODUCTION

This chapter has been inspired by a painting entitled *Building of the
Roman Wall*, which may be viewed at Wallington Hall in Northumberland
(Figure 9.1). This imposing composition, completed in June 1857, shows the
rebuilding of Hadrian's Wall from its foundations. Wallington Hall is a
neoclassical country house that is maintained for visitors by the National
Trust. The central hall is hung with a series of eight paintings by William
Bell Scott, which portrays scenes from the history of Northumberland. Scott
(1811–1890) was born in Edinburgh and was director of the Newcastle School
of Design at the time that these paintings were commissioned (Figure 9.2). He
was a well-known artist, poet, and friend of the Pre-Raphaelite painter Dante
Gabriel Rossetti.[2] The painting depicts ancient Britons and also Roman
soldiers from across the empire and it would appear that Scott was casting a
reflective gaze on Britain's imperial concerns at a time of particular pressure
by effecting an opening-up of the Roman frontier that drew upon the evidence
for the diverse communities along this ancient Wall.

FACT AND FICTION IN PAINT

The scene in the painting is set at the base of Hotbank Crags, two kilometres
to the west of Housesteads, looking westwards towards Crag Louch and Peel

---

[1] Rossetti made these comments about a calotype of William Bell Scott's painting, *Building of
the Roman Wall*, which the artist had sent to him.
[2] Batchelor (2004); R. Trevelyan (1994), 56.

Fig. 9.1. The painting by William Bell Scott at Wallington Hall entitled *Building of the Roman Wall*. Reproduced by permission of the National Trust.

Crag. It depicts the partly built curtain Wall under attack by Caledonians. The owners of the Wallington estate, Sir Walter Calverley Trevelyan and his wife, Paulina Jermyn Trevelyan, commissioned these paintings. Sir Walter was a liberal with interests in geology and antiquity, whose works included a contribution to Hodgson's *History of Northumberland*.[3] He was also one of the

---

[3] Morrell (2004).

Fig. 9.2. A photograph of William Bell Scott, with John Ruskin and Dante Gabriel Rossetti (from left to right), taken on 29 June 1863 by William Downey. Reproduced by permission of National Portrait Gallery, x128797.

subscribers to the first edition of John Collingwood Bruce's monograph, *The Roman Wall* (1851). He had travelled extensively with his wife in Europe, including visits to Rome. The Trevelyans had been remodelling their house for some years; the central hall had been designed by the Newcastle architect, John Dobson.[4] Scott was paid £100 for this painting of the Roman Wall.[5] He wrote regular letters to the Trevelyans, some of which elucidate this important work.

Scott painted *Building of the Roman Wall* between January and June 1857.[6] He had already begun to think about the composition by 11 January, since he writes to Sir Walter, 'Will you please say to Lady Trevelyan which I forgot to do the other day, that Dr Bruce, the enthusiast of the Roman Wall, hopes if she ever visits the Wall, that she will allow him to offer his services as guide and expositor'.[7] By 12 March, Scott had decided to focus on this particular painting and to postpone two of his other paintings of Danes and Saxons.[8] On 15 March, Scott records that he had produced a 'picture', presumably a mock-up of the Roman Wall painting.[9] In a letter dated 21 April, he mentions that he had been discussing details for the image with John Collingwood Bruce.[10] On 26 May, Scott told Lady Trevelyan that 'The

---

[4] R. Trevelyan (2009), 16. [5] W. C. Trevelyan (1857).
[6] R. Trevelyan (2009), 18. [7] W. B. Scott (1857a).
[8] W. B. Scott (1857b). [9] W. B. Scott 1857c).
[10] W. B. Scott (1857d).

Roman Wall goes on...in a rather triumphal manner' and by 5 June, the artist stated that she would be able to examine the finished painting by the end of the month.[11]

Building of the Roman Wall is hung at the beginning of a series of eight of Scott's paintings depicting the history of Northumberland from the Roman period to the nineteenth century. The last painting in this sequence is an image of the Industrial Revolution in Victorian Newcastle.[12] Within this series, the Roman painting equates the construction of the Wall with the early stages of England's progress towards contemporary Christian imperial order.[13] The industry portrayed in the building of the Wall is equated with the growing industrial significance of Newcastle and Tyneside.[14] The later paintings in the sequence, together with the accompanying sculpture by Thomas Woolner, articulate the victory of Protestant Christian morality over ancient British and Roman paganism;[15] this echoes the theme that had been addressed by Bruce at *Borcovicium* in 1851.

In his imaginative portrayal of the Roman Wall, Scott aimed for a degree of historical accuracy.[16] His letters suggest that he consulted John Collingwood Bruce on several occasions about some details.[17] Bruce was the obvious authority to approach, since he had done so much to publicize and promote the monument since the first Pilgrimage. Scott also consulted the antiquary John Clayton at Chesters, noting in a letter that Clayton had sent him a stone, 'a good fresh sample of the Wall to paint into my foreground'.[18] Scott must have visited the Wall when preparing his work, although it is impossible to reconstruct his exact viewpoint since the course of the Wall does not exactly fit with the composition (Figure 9.3).[19] Scott's examined images of Trajan's Column in order to portray Roman soldiers with as much accuracy as possible.[20] His interest in detail is apparent from his comment that the Roman Wall painting included 'an immense number of historic points for Sir Walter to discover accuracy or the reverse in my treatment of it'.

Some of the individuals portrayed in Scott's Wallington Hall paintings are carefully worked portraits of his contemporaries,[21] but he only appears to have used one person as a model for the Roman scene. Scott observed of the Roman Wall painting that, 'The only portrait here is that of Dr Bruce the historian of the

---

[11] W. B. Scott (1857e); W. B. Scott (1857f).

[12] R. Trevelyan (2009), 18; Smiles (1994), 143–5.

[13] Batchelor (2006), 125; Smiles (1994), 144–7; Usherwood (1996), 153.

[14] Usherwood (1996), 153.

[15] Batchelor (2006), 125.

[16] R. Trevelyan (1994), 18.

[17] W. B. Scott (1857b); W. B. Scott (1857c); W. B. Scott (1857d).

[18] W. B. Scott (1857d).

[19] Batchelor (2006), 134; There are traces of a milecastle shown in the painting just behind the figures and this must be intended to represent the Milking Gap Milecastle (*MC 38*). The view from the painting, however, fits better a lower-lying area 200 metres to the south-west.

[20] W. B. Scott (1857e).

[21] W. B. Scott (1879); cf. Batchelor (2006), 135.

Fig. 9.3. Hadrian's Wall close to the location shown on William Bell Scott's painting, just below Hotbank. Photograph by Richard Hingley, 2011.

Wall, who gave me a setting for the profile near the middle of the picture, of one of the labourers on the Wall'.[22] This figure is immediately behind the left knee of the Roman officer in the foreground. Scott noted that, after meeting Bruce on 21 April 1857, he was 'going to have the historian's head on Roman shoulders in the picture after all. Not an important head, but secondary.'[23] The figure modelled on Bruce is shown glancing at the attacking Caledonians while engaged in the vital work of building the Wall. A review of the third edition of Bruce's *The Roman Wall* states, with regard to the painting, that:

> one of the most striking figures in the picture, a builder with a fine attenuated face, intense in expression as Caesar's himself, who is throwing his whole heart and strength and soul and mind into the work, is . . . the portrait of Dr. Bruce. And Dr. Bruce is as truly a builder of the Wall as the emperor Hadrian himself. He has built it up once more in his work absolutely unique in literature. Of that great historical structure there can hardly remain a stone that is strange to him. He has not, indeed, left any stone of note that can hereafter be strange to anybody . . .[24]

It has been suggested that the Roman officer who dominates the painting in the foreground is a portrait of John Clayton (1792–1890),[25] but Scott's comments contradict this idea. Nevertheless, that this figure is based on Clayton is

---

[22] W. B. Scott (1879).   [23] W. B. Scott (1857d).   [24] Anon (1867).
[25] R. Trevelyan (1994), 58–9; Crow (2004a), caption to colour fig. 19.

Fig. 9.4. A portrait of John Clayton. From Hodgkin (1892).

attractive, since he also greatly inspired Wall studies during the mid-nineteenth century (Figure 9.4). He lived at the mansion beside the Roman fort at Chesters on the line of the Wall and excavated many of the Roman sites, acquired four Roman forts, and involved himself in the rebuilding of a substantial section of the Roman curtain Wall. The partial completeness of the Wall in Scott's painting drew upon the contemporary appearance of the rebuilt curtain Wall on the Crags just to the east of the location at where the painting was set. At the time, however, Clayton would have been sixty-five and the Roman officer is shown to be a much younger man.

The painting clearly supports the argument that the curtain Wall was built by Hadrian and counters the previously dominant idea that it was the work of Septimius Severus. In 1840, John Hodgson had argued that the whole of the Wall was the work of Hadrian, a suggestion that was then popularized by Bruce.[26] The caption in Latin above the painting draws upon the *Historia Augusta, de vita Hadriani* (XI, 2) to state that 'Hadrian built the Wall to divide the barbarians from the Romans'.[27] There is also a Latin inscription on a stone set into the outer face of the curtain Wall that reads:

---

[26] J. Hodgson (1840), 309; J. C. Bruce (1851), 382–3.
[27] At the bottom of the painting a Victorian reinterpretation of the Latin phrase is provided, stating that 'The Romans caused a Wall to be built for the protection of the south'.

IM[P]. CÆS. TRAIAN
HADRIAN. AVG
LEG. II. AVG
A.P. NEPOTE. L.P.P.

This is based on the important example that had been found among the remains of the Milking Gap Milecastle (*MC 38*) in the 1750s (Figure 9.5).[28] This had clearly identified the milecastle's builders as the Second Legion Augusta under Hadrian and named the governor of Britain at the time of its construction, Aulus Platorius Nepos.[29]

Fig. 9.5. The Roman inscription from Milking Gap Milecastle (*M 38*). From J. C. Bruce (1863), 143.

During the 1850s, there was a lively debate regarding on whose orders the Wall had been built, entitled the 'mural controversy', since many had rejected Hodgson's and Bruce's argument that Hadrian ordered the construction of the curtain Wall, turrets, and milecastles.[30] In his letters, William Bell Scott discussed the likely date of the monument, using 'Dr Bruce's controversial botherings' to suggest that the curtain Wall was built by Hadrian rather than Severus.[31] Scott noted that this particular question was agitating people 'as if the British empire depended on it'. Richard Abbatt, drawing on Gildas and Bede, argued that the stone curtain Wall was built in post-Roman times, dating the construction to AD 409–18.[32] Abbatt considered that the earth wall (the Vallum) was constructed at an earlier date and that the various Roman stations lay to the north of this barrier. Most antiquaries,

---

[28] See J. C. Bruce (1851), 383; Breeze (2006a), 255; RIB, n. 1638. The final line on the painted stone has been shortened and the 'P' is missing from the first word.

[29] Clayton (1855), 55–6; cf. Breeze and Dobson (2000), 63–6. In fact, a rendition of the stone is show on the painting built into the outer face of the curtain Wall.

[30] cf. Collingwood (1921a), 56; Maxfield (1982), 59.

[31] W. B. Scott (1857c); W. B. Scott (1857b).

[32] Abbatt (1849), 9–10.

however, continued to believe that Severus constructed the curtain Wall during the late second or early third century,[33] influenced by the writings of John Horsley.[34] Despite the support of Bruce and Clayton for the Hadrianic construction of the curtain Wall, arguments about its exact dating were to continue until the 1920s.

NATIVE TROOPS UPON THE WALL

Perhaps the most interesting aspect of this painting relates to the variety of people it portrays. *Building of the Roman Wall* drew deeply upon Victorian concepts concerning the ethnology of the Romans and ancient Britons, although it is unfortunate that William Bell Scott did not reflect on this issue in his letters to the Trevelyans, making his motivation difficult to comprehend. The painting appears to reflect imperial problems of the mid-Victorian period, drawing messages from the ethnologically mixed nature of the communities responsible for constructing and guarding the Roman Wall. In his seminal study of representations of British antiquity, Sam Smiles has drawn upon Victorian phrenology to consider some of the racial character-istics of the people represented in this painting.[35] He has also suggested that problematic military events in Afghanistan and India during the 1840s and 1850s provided a meaningful context for the painting, which appears to include at least three categories of people.

First, there are three Roman soldiers in legionary dress, one the imposing figure in the foreground, another in the middle ground standing at the edge of the curtain Wall, and a third before a pagan altar at the left of the painting. There are also auxiliary soldiers, clearly drawing upon evidence for the Roman units stationed along the Wall. Second, partly clothed ancient Britons, both men and women, are building the Wall. Third, to the north of the line of the Wall to the right, a small band of lightly clothed barbarian Caledonians is advancing up the slope towards the curtain Wall. They are attacking from outside the province, provoking an armed response from the Roman soldiers on the curtain Wall.

The Roman soldiers comprise a particularly interesting group (Figure 9.6). The appearance of at least three of them seems to be drawn from information in Roman inscriptions from the Wall, while also referencing the Victorian military policy of recruiting 'native soldiers' to serve the British empire.

[33] E. Birley (1961), 61–2.
[34] Collingwood (1921a), 56.
[35] Smiles (1994), 144–6. Phrenology focused on the idea that the shape of the head reflected the mental faculties of an individual.

Fig. 9.6. Details of the painting entitled *Building of the Roman Wall* by William Bell Scott, showing native soldiers. Reproduced by permission of the National Trust. Photograph by, Richard Hingley, 2011.

During the nineteenth century, the British recruited native soldiers from India and elsewhere, both for war and to defend the imperial frontiers, and by the middle of the century the majority of troops in the Indian army were indigenous mercenaries.[36] Comparisons were sometimes drawn between the auxiliary soldiers of the Roman empire and the native soldiers used by the modern British,[37] as demonstrated by the Wallington Hall painting.

Facing the oncoming barbarians, the legionary standing on the edge of the curtain Wall has dark skin and facial features that appear to suggest African descent.[38] He holds an article of surveying equipment in one hand and a shield in the other, which has an arrow fired by one of the Caledonians sticking into its outer face. This soldier may represent one of the African or Near Eastern soldiers identified by Bruce in the Roman inscriptions found along the Wall. The soldier's legionary equipment indicates that he is a citizen of the Roman empire, with a status higher than anyone else in the scene apart from the officer in the foreground. Two other characters that are working on the Wall

[36] Streets (2004), 25.   [37] cf. Thorne (2010), 101–4.
[38] Usherwood (1996), 162 n. 6; Hingley (2010b), 234.

close by increase the probability that this figure is intended to represent an African. A second soldier is using a bow and arrows to ward off the attacking Britons—he presumably represents a member of the First Cohort of Hamian Archers from Syria,[39] since an inscription from this unit had recently been found at the Roman site at Carvoran on the Wall, a few miles to the west of the location shown in the painting.[40] A third man in this group wears a 'Phrygian cap' and appears to be intently involved in building the Wall.

These figures in the Wallington Hall painting reflected contemporary knowledge of the Roman population of the Wall. There was a growing interest at this time in the geographical and ethnological origins of the peoples who had settled in Roman Britain, including those who had lived along the Wall.[41] From the late sixteenth century, the widespread geographical origins of those serving in the Roman army on the Wall had gradually become evident as a result of the recognition of evidence for origins derived from the Roman stone inscriptions and the *Notitia Dignitatum*. Antiquaries describing the Wall prior to the mid nineteenth century often listed the information for the origins of these soldiers but made little comment on the significance of the observations.[42] The absence of discussion of this theme prior to this time presumably reflects the lack of knowledge about the Roman cultures of other areas of the empire due to an absence of detailed archaeological work. Consequently, it was impossible to place the information for these overseas soldiers from other parts of Europe, North Africa, and the Near East in any sort of cultural context. What did it mean to have a soldier from Germany, Spain, Syria, or North Africa stationed on the Wall when there was little understanding of Roman material culture across the empire?

It is significant that the increasing interest of antiquaries in the ethnology of the population of the Wall occurs alongside the development of racial concepts about the identities of the contemporary peoples of Europe and the British empire.[43] In *The Roman Wall*, Bruce discussed the available evidence for the geographical origins of the soldiers who had served and settled on the frontier, including many military units from Germany and Spain.[44] He noted that some of these men originated from places far from Britain and that the *Notitia Dignitatum* lists a detachment of Moors at 'Aballaba'.[45] Bruce connects this place name with a Roman fort at Watch-cross (Burgh-by-Sands, Cumbria) and records that this fort was 'garrisoned by a *numerus* of troops of Moors, under a prefect'.[46] Elsewhere, he drew attention to an altar from *Magna* (Carvoran) dedicated by Titus Flavius Secundus, Prefect of the First Cohort of Hamian Archers.[47]

---

[39] cf. Breeze and Dobson (2000), 283.   [40] J. C. Bruce (1857b), 249–50.
[41] Hingley (2010b), 231–2.   [42] ibid., 231.
[43] cf. Ballantyne (2002); Smiles (1994), 120–6; R. Young (2008).
[44] J. C. Bruce (1851), 60–4.
[45] ibid., 60.   [46] ibid., 297; see Breeze (2006a), 351.
[47] J. C. Bruce (1857b), 249–50; RIB, n. 1778.

In his influential but problematic book, *The Celt, the Roman and the Saxon* (1852), Thomas Wright focused particularly on the ethnological nature of the population of Britain in Roman times. In relation to the Wall, he drew upon the work of Bruce to observe that there were many semi-distinct 'races' living in the 'towns' along the line of the Wall, including Asturians from Spain at Chesters, Dacians at Birdoswald, and Moors at Watch-cross.[48] Evidence for these people was derived from the *Notitia*, but Wright also noted that inscriptions on altars and tombstones indicated that many of them had stayed in place, becoming 'possessors of the land'.[49] He argued that settlers in Britain had been accompanied by 'relations and friends, and as evidently they were recruited from their own countries, they must have gone on and on increasing and strengthening themselves.' This idea reflects the mid nineteenth-century concept that racial groups are self-contained and relatively immutable.[50] Wright effectively sees the overseas settlers as self-contained colonies living in their own particular places along the line of the Wall. In contrast, the native soldiers in the Wallington Hall painting appear to represent a mixed community of soldiers from across the empire, united through the desire to construct and defend the Wall.

Noting the 'otherness' of the dark, rainy stretch of land on the right ('barbarian') side of the Wallington Hall painting, Paul Usherwood has suggested that this represents the anticipation of future trouble,[51] but he also saw the attack from the north by the barbarian Caledonians as desperate and entirely futile.[52] The symbolism of the painting, however, is particularly complex.[53] Certain Victorians considered that Rome had successfully addressed the issue of imperial incorporation that the British were beginning to find problematic by the late 1850s. William Bell Scott's painting appears to be playing with ideas of military identity, crossing geographical boundaries in a search of a viable analogy for the defence of the frontiers of the British empire. The idea that certain colonized peoples represented 'martial races' had a growing impact in Britain during the nineteenth century.[54] In the Wallington Hall painting, the native soldiers of the Roman army are helping to organize and defend ancient British women and children, depicted behind the curtain Wall, from an attack by Caledonians. By the time *Building of the Roman Wall* was being completed in June 1857, this concept may have appeared problematic.[55]

In May 1857, the so-called 'Indian Mutiny' broke out,[56] raising issues about the relationship between the British and the native troops of the empire.[57]

---

[48] Wright (1852), 250–1.
[49] ibid., 251.   [50] cf. Hingley (2008a), 266–71.
[51] Usherwood (2007), 251–2.   [52] Usherwood (1996), 153.
[53] Hingley (2010b), 234–5.   [54] Streets (2004), 1.
[55] Hingley (2010b), 234–5; cf. Streets (2004), 18–19.   [56] David (2002).
[57] Streets (2004), 29–30.

Prior to this, the British had been rapidly acquiring new territories but the events in India of 1857 precipitated a significant psychological shock, leading to a reduction in confidence regarding the invincibility of Britain's control over its colonies.[58] *Building of the Roman Wall* appears to contain an optimistic view of imperial progress, since the Romans dominate both the barbarian Britons and Caledonians and also because the painting is part of a series that championed imperial progress and the triumph of Christianity. There are, however, elements of insecurity present.

The siege of Cawnpore (Kanpur) during late May and early June 1857 led to the surrender of the British garrison to Nana Sahib, who ordered the execution of all of the prisoners.[59] Almost all the Christian civilians were slaughtered, including Anna Halliday, the daughter of Walter Trevelyan's sister, Emma Wyndham, together with her husband and children.[60] Although Scott's painting was clearly not a direct response to the events at Cawnpore, the view it expressed of imperial cooperation between the races of the empire must have appeared particularly apposite in the context of the events on June 1857. Two of the artist's letters to the Trevelyans reflect on the context of the tragedy at Cawnpore. Writing to Lady Treveleyan on 26 May, Scott refers to Sir Walter's visit to his sister, commiserating 'we are very sorry for the reason'.[61] In a letter to Sir Walter dated 5 June, Scott observed that he wrote that he hopes that the Trevelyans would examine the painting before the end of the month, reiterating that 'We were very sorry to hear from Lady Trevelyan of the great loss you have sustained, so suddenly.'[62] In the context of the news that was arriving from India during the early summer of 1857, the presence of British women and children behind the Roman curtain Wall might have taken on the significance of reflecting concern for the security of British families in India,[63] over which there was a sensation in the media around the time of the painting's completion.[64]

During the siege at Cawnpore, a loyal band of Indian troops had fought alongside the British.[65] Native troops remained fundamental to the British imperial effort and parallels between the imperial policies of Rome and Britain continued to be drawn.[66] A direct reference to the Roman Wall and the 'Indian Mutiny' was published in an anonymous editorial in *The English-woman's Review and Home Newspaper* of 5 December 1857.[67] Placed after Queen Victoria's speech to Parliament, the article recorded the opening of 'probably, one of the most momentous Parliamentary Sessions ever held'. The editorial emphasized that 'The interests of Britain, of the empire at large, and

---

[58] Hall (2010), 33.   [59] Batchelor (2006), 194–5; David (2002), 198–9.
[60] Batchelor (2006), 194–5.
[61] W. B. Scott (1857e).   [62] W. B. Scott (1857f).   [63] cf. Paxton (1992).
[64] cf. Nagai (2005), 85.   [65] David (2002), 198.
[66] cf. Hutchins (1967), 145.
[67] cf. Hingley (2010b), 234–5.

our vast dependency of Hindostan—of civilisation itself—are at stake'.[68] Drawing attention to the supposed general benefits of the activities of the East India Company, to which 'a deep debt of gratitude is due', some of the reported atrocities committed by the rebels are recorded and the problems faced by the British in the context of the Mutiny considered. Parallels between the British in India and the Roman empire are then suggested and it is noted that:

> Another point which must be settled soon is the constitution of the Indian army. The Romans knew how to govern a conquered country, their motto was *'divide et impera'*. They did not attempt to hold Britain with British soldiers, or Gaul with Gauls, they sent the Britons abroad, and brought foreigners to Britain; for instance, along the line of the Roman wall were Spaniards, *Tungrians*, &c. But we recruited our Bengal army almost entirely from Oude—brothers, cousins, and other near relatives, connected too, by religious ties, formed a vast military clan. To complete the folly of our system, we under-officered our regiments . . . [69]

The folly of allowing native troops to serve close to their homelands was emphasized, to which the current troubles in India are attributed and it was suggested that the Romans had followed a better policy in this regard.[70] The editorial further reflected that, 'The advantages of mixing the races in the composition of the army has been shown by the fidelity of the Sikhs and Ghorkas, which has probably saved India'.[71] The use of native troops is viewed as vital to the success of the British, but in future they should always be stationed in mixed groups and far from their homelands in order to avoid further problems.

From this perspective, the mixed character of the Roman soldiers portrayed on the Wallington Hall painting represented good practice for an imperial power under pressure. Perhaps the armed resistance of some of the Britons in this painting and the indolence of the others also represents the folly of stationing soldiers too close to their home ground.

BRITONS ON THE WALL

Victorian commentators were aware of foreigners serving in Roman Britain, but what role did indigenous Britons play in constructing and guarding the Wall? Scott's response to this is complex, since Britons are portrayed as both builders and attackers.[72] Victorians inherited contrasting views of the ancient population of Britain, of both noble and ignoble savagery.[73] The work of

---

[68] Anon (1857), 241.   [69] ibid., 242.   [70] cf. Hutchins (1967), 145.
[71] Anon (1857), 242.   [72] Hingley (2010b), 235.   [73] Smiles (1994), 2.

antiquaries and artists supported contradictory images of the ancient population as either the valiant upholders of British national freedom or primitive savages more akin to certain colonized peoples within the British empire. Some commentators considered that the ancient Britons were the ancestors of the current Scots, Irish, and Welsh, while the English were descended from Anglo-Saxon settlers; in any case, the ancient past had a vital contemporary relevance.

Smiles has explored how both the Wallington Hall painting and Ford Maddox Brown's painting of the building of a Roman fort at Manchester (in Manchester Town Hall) portray Victorian ideas about phrenology, with the ancient Britons in the guise of working-class Celtic labourers.[74] The three Britons on top of the Wall to the left of the Wallington Hall painting are cooperating to a degree with their imperial masters, but they do not have the Roman demeanour or apparel, retaining the partly naked character of the Caledonians who are shown attacking the Wall. The figures on top of and behind the Wall to the left are Lowland Roman Britons; they have been subdued by their conquerors and have been put to work as labourers under the control of Roman officers, an idea that drew upon the sixth-century writings of Gildas.

William Hutton had written that, during the construction of the Wall, 'In all laborious undertakings, the Britons were pressed into the service, and charged with the drudgery'.[75] Bruce drew on this idea when he observed that, during the construction of the Wall:

> There can be no doubt that the unfortunate inhabitants of the country were by the Romans compelled to do much of the servile work that was required. Most unwillingly they were forced, with something more potent than the centurion's vine twig, to quarry the stone, to raise the ramparts, and grind the mortar. Had they an historian amongst them, 'The Groans of the Britons' of the early half of the second century would have been a tale fitted to move the heart of the modern Englishman.[76]

The two male ancient Britons in the foreground of the painting, however, have put down their tools and are involved in cooking and gambling with dice.[77] This indolence presumably recalls Gildas' (19.2) that the Britons 'sat about day and night, rotting away in their folly' when they should have been defending the Wall. Women are also depicted, perhaps partly reflecting their presence on the first Pilgrimage along the Wall and also drawing upon the classical texts that described ancient British women fighting alongside men. Norman Vance has suggested that the woman with a child in the painting promises the eventual possibility of a settled Romano-British social life

---

[74] ibid., 146. [75] Hutton (1802), 21. [76] J. C. Bruce (1875), xi.
[77] Usherwood (1996), 153; R. Trevelyan (1994), 58–9.

in this region,[78] but a rather less optimistic suggestion may have derived from the contemporary international situation.

To the right of the painting, partly clothed Caledonians are advancing to threaten the progress of civilization by attacking the Wall. The representation of Britons as both building and attempting to overthrow the Wall demonstrates a lack of unity among the ancient population, with the result that Roman soldiers must control the construction and defence of the imperial frontier. Despite their supervision of the subservient Britons, there is a feeling of doubt that the Wall will ever be completed. The attacking barbarians echo the theme of Scott's cartoon, 'The Free Northern Britons', but the Caledonians in the painting at Wallington Hall look unlikely to achieve their objective of overrunning the Wall. The painter's reflection of the Hadrianic dating of the Wall illustrated that the Roman empire would survive for a further three centuries, so this was not the time at which the Wall would be destroyed.

The ambivalent role of the ancient Britons in the Wallington painting is also represented in another Victorian scene from the Wall. This engraving is taken from an image by C. Cattermole, presumably the painter Charles Cattermole, and portrays a young man at *Cilurnum* (Chesters; Figure 9.7). It accompanied a poem, by 'H. P.', in the April 1876 edition of *Belgravia*.[79] The poem and engraving both draw upon the Roman remains at *Cilurnum* as a source of contemplation, noting the 'hundred relics' from the site, but that there is:

> Not one o'er which the heart could say
> 'These Romans were of kindred clay.'
> Yes one! I found a broken tile—
>   Among the rest 'twas little worth;
> It could not tell the name or style
>   Of any god in heaven or earth;
> It did not in the least bring home
> The might or majesty of Rome.
> But on its unpretending face,
>   Of greater price than virgin gold,
> Some childish hand had striven to trace
> The semblance of a warrior bold.[80]

The ancient Briton in the engraving is using a broken Roman tile to sketch a warrior, a reflection upon the connections between the Roman past and the imperial present drawing on the excavated material from John Clayton's excavations at Chesters. As will be discussed in detail in the following chapter, Clayton had undertaken extensive excavations at the site since the 1840s,

[78] Vance (1997), 245.
[79] The identity of this poet is unclear (Renato Pinto pers. comm.).
[80] Anon (1876), 214.

Fig. 9.7. An engraving by W. A. Cranston from an image by C. Cattermole titled *There sits a noble boy... intent upon a work of art*. From *Belgravia* 1876, 3rd Series, 9, 213–217. Reproduced by permission of Tyne and Wear Museums on behalf of North Tyneside Council, John Collingwood Bruce Archive.

Fig. 9.8. One of the Roman inscribed stones at Chesters Museum showing two warriors. It was supposed in Victorian times that a number of these carved stones had been produced by boys. Photograph by Richard Hingley, 2011. Reproduced by permission of English Heritage and the Trustees of the Clayton Collection.

uncovering much of a plan that he considered to represent a military city. Stones individually inscribed with figures of soldiers had been found during the excavations and were interpreted as the work of children (Figure 9.8).[81] The poem makes it clear that the boy is 'a Briton born and bred' and, in the illustration, he is clearly distinguished from the Roman soldier patrolling on

---

[81] cf. Whitworth (2009a), 27.

the tower in the background by his semi-clothed appearance and also by the torc around his neck and his arm ring. On the stairs at his feet is a small shield of Bronze Age style together with a spear, but this young figure seems unprepared to defend the Wall.

The inner face of the stone Wall on which the boy is sitting is inscribed SPQR, making a clear Roman claim to its construction. As the poem observed, the boy is not engaged in the Roman practice of writing, but is drawing an image of a warrior on the Roman tile, possible suggesting that he is illiterate. Evidently, this native Briton is living at peace with his Roman masters but he is not at all engaged in the defence of the imperial realm. Nor is he assimilated into the responsibilities of imperial defence, since it is left to the Roman soldiers to survey the hills to the north of the turret on which they stand. The poet concludes by pleading:

> Ye guardian powers! Shield them well
>   When all the shudd'ring banks of the Tyne
> Give back the Caledonian yell,
>   And 'gainst the calm-eyed Roman line,
> Wave behind wave, tumultuous roar
> The torrents of Barbarian war.[82]

As in the case of the Wallington Hall painting, the threat to the Lowland Britons was perceived as coming from the barbarians to the north, reflecting Gildas' comments both on the function of the Wall and the failure of the ancient Britons south of the Wall to defend their territory after the Romans had withdrawn from Britain.

One dominant idea in nineteenth-century England was that Roman control had not greatly influenced the ways of life of ancient Britons to the south of the Wall, although it had removed their independence and fighting spirit.[83] From the first surviving depiction of ancient Britons during the late sixteenth century, their nakedness and barbarity were often emphasized.[84] This image drew on the influential idea that the English were themselves descended from post-Roman Anglo-Saxon invaders, people who had overwhelmed the Roman empire and then adopted its civilization. In the Wallington Hall and *Cilurnum* images, the colonized ancient Britons within the line of the Wall are, therefore, peaceful and compliant but not in any real sense Romanized in their language, manners, or dress, nor are they ready to defend the empire.

By the time the poem was published in 1876, four inscriptions had been found that mentioned individual British *civitates* and these could, perhaps, have been used to tell a different story of active British involvement in the construction and defence of the Wall. Wright observed, however, that

---

[82] Anon (1876), 215.   [83] Hingley (2008a), 269.   [84] Smiles (1994), 129–32.

although several 'British tribes' were involved in building the Roman Wall, the descendants of the ancient population of Britain were reduced to the 'lowest degree of dependence'.[85] He observed: 'In the towns of the legions or of the auxiliaries they would not be allowed to enjoy any rights, and it is probable that in the later part of the Roman period the British blood in the south was found chiefly in the peasantry. The name of Britons was then applied almost exclusively to the independent tribes of Caledonia.' These writings reflect a current view of the native population of Roman Britain as slaves, an idea that was beginning to replace earlier images of noble resistance to Roman rule.[86] Victorian artists often shared this belief and drew upon the idea of the ancient Britons of the area within the Wall as semi-naked barbarians, unable to defend their own liberty, and requiring the armed protection of Rome.[87] This is an image that, to an extent at least, draws the populations of ancient Lowland Britain and contemporary English apart.

SUMMARY: AN INCLUSIVE WALL

Although William Bell Scott's painting was produced for display in a private house, the impact of its message was felt across the north-east and further into England. The eight paintings of the Wallington Hall sequence were exhibited at the French Gallery in Pall Mall at the end of June 1861. Although Scott noted dejectedly that the exhibition 'did little good',[88] John Batchelor has argued that this painting cycle represented an innovation of national as well as regional significance.[89] The *Illustrated London News* of 20 July 1861 reported the display of the paintings and reproduced engravings of two of them, noting 'These pictures...present a freshness and an originality which would hardly have been attained by an artist less acquainted with the country and its by-gone history'.[90] The paintings were also widely reviewed in the national press. Engravings were produced from the individual paintings for a number of publications, including a London newspaper.[91] It will be seen that later images of the Wall appear to draw on William Bell Scott's innovative painting, but artists often demonstrated less concern for the accuracy of the details that they portray.

Discoveries of Roman tombstones during the late nineteenth century were to encourage an increasingly international focus of attention on the evidence for the communities that occupied the frontier zone of Roman Britain, helping to break down the national focus of much of the previous scholarship on the

---

[85] Wright (1852), 255.   [86] Smiles (1994), 126.   [87] ibid., 146–7.
[88] Quoted by Minto (ed. 1892), 67.   [89] Batchelor (2006), 200.
[90] Illustrated London News (1861).   [91] W. B. Scott (1879).

Wall. In particular, this was a result of contact with German scholars who were taking an increasing interest in the Roman frontier works along the rivers Rhine and Danube.[92] The international focus of *Building of the Roman Wall* on the ethnology of the Roman population of the Wall appears truly remarkable. Although Bruce and other contemporary antiquaries were aware of the origins of Roman soldiers who served along the Wall, Scott had a particular desire to draw this issue to the attention of viewers of his painting. Victorian society's interest in race extended to the ethnology of the population of the Roman Wall. This is evident in the writings of Bruce and Wright, but is particularly graphically represented by the appearance of the three native soldiers in this remarkable painting.

[92] cf. Buchner (1822); W. Bell (1854); Yates (1858).

10

The Clayton Wall: 'A New Era in Antiquarian Research'

Some excavations recently made at Cilurnum and Borcorvicus, shew us, that were the requisite skill and labour bestowed, we might in our own land walk in Roman streets, and traverse Roman temples, little inferior in interest to those of Pompeii.

John Collingwood Bruce (1850), 203

INTRODUCTION

This chapter will explore the contributions of John Clayton and John Collingwood Bruce to knowledge of the Wall. Later commentators have not always been very generous in acknowledging the significant work of these two antiquaries. In an obituary for Bruce, Thomas Hodgkin observed that the time for 'great discoveries in connection with the Roman Wall was probably ended when John Horsley...settled the names of the Roman stations',[1] effectively dismissing the studies of the Victorian antiquaries. Francis Haverfield reviewed previous work on the Wall, noting the 'surface descriptions' of the earthwork remains produced by Horsley, Hutton, Hodgson, and Bruce.[2] He argued that:

> The spade was rarely used to prove theories which were suggested by the appearance of the ground, and the excavations made in some of the forts were incompletely recorded or more often not recorded at all. The result is inevitable. Our best descriptions of the Wall contain many statements which are guesses, others which are actually wrong, and our maps lay down the lines of Roads or Wall or Vallum with a false and misleading precision.

This criticism of the excavation works undertaken by the Victorian antiquaries is accompanied by an overt claim that archaeological work can produce certainty to replace guesswork, as will be discussed in Chapter 12.

---

[1] Hodgkin (1892), 367.   [2] Haverfield (1899a), 337.

R. G. Collingwood mentioned that:

> Clayton, the owner of Chesters, devoted both his wealth and his scholarship to the study of the Wall, which indeed he 'collected' by systematically buying up the land on which it stood, as opportunity offered, and excavating what he bought. It was, of course, not what we call scientific digging. That had not yet been invented. It was pioneer work, and inevitably destroyed much evidence which to-day would be valuable: for Clayton's main object was only to clear the chief walls and to collect inscribed stones.[3]

Haverfield and Collingwood play down the significance of the contribution of Bruce and Clayton in order to emphasize the importance of a sustained new programme of archaeological research that commenced during the final decade of the nineteenth century.

Eric Birley was more generous when he stated that Clayton's 'progressive disinterment of individual structures, and loving restoration of long stretches of the Wall' provided increasingly more for visitors to see.[4] It should be stressed that Clayton and Bruce added significantly to the available knowledge of the Wall by focusing the attention of local antiquaries onto its remains. The detailed chronology of the construction of the Wall would await the more systematic excavations undertaken by the Cumberland and Westmorland and the Newcastle societies from the 1890s, but the focus of interest on the Wall due to Clayton's excavations and Bruce's publicizing led to important new discoveries about the physical character of the monument and the revision of earlier ideas.

The particular location drawn upon in this chapter is the section of curtain Wall reconstructed by Clayton along the central upland section of its course— the so-called 'Clayton Wall' (Figure 10.1). While William Bell Scott was painting the canvas for Wallington Hall, Clayton was engaged in uncovering and rebuilding the physical fabric of the Wall. This chapter will assess the idea of the metaphorical and physical rebuilding of the Wall through an assessment of the contributions of Clayton and Bruce to Wall studies, by selecting themes related to the way that knowledge and understanding were built up during the second half of the nineteenth century. The development of knowledge about the history and structure of the Wall at this time resulted in a fundamental re-conceptualization of its significance and a growing international appreciation of the monument.

---

[3] Collingwood (1921a), 55. [4] E. Birley (1961), 28.

Fig. 10.1. The 'Clayton Wall' on the east side of Winshield Crags. John Clayton's workmen created a turf cap for the reconstructed curtain Wall and this approach was followed by the National Trust when it consolidated additional sections of the monument during the twentieth century. Photograph by Richard Hingley, 2011.

BRUCE'S ITINERARIES OF THE WALL

Bruce publicized and communicated information about the Wall through lectures, the Pilgrimage of 1849, and publication. Bruce's two main works were *The Roman Wall* (1851) and *The Wallet-Book* (1863), in which he adopted a method of study with antecedents in earlier accounts. The core of each of these volumes is an itinerary describing the remains of the Wall, starting at Wallsend in the east and ending in the west at the Solway.[5] Bruce's itineraries followed the model of earlier writings. In his account of Roman Britain, John Horsley had addressed 'The Present State of *Hadrian's vallum* and the Wall of *Severus*' by describing the surviving remains from east to west.[6] This approach drew upon the classical itineraries, which listed specific places along the lines of particular roads.[7] The *Notitia Dignitatum* named Roman stations along the line of the Wall from east to west, and subsequent accounts of the Wall, including the various editions of the *Handbook* and the *Hadrian's Wall Path National Trail Guide*,[8] have adopted the same approach.

Horsley used his itinerary to provide an account of the state of the Wall's Roman remains, including the surviving traces of Roman structures and the inscriptions and carved stones found along its line. Bruce drew upon this approach but also included additional material, since *The Roman Wall* and

---

[5] J. C. Bruce (1851), 103–314; (1863), 38–217.   [6] Horsley (1732), 135–58.
[7] Rivet and Smith (1979), 148–9.   [8] ibid., 220; Breeze (2006a); Burton (2003).

The Wallet-Book drew upon a tradition of chorographical writings in which the spirit of a place relates to the sum of its history. Both books contain historical and architectural asides that describe significant medieval and later buildings along the Wall, drawing on the connection that had long been made by authors such as Camden, Warburton, and Hutton, between Roman and medieval border warfare. That the medieval strongholds along the Wall's line were built out of stone derived from the Roman remains, created a material link between structures constructed many centuries apart. At other places along the line of the Wall, Bruce used landscape features to create very different associations.

One of the best known folk tales referenced by Bruce in *The Roman Wall* relates to King Arthur.[9] He provided a two-page quotation from John Hodgson giving details of Arthurian stories that are associated with the area around Sewingshields in the central section of the Wall. Bruce repeated and elaborated upon these tales in *The Wallet-Book*.[10] Bruce endeavoured to engage his readers in the living significance of the monument through 'a fine vein of enthusiasm' that runs through both of his books on the Wall.[11] On one occasion, he described the folk tale of Bogle Hole (close to Shield on the Wall); the curtain Wall crosses a steep nick, which according to popular accounts was 'the abode of an evil spirit'.[12] Bruce quotes the writings of Procopius in *De bello Gothico* (4.20. 42–55), describing that 'in this isle of Brittia [Britain], men of ancient times built a long wall, cutting off a great portion of it.' He adds a story that the souls of the dead are brought to Brittia.[13] Bruce remarks that 'We can readily conceive that at a period when the inroads of the Caledonians were still fresh in the memory of the inhabitants, the country north of the Wall would be regarded with superstitious dread.'[14]

It is possible that folk tales may once have been very common along the Wall, although Bruce's accounts do not provide many further examples. At Rudchester, he recorded a trough-like depression to the west of the farmhouse that was once popularly called 'the Giant's Grave', but which appears to have been a cistern.[15] Bruce also recalls another tradition communicated to him by a correspondent:

> Even in my own day it was the custom of the superstitious, on the line of the Wall, especially between Birdoswald and Cambeck Fort to pound the stones, bearing inscriptions, into sand for their kitchens, or bury them in the foundations of houses or walls, for the simple reason that they considered them unlucky—calling

---

[9] J. C. Bruce (1851), 205–7.   [10] J. C. Bruce (1863), 109–11.
[11] cf. ibid., 3.   [12] J. C. Bruce (1851), 244–5.
[13] ibid., 245–6. Procopius was writing in the sixth century and lived in the eastern Mediterranean. For a modern translation of this text, see A. Birley (2005), 465.
[14] J. C. Bruce (1851), 245.   [15] J. C. Bruce (1863), 60.

them 'witch stones'. When one was found, the *old wives* fearing that the butter might not form in the churn, took good care that it should never again make its appearance. Thus down went many a splendid Roman altar . . . [16]

Bruce used a rational argument to suggest that this practice helped explain the general scarcity of Roman inscribed stones along this section of the Wall.

That tales of spirits connected with particular places along the Wall were once common is suggested by the writings of another influential Victorian antiquary, Charles Roach Smith. He visited the Wall on a number of occasions, discovering the tale of the Bogle Hole and noted that 'evidences are found throughout the entire length of the Roman wall of unlimited beliefs in local divinities.'[17] Some of these tales were written down but many will have been lost. The tale of two giants at Risingham had been recorded in Camden's *Britannia* and retold in a different form by Walter Scott in his poem *Rokeby*.[18] A nineteenth-century guidebook recalls an additional tale told by the local inhabitants in which the stones that made up the Roman Wall were 'conveyed in the apron of an old woman, and that the Wall was built in one night'.[19]

RECOGNIZING THE WALL'S NATIONAL AND INTERNATIONAL SIGNIFICANCE

These tales and asides about the Wall evidently interested Bruce's audience but his main objective in his lectures and books was to emphasize the importance of the Roman Wall and to encourage people to go to visit its remains. In 1850, shortly after he first took an interest in the monument, Bruce wrote about the potential of excavating sites along the Wall, in order to uncover Roman streets and temples 'little inferior in interest to those of Pompeii'.[20] Such a claim countered earlier dismissive views of the Roman military remains of Britain, which had suggested that these provincial works were markedly inferior to those of Rome and Italy. On the first page of *The Roman Wall* (1851), Bruce stated that 'Every other monument in Britain yields in importance to THE WALL. As this work, in grandeur of conception, is worthy of the Mistress of Nations, so, in durability of structure, is it the becoming offspring of the Eternal City.'

Bruce had yet to visit Rome and, after he had explored of the remains of the empire's capital, his comments on the character of Roman sculptures from the

---

[16] J. C. Bruce (1851), 64, n. e.   [17] C. R. Smith (1883), 181.
[18] W. Scott (1813), xxi–xxii.   [19] Jenkinson (1875), 173–4.
[20] J. C. Bruce (1850), 203.

Wall became a little more circumspect.[21] For example, in 1857 he observed that:

> The materials employed in the formation of these statues and slabs and altars—sandstone—is unquestionably inferior to that which the lapidarian treasures of the Vatican consist; and they are, for the most part, immeasurably below them in artistic design and skilful execution. To Englishmen, however, they have an interest which all the glories of the Vatican and the Capitol can never surpass.[22]

The considerable impact of Bruce's publicizing of the Wall may be judged in the writings of the London-based antiquary, Charles Roach Smith. Smith first visited the Wall in June 1851 and wrote a lengthy description that drew upon Bruce's *The Roman Wall*.[23] Smith argued that this Wall was poorly known but also observed that John Collingwood Bruce and his co-investigators were striving to change this situation.[24] On Saturday 6 September 1851, the *Illustrated London News* included a well-illustrated article on the Roman Wall, presumably produced at the instigation of Smith. This described 'The noble design of his Grace the Duke of Northumberland, comprising an extensive examination of this ancient barrier of Northern Britain, and a liberal invitation to the body of antiquaries to take part in the proposed investigation'.[25] This article indicates the central role played by Algernon Percy, the Fourth Duke of Northumberland, in research on the Wall during the 1850s.[26]

Smith visited the Wall for a second time in 1857, exploring Housesteads, the course of the Wall across Cuddy's Crag, and the outpost forts at Risingham and High Rochester. He observed that, 'A few enthusiastic men have made it their study; but to the many its pages have been unread, its language unknown. It is commendable to institute Societies for researchers at Nineveh and Babylon; but it is somewhat inconsistent to leave the no less wonderful monument of our own country unexplored'.[27] Smith noted that Bruce and the Duke of Northumberland had recently proposed to the Society of Antiquaries of London that a deputation composed of its members, together with those of the two 'Metropolitan Archaeological Associations' (the British Archaeological Association and the Royal Archaeological Institute) should be appointed, in order 'to consult about the best plan of examining the stations on the line of the wall, or such of them as are within his Grace's domains, with a view to excavate them'.[28] In 1852, the Duke of Northumberland had begun these works by organizing the excavations of the outpost fort at High Rochester, which was run by his own mining engineer, Mr T. J. Taylor. Smith visited this site and described the new excavations that were now

---

[21] G. Bruce (1905), 187.
[22] J. C. Bruce (1857b), 221.   [23] C. R. Smith (1852), 171–202.
[24] Ibid., 172.   [25] *Illustrated London News* (1851).   [26] cf. Thompson (2004).
[27] C. R. Smith (no date), 155.   [28] ibid., 155–6.

being conducted by the Newcastle Society.[29] The Duke also funded Henry MacLaughlan's important 1857 survey of the remains of the Wall, which was published as a map.[30]

Charles Roach Smith's accounts provide an insight into the growing international interest in Roman frontiers. In the account of his first visit,[31] Smith drew attention to an article on the Roman frontiers in Germany by Professor Bückner, published in the first volume of *Archaeologia Aeliana*.[32] Smith also commented on some recent work on the German frontier lines, including information that Dr William Bell had provided.[33] He concluded by arguing that 'The Wall in Germany, and the Wall in England, should obviously be studied together'.[34] In 1854 William Bell wrote to Smith with a more detailed account indicating that serious plans for the mapping, excavation, and interpretation of the German frontiers were underway.[35] Bell observed that:

> You are fully aware of the spirit of enterprise that now incites the zeal and industry of our brother antiquaries in Germany to investigate their Roman Wall, which they designate 'Limes Romani Imperii,' in its full extent. It may probably be owing to Dr. Bruce's volume, and to your own remarks in the Colletanea, that we owe much of this awakened interest.[36]

The term *Limes* was increasingly used to refer to the Roman frontier along the rivers Rhine and Danube during the nineteenth century.[37] It is not clear to what extent the work on England's Roman Wall had actually inspired the Germans to take a more direct interest in their own Roman frontiers, but some German antiquaries were evidently very interested in the research taking place in Britain. Bell observed that Mr Habel of Schierstein was 'the principle promoter of these enquiries; he is placed at the head of a Commission to carry them on systematically and generally through all the districts that the Pfahlgaben ("Limes") passes.'[38] Bell explains that Habel had been undertaking some excavations.[39] Habel was also a foreign member of the British Archaeological Association. English antiquaries were starting to explore the German frontiers at this time. James Yates presented a detailed lecture on the 'Limes Rhæticus and Limes Transrhenaus' at the Archaeological Institute's visit to Newcastle in 1852.[40] This was based on his inspection of the monument and included cross-sections and a three-page list of publications that had addressed the German *Limes*.

The Duke of Northumberland intended to institute a large-scale project on the Roman Wall and encouraged various archaeological societies to undertake

---

[29] cf. J. C. Bruce (1857a).
[30] Breeze (2003), 3; E. Birley (1961), 63; Charlton and Day (1984).
[31] C. R. Smith (1852), 196–7.   [32] Buchner (1822).   [33] C. R. Smith (1852), 197–8.
[34] ibid., 198.   [35] cf. Baatz (2000), 81.
[36] W. Bell (1854), 210.   [37] cf. Isaac (2000), 408.
[38] W. Bell (1854), 210.   [39] Ibid.   [40] Yates (1858).

survey and excavation,[41] but little came of these ambitious plans. The excavations undertaken by John Clayton did, however, help to provide vital new information about the Wall, uncovering Roman sites and impressive finds for visitors to marvel over.

THE CLAYTON WALL

Most of John Clayton's papers were lost after his death,[42] but some records survive which help to document his activities on the Wall. His father, Nathaniel, had purchased the Chesters estate in 1796 and levelled the site to form a park between the garden of his mansion and the river, during which many Roman remains were found.[43] Clayton noted that, 'My studies were a little varied by the interpretation of Roman inscriptions, found in the Fortresses erected by the Romans as a protection against the Scottish invaders, to which my attention was occasionally drawn by my father, who had received a good classical education at the public school at Newcastle-upon-Tyne.'[44] As Town Clerk of Newcastle for forty-five years, Clayton was partly responsible for the development of the city through his association with the architect Richard Grainger.[45] He became a member of the Newcastle Antiquaries in 1832 and, from the 1830s, added to his father's lands by systematically buying up farms along the line of the Wall, establishing a substantial estate to protect the Roman remains from stone robbing.[46]

Clayton was responsible for some of the earliest excavations on the Wall. Earlier excavations had been conducted, for example at Housesteads, Vindolanda, and Birdoswald,[47] but Clayton's projects were on a different scale from those of his predecessors. John Collingwood Bruce stated, without too much exaggeration, that John Clayton's endeavours had led to discoveries that 'may almost be said to have formed a new era in antiquarian research'.[48] Clayton's uncovering of Roman structures and reconstruction of the curtain Wall across his extensive estate was an attempt to display these remains to visitors, presumably with the intention of impressing them with the scale and importance of the monument. Alison Ewin has suggested that his actions were the single greatest act of conservation in the history of the Wall.[49] It should be noted that, at the time when John Clayton commenced his work, the curtain

---

[41] E. Birley (1961), 27.   [42] Ewin (2000), 12.   [43] ibid., 173.

[44] Letter reproduced in C. R. Smith (1891), 171–2.

[45] Ayris (1997), 61–2; Ewin (2000), 11.

[46] Budge (1903), 6; Crow (2004a), 131; Woodside and Crow (1999), 102–4.

[47] R. Birley (2009), 19–25; J. Hodgson (1822); Wilmott (2001), 156.

[48] J. C. Bruce (1892), 94.   [49] Ewin (2000), 42.

Wall along much of its central sector would have been far less visible than it is today.

There are a few sources of information for the condition of the curtain Wall in the century prior to Clayton's restoration. The military survey undertaken by Campbell and Debbieg in 1749 illustrated the face of a section of the curtain Wall half a mile to the west of Harlow Hill, indicating the survival of four layers of Roman masonry. Their cross-section of the curtain Wall at Port Gate suggests that eight or nine courses of masonry survived, but the remains also appear to have been deeply buried in a bank of material with only the top courses visible (Figure 7.4). Another cross-section that Campbell and Debbieg provided of the Wall at Wall Fell, near St Oswald's, appeared to have been nine courses high, although it is not clear whether the narrower top section had been rebuilt. Debbieg and Campbell mentioned the clearing of rubbish from this section of Wall, which suggests that its cross-section had not been fully evident. William Hutton also provided some information about the condition of the curtain Wall, describing a section on Whin Sill opposite Crag Lough as 'three feet high; but deprived of all the facing-stones'.[50] At another point on the Crag, Hutton stated that 'the Wall is eleven courses high on one side, and from three to five on the other; and, for sixty yards, is eight feet high'. William Collard's 1837 engraving of the curtain Wall at the Nine Nicks of Thirlwall also shows a good deal of standing masonry (Figure 10.2). Many of the other parts of the curtain Wall examined by Hutton were, presumably, not so well preserved and some of the sections visible today that have not been refaced indicate the appearance of much of the Wall prior to Clayton's activities (Figure 10.3).

Clayton had the remains of the curtain Wall cleared and partially rebuilt, probably between 1848 and 1873.[51] Sections of what is today known as the 'Clayton Wall' run through the central part of the Wall's course where the majority of visitors walk today, on Peel Crag, Hotbank Crags, and Housesteads Crags. Clayton aimed to recreate the 'Romanness' of this curtain Wall by clearing the debris from the surviving masonry and rebuilding it using the materials removed, including the relaying of face stones, the effective rebuilding of much of the structure, and sealing the top with a turf cap.[52] Collard's engraving, together with the detail of the Harlow Hill section of curtain Wall on the map produced by Campbell and Debbieg, shows that particular sections of the monument may often have possessed a turf cap prior to Clayton's rebuilding.

John Collingwood Bruce described how, on Winshields, 'we find the Wall in an encouraging state of preservation. A little friendly help has been used to

---

[50] Hutton (1802), 239.
[51] Woodside and Crow (1999), 103.
[52] Whitworth (2009b), 65–6; Woodside and Crow (1999), 103.

Fig. 10.2. William Collard's engraving of the Nine Nicks of Thirlwall, 1837. From J. Hodgson (1840), opposite p. 288. Reproduced by permission of Durham University Library.

Fig. 10.3. An unreconstructed section of the Roman curtain Wall marked by a tumbled stone wall close to the farm at Hotbank, showing how much of the curtain Wall might have appeared prior to Clayton's attempts to reconstruct it. Photograph by Richard Hingley, 2011.

make the facing-stones on each side equal the height of the core of the interior.'[53] Clayton's reconstruction of the Wall was so successful that in some places it can prove difficult to distinguish the rebuild from the original without careful excavation.[54] At the same time, Clayton moved people and structures away from the line of the Wall in order to increase its visibility. Woodside and Crow have noted that, on Cuddy's Crag, just west of House-steads, the appearance of today's landscape probably owes more to the work of Clayton and his successors than to the Romans, and that 150 years ago this impressive section of curtain Wall would have been no more than a pile of rubble.[55]

The rebuilding instigated by Clayton created far more for the visitor to view along the best-preserved central section of the monument. These operations continued after his death and until the 1970s. Bruce noted that before Clayton commenced his operations, the turrets were 'completely excluded from view.'[56] In 1863, the foundations of just one turret were visible along the Wall's entire length, while the stone remains of three milecastles could be seen—Clayton had disinterred all of these features since 1848.[57] By 1907, a purposeful campaign of excavation on Clayton's estate had uncovered the foundations of at least seven turrets.[58] The substantial physical remains of six excavated milecastles and around seventeen turrets are now visible along the National Trail.[59] Clayton began the physical process of uncovering the mile-castles, turrets, and forts along the Wall, with consequent benefits for visitors.

Clayton's excavations, undertaken from 1843 until his death, have long been criticized for their haphazard nature and the lack of recording, but there was little established methodology for archaeological excavation and record at this time. Clayton's main objectives at the sites he excavated was to clear the soil from stone structures to reveal their plan so that visitors could appreciate the remains, and to recover inscribed stones and other artefacts to display at his house at Chesters.[60] The legacy of his work might have been rather different had these excavations followed the methods of recording and pub-lishing practised by Samuel Lysons who had uncovered a number of Roman villas in southern Britain during the early years of the nineteenth century.[61] Nevertheless, it is wrong to be too critical of Clayton's excavations, since they provided a major inspiration for the growth of interest in the Wall.

Clayton worked on sites across his estate, uncovering part of the command-ing officer's house at Chesters in 1843. In 1849, he commenced excavations at

---

[53] J. C. Bruce (1863), 155.
[54] Whitworth (2009b), 66; Woodside and Crow (1999), 103; Jim Crow (pers. comm.).
[55] Woodside and Crow (1999), caption to colour Plate 6.
[56] J. C. Bruce (1892), 93.   [57] See J. C. Bruce (1863).
[58] See J. C. Bruce (1907).   [59] See Breeze (2006a).
[60] Ewin (2000), 25.   [61] See Hingley (2008a), 247–53.

Fig. 10.4. John Clayton's house at Chesters. From Budge (1903), opposite page 6.

Housesteads, probably inspired by the visit of the Pilgrimage.[62] His workmen uncovered the walls and gates of the fort and some of the internal buildings.[63] Clayton also continued the excavations close to his country house at Chesters, where he superintended work that uncovered much of the plan of the Roman site close to his house (Figures 10.4 and 10.5).[64] During the eighteenth and early nineteenth centuries, members of the landed gentry of southern Britain sponsored antiquaries to excavate Roman villas on their estates, enabling them to imagine a genealogical connection between the Roman past and their neo-classical country houses and surrounding landscapes.[65] Clayton conducted a serious search for Roman civilization at Chesters that drew upon their example.

The Roman remains from Clayton's excavations on his Wall-properties—including numerous inscriptions—were collected at Chesters and were 'disposed in various places in the house and in the gardens'.[66] These finds were then placed in a small 'Antiquity House', but they overflowed into Clayton's house and garden.[67] In 1896, after John Clayton's death, his collection was placed in a specially built museum at the edge of the site (Figure 10.6), where they can still be examined.[68] This important assemblage includes

---

[62] E. Birley (1961), 180.   [63] Crow (2004a), 131; Rushworth (2009), 4–5.
[64] Ewin (2000), 25.   [65] Hingley (2008a), 170–3; 247–54.
[66] J. C. Bruce (1892), 95.   [67] Ewin (2000), 25–6.
[68] ibid., 25; Lindsay Allison-Jones (pers. comm.).

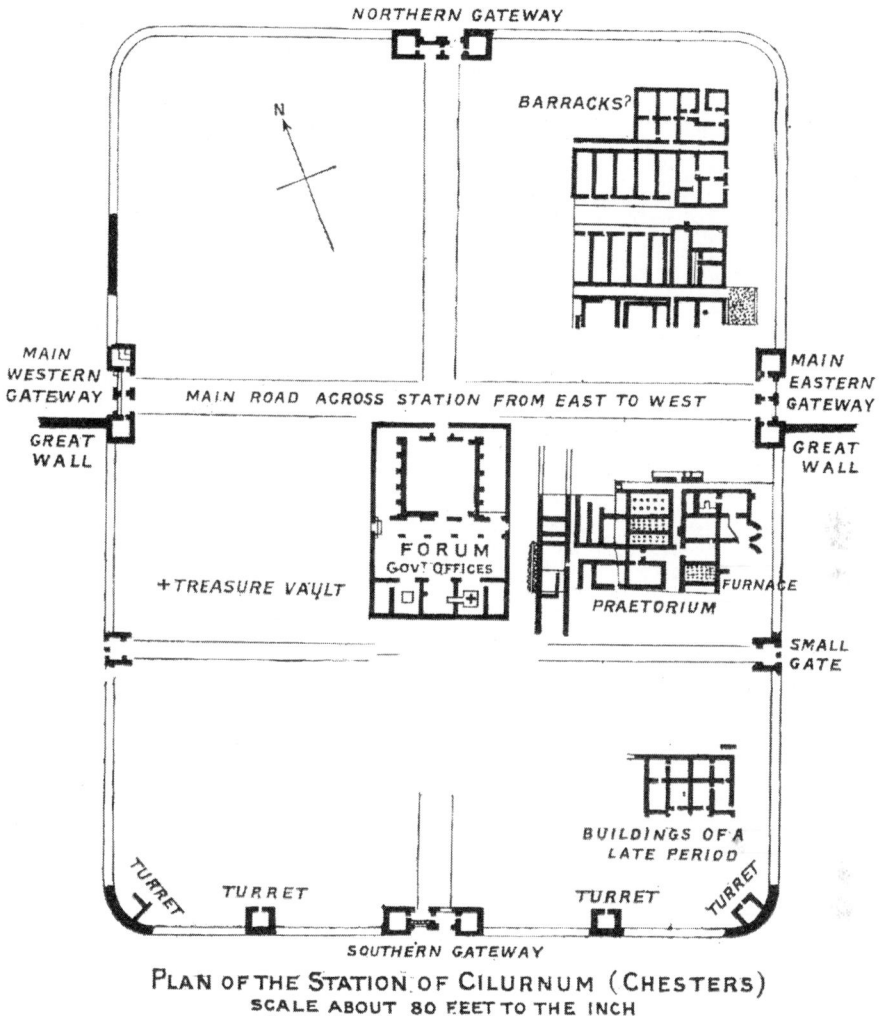

Fig. 10.5. The Roman site at Chesters (*Cilurnum*) showing the excavated areas and 'forum'. From Budge (1903), opposite page 98.

Roman material gathered by Clayton and his successors from the forts of Chesters, Carrawburgh, Housesteads, Chesterholm, and Carvoran.[69] Clayton's excavations made significant contributions to the comprehension of the Wall and its stations, including knowledge of the structure of the Wall and information about religion and settled life along its line.

[69] E. Birley (1961), 175.

Fig. 10.6. The museum at Chesters during the early twentieth century. From Budge (1903), opposite page 26.

THE FUNCTION OF THE WALL:
AN IMPENETRABLE FENCE?

One of Clayton's most lasting contributions was the discovery that regular gateways occurred along the line of the Wall. John Horsley had undertaken a detailed study of the remains of the curtain Wall and its associated structures but he did not discover 'any gates . . . or passes through it, except it be just in the stations, or where the grand military ways have crossed it'.[70] His detailed maps show entrances through the curtain Wall at some of the forts, but it was

---

[70] Horsley (1732), 121.

unclear to him whether these were Roman in date or had been created in later times. Antiquaries did not discuss movement though the Wall in any detail prior to the mid nineteenth century, since emphasis was usually placed on the impenetrability of the curtain Wall, promoting the defensive explanation for the fortification. Bruce, for example, repeated Gildas' comments that the Picts and Scots used hooked weapons to drag 'our wretched countrymen' from the Wall, where they were dashed on the ground,[71] an idea that supported the need for a secure line of defence.

Clayton's excavations indicated, however, that the Wall had numerous gateways providing access across its line, a significant discovery that was to inspire new approaches to the function of the frontier. Clayton's excavation at Cawfields Milecastle (*MC 42*) between 1848 and 1851 revealed a 'massive gateway' through the curtain wall (Figure 10.7).[72] Bruce emphasized the importance of this discovery on several occasions, since it suggested that gates occurred at intervals of one Roman mile along the line of the Wall.[73] During road works at Walbottle Dene (*MC 10*), Bruce, emphasized the importance of the discovery of another milecastle gateway:

> At one time it was thought that the Wall was the northern boundary of the Roman empire. On this theory, no one looked for northern gateways in the stations or the milcastles. Mr. Clayton's instructive explorations, first at Cawfields Mile Castle, and afterwards at Borcovicus, and then at the mile castle to the west of it, and at Castle Nick, showed us how much we were mistaken in this particular. This new discovery confirms the supposition that every milecastle and every station had a portal opening boldly upon the north. The Wall, therefore, was not a fence or boundary line, but a line of military operation.[74]

The discovery of gates at the milecastles and forts persuaded Bruce that the Wall was a more permeable barrier than had been supposed, but his interpretation of its function remained distinctly military. In *The Wallet-Book*, Bruce wrote 'THE ROMAN WALL . . . is a great fortification intended to act not only as a fence against a northern enemy, but to be used as the basis of military preparations against a foe on either side of it.'[75] He saw it as 'a line of military works for the better managing their assaults upon' the Caledonians, with the multiple access-ways through the curtain Wall providing the Roman soldiers with a tactical advantage to the north and south of the line.[76] The potential permeability of the curtain Wall proved to be a vital discovery and it was to have a considerable impact on interpretations of the Wall during the twentieth century.

---

[71] J. C. Bruce (1851), 29.
[73] e.g. J. C. Bruce (1851), 249.
[75] J. C. Bruce (1863), 16.
[72] Clayton (1855), 59.
[74] J. C. Bruce (1865), 223.
[76] J. C. Bruce (1892), 93.

Fig. 10.7. An engraving of the remains of the milecastle at Cawfields (*MC 42*), uncovered by John Clayton's workmen in 1848. From J. C. Bruce (1851), opposite page 248.

RELIGION AND URBAN LIFE ON THE WALL

Clayton's excavations also contributed significantly to ideas about life at the Roman stations along the Wall. For 300 years, antiquaries had concentrated on the religious dedications along the Wall and Bruce explored this information at length in his publications. One particular discovery, the location and excavation of Coventina's Well at Carrawburgh in 1876, brought Bruce and Clayton face to face with the impressive evidence for pagan worship. John Horsley had been the first to record the remains of the well,[77] and the spring had been known as a source of pure water for some time. The remains of the shrine of Coventina were located in October 1876 by John Clayton and his foreman William Tailford and then excavated on a substantial scale over the following year.[78] Clayton noted that the excavation excited much interest in the neighbourhood, including the naming of a yacht after the goddess and also

---

[77] Horsley (1732), 145–6.
[78] Clayton (1876); Clayton (1877); Allason-Jones and McKay (1985), 2.

the idea that the name Coventina might be used for 'infant beauties hereafter born on the banks of the Tyne'.[79]

Clayton's men uncovered the massive masonry structure of the well, the traces of an enclosure or building that surrounded it, and a substantial and very impressive group of finds, including many Roman coins and other objects of bronze, bone, pottery, stone, glass, lead, leather, and shale.[80] These dated from the second and third century, with evidence for some limited activity in the fourth.[81] The most impressive of these finds were included in Clayton's collection of Roman objects at Chesters, where they can still be seen today. They include several representations of Coventina as a nymph, either singly or in triplicate. A dedication by Titus Cosconianus, prefect of the First Cohort of Batavians, depicts Coventina reclining by a flowing urn and holding a water plant, in the normal manner of a Greek or Roman nymph (Figure 10.8).[82] Coventina's name is found on most of the inscribed stones from the well, spelt in several different ways.[83]

Bruce's published accounts of the Wall reviewed the plentiful evidence for pagan worship along its line and the focus of his comments on Roman religion reflect his role as a non-conformist minister. In *The Roman Wall* he noted that, notwithstanding the 'example and teaching' of Christians along the Wall, 'it is a lamentable fact, that heathenism continued to rear its head in Britain until near the close of the period of Roman occupation, as several of the altars found on the line of the Wall clearly testify.'[84] Bruce included a study of pagan inscriptions found along the Wall.[85] His judgemental comments about religion were also expressed in later work: 'However, corrupt and impure their religion was, they carried it with them wherever they went, and boldly professed it'.[86]

The writings of Gildas emphasized the Christian identity of the Lowland Britons who were overwhelmed by the barbarians at the end of Roman rule, and the Wall could be perceived as a prime location at which to search for evidence of Christian worship. Bruce observed that some writers had suggested that Christianity was introduced to Britain around AD 60, noting that around this time some of the 48,000 Roman soldiers in Britain must have been acquainted with the religion, but 'these Christian soldiers have, along the line of the Wall, left no memorial of their faith. The God whom they served required not the erection of an altar of stone, or an offering of frankincense. Their "inscription" was, a holy life, "seen and read of all men".'[87] He was very alert to any potential connections with Christianity on the Wall, as the caption

---

[79] Clayton (1876), 1; Clayton (1877), 22. There is no evidence that Coventina was actually used as a personal name (Lindsay Allason-Jones pers. comm.).
[80] Allason-Jones and McKay (1985), 6.
[81] Ibid., 12.   [82] Henig (1984), 63.   [83] Allason-Jones and McKay (1985), 3.
[84] J. C. Bruce (1851), 423.   [85] ibid., 422–9.   [86] J. C. Bruce (1857b), 268.
[87] J. C. Bruce (1851), 422–3.

Fig. 10.8. One of the commemorative stones from Coventina's Well at Chesters, now at Chesters Museum, showing the goddess in the guise of a classical nymph. Photograph by Richard Hingley, 2011. Reproduced by permission of English Heritage and the Trustees of the Clayton Collection.

to a plate that shows a pier of the Tyne Bridge in Newcastle illustrates.[88] Bruce believed the structure that had been uncovered to be Roman in date and noted that, 'The oak trees which supplied the timber must have been growing on the banks of the Tyne when our blessed Saviour was walking the streets of Jerusalem.'[89] Bruce argued that 'The struggle between light and darkness prevailed long before it was fully day. This circumstance may encourage those whose hearts experience the sickness of hope deferred in reference to the teaming millions of others lands.'[90] Elsewhere, Bruce also drew attention to the absence of evidence for the presence of 'a temple to the purpose of Christian worship'.[91]

Others antiquaries were also enthusiastic about the possibility of finding evidence for Christian worship along the Wall, but with no greater success. The Reverend Robert Hooppell suggested that the excavations at South Shields (Tyne and Wear) had uncovered a possible Christian church, although he had no conclusive information to support his claim.[92] Specific evidence for Christians on the Wall remained entirely absent at this time.

Clayton and his contemporaries drew upon the impressive objects and structures from the excavations at Chesters to suggest that this site was a Roman town. Clayton, who played a significant role in the civic life of Newcastle, evidently considered that he was uncovering the remains of a small classical city. This concept was reinforced by a strong tradition derived from Gildas and Bede that focused on the idea of urban life along the Wall, and the impressive discoveries made at the site. Influential visitors to Chesters admired Clayton's estate. In his reminiscences, Charles Roach Smith wrote of his visits in the 1850s, noting that 'Just above is the noble mansion with its flowered lawns, its gardens, groves, and all the comforts and elegancies of life; below, the widespread park in its velvety green mantle shrouding one of the great strongholds of imperial Rome which held in subjection a province'.[93] Chesters was also frequented by artists, poets, and clerics.[94]

In *The Roman Wall*, Bruce referred to Chesters as a 'station' and drew attention to an ornate building with a hypocaust that he described as a 'mansion'.[95] The subsequent excavations at Chesters produced further information, which was fitted into this urban explanation. In 1876, Bruce reported on the recent excavations of the rectangular building at the centre of the station (Figure 10.5), noting, with regard to the rooms at the rear, that

---

[88] Paul Bidwell (pers. comm.).
[89] This text is shown on a plate in the John Collingwood Bruce Collection at South Shields, which is published in Bidwell and Holbrook (1989), figure 72. This timberwork was actually medieval in date (Paul Bidwell pers. comm.).
[90] J. C. Bruce (1857b), 269.   [91] J. C. Bruce (1875), xv.
[92] Hooppell (1878), 376–7.   [93] C. R. Smith (1883), 176.
[94] Anon (1876); G. Bruce (1905), 172; cf. Whitworth (2009a).
[95] J. C. Bruce (1851), 171–8.

'Mr Clayton was struck with the resemblance which these apartments bore to the halls which he had seen at Pompeii at the southern end of the forum of that famous city'.[96] He remarked that the discovery of this building indicated 'how thoroughly the Romans occupied the country; how systematically they proceeded to bring the whole population under the influence of Roman law and Roman civilization'.[97] Excavations at the Roman towns of Bath, Silchester, and Cirencester in southern Britain had begun to uncover impressive urban remains, illustrating the remarkable civic life of the province.[98] The excavations at Chesters appeared to be producing a comparable record from the northern frontier. In the third edition of the *Handbook*, Bruce repeated the idea of the urban role of the 'forum' at Chesters, arguing that *Cilurnum* was not 'a mere garrison, but a military city commanding an extensive district'.[99]

The discovery of an elaborate building to the east of the walled circuit at Chesters in 1885, was to 'interest and perplex' the antiquaries, leading to the suggestion that the structure with five semi-circular chambers formed part of a villa situated to the east of the walled area (Figure 10.9).[100] Further research and excavation was required to indicate that this structure was a substantial bath-house connected with the Roman fort and *vicus*. The identification of a forum at Chesters led to a comparable claim that the central building inside the 'station' at South Shields (Tyne and Wear), and a similar structure inside the fort at Hardknott (Cumbria), represented urban public squares. At South Shields, the Reverend Hooppell identified the 'ancient forum' and other 'fine buildings, as well as houses inhabited by individuals of taste and wealth' (Figure 10.10).[101] He also inferred that the 'station' or its immediate neighbourhood, 'Was thickly peopled, for the evidence of the passage along its streets, and over the pavements of its forum, and through its halls, of innumerable feet, are unmistakable'. The excavations at South Shields, undertaken during urban regeneration, were of significant public interest and, during 1880, a 'Roman Remains and People's Park' was established.[102] The Victorian excavators and visitors to the site conceived of an earlier period of settled civic life on this exposed hilltop close to the modern port of South Shields. These works resulted in considerable interest across Britain and also the publication of an article in a German journal.[103]

The idea of the urban function for the central buildings at Chesters and South Shields was challenged during the final decade of the nineteenth century. R. S. Ferguson discussed the central building at the Roman station at Hardknott in the Lake District and noted that the Oxford ancient historian

---

[96] J. C. Bruce (1876), 3.   [97] ibid., 8.
[98] Hingley (2008a), 279–93.   [99] J. C. Bruce (1885), 89.   [100] Anon (1885), iv.
[101] Hooppell (1878), 374.   [102] Allason-Jones and Miket (1984), 12.
[103] Bidwell and Speak (1994), 1.

Fig. 10.9. The excavations on the bath-house at Chesters, initially thought to represent part of a villa. From Budge (1903), opposite page 108.

Fig. 10.10. Victorian gentlemen inspecting the excavated remains at South Shields in 1875. The building that is being uncovered is titled the 'forum' on this photograph and the structure would now be interpreted as the headquarters building of the fort. Reproduced by permission of the Great North Museum and Society of Antiquaries of Newcastle upon Tyne, Hadrian's Wall Photograph Collection, 6548.

Francis Haverfield had claimed that it represented the *prætorium*, the commanding officer's house, of a Roman fort, rather than a forum.[104] Despite this, Ferguson remarked that 'we shall call this building the *forum*'. Haverfield's international knowledge of Roman archaeology prompted him to claim that these central buildings were military rather than urban in character. It later came to be recognized that the term *prætorium* was inaccurate for these buildings and they are now identified as the individual headquarters (*principia*) of each fort, the focus of the military life of the garrison.[105]

Knowledge of the Roman forts of Britain and Germany was increasing at this time and the civil interpretation for the Roman stations of the Wall was slowly being challenged. In the fifth edition of the *Handbook*, Robert Blair, while repeating much of Bruce's earlier text, refers to the 'so-called Forum at CILURNUM'.[106] The eventual overturning of a civil interpretation for such structures along the Wall undermined the ancient idea that the stations of the military north were Roman cities or towns and also, eventually, led to the drawing of a distinction between military sites—such as Chesters, South Shields, and Housesteads—and the Roman towns of the south of the province, including London, Silchester, and Cirencester.[107] The idea of urban life at *Cilurnum*, however, continued for some time in popular accounts. Maria Hoyer, who visited Chesters while on summer holiday, described the market that would have been held in the forum and the government business that was conducted there.[108]

SUMMARY: INTERNATIONAL FAME

This chapter has assessed the considerable contributions to Wall studies made by John Clayton and John Collingwood Bruce. Later archaeologists often played down their contributions, but these two Victorian antiquaries had a vital role in the interpretation of the monument. As a result of Bruce's initiatives, the Wall's fame spread across Britain, making it a tourist destination.[109] Warburton and Stukeley had sought to encourage the gentry to visit the monument, but it is only from the mid nineteenth century that significant numbers of people began to explore its remains.[110] The publication of Bruce's *The Wallet-Book* in 1863 coincided with the improvement of transport in the region, with the construction of the Newcastle and Carlisle Railway in the

---

[104] R. S. Ferguson (1893), 386.
[105] Haverfield (1924a), 135; Breeze and Dobson (2000), 168–70.
[106] J. C. Bruce (1907), 141.   [107] Hingley (2008a), 319.   [108] Hoyer (1908), 5.
[109] Witcher (2010a), 131–2.   [110] J. C. Bruce (1863), iii.

1830s and improvements being made to the local roads.[111] Despite this, *Jenkinson's Practical Guide to Carlisle, Gilsland, Roman Wall and Neighbourhood* referred to the area as being little known but discussed the considerable interest of the region.[112] By the early twentieth century the Wall was becoming better known and visitors more common.[113] New accounts encouraged people to tour the area and visit the remains. In *Country Life*, 'Martia' provided a well-illustrated article on the remains, urging that 'no more interesting expedition may be planned than a few days' walking along "the Picts' wall".'[114]

Bruce's writings led to a greater appreciation of the significance of the Wall across Britain and also in Germany. Correspondence between scholars of the Roman Wall in Britain and those studying frontiers in Germany had been developing for some time and Clayton and Bruce had developed significant contacts with Theodor Mommsen and Emil Hübner.[115] In 1881, Thomas Hodgkin visited the limit of the barrier of the Roman empire between the Rhine and Danube.[116] His detailed article contained a description of the discoveries to date and included the stated intention to stimulate further interchange of views between English and German archaeologists.[117] In 1884, Hodgkin translated an article by an internationally famous German classical scholar, Professor Emil Hübner, which described the Roman annexation of Britain.[118] Hübner had edited the *Corpus Inscriptionum Latinarum* Volume VII in 1873 and had a deep knowledge of the Roman inscriptions of Britain.[119] His paper included seven pages addressing England's Roman Wall, a monument about which, according to Hübner, 'every English boy, and many a German, learns at school'.[120] That knowledge of the Wall was spreading beyond Britain and Germany is indicated by Henry W. Haynes' lengthy discussion on the Roman Wall in the *Journal of the American Geographical Society*.[121]

Theodor Mommsen, an extremely influential ancient historian,[122] was elected an Honorary Member of the Newcastle Antiquaries in 1883. In 1885, he described Hadrian's Wall as 'the best known of all the great Roman military works',[123] a very positive reflection on the works of Bruce, Clayton, Hooppell, and others. Francis Haverfield noted that Mommsen's 'words were an honour to English archaeology'.[124] From the mid 1870s, Mommsen had been attempting to focus the interest of German antiquaries on the study of the *Limes*, and the work on England's Roman Wall probably provided part of the stimulus for the creation of the German Imperial Limes-Commission during the 1890s, a topic that will be considered further below. Professor Hulsebos travelled

---

[111] Ewin (2000), 60; Witcher (2010a), 132.   [112] Jenkinson (1875), 1–2.
[113] Ewin (2000), 61–3.   [114] 'Martia' (1899), 238.
[115] cf. J. C. Bruce (1879), 216–21.   [116] Hodgkin (1883).   [117] ibid., 73.
[118] Hübner (1884).   [119] Tomlin (1999).   [120] Hübner (1884), 104.
[121] Haynes (1890); cf. Shannon (2007), 2 n. 8.   [122] Mouritsen (1998).
[123] Haverfield (1899a), 337; cf. Freeman (2007), 269.   [124] Haverfield (1899a), 337.

from Utrecht to be part of the Second Pilgrimage in 1886,[125] the only participant from overseas.[126]

Bruce's writings elevated the significance of the Roman Wall, establishing it in the minds of many antiquaries as a nationally important monument and giving increased prominence to the Newcastle Antiquaries. The Cumberland and Westmorland Antiquarian and Archaeological Society was established in 1866, since the Newcastle antiquaries tended to focus their attention on the eastern part of the Wall.[127] In the final decade of the nineteenth century, these two societies conducted a substantial campaign of excavation concentrating on the form and sequence of the Wall, a programme of work that will be addressed in Chapter 12. For Bruce and Clayton, however, the significance of the Wall was not entirely characterized by its form and sequence. Bruce's broadly chorographical approach to places along its line acknowledged the importance of the living monument. Both William Hutton and John Collingwood Bruce sought to bring the Wall's ancient remains into a living engagement with their contemporary times. Clayton's efforts in acquiring, excavating, and displaying the Roman remains along the Wall's central section also attracted the attention of writers and artists, promoting the Wall's regional and national significance. Bruce and Clayton were prominent in promoting the living significance of the Roman Wall, without which the monument would have been far less well known in Britain and Germany at the end of the nineteenth century. Nevertheless, after the death of both men in the early 1890s, a new generation of research on the Wall commenced.

[125] E. Birley (1961), 28.   [126] Breeze (2008b), 142.   [127] E. Birley (1961), 28.

PART III

Hadrian's Wall

By the mid nineteenth century, the name 'Hadrian's Wall' was beginning to be widely used. Although John Collingwood Bruce had entitled his detailed studies *The Roman Wall* (1851) and *The Wallet-Book of the Roman Wall* (1863), he also addressed the monument as 'Hadrian's Wall' in these works. In his survey of five years of excavation, Francis Haverfield continued to use the name 'The Roman Wall',[1] as did Rudyard Kipling in his popular novel *Puck of Pook's Hill*.[2] Indeed, the exact dating for the various elements of this complex monument remained uncertain, since many commentators continued to believe that the Vallum was built by Hadrian and the curtain Wall by Severus. During the 1920s and 1930s, R. G. Collingwood published a number of influential reviews of the work on 'Hadrian's Wall'. A sequence of excavations had provided evidence for the construction of the major elements of the monument, including the curtain Wall, during Hadrian's reign, from which time Hadrian's Wall became the most commonly used term.[3] This name also helped to distinguish the monument from the Antonine Wall. Some accounts nevertheless continued to use the title of *the* Roman Wall, and the *Handbook of the Roman Wall* has retained this name throughout its 13 reprints.[4] The name 'The Roman Wall' continued to emphasize the scale and monumentality of these frontier works, drawing upon eighteenth-century roots. As has already been shown, change often comes slowly to the Wall.

[1] Haverfield (1899a).
[2] Although Kipling also addressed the monument as 'Hadrian's Wall' (e.g. 1906, 154).
[3] Collingwood (1921a), 61–2.
[4] Breeze (2006a).

11

The Roman Gate at *Hunnum* (Halton Chesters): Ethnographic Time

only here and there are the facing-blocks of the foundation course still to be seen, like fragments of an almost vanished pavement, lying where the legionaries placed them more then seventeen hundred years ago, so that bicycles and motor-cars may run upon stones which were wrought in the days of Hadrian.

Robert Forster (1899), 202–3

INTRODUCTION

Initially, this chapter will address the writings of Robert Henry Forster, who called himself an 'Amateur Antiquary'. Despite his claim to amateur status, Forster combined an interest in creative writing with considerable skills as an archaeological excavator and made a significant contribution to the Edwardian excavations at Corbridge. In his writing, Forster drew deeply on the perspective of William Hutton who had toured the Wall a century earlier.

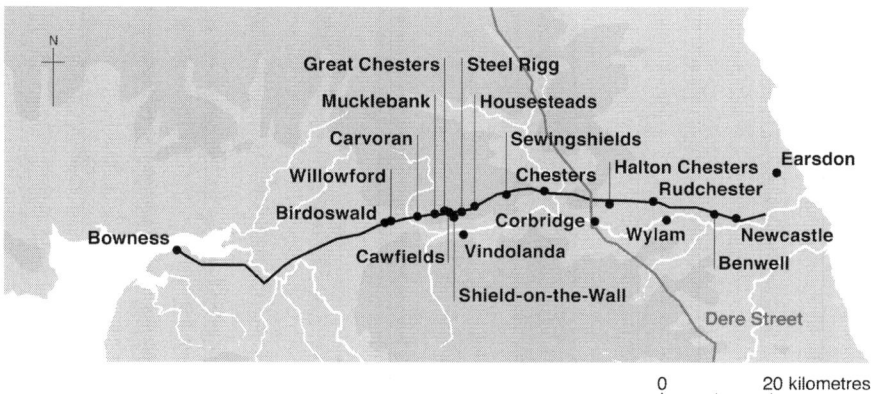

Fig. 11.1. Places mentioned in Chapters 11, 12, and 13. Drawn by Christina Unwin.

The methods used by Forster to animate the Wall in his book *The Amateur Antiquary* (1899) will be discussed, together with Rudyard Kipling's influential image of the monument in his children's novel, *Puck of Pook's Hill* (1906). These two creative accounts help to demonstrate the growing public appreciation of the Roman Wall at the beginning of the twentieth century. Both authors erode the division between the Roman past and contemporary time by bringing the Wall to life in what might be termed 'ethnographic time'.[1] The tales about the Wall these two authors told are linked by the Roman gate through the curtain Wall close to the Roman station of '*Hunnum*' (Figure 11.2; Halton Chesters, Northumberland). One of the Roman forts along the Wall, the name of the site is recorded in the *Notitia Dignitatum* as *Hunnum*, but the correct version is now thought to be *Onnum*.[2]

A few hundred metres to the west of the fort, the Roman road—known to the Victorians as Watling Street and today as Dere Street—passed through the line of the Wall at a gate called the Port Gate.[3] John Horsley noted that 'there has been a square *castellum* half within the wall and half without, in which respect it differs from the other *castella*'.[4] Both Forster and Kipling drew upon this substantial gateway, although its remains were not visible at the start of the twentieth century.[5] Dere Street was one of the major Roman roads crossing the line of the Wall and the Port Gate had a particular strategic significance in Roman times, explaining why Forster and Kipling were interested in this particular location. This gateway was located and a few blocks were exposed in 1966, but there is nothing to be seen on the site today.[6]

THE AMATEUR ANTIQUARY

Forster's imaginative work, *The Amateur Antiquary: His Notes, Sketches, and Fancies concerning the Roman Wall*, is not commonly discussed today, but has been an inspiration for the approach adopted in this book as it effectively brought the remains of the Wall to life. Forster (1867–1923) was born at Backworth, Earsdon, just a few miles to the northeast of Newcastle (Figure 11.3). He gained a First Class Degree in Classics Tripos at St John's College, Cambridge,

---

[1] cf. Colls (2002), 261.
[2] Breeze (2006a), 178.
[3] ibid., 184.
[4] Horsley (1732), 142–3.
[5] J. C. Bruce (1907), 66.
[6] Breeze (2006a), 184; Paul Bidwell (pers. comm.).

Fig. 11.2. An imaginative reconstruction of Hadrian's Wall close to the gate at *Hunnum* by H. R. Millar titled *And that is the Roman Wall.* From Kipling (1906), 172.

and was called to the Bar in 1892.[7] During the 1890s he developed a serious interest in the archaeological remains of Hadrian's Wall and subsequently published a significant study of the structure of the monument.[8] In 1906 Forster became involved with the excavations at Corbridge, helping to direct

---

[7] Bishop (1994), 10–12.   [8] Forster (1901); cf. E. Birley (1961), 87, 105, 201, 270.

Fig. 11.3. Robert Forster outside the site museum at Corbridge. Reproduced by permission of the Corbridge Excavation Fund and the Great North Museum.

them from 1907 until the completion of the project in 1914 (Figure 11.4).[9] Forster travelled to Corbridge from his home in Putney each year to stay for the duration of the excavation season.[10]

In *The Amateur Antiquary*, Forster stressed his amateur status, drawing on a number of imaginative methods to give a voice to the Wall. The central third of the book explores one particular technique that appears very familiar today but which was quite innovative in 1899—an imaginary 'Second Century Tour' of the Wall. Forster drew upon the archaeological remains of the frontier and its stations to construct this tale, which involved travelling around the local

[9] Freeman (2007), 281–98.   [10] Bishop (1994), 12.

Fig. 11.4. The Edwardian excavations at Corbridge, showing workmen clearing an area to the east of the excavations. Reproduced by permission of the Corbridge Excavation Fund and the Great North Museum.

landscape in an 'attempt to honour the memory of that intricate tangle of things and persons, which once formed the life and society of this corner of Roman Britain'.[11] This journey took Forster's narrator from his home to Godmanchester, Lincoln and then northwards along Watling Street to York and Corbridge. His account considered the thriving town at *Corstopitum* (Corbridge) before arriving at a gap in the Vallum and exploring the Wall just to the west of *Hunnum*.[12] At the Port Gate, Forster recalls:

[11] Forster (1899), 69.
[12] The name '*Corstopitum*' was used in the nineteenth century to address the Roman site at Corbridge, but the exact Roman name for this site is now unclear as a result of further discoveries (Breeze 2006a, 416).

But we were impatient to examine the Wall . . . For some time we gaze in silence at the huge mass of masonry, with heads thrown back and necks in danger of much stiffness to-morrow; for even the paved walk, where the sentry paces, is twenty feet above the road, and the coping of the parapet rises some four feet higher still. Eastward and westward the great work stretches, till on either hand it passes out of view over the farthest visible hill. There are some two and a quarter million cubic feet of masonry in sight, and a quarter of a million square brown facing-stones. Ah! (we cannot help sighing) if only one had a denarius for each of them! We might even be content to accept that number of humble sesterces.

But the long range of stonework is not one bare, monotonous face: the gateway, through which the road passes on its way to Bremenium, breaks the continuity, and varies the aspect of the Wall. The double-arched passageway is flanked by strong towers on the northern side . . . The northern view of the Wall is grimmer and more impressive: except for its regularity, one might imagine it to be a long line of sandstone cliffs,—a rock-bound coast, ready to combat any sea of northern rebellion that may try to encroach upon the fertile soil of a Roman province.[13]

At this point in the story, Forster's narrator is befriended by the Prefect of *Hunnum*, Marius Longus, an elderly man from Italy. Forster's narrator is then taken on a tour of the Wall, travelling west to Chesters and beyond. The lengthy account of the 'stoutly-walled little city' at Chesters is embellished with descriptions of the buildings that had been uncovered by John Clayton during the second half of the nineteenth century.[14]

The men then travel to *Borcovicium*, where a ballista is described in detail,[15] before marching to the north of the Wall to suppress a native insurrection. The programme of excavations that had been undertaken by R. C. Bosanquet at Housesteads in 1898 had suggested that a ballista was sited on one of the towers of the Roman fort.[16] Forster's account of the ensuing battle, and the consequent destruction of the native men and enslaving of the women and children, conveys considerable sympathy for the local people who are captured by the Romans: 'Only an hour ago these were the wives and children of heroes and patriots: now the high resolve is broken and the proud boasts belied; the wives and children are widows and orphans, and, saddest of all, the free are slaves'.[17] Although Forster's narrator identified himself as Roman, he shows considerable understanding for those who fought against Rome. After describing the destruction of their homes, he observed, 'But we are Romans and must harden our hearts to fit our characters'.[18] This is an interesting observation in the context of Britain's imperial activities of 1899, the year that witnessed the outbreak of the serious conflict in South Africa.

---

[13] Forster (1899), 84–5.   [14] ibid., 93–105.   [15] ibid., 117–23.
[16] J. C. Bruce (1907), 144.   [17] Forster (1899), 138.   [18] ibid., 139.

Forster also animated the Wall by other means. At the beginning of his book, he drew on William Hutton's account of his journey along the Wall in 1801 to define the 'two divisions into which antiquaries may be divided'—'the pedantic and the imaginative'.[19] He then defined the natures of these two idealized characters, without naming any individuals. With regard to the 'pedantic antiquarian', Forster wrote:

> Not that we ought to decry the former: perhaps we had better rename him the microscopic, omnivorous and predatory. He is a seething mass of multifarious learning, proficient in many arts and sciences . . . As a proof of his mathematical, critical, strategical, topographical, epigraphical, and other capacities . . . he can decipher obliterated inscriptions, till they mean whatever he has previously assumed their purport to be. His only faults are in the absence of imagination, and a deficient sense of perspective: but knowing, as he does, everything knowable, and a great deal besides, there is no sphere of imagination left for him; and its absence can therefore hardly be accounted a fault: in fact he imagines nothing, because, to his own satisfaction at least, he proves everything.

The emphasis placed on the reading of inscriptions may suggest that he had John Horsley's work in mind, but it is more likely that he was commenting on the stifling debates over the dating and attribution of various elements of the monument that had dominated Wall scholarship since the 1840s.[20]

Forster had a rather less pedantic approach to the Wall in mind, observing that:

> The imaginative antiquary is a different, and perhaps more humane person: he is usually endowed with less learning and more equanimity. Compared with the other, he is somewhat of an impressionist, being devoid of that passion for minutiae, that enthusiasm for the comparatively trivial, which forms so marked a feature in his brother antiquary's character . . . But to the imaginative antiquary the coin, the inscription, the ruin, or the manuscript are but husks of the past: their interest lies in the fact that they contain, as it were, a kind of residual magnetism, upon which his imagination and his knowledge of human nature can work, till he reproduces some picture of bygone times, some chapter of a lost romance, or some echo of long silent poetry: for the true interest of antiquities is, after all, the interest of human life.[21]

This idea of using archaeological objects and ancient texts to reflect on life in the ancient past drew on the Romantic antiquarianism of authors such as Walter Scott, and of painters and illustrators, such as William Bell Scott, while also prefiguring Kipling's use of archaeological knowledge.[22] Forster developed the concept of an imaginative antiquarianism in some detail through his account of the history of the Wall.

---

[19] ibid., 5–6.   [20] cf. Bates (1895), 7.
[21] Forster (1899), 6–7.   [22] cf. Mackenzie (1993), xiv.

In the first third of the book, Forster brings the Wall to life by discussing the famous Romans associated with the Wall by earlier writers, including Julius Caesar, Agricola, Hadrian, and Severus, and by addressing 'The Stones and their Story'. Here Forster described those who excavate as:

> imaginative rag-pickers, rubbish-sorters of cities which have been dead and buried these fourteen hundred years,—scraping and ferreting among stones and earth, sifting out old broken bottle necks, rusty nails, and odd pieces of crockery, and endeavouring to apply to each fragment a kind of Sherlock Holmes method of reasoning, that we may gain some clue to the lives and histories which once circled around it.[23]

These comments may well reflect on the contemporary programme of excavation on the Wall, deriving perhaps in particular from the excavations at Housesteads in 1898 where R. C. Bosanquet had produced a plan of the fort by following the walls of the main buildings.[24] Forster may also be reflecting on the intensive new excavation campaign that had commenced earlier in the decade to uncover the form, structure, and sequence of the Roman Wall.[25]

Forster considered that archaeological finds, such as coins, inscriptions, and ruins, or manuscripts, were of interest since they could serve to encourage the imagination, enabling the development of an image of bygone times. Reflecting on the stones from the Wall, Forster observed:

> Here is the record of an emperor or imperial legate, here of an obscure barbarian soldier, or a humble Briton's dead child; here is the great altar which a prefect dedicates to a fashionable deity of the day; here is another . . . which betokens the clumsy workmanship of a slave or peasant, and his devotion or gratitude to some uncouthly named god of his forefathers. Here a large and not inartistic image presents to us Cybele or Hercules; and here is the rough flagstone, on which some budding six-year-old artist has scratched his earliest masterpiece . . . [26]

Inscriptions enabled Forster to explore the lives, beliefs, and deaths of the people who had lived along the Wall, indicating 'a perfect hotch-potch of religions, a medley of faiths dead and dying, which perhaps only Rome or Alexandria could have matched'.[27] He reviewed the official religion of the Roman gods and also noted the wide variety of subsidiary spirits. Interestingly, in exploring these inscriptions Forster focused on what may be termed the ethnic origins of the soldiers and their religious beliefs.[28] He did not dwell in any detail on the military organization of the Wall's population, the particularly defensive role of the frontier at the margin of Roman civilization or the absence of evidence for Christianity; a marked contrast with John Collingwood Bruce. In Forster's account, the Romans are in full control of the landscape from their elevated position on the Wall.

---

[23] Forster (1899), 35.
[24] Bosanquet (1904); Crow (2004a), 133–4; Rushworth (2009), 5.
[25] Haverfield (1899a).   [26] Forster (1899), 36–7.
[27] ibid., 42.   [28] ibid., 42–57.

Fig. 11.5. The Roman Wall visible in the road surface close to Walwick. From J. C. Bruce (1863), 99.

The final part of Forster's book explored the Wall 'Through the Centuries'.[29] He writes that 'through the castles, churches, priories, and towers, which have sprung from its remains, it may claim a connection with many events of interest, and some of even national importance'.[30] He also presents a detailed account of the later use of the monument and the stories adhering to its remains, including tales of King Arthur, King Oswald's battle at Heavenfield, and Michael Drayton's rendition of 'aged *Pictswall*'.[31] Forster emphasized a sense of place through the idea of continuity between the Roman past and the present day, such as when he discussed the eighteenth-century military road, noting that 'the unlucky Wall suffered vicarious punishment for the unconscious Jacobitism of the Tynedale mud'.[32] He also observed that, in certain sections, parts of the curtain Wall remained visible (Figure 11.5); and argued, 'only here and there are the facing-blocks of the foundation course still to be seen, like fragments of an almost vanished pavement, lying where the legionaries placed them more then seventeen hundred years ago, so that bicycles and motor-car may run upon stones which were wrought in the days of Hadrian.'[33]

---

[29] ibid., 142–208. [30] ibid., 142–3.
[31] ibid., 143, 149, 157–61. [32] ibid., 202. [33] ibid., 202–3.

Forster concluded his book by comparing Roman engineering works with contemporary examples. He referred to George Stephenson, the famous colliery and railway engineer,[34] who was born in 1781 just a few miles to the south of the line of the Wall at Wylam, to the west of Newcastle.[35] Remarking that a number of other road engineers and industrialists were born close to the Roman roads of the North, Forster observed, 'we might almost imagine that the spirit of the Roman engineers haunted the scenes of their labours, and in some mysterious manner inspired their unconscious successors,—that the walls, roads, and bridges of the Romans are in some fashion the parents of the great engineering achievements of the present century.'[36] Forster conceived that the construction of the eighteenth-century turnpike road was another stage in the cycle of life of the Wall, symbolized by the fact that bicycles and motorcars could travel over stones that had been put in place during Roman times.

The increasing scale of archaeological works undertaken on Hadrian's Wall during the 1890s is not at all evident from the text of *The Amateur Antiquary*. Forster reflected on an older tradition when he wrote that 'the Wall can speak, and, if we may credit old Michael Drayton, can speak in somewhat vainglorious tones'.[37] His approach is entirely different from contemporary archaeological endeavours, presumably explaining his claims to amateur status. He consciously used his imagination to animate the static materials along the Wall's line and to construct a living picture of the monument.

Also published in 1899 was Francis Haverfield's summary of the first five years of an archaeological project that was seeking to define and tie down the Wall's form and chronology.[38] Haverfield (1860–1919) was the foremost scholar of Roman Britain from the late 1890s until his death in 1919. Although Forster and Haverfield epitomize two different ways of thinking about Hadrian's Wall, both their approaches originate in preceding accounts. Forster drew particularly deeply upon the work of William Hutton who had created a more impressionistic, immediate, general, and less pedantic image of the Wall.[39] It will be seen in the following chapter that Haverfield drew upon an alternative genealogy of knowledge and focused on the commencement of the scientific study of the Wall in the work of the eighteenth-century antiquary John Horsley.

It is important to understand that Forster was not arguing that archaeological detection work is inherently pedantic, since his 'rag-pickers' are 'imaginative' and seek to tell stories that focus on fragments from the past. Forster's writings clearly express his view of imaginative antiquarianism, an approach that aims to bring Roman artefacts, sites, and landscapes to life. In

---

[34] cf. Kirby (2004).   [35] Forster (1899), 203.
[36] ibid., 204.   [37] ibid., 143.   [38] Haverfield's (1899a).
[39] Hutton (1802); cf. Sweet (2004), 313–14.

this context, it is significant that Forster also undertook archaeological field-work, and his contribution to knowledge of the Wall, through both this and his imaginative writings, combined a desire to bring the remains of the Wall to life with the skills of an acute observer of archaeological remains.[40] Although later writers have recognized Forster's contribution to the archaeological study of the Wall,[41] few have mentioned his imaginative antiquarianism.[42] From the 1890s, a more distinct division came to be drawn between the science of archaeology and the speculations of novelists and artists, making Forster's approach appear irrelevant. Despite this, some popular writings on the Wall have had a distinct impact on academic perceptions during the past century.

RUDYARD KIPLING'S ROMAN WALL

Kipling provides a very different account of the Wall, but one that also aimed to bring the remains of the monument to life. Kipling (1865–1936) was born in India and travelled widely, both in Britain and overseas. He wrote numerous works of fiction exploring contemporary imperial issues that had a signifi-cantly wide readership.[43] A Tory with a stout conviction of the justice of British imperialism, Kipling's early twentieth-century works addressed the state of England and its empire.[44] They exhibit his conservative pessimism and sense of irony and express some of the moral and ethical ambiguities of empire.[45] His works include three references to Hadrian's Wall, the first and most significant is incorporated into his influential novel, *Puck of Pook's Hill* (1906). He also contributed poems to the *School History of England* and referred to the Wall during a speech to the Royal Society of St George in 1920.[46]

It is clear that Kipling had some knowledge of the Wall, having visited it on several occasions.[47] His account also drew upon recent discoveries from the Wall,[48] following much the same approach as Forster's imaginative

---

[40] Bishop (1994), 10; Freeman (2007), 296.

[41] e.g. E. Birley (1961), 87, 105, 201, 270; Bishop (1994), 10–12; Freeman (2007), 281–98.

[42] The only reference to *The Amateur Antiquary* in Birley's *Research on Hadrian's Wall* is that Forster was the first to assert confidently that there were only two turrets for each mile of the Wall's length (E. Birley 1961, 299).

[43] Betts (1971), 158; Larson (1999), 222; Pinney (2004).

[44] Hynes (1991), 18–19.   [45] Roberts (2007).

[46] Fletcher and Kipling (1911); Kipling (1920).

[47] Mothersole (1924, 82), mentions that Kipling's name was in the visitors' book at the George Inn, Chollerford. Kipling was also a regular visitor to the Straker family of Stagshaw House near Corbridge (Leach and Whitworth 2011, 27).

[48] Rivet (1976), 7–8.

antiquarianism, but with a more directly political message. Kipling's writings on the Wall have been the subject of a number of studies. Initially the inaccuracies of the archaeological picture of the Wall conveyed by his writings were explored.[49] For example, Collingwood observed that Kipling referenced the Roman Wall as an allegory of British India and not in the context of writing a history of Roman Britain, stating that the two topics 'go on quite different lines'.[50] More recent accounts have explored the context of Kipling's imperial thoughts, addressing how he came to imagine a Roman Britain that could serve contemporary imperial needs.[51]

Puck was a long time in gestation. In a letter of 1897 Kipling remarks, that he and 'Uncle Ned' 'are deep in the Roman occupation of Britain (this with an eye to stories)'.[52] Kipling's 'Uncle Ned' was the painter Sir Edward Burne-Jones, married to Kipling's mother's sister, who died in 1898.[53] Kipling's aim was to make the history of England relevant to the young reader through his main characters of two children, Dan and Una.[54] In his narration, the Roman past is one of three main periods of time visited by the children and their guide, Puck. The book begins with the Normans, the Romans coming later in the narrative, perhaps because Kipling identified the Norman period with the beginning of English history. The sequence of time is unimportant, since the tales present the complexity of the multilayered past in particular places,[55] an approach which drew on earlier accounts of the landscape of England. Kipling wished to emphasize the complexities of the history of England, drawing on ancestral strains from ancient Britons, Romans, Normans, and Anglo-Saxons. The Roman tales in *Puck* were particularly popular with Kipling's readers and this part of the novel will be discussed here.

Kipling introduces two main Roman characters, Parnesius and Pertinax. Parnesius is a pro-Roman Briton, born in southern Britain and descended from a Roman family given lands in the Isle of Wight by Agricola.[56] This appears to have been an idea that was inspired by the recent excavation of the Roman villa at Brading.[57] Parnesius' character is partly derived from the idea of the Anglo-Indian subaltern, but he is a more complex figure with a particular loyalty to Roman Britain.[58] Pertinax, by contrast, is from a Roman family background in Gaul. These men lead a spirited defence of the frontiers of *Britannia* as centurions of Rome, burdened with this task for three years

---

[49] Haverfield (1906), 190; Collingwood (1921b), 6; Rivet (1976). This archaeological critique of the details of Kipling's rendition of the Wall formed part of the development of a scientific approach to the study of the Wall that is explored in the following chapter.

[50] Collingwood (1923), 15.

[51] Hutchins (1967), 145–9; Hingley (2010a), 37–9; Roberts (2007); Roberts (2010).

[52] Kipling (1897), 324; Ricketts (1999), 290.

[53] Pinney (2004).   [54] Roberts (2007).

[55] Gilmour (2002), 172; Ricketts (1999), 289.   [56] Kipling (1906), 147.

[57] Rivet (1976), 7.   [58] Ricketts (1999), 291.

during the decline of Roman power that occurred under the commander Magnus Maximus during the late fourth century.[59] Maximus, who was probably born in Spain, overthrew the emperor of the Western Roman empire and ruled Britain from 383 to 388. He was later remembered as the last ruler of Roman Britain and thought of as an independent king from whom Welsh dynasties claimed descent.[60] Kipling chose Maximus' reign as the focus for his Roman tales because the novel draws deeply on Gildas' account of the Wall and emphasizes his aim to find evidence for British nationhood in its ancient history.[61]

Parnesius and Pertinax are sent to defend the Wall against the northern attackers and manage to hold the line until a relief force is dispatched by Maximus' successor, the Emperor Theodosius. On his journey to the Roman Wall from the south of the province, Parnesius describes the gradual deterioration of landscape, and then:

> Just when you think you are at the world's end, you see a smoke from East to West as far as the eye can turn, and then, under it, also as far as the eye can stretch, houses and temples, shops and theatres, barracks and granaries, trickling along like dice behind—always behind—one long, low, rising and falling, and hiding and showing line of towers. And that is the Wall![62]

Kipling provides a detailed and imaginative description of the Wall, describing a 'thin town eighty miles long following the south of the rampart'.[63] In his description of the structure of the Wall, which may be partly taken from Forster's book, Parnesius notes that:

> It is *the* Wall. Along the top are towers with guard-houses, small towers, between. Even on the narrowest part of it three men with shields can walk abreast, from guard-house to guard-house. A little curtain wall, no higher then a man's neck, runs along the top of the thick wall, so that from a distance you see the helmets of the sentries sliding back and forth like beads. Thirty feet high is the Wall, and on the Pict's side, the North, is a ditch, strewn with blades of old swords and spear-heads set in wood, and tyres of wheels joined by chains.[64]

He arrives at the Wall at the point where Watling Street passes through a gate, close to the Roman fort of *Hunnum*.

Kipling exaggerated the height of the curtain Wall at this location. Forster had suggested an external elevation of twenty-four feet, but Parnesius states that is was thirty feet high. Kipling's reference to three soldiers marching along the Wall abreast drew upon the comments of 'aged *Pictswall*' in Michael Drayton's poem.[65] One of the reasons for the exaggeration of the height and width of the curtain Wall appears to be the Roman soldier's desire to impress

---

[59] Rivet (1976), 5.   [60] Robbins (1998), 24–5; Casey (2002), 90.
[61] Higham (1991), 4; Hingley (2000), 177 n. 34.   [62] Kipling (1906), 173.
[63] ibid., 174.   [64] ibid., 173.   [65] Drayton (1622), 159.

his young audience, since he is responding to a child's innocent question, 'Is it just *a* Wall? Like the one around our kitchen-garden.' Over-emphasizing the scale of the curtain Wall also exaggerated its physical significance, a device also used by a number of Edwardian illustrators such as H. R. Millar in the first edition of *Puck*. One of Millar's images shows the gate through the Wall close to Halton Chesters (Figure 11.2), while the other illustrates Roman soldiers involved in a battle outside the Walls of South Shields fort (Figure 11.6).

Fig. 11.6. An imaginative image of a battle at South Shields by H. R. Millar titled *We dealt with them thoroughly through a long day*. From Kipling 1906, 204.

Ballistas are mounted on the towers in these images, repeating an idea developed by Robert Forster in his account of *Borcovicium*.

Kipling's approach to the Wall differed markedly from Forster's. While Forster appears to have been genuinely interested in the structure of the monument and shows some concern for the way that the Romans had treated free Britons beyond the frontier, Kipling recreated Hadrian's Wall as an analogy for the British imperial North-West frontier in India and for concerns about the potential state of decadence in the British empire, that drew, in particular, upon the problematic recent events in South Africa and India.[66] Kipling's three Roman chapters were, not so much a contribution to the history of Britain, as parables of empire and civilization that projected contemporary morals for the British.[67] His main emphasis in this part of the book is, in Kipling's own words, on the 'ultra-Roman Britons, and ultra-British Romans, and tame tribesmen pretending to be civilised'.[68] The character and actions of Parnesius and Pertinax were deeply informed by Kipling's view of the correct attitudes for British officers in India and his opinions about the Anglo-Indian population. The imperial allusions in the stories are deeply ingrained. Deborah Roberts has argued that the relationship of Parnesius and Pertinax to the Picts to the north of the Wall is in keeping with the behaviour of the 'best' of the colonial administrators in Kipling's stories of India.[69]

Kipling's novel *Puck of Pook's Hill* also drew on the deep sense of history of place that resulted from the relics, dating from Neolithic to modern times, discovered on land that he owned in Sussex.[70] He transported the characters from a location close to his own home to places across England, including Hadrian's Wall. Harry Ricketts has observed that the stories in *Puck* do not assert that Roman, Norman, Anglo-Saxon, or any other single strain represented the English people, but that they originated from the mixing of these different elements.[71] In this context, a transformed idea of Englishness gained powerful support during the early twentieth century, as the Britons sought to distinguish themselves from the German peoples by contesting the simple idea of pure Teutonic or Anglo-Saxon origin.[72]

Ancient history helped with this process and, by Edwardian times, the writings of the German ancient historian, Theodor Mommsen, had begun to communicate a transformative perspective for Roman imperial culture. This concept enabled Francis Haverfield to develop a new approach to the Romanization of Roman Britain.[73] The interpretative framework that had dominated the nineteenth century had made it difficult to imagine Romanized Britons,

---

[66] Ricketts (1999), 305–6; Roberts (2007), 114.   [67] Gilmour (2002), 171–2.
[68] Kipling (1906), 149.   [69] Roberts (2007), 114.   [70] Mackenzie (1993), xiii.
[71] Ricketts (1999), 291; cf. Hingley (2000), 86–95.   [72] Hingley (2000), 62.
[73] Haverfield (1906); cf. Dowling (1985), 596.

who were represented as semi-clothed barbarians in the Wallington Hall painting and other Victorian and Edwardian images and writings. In 1905, Haverfield presented his seminal lecture, 'The Romanization of Roman Britain', published the following year and republished several times,[74] enabling a challenge to this inherited image.

In this lecture, Haverfield argued that, 'In Britain, as it is described by the majority of English writers, we have a province in which Roman and native were as distinct as modern Englishmen and Indian, and "the departure of the Romans" in the fifth century left the Britons almost as Celtic as their coming had found them.'[75] Haverfield noted that this image had been caused by an over-reliance on the writings of Caesar and Tacitus and also by 'the analogies of English rule in India'. Many nineteenth-century accounts of Roman Britain had drawn deeply upon cultural models derived from British rule in India, just as British officers in India had drawn upon Roman parallels to inform their actions and policies.[76] Haverfield probably had Kipling's Romans and Britons in mind when he made these comments.[77]

As a result of Haverfield's work, ideas about Romano-British society began to address the idea that ancient Britons, especially in the civil regions of *Britannia*, could become Roman in appearance and character.[78] Ideas of Roman civilization began to be incorporated into the origins of the English,[79] but evidently this had only a limited influence on Kipling. Deborah Roberts has argued that, although we might expect Kipling to show us 'a prospect of the coming together of Britons and Romans', his particular identification of imperial Rome with imperial England actually serves to challenge the idea of the 'blending of subject races and rulers'.[80] There is no straightforward fusing of Romans and Britons in Kipling's stories since, as in many Victorian accounts, they remain as fairly exclusive racial groups.[81] Parnesius is an Anglo-Roman with an effectively fully Roman character, although his loyalty is really to England. The other ancient Britons in the story are distinctly un-Roman. As such, Kipling develops a rather conflicted view of Britain and Rome that undermines the concept of multicultural empire.[82]

This indicates that there is a contradiction in Kipling's idea of the Roman history of Britain, since he views the English as a product of the mixing of the races that had occupied Britain in the past, while at the same time drawing his main characters from his conception of typical British colonial officers. Perhaps the idea of a full synthesis of Roman and Briton did not suit Kipling's particular purpose in *Puck*. In any case, his writings reflected upon colonial

---

[74] Haverfield (1906); Haverfield (1912).   [75] Haverfield (1906), 190.
[76] Alston (2010); Hingley (2008a), 240–1.   [77] cf. Rivet (1976), 14.
[78] Hingley (2005), 33–5.   [79] Hingley (2008a), 298–306.
[80] Roberts (2007), 116–17; cf. Shumate (2006), 108.
[81] Rivet (1976), 13; Roberts (2007), 116–17.   [82] cf. Shumate (2006), 110.

identities in the British empire rather than providing a scholarly and accurate portrayal of Roman Britain or the Roman Wall. His tales are told by drawing upon archaeological finds and structures, giving his stories some degree of genealogical authority through the creation of a sense of place derived from the depth of the history evident in the English landscape.

Kipling remarked that 'the Wall was manned by every breed and race in the Empire. No two towers spoke the same tongue, or worshipped the same Gods'.[83] This image drew upon the ideas explored by earlier writers—including John Collingwood Bruce, Thomas Wright, and Robert Forster—but it also suited Kipling's agenda for the idea of an ethnically varied but unified imperial defense for the British empire. Francis Hutchins suggests that Kipling took his personal religion from Rome, since he clearly preferred the Mithraism of Parnesius to contemporary Christianity.[84] Kipling had become a freemason in 1885 and drew analogies between Mithraism and Freemasonry in terms of their potential to integrate troops from across empires.[85] Kipling was hinting at a vision of the need to construct a unified British imperial army spread across the world and with a common bond of devotion to the empire.[86] Kipling may well have drawn upon Bruce's allusion to Mithras in his speech at Housesteads. Information for the worship of Mithras on the Wall was also available to Kipling in the form of altars from Rudchester and particularly at the Housesteads temple, the remains of which had been uncovered again in 1898.[87]

The contemplation of the significance of imperial decline and fall was becoming fashionable at the time when Kipling published *Puck*, as the military and imperial ambitions of Germany were creating increasing problems for the British overseas.[88] By the early twentieth century, Britain was facing a difficult imperial situation and many writers looked to the Roman past for military, imperial, and cultural morals that would help to bring stability to Britain's empire. In this context, Kipling drew upon the theme of the genealogy of English identity to create a mythic text for empire.[89] The Tory politician and author, George Wyndham, wrote a letter to Kipling, immediately after the publication of *Puck*, remarking, with regard to the tale of the two Roman officers:

> That parable tells the men and women and children what they have got to do in the everlasting sunlight, and, even, why they have got to do it. They may now understand that the world rots in the everlasting sunlight; and that they must

---

[83] Kipling (1906), 176.   [84] Hutchins (1967), 146.   [85] Rivet (1976), 12–13.
[86] Hutchins (1967), 146–8.   [87] Bosanquet (1904), 225–63; Rivet (1976), 12.
[88] cf. Hynes (1991), 18–20. Elsewhere, I have explored the interest of educationalists, politicians, military men, and academics in Roman frontiers at this time (Hingley 2007b).
[89] Low (1996), 256.

delay the rot, year in and year out, on the chance that, once in 100 years, a saviour, and once in 500 years, a creator, may—or may not—appear. That is their glory. Your glory is that you have told them so![90]

As under-secretary at the War Office, Wyndham had played a significant role during the South African War of 1899–1900, but the Tories were voted out of power by the time *Puck* was published.[91] Kipling's novel publicized a topic that was of considerable importance to politicians, academics, and military men. In the years between 1906 and 1914, a number of authors explored the potential parallels between the frontiers of contemporary imperial Britain and those of ancient Rome, including Lord Cromer, Sir Charles Lucas, James Bryce, and Francis Haverfield.[92]

The Roman tales in *Puck* were to prove highly influential since they communicated the supposed imperial lessons of classical Rome to a broad audience, helping to inform members of the British public of the supposed benefits of the rule of empire and the necessity of becoming involved in military and political action.[93] Kipling's image of the valiant defence of the Roman Wall had an immediate impact on educationalists, which partly explains its popularity during the succeeding years. A pamphlet published by Goldsmith's College in 1909, for example, presented 'A Suggested History Course for the Elementary School, Standards I-VII'.[94] For Standards II and III, it was proposed that a series of stories should be brought together from English history, including Boadicea or Caratacus, 'on the Great Roman Wall (see Puck of Pooks Hill by Kipling)', Vortigern, Hengist and Horsa, and other themes.[95] There was to be a different emphasis in Standards IV to V, but the teaching was still historically based. The course began by emphasizing the ancient Britons, the coming of the Romans, and 'the Roman occupation of Britain on its social side. N.B.—A helpful book is Kipling's Puck of Pook's Hill'. Over the next three decades Kipling's book ran through thirty editions and had a deep impact on generations of adults from the Edwardian era until the present.[96]

KIPLING'S LATER WRITINGS ON THE WALL

In 1911 Kipling contributed poems to C. R. L Fletcher's *A School History of England*,[97] an extreme piece of Tory propaganda that drew the Roman occupation of Britain into a direct relationship with the contemporary state

[90] Wyndham (1906), 553.   [91] Jackson (2004).
[92] cf. Hingley (2000), 44–8; Hingley (2007b), 137–8.   [93] Larson (1999), 222.
[94] Anon (1909).   [95] ibid., 7.   [96] Usherwood (1996), 157.
[97] Fletcher and Kipling (1911); cf. Ricketts (1999), 289.

of Britain and its empire. In their discussion of *Britannia*, Fletcher and Kipling noted that:

> It was, however, a misfortune for Britain that Rome never conquered the whole island. The great warrior, Agricola, did, between A.D. 79 and 85, penetrate far into Scotland; but he could leave no trace of civilization behind him, and Ireland he never touched at all . . . Then there was always a 'Scottish frontier' to be guarded, and along this frontier the Emperor Hadrian, early in the second century, began the famous Roman Wall. His successors improved upon it until it became a mighty rampart of stone, eighty miles long, from Tyne to Solway, with ditches in front and behind and a strong garrison kept in its watch-towers.
>
> To the north of the wall roamed, almost untouched, certainly unsubdued, the wilder Celts whom the Romans called 'Picts' or painted men; the screen of the wall seemed a perfectly sufficient defense against these. But prosperity and riches are often bad for men; they lead to the neglect of defence. I fear that Roman Britain went to sleep behind her wall, recruiting fell off, the strength of the legions became largely a 'paper strength'.[98]

The text of this book is racist, bigoted anti-Irish, and anti-Parliamentary.[99] It may be thought to be surprising that Kipling cooperated in the production of such a publication, but he was strongly conservative and deeply worried about the state of the British empire.

Kipling's poem 'The Roman Centurion speaks' was printed in this volume. It places distinctly pro-British sentiments into the mind of the Roman soldier who has 'served from Vectis [the Isle of Wight] to the Wall', but has just been ordered to return to Rome.[100] In this poem, the centurion contemplates his loyalty in a manner reminiscent of the two Roman officers in *Puck*:

> Legate, I had the news last night. My cohort's ordered home
> By Ship to Portus Itius and thence by road to Rome.
> I've marched the companies abroad, the arms are stowed below:
> Now let another take my sword. Command me not to go!
> I've served in Britain forty years now, from Vectis to the Wall
> I have none other home than this, nor any life at all.
> Last night I did not understand, but, now, the hour draws near
> That calls me to my native land, I feel that land is here.
> Here where men say my name was made, here where my work was done,
> Here where my dearest dead are laid—my wife—my wife and son;
> Here where time, custom, grief and toil, age, memory, service, love,
> Have rooted me in British soil. Ah, how shall I remove?

A rather different idea of Hadrian's Wall is evident in a speech on *England and the English* presented by Kipling to the Royal Society of St George in April 1920, after the death of his son in the First World War and during a

---

[98] Fletcher and Kipling (1911), 21–2.   [99] Gilmour (2002), 176–7.
[100] Kipling (1911), 19–20.

particularly introspective period in his life.[101] There are some similarities in this speech with ideas about the mixed nature of English origins he had developed in *Puck*,[102] but the tenor of the argument is rather different.[103] At the beginning of the speech, Kipling remarked:

> About sixteen hundred years ago, when Rome was mistress of the world and the Picts and Scots lived on the other side of the Wall that ran from Newcastle to Carlisle, the story goes that Rome allowed all those peoples one night in the year in which they could say aloud exactly what they thought of Rome, without fear of consequences. So then, on that one night of the year, they would creep out of the heather in droves and light their little wandering fires and criticise their Libyan Generals and their Roman Pontiffs and the Eastern camp followers, who looked down on them from the top of their great high unbreakable Roman Wall sixteen hundred years ago.
>
> To-day, Imperial Rome is dead. The Wall is down and the Picts and Scots are on this side of it, but thanks to our Royal Society of St. George, there still remains one night in the year when the English can creep out of their hiding-places and whisper to each other exactly what we think of each about ourselves.[104]

Kipling's observations about the Picts and Scots having crossed the Wall repeated an earlier motif expressed in some nineteenth-century accounts about immigration, while his comments on Libyan Generals and Eastern camp followers highlighted the multi-ethnic nature of the Roman empire. In fact, he viewed the Wall's ruination as having partially inverted its significance, since it was now the English, rather than the Scots and Picts, who met to talk together, and the Picts and Scots now lived on the near side of the Wall, within England.

Later in this speech, Kipling drew on Daniel Defoe's 'The True-Born Englishman', conceiving the English as a mixed race.[105] Kipling argued that the English were 'taught' by the Phoenicians and the Romans, as well as by the Normans.[106] The ruined condition of the Wall was taken to represent the partial collapse of the barriers between peoples. As Robert Young has argued, in Kipling's works the real England had become the much larger civilization found across the British empire.[107] The Wall, as a ruin, could no longer serve to define the boundaries of English identity, but there is an ambiguity here since the whole speech appears to be based on the premise that the English could still identify themselves and meet together to discuss common kin-ship.[108] Moreover, Kipling only mentions certain ancestors for the English— 'Roman, Dane, Norman, Papists, Cromwellian, Stuarts, Hollander, Hano-verian, Upper Class, Democracy'.[109] This continues to exclude non-Western

---

[101] Pinney (2004).   [102] Ricketts (1999), 291.   [103] Hingley (2010a), 38–9.
[104] Kipling (1920), 177–8.   [105] ibid., 178; cf. Ricketts (1999), 291.
[106] Kipling (1920), 179.   [107] R. Young (2008), 230.
[108] Hingley (2010a), 38–9.   [109] Kipling (1920), 180.

peoples from across the empire who had settled in England, the Scots and, apparently, also the Germans (Anglo-Saxons), unless the latter are included in the Hollanders or the Hanoverians.

Kipling's concept of Englishness, as expressed here, appears both ethnically permeable and impermeable, an issue that reflects in an interesting way on the role of the Roman Wall as both an inclusive and a divisive structure—an idea developed further in Chapter 15 of this book. Despite its ruination, for Kipling the Roman Wall continued to serve as a referent for the exclusion of certain peoples from the common kinship of the English. It is easy to focus on the peoples left out of Kipling's account but his concept was rather less exclusionary than many contemporary writings on colonial identities, including those penned by Fletcher.[110]

REPRESENTING THE WALL

A number of Edwardian images of the Wall feature its construction and its Roman population. Fletcher and Kipling's book included images of key events from English history by Henry Ford, a contemporary illustrator of children's books, including one that shows the construction of the Roman Wall (Figure 11.7). In this image, a very high curtain Wall is portrayed with a milecastle that appears to be at least ten metres in elevation. Both Ford and Millar represent Hadrian's Wall as largely rebuilt and the scale of the curtain Wall in their three images suggests that both artists were inspired by medieval town walls, or perhaps that they were familiar with the late Roman fort at Pevensey.[111] The idea of the national and imperial importance of Hadrian's Wall appears to have led to an exaggeration of its scale and magnificence. Ford's illustration shows Britons involved in laborious activities under the watchful control of Roman legionaries. These Britons are not the romanticized Celts of the Wallington Hall painting but individuals who look distinctly Palaeolithic in character. The figure at the bottom right is in chains and the style of his hair might have been intended to draw colonial parallels with certain native peoples of the British empire for schoolboy readers.[112] Other figures in the scene represent unreconstructed Celts, possibly projecting Fletcher's highly racist views of the Irish.[113] Ford also appears to draw upon John Collingwood Bruce's observations: 'We cannot . . . view from the vicinity

---

[110] As we shall see, Kipling also became involved in the defence of the Wall in 1930, when its central section was threatened with quarrying.

[111] Kipling had some involvement with archaeological work occurring at this site.

[112] cf. Smiles (1994), 15.

[113] cf. Hingley (2000), 128.

Fig. 11.7. Henry Ford's image of *The Building of the Wall*. From Fletcher and Kipling (1911), 23.

of BORCOVICUS the thin lines of ways leading from the quarries on the opposite site of the valley, without fancying we see moving along them a string of half-naked, half-famished savages, bearing upon their galled shoulders the stones wherewith to construct the Wall intended to keep them in perpetual subjection . . .'[114]

Two additional paintings of the Wall were produced in the early second decade of the twentieth century. Robert Spence's painting *Night Attack*, completed in 1912 and now stored in the Great North Museum in Newcastle, drew on a common concern with the security of the frontiers of civilization (Figure 3.4). Spence showed this painting, which he initially entitled *Day Time Attack on the Wall*, to some members of the Society of Antiquaries of Newcastle upon Tyne and, as a result of their criticisms of the detail, reduced its

---

[114] J. C. Bruce's (1875), xi–xii.

size and made it darker.[115] The Council of the Newcastle Antiquaries' report for 1912 observed that:

> The scene depicted is at the north-eastern gateway of *Borcovicius*, a point from which, looking eastward, the Wall is seen following the edges of the basaltic escarpments, half revealed in the moon-light. Sleepers of the garrison, aroused by the alarm, have turned out in hurriedly donned armour to find the inner pair of gates already forced by aid of fire and battering ram, whilst the crowding assailants are indicated by the escalade of the Wall, and the half-nude figures of the press of men who have won its crest and are hotly engaged in the mêlée with the defenders within. The picture will henceforth be regarded as one of the art treasures of the City, and its position on our walls will be the more appreciated as probably the most successful effort of the painter in visualizing one of the scenes that our recent excavations show must have been repeatedly enacted during the period of the Roman occupation.[116]

A further published note records that the painting depicts a Caledonian raid on the 'Roman fort of Borcovicium (now called Housesteads) during the Second Century'.[117] Excavation work on a number of forts and milecastles along the Wall during the 1890s and 1900s had produced evidence that was taken to indicate that the Wall had been destroyed in AD 181,[118] but this painting may also reflect contemporary concerns about German ambitions for military expansion.[119] The barbarians who are overrunning *Borcovicium* are not the valiant defenders of liberty shown in William Bell Scott's Houses of Parliament cartoon (Figure 8.2). Nor are they involved in what is evidently a pointless attack on the Wall, as in Bell Scott's painting at Wallington Hall (Figure 9.1). It seems as if the Romans will be unable to resist this attack, although—unlike the context described by Kipling in the Roman stories included in *Puck*—this scene is staged more than two centuries before the end of Roman rule, so Roman imperial order will be restored shortly. The scale of the northern defences of Housesteads and the curtain Wall in Spence's image is more realistic than the other illustrations discussed above.

An article published in the *Illustrated London News* entitled 'The Making of the Modern Englishman. No. 1: England under the Roman Empire' was illustrated with a black and white image, 'From the Painting by R. Caton Woodville' (Figure 11.8).[120] Woodville (1856–1927), a well-known Victorian and early twentieth-century war artist employed by the *London Evening News*,

[115] Lindsay Allason-Jones (pers. comm.).

[116] Anon (1913), xii–xiii. I am grateful to Lindsay Allason-Jones for drawing my attention to this source.

[117] *Illustrated London News* (1930b).

[118] Collingwood (1921a), 61.

[119] cf. Hynes (1991), 352–9.

[120] *Illustrated London News* (1911). I am very grateful to Hella Eckardt for bringing this image to my attention.

Fig. 11.8. An engraving taken from a painting by R. Caton Woodville (1911) titled *The Building of Hadrian's Great Wall*. Reproduced by permission of the Mary Evans Picture Library and the *Illustrated London News*. From *Illustrated London News*, 1 April 1911, 468–469.

lived in London.[121] The image is printed over a double-page spread and is captioned, 'Sign of the military genius of an emperor: the Building of Hadrian's Great Wall across England from the Solway to the Tyne'. It notes, with regard to the drawing that:

> The group in the foreground is on top of the mile-castles constructed in the wall, with smaller turrets at shorter intervals, for use as watch-towers. The Emperor Hadrian is shown seated, while an architect shows him a plan of the wall. It will be noted that, with the exception of the Emperor and the general at his side, the faces of most of those shown are of a Northern type, an illustration of the fact that the armies in the Roman provinces consisted largely, not of Romans, but of men from various provinces trained by Roman officers. On the northern side of the wall was a ditch; on the south side a series of mounds, with a military way between them and the wall. Thus the structure could be manned and defended from the southern side; and its steep side faced in the direction by which the enemy would come. It was built to keep out, not an army equipped with scaling-ladders and battering-rams, and other engines of war, but the wild tribes of Scotland, who were continuously making incursions across the border into Britain. It was both wall of defense and line of advance.

[121] Stearn (2004).

As seen in the illustrations of Ford and Millar, the curtain Wall is represented as far too substantial. The milecastle in the distance resembles a blockhouse, while the turrets project beyond the front of the curtain Wall. The latter resembles a railway line with a cart on top, perhaps drawing on the industrial achievements of George Stephenson, who had been born just over a century earlier close to the line of the Wall.

The reference to 'Northern type' faces draws upon the nineteenth-century view that races could be defined through craniological considerations.[122] These soldiers presumably stand for the Germanic recruits well known from inscriptions along the Wall, people who, according to the Germanic myth of origin, had a direct genetic relationship to modern Englishmen. A black-skinned man is sitting to the left, partly out of the frame and watching the architect and the emperor. He has a ring in his ear and wears a torc or neckring. Once more echoing the Wallington Hall painting, ancient Britons are represented, since there is a figure who is presumably intended to represent a Celt or druid in the background to the right; a second comparable figure is helping with the construction of the Wall.

It is significant that popular accounts of the Wall during the early twentieth century remain fascinated by the idea of a mixed population, drawing on the concept popularized by Kipling. Nevertheless, these accounts sometimes suggest that the blood of the Roman settlers mixed with the local population to leave a living inheritance. In both the Wallington Hall painting and in *Puck of Pook's Hill*, the communities along the Wall consist of peoples from across the empire, but there is no clear evidence for the mixing of blood between the distinct ethnological groups, but attitudes appear to have been changing. In *The Romance of Northumberland*, A. G. Bradley argued that the blood of the Tungrian, Batavian, Spanish, and Moorish soldiers stationed along the Wall had 'merged' into the population of northern Britain, although the author used contorted logic to attribute such racial strains to the modern Welsh.[123] Arthur Weigall's *Wanderings in Roman Britain* contains a lengthy discussion of Hadrian's Wall in which he wrote that, 'In the Roman Empire there were no frontiers dividing one compact nation from another. The conquered people did not long remain subject nations, but they soon styled themselves Romans'.[124] Weigall used the evidence of the inscription naming Regina and her husband Barates from Palmyra, to illustrate this point—'He was a Roman, and therefore it did not matter in the least whether he was by blood a Syrian or a Briton' (Figure 11.9).[125] Turning to Hadrian's Wall, Weigall suggested that:

> The troops who manned the Wall . . . were drawn from all parts of the Roman Empire; and the bulk of these forces lived here for the next 300 years of so,

[122] R. Young (2008), 71–93.   [123] Bradley (1913), 237–8.
[124] Weigall (1926), 17.   [125] ibid., 17–18; *RIB*, n. 1065.

Fig. 11.9. The Roman tombstone of Regina from South Shields. From J. C. Bruce (1907), 242.

intermarrying freely with the British inhabitants, and regarding Northumberland and Cumberland as their home, where they continued to live after their discharge. Thus it can be stated beyond doubt that the modern inhabitants of these counties are in large part directly descended from the Roman troops.[126]

---

[126] Weigall (1926), 102–3.

Weigall wrote of a 'curious mix of blood', although his list of soldiers included only peoples from Spain, Gaul, and the German provinces. He was one of the scholars who was seeking to find an origin for the character of the contemporary population of England in the mixed populations of Britain's past, to glorify England and its empire through this process.[127] This included a wider range of people within the definition of the origins of the English, suggesting a very varied source for the English genetic strain.

SUMMARY: EDDIES IN TIME

In a discussion of the identity of England, Robert Colls has argued that 'Serious travelers...stand in ethnographic time (which was no time), in order to be entranced by their own reveries'.[128] One of the writers drawn upon in this discussion is Rudyard Kipling who, as has been seen, perhaps followed Robert Forster's example and collapsed time into place in his account of the Wall to reveal how several worlds and times intersect.[129] The remaining chapters of this book will show that this approach to time and geography grew in popularity in accounts of the Wall during the course of the twentieth century. These reconstructions of the Roman past draw upon archaeological materials to create 'eddies in time' that bring the writer and reader into contact with the Roman population of the Wall. It is also an approach that, in the works of certain popular writers such as Kipling, has drawn upon mythical accounts of the Wall.[130] The objective of such an approach is usually to communicate an accessible view of the Wall, an idea that draws deeply on the chorographical tradition developed by earlier writers, including Camden, Drayton, and Hutton. Before exploring the creation of temporal eddies in certain twentieth-century accounts of the Wall, Chapter 12 will address a very different tradition of scholarship, an archaeological approach that aimed to create an enhanced appreciation of the temporal distance that separates the Roman past from the present.

[127] Hingley (2000), 103–4.
[128] Colls (2002), 261.
[129] Mackenzie writes that Kipling opens up a sense of 'archaeological time', of gaps and discontinuities, by the movements that drive his narrative backwards and forwards through history (1993, xxi).
[130] cf. Walsh (2010), 150.

12

Birdoswald: Scientific Archaeology

Nine years ago at Bainbridge gate
You taught me how to excavate
With patient trowel to assess
Remains that else were meaningless
To note what layers ran over what
If finds were made to mark the spot
Eric Birley (1935)[1]

INTRODUCTION

This chapter will explore a programme of archaeological research conducted from the last decade of the nineteenth century to the 1940s. This work explored the date of construction, identity, and signature of these frontier works, by addressing the location, form, and sequence of the individual features of the frontier.[2] R. G. Collingwood, one of the most influential archaeologists involved in this work, defined 'The period of scientific excavation' in his important article 'Hadrian's Wall: A History of the Problem', arguing that it commenced in 1891 and lasted until his own time.[3] Collingwood observed that the scientific study of the Wall commenced with the work of a number of researchers, primarily the ancient historian and archaeologist Francis Haverfield, who had become deeply involved in excavating sites along the Wall in 1894 and had continued his interest until 1906 (Figure 12.1). From 1920, Collingwood followed Haverfield's example and maintained his own curiosity until the early 1930s.[4] Between them, Haverfield and Collingwood helped to plan, publicize, and encourage a sustained programme of research-based excavation, the theme of this chapter. Both of these men held academic posts at Oxford and the importance of their writings has been emphasized at

---

[1] These are the first six lines of a poem sent to R. G. Collingwood at Christmas 1935. Eric Birley sent Collingwood poems every Christmas to thank him for introducing him to Hadrian's Wall (Anthony Birley pers. comm.).
[2] cf. Baudrillard (2005), 81.
[3] Collingwood (1921a), 59–66.   [4] Freeman (2007), 539–41.

Fig. 12.1. A photograph showing Francis Haverfield with a group of workmen, taken in 1898 at Birdoswald. Haverfield is the standing figure at the back left of the photograph. The notes on the photograph indicate that the fort is not visible since the photograph is taken up with the figures. The section has been taken across an earth feature, possibly the turf Wall. Reproduced by permission of the Great North Museum and Society of Antiquaries of Newcastle upon Tyne, Hadrian's Wall Photograph Collection, 6519.

Fig. 12.2. F. G. Simpson standing on the north-west angle tower of the fort at Great Chesters, explaining the structure to members of the Society of Antiquaries of Newcastle upon Tyne. Reproduced by permission of the Great North Museum and Society of Antiquaries of Newcastle upon Tyne, Hadrian's Wall Photograph Collection, 6937.

the expense of the efforts of other fieldworkers from Carlisle, Newcastle, and elsewhere who undertook much of the archaeological work synthesized and publicized by Haverfield and Collingwood.[5] In particular, Frank Gerald Simpson undertook some of the most important excavations (Figure 12.2), including a sustained campaign of archaeological fieldwork close to the Roman fort at Birdoswald (Cumbria). Haverfield and Collingwood were, however, the most widely recognized Wall scholars at the time, since they published the most influential general accounts.

The archaeological methods championed by Haverfield and Collingwood involved the excavation of small trenches at different sites, a technique that was considered to provide the best means for studying the Wall.[6] Collingwood argued that this method, throughout the period of scientific excavation, had led to dramatic advances in knowledge about the Wall.[7] This approach to the

---

[5] See E. Birley (1961), 30, 66–8.
[6] Freeman (2007), 275.   [7] Collingwood (1921a), 59.

selective excavation of the various features of the frontier at points that might be expected to show their relative dates was developed from the 1890s to the late 1940s by archaeologists including Haverfield, F. G. Simpson, and Ian Richmond. Haverfield, Collingwood, and Richmond publicized this work during the first five decades of the twentieth century through a number of review articles published in the *Journal of Roman Studies*.[8]

David Breeze has called this the 'great era of investigation on Hadrian's Wall', characterized by a new analytical approach to the date, structure, and sequence of the individual features that made up the frontier.[9] Large-scale excavations were undertaken at this time on the Roman sites at Housesteads and Corbridge, but this chapter will focus on the excavations that explored the sequence and character of the Wall's linear elements. Breeze has emphasized the importance of this work but has argued that the legacy of this period was to create a focus on question and answer that led, by the 1930s, to the idea that all the main problems of Hadrian's Wall had been solved.[10] As a result, the 'great era of excavation' was succeeded by what Breeze has called 'The Age of Certainty'.[11] He has suggested that the emphasis on the certainty of knowledge about the Wall has, in turn, had a deeply detrimental effect on research since the 1950s by suggesting that further additions to knowledge are likely to be very limited in nature. The main point here is that an emphasis on the certainty of interpretation might be considered to hold back innovative research on the Wall today, although it should be stressed that Hadrian's Wall is certainly by no means a moribund topic.[12]

Others have addressed the systematic ways in which the work was undertaken and the major contribution that this campaign made to knowledge of the Wall's form and sequence.[13] These excavations remain fundamental to current ideas of the chronology and sequencing of the Roman Wall. They also settled the controversy about the authorship of the monument, indicating that all the main elements—the stone curtain Wall, Vallum, milecastles, and turrets—had been built during the reign of the Emperor Hadrian. At this time scholarly attention was focused on the anatomy of the Wall, exploring the Vallum and the structure of the stone curtain Wall. An entirely new element of the frontier, the turf Wall, was recognized in 1895 close to Birdoswald and this was examined in detail during the subsequent four decades.[14] At Birdoswald, the turf Wall ran to the south of the stone curtain Wall for approximately two miles, the two phases of the Wall converging at either end, enabling a detailed consideration of their form and sequence.

---

[8] E. Birley (1961), 120.
[9] Breeze (2008a), 3.   [10] Breeze (2003), 12.   [11] ibid., 13.
[12] cf. N. Hodgson (2009b), 50–1.
[13] e.g. Browning (1991); Browning (1995); RFb, 9.
[14] Couse (1990), 64; Freeman (2007), 260–1; RFa, 41.

This chapter will examine the general increase in knowledge and, in particular, will explore Collingwood's claim that archaeological studies of the Wall had become more professional and scientific. The extent to which the great era of excavation resulted in a philosophy of thought that has damaged subsequent research on the Wall will also be considered. For those who wish to study the details of the archaeological work, Phil Freeman provides an extensive discussion and further references.[15]

THE TURF WALL, THE VALLUM, AND THE INTERNATIONALIZATION OF RESEARCH

Founded in 1866, the Cumberland and Westmorland Antiquarian and Archaeological Society increased the scholarly attention paid to the western part of the Wall.[16] The Cumberland Excavation Committee was created as an offshoot of the Society in 1894 and began a long series of excavations on the western part of the Wall under the direction of Francis Haverfield.[17] The Newcastle Antiquaries also undertook significant work on the Wall at this time.[18] This increased interest in Hadrian's Wall was partly the result of a campaign of excavation on the Antonine Wall that had been conducted from 1890 to 1893 by the Glasgow Archaeological Society.[19] The Vallum was the initial focus of archaeological attention, in a sustained effort to establish its chronological and topographical relationship to the curtain Wall and Wall forts.[20]

Collingwood later reviewed the significance of this work when he explored the scientific method of excavation adopted by Haverfield and developed by subsequent Wall scholars, observing:

> The problem of the Vallum was seriously attacked by ... scientific excavation ... In 1894 the late Professor Haverfield ... began the long series of diggings ... in which this problem was for the first time attacked with adequate weapons. At first the object was merely to trace the course of the Vallum in places where it was not revealed by surface indications; but in 1895 startling results began to emerge. At Birdoswald it had long been known that there was an extra fosse between the Vallum and the Wall: and ... the turf Wall was actually found by Haverfield's excavations ...[21]

The excavations close to Birdoswald helped to demonstrate the sequence of frontier works constructed there, including the newly-discovered turf Wall,

---

[15] Freeman (2007), 247–98. [16] E. Birley (1961), 28.
[17] ibid., 28–31, 65; Freeman (2007), 250, 255–72. [18] Freeman (2007), 255.
[19] Maxwell (1989), 13. [20] E. Birley (1961), 119.
[21] Collingwood (1921a), 59–60.

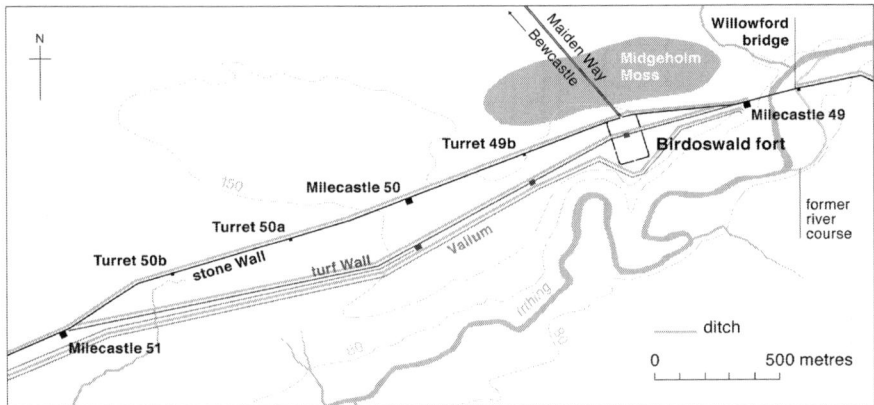

Fig. 12.3. A map of the major features of the Wall close to Birdoswald, where the turf Wall and the curtain Wall are built along different alignments. Drawn by Christina Unwin, after Wilmott (2009b), figure 307.

the stone curtain Wall, the Vallum, and the fort (Figure 12.3).[22] It swiftly became apparent that the turf Wall at Birdoswald had been replaced after a few years by the curtain Wall on a slightly different alignment further to the north. Later, it was shown that this turf Wall formed the first stage in construction from just east of Birdoswald to its western end at Bowness-on-Solway. These excavations revealed the structure and sequence of the turf and stone Walls and also confirmed the Hadrianic dating of the whole complex, including the Vallum, turrets, and milecastles, although the full picture of the sequence was only to emerge during the 1920s.

In 1899 Haverfield published an assessment of the results of the first five years of this project particularly addressing the turf Wall and discussing the evidence for the function and dating of the Vallum. He argued that the Vallum and turf Wall were both Hadrianic in date,[23] but by 1901 his confidence in this idea had been undermined by evidence from further excavation, leading him to draw a different conclusion. Haverfield then argued, on the basis of the discoveries around Birdoswald, that a Hadrianic turf Wall had once extended from sea to sea and that the curtain Wall actually dated to the reign of Severus.[24] This came to be known as 'The Turf Wall Theory', an idea that

---

[22] Simpson and Richmond (1935), 1; Wilmott *et al.* (2009), 204–6.
[23] Haverfield (1899a), 342.
[24] E. Birley (1961), 65; Freeman (2007), 271.

was, in turn, revised by information from excavations during the second decade of the twentieth century.[25]

Haverfield's work focused scholarly attention on the structure and chronology of the elements that made up the Wall. His other significant contribution to Wall studies was to formalize the international contacts that had been developing between British and German scholars. During the second half of the nineteenth century, John Collingwood Bruce and Thomas Hodgkin had made important contacts with a number of German ancient historians, including Theodor Mommsen and Emil Hübner.[26] Haverfield observed that in 1885 Mommsen had described the Roman Wall in England as 'the best known of all the great Roman military works', but noted that this was no longer the case as the 'Imperial Limes-Commission' (*Reichslimeskommission*) had been formed in 1892.[27] Representing a confederation of German archaeologists and antiquaries dedicated to the study of the Roman frontiers in Germany, this organization has been called a large 'patriotic-scientific project'.[28] The Reichstag had voted supplies to the Commission, together with the appointment of district commissioners superintended by a military and an archaeological director.[29] Efforts had been made over the previous three hundred years to locate and study the remains of the Roman frontier works along the Rhine and Danube, but the Limes-Commission led to far more systematic, sustained, and detailed study taking place. Contacts between those working on the Roman frontiers in Germany and Britain began to develop. The military director of the Limes-Commission, General Otto von Sarwey, visited the two Roman Walls of Britain in 1893, accompanied by Haverfield on a return trip to the German *Limes* later the same year.[30] In 1894 two men from Oxford, J. L. G. Mowat, and T. M. Crowder, accomplished the highly impressive objective of walking the entire length of the German frontier.[31]

Mommsen, who had played a significant role in the establishment of the Imperial Limes-Commission, was made an honorary member of the Society of Antiquaries of Newcastle of Newcastle upon Tyne in 1883. Haverfield was later to note that this was highly appropriate:

> For he had a sincere regard for our country, and, though he did not admire all our statesmen (he disliked Gladstone and Chamberlain about equally), he desired amity between England and Germany, and had many English friends. He took a vivid interest, too, in our northern antiquities of Roman date. He recognized that our Wall and military inscriptions were the most valuable evidences both for the history of the Roman army and for the history of the imperial frontier defenses.

---

[25] Collingwood (1921a), 61.
[26] Browning (1991); Freeman (2007), 251–5.
[27] Haverfield (1899a), 337; cf. Marchand (2003), 173; Struck (2001), 105.
[28] Marchand (2003), 174.   [29] Pelham (1906), 19–20.
[30] Freeman (2007), 252.   [31] Pelham (1906), 19 n. 2; Freeman (2007), 254 n. 29.

In particular he hoped that further comparison of our Wall and the German Limes would illuminate each work.[32]

Henry Pelham, who had been Haverfield's mentor in Oxford, was highly impressed by the work undertaken by the Limes-Commission. He observed that it had established the exact course of the German barrier, excavated more than seventy forts and studied smaller posts, watchtowers, and roads.[33] The interest of the German government in mapping and understanding the *Limes* at this time demonstrates the growth of their fascination with measures of Roman imperial control. During the 1890s Haverfield attempted to establish a state-supported project on Hadrian's Wall of a scale comparable with the German programme but, as Pelham noted, research in England remained in the hands of 'single scholars and local societies'.[34]

With regard to the excavations undertaken by Victorian Wall specialists, Haverfield observed that 'The spade was rarely used to prove theories which were suggested by the appearance of the ground'.[35] Haverfield's new programme of works on Hadrian's Wall drew upon the German example, developing their approach to targeted excavation. Margot Browning has argued that Haverfield's project was driven 'by a theoretical, comparative context that guided how and where excavations were planned and carried out', and that under the direct influence of Mommsen, the 'object of archae-ological enquiry' on Hadrian's Wall was 'historicized' by a technique of exca-vation which was informed by historical theory and method.[36] She has argued that this procedure was used to select sites for excavation according to questions in which 'the demands of theory and the realities of observation coincided'.

The immediate impact of Haverfield's work is evident in the arguments used by General Pitt-Rivers to justify an ambitious plan to excavate native settlements on his estate at Cranborne Chase (Dorset). Pitt-Rivers's aim was to study the 'agricultural districts' of southern Britain during the Roman period and he cited programmes of work already conducted on the 'towns and military works of the Roman Age',[37] a reference to the major project then being undertaken to provide a complete plan of the Roman city of Silchester in Hampshire.[38] For military works, Pitt-Rivers drew upon the excavations on the Roman Wall in Northumberland 'by a committee of North Country Antiquaries'.[39] At the start of the twentieth century, a new comprehension of the Roman province of *Britannia* began to develop, based on the study of

---

[32] Haverfield (1904), 187–8.
[33] Pelham (1906), 20.   [34] ibid., 19.   [35] Haverfield (1899a), 337.
[36] Browning (1991), 356. Browning does not draw sufficient attention, however, to the significant impact that the Victorian works on Hadrian's Wall had upon the research of the Limes-Commission (Anthony Birley pers. comm.).
[37] Pitt-Rivers (1898), 12.
[38] see Hingley (2008a), 302–6; Fulford (2007), 353–6.
[39] Pitt-Rivers (1898), 12.

Roman towns, villas, forts, and native settlements of which the new knowledge emerging about Hadrian's Wall formed a vital element.[40]

Haverfield's direct interest in fieldwork on the line of the Wall appears, however, to have ended in 1906. Eric Birley has argued that the fourth Pilgrimage to the Wall in 1906 was his 'farewell to excavation on the Wall',[41] although Haverfield was involved in the early years of the major excavations at Corbridge, which ran from 1906 to 1914.[42] Other excavators continued Haverfield's work, supplying valuable information that was drawn upon by Collingwood when he turned his attention to the scientific study of Hadrian's Wall during the early 1920s.

DEVELOPING THE SCIENCE OF ARCHAEOLOGY

Collingwood (1889–1943), who had been taught by Haverfield at Oxford, contributed to his mentor's fieldwork and publications, including the excavations at Corbridge.[43] Collingwood became a philosophy tutor at Pembroke College in 1912 and, after Haverfield's death in 1919, continued to teach philosophy and courses on Roman Britain.[44] He also maintained his fieldwork activities in northern Britain, but in 1934 he became Waynflete Professor of Metaphysical Philosophy in Oxford and his interest in Roman archaeology and the Wall subsequently declined. In a series of works published during the 1920s, Collingwood made a truly significant contribution to the archaeology of Roman Britain, an area of work that he called 'a small [field] ... and ripe for intensive cultivation'.[45] In particular, Collingwood was determined to continue Haverfield's collation of the evidence for the *Roman inscriptions of Britain*.[46] He also began a campaign to synthesize new information about the Wall, communicating important ideas through a number of highly influential papers.[47]

Collingwood appears to have had three main objectives for his work on the structure of the Wall: to establish the dates within which the construction of the system took place, the building sequence of its various components, and the purpose of the frontier system. Some of Collingwood's papers were highly significant since they challenged received ideas about the Wall's structure and purpose, and provided systematic summaries of current knowledge. He

---

[40] Haverfield (1906); Haverfield (1912); Haverfield (1924b); cf. Hingley (2008a), 307–21.
[41] E. Birley (1961), 32.
[42] Bishop (1994); Ewin (2000), 27–9; Freeman (2007), 281–98.
[43] Freeman (2007), 538–9.   [44] ibid., 36, 439.
[45] Collingwood (1939), 120.   [46] Collini and Williams (2004).
[47] including Collingwood (1921a); Collingwood (1921b); Collingwood (1929); Collingwood (1931).

worked very closely with F. G. Simpson, who had developed the earlier excavation methods and focused serious attention on the Stanegate, milecastles, Vallum, and turf Wall during the earlier years of the twentieth century.[48] Collingwood's summaries of research on the Wall, published in 1921 and 1931, will be examined in order to provide an idea of his approach.

Collingwood's paper, 'Hadrian's Wall: A History of the Problem', drew on the concept of 'science' as part of his search for a more rational approach to history.[49] In his study of antiquarian work on the Wall, Collingwood constructed a genealogy for the scientific approach he had derived from Haverfield. With regard to John Horsley's monograph of 1732, he proposed that 'we feel that we have emerged from a tentative and amateurish, a prescientific, study of the subject, in which grave oversights and fundamental errors are expected and pardoned, into an age of clear thinking, where problems are faced and evidence mustered in a scientific spirit.'[50] Collingwood is suggesting that Horsley's focus on science provided an excellent example, but it evidently did not result in the ending of amateur work. According to Collingwood, for example, John Clayton had 'systematically' bought up land along the line of the Wall, but his excavations at Chesters were 'not what we call scientific digging', since they destroyed much evidence without the types of detailed records that are considered important today.[51] Collingwood argued that, before Haverfield, antiquaries and archaeologists had dug sites simply because they were there. He quoted the Edwardian work at the Roman town of Silchester to provide an example of such relatively unplanned work, but he evidently also had in mind the earlier excavations that had been undertaken by Clayton along the Wall.

In his survey of the final phase of the study of the Wall, 'The Period of Scientific Excavation', Collingwood updated earlier arguments about the dating and nature of the various parts of the Wall. Collingwood stressed the significance of the work of John Pattison Gibson between 1891 and 1897 at Mucklebank Turret and Great Chesters.[52] Gibson had found three layers of occupation on the sites and began the process of establishing the chronology for the construction and occupation of the Wall. This new approach was based on the stratigraphy of the archaeological layers in some of the excavated structures along the Roman Wall together with the dating of artefacts.[53] Collingwood then demonstrated how 'the Turf Wall theory' outlined by Haverfield came to be undermined as a result of Gibson and Simpson's excavations on the curtain Wall at Birdoswald during 1909–11. Gibson and Simpson had conducted this work in the belief that it might establish the chronology of the

[48] E. Birley (1961), 65–6; Couse (1990).
[49] Collingwood (1921a); cf. Couse (1990), 74.   [50] Collingwood (1921a), 52.
[51] ibid., 55.   [52] Collingwood (1921a), 59; cf. Breeze (2003), 10.
[53] Collingwood (1921a), 59; cf. Breeze (2003), 10.

building of various sections of the Wall.[54] At one milecastle and three turrets, the excavators found evidence for three phases of use, the initial phase apparently dating to the early part of the second century. Gibson, Simpson, and Collingwood provided evidence that the stone curtain Wall was built under Hadrian and not under Severus,[55] an argument that is still accepted today.

Collingwood reprised Haverfield's earlier arguments by proposing that all the major elements of the frontier—the turf Wall, curtain Wall, Vallum, milecastles, and forts—had been built under Hadrian. He argued that they were constructed over a short period of six or seven years and then used for a considerable period of time, resulting in the three successive stratified deposits represented in the excavated structures. In a later article, Collingwood summed up research on the Wall by 1921, arguing that the sequence of building appeared to include the following successive steps: '(a) the Stanegate frontier, (b) the Vallum with small forts, (c) the enlargement of certain forts, and (d) the Wall'.[56] He noted that the *terminus ante quem* for the building of the curtain Wall was provided by the inscriptions naming the provincial governor Aulus Platorius Nepos (*c.* AD 122 to 127) found at several milecastles. Collingwood observed that from then on, attention could be focused on the chronology of the forts and details of the structural elements of the frontier, since the major issues of chronology had apparently been solved.[57]

Collingwood's article 'Hadrian's Wall: 1921–1930' focused on the changing ways in which work on the Wall had been conducted during the previous forty years with an emphasis on the increasing professionalization of the workforce.[58] He observed that the 'peculiarity of the problem' of the Wall related to the fact that the site was '73 miles long by, say, a quarter of a mile broad', and that, 'The strongest staff in the world, backed by all the financial resources at the disposal of British archaeology, could never have excavated these sixteen square miles in the way in which the Society of Antiquaries excavated Silchester. The excavation of Silchester took twenty years at that rate, to excavate the Wall would have taken two thousand.'[59] Collingwood then discussed a method of study primarily developed by Haverfield, observing that:

> The method of selective excavation is not the method traditionally employed by professional archaeologists. They have generally begun by thinking of a site as a unit that admits of complete excavation, and their ideal is to excavate it completely. While part of a site remains unexplored, they think that their duty to that site remains undone. Therefore, when they look at the digging hitherto done on the Wall, and this they have begun to do oftener in the last ten years, they are offended by its scrappiness, its incompleteness, in a word, its selectiveness. They would prefer, and they have been heard to advise, the complete excavation

[54] Collingwood (1921a), 61–2.   [55] ibid.; Couse (1990), 64; Freeman (2007), 277.
[56] Collingwood (1931), 40.   [57] Collingwood (1921a), 62.
[58] Collingwood (1931).   [59] ibid., 37.

of some chosen site on the Wall; in order that, in this one instance at least, we should know what the facts in their entirety are.

To this I would reply: the methods here in question are methods intended to increase our knowledge, not of Housesteads or Birdoswald or Chesterholm, but of the Wall. The Wall is our unit; and the Wall is a hundred times the size of Silchester. The only way in which we can hope to solve the problems of a site is to keep steadily before our minds an idea of the site as a whole, and to direct every detail of our work towards that idea. Where a site is so large as this, the difficulty of seeing it as a single unit is correspondingly great; and it is all the more necessary to insist on the idea, and to reject any proposed method of work that is not based upon it.[60]

Drawing on Haverfield's earlier observations, Collingwood noted that the tradition of study on the Wall had previously been largely amateur and, although this method had yielded dramatic results, since 1921:

there has grown up a generation of workers trained in Roman history and in the archaeology of the Roman provinces, who have turned to the Wall as a promising field for specialisation. They accept, as any one must who understands the problems of the Wall, the method of selective excavation; in fact, they delight in it, as a method scientifically superior to that of complete excavation.[61]

The scientific excavation methodology for work on the Wall that had emerged, according to Collingwood, during the 1890s had developed through the succeeding years.

He was to later observe in his autobiography that:

Haverfield and his colleagues in the Cumberland Excavation Committee in the eighteen-nineties had been consciously and completely Baconian in their methods. They never dug a trench without knowing exactly what information they were looking for . . . That is why they could settle highly intricate and abstruse problems at a cost of never more, and often much less, than thirty or forty pounds a year.[62]

In his own research on the Wall, Collingwood argued that he had used a 'logic of question and answer' to study the archaeological evidence.[63] This involved formulating the question to be answered before undertaking the digging work. Collingwood argued that, in turn, he had deliberately used the study of Roman Britain as an attempt to encourage a 'Baconian revolution' in historical studies.[64]

The nature of the work force was also changing. Collingwood observed that the study of the Wall had arrived at a point where 'professional archaeologists are willing to take it up and make it their chief occupation', although he noted

---

[60] ibid., 38.   [61] ibid., 38–9.   [62] Collingwood (1939), 124.
[63] ibid., 122.   [64] ibid., 133; cf. Browning (1995).

Fig. 12.4. A photograph of Eric Birley. Reproduced by permission of the Archaeology Department, Durham University.

that their number was 'small'.[65] The study of the Wall had clearly been put on a more serious footing by this time as part of the general professionalization of archaeology that took place during the 1920s and 1930s.[66] In 1926, the North of England Excavation Committee had been established and had already conducted some excavation work by the time Collingwood was writing.[67] The most significant of the new scholars involved in the study of the Wall was Eric Barff Birley (1906–1995; Figure 12.4).[68] This same year Collingwood had taken Birley to the Wall with a group of undergraduate students from Oxford, and, in addition, Birley dug with Collingwood at Bainbridge. After graduating from his degrees in Classics in 1928, Birley turned his attention to the Roman Wall.[69] Deciding that it would be vital to acquire a Roman fort if any long-term excavation was to be contemplated, with his father's assistance he purchased the Roman site of Vindolanda and the surrounding lands in 1929.[70] In 1930 Birley succeeded Simpson as director of the North of England Excavation Committee and in 1931 was

---

[65] Collingwood (1931), 39.
[66] cf. Hudson (1981), 129–30.   [67] E. Birley (1961), 66–7.
[68] It is notable that, of those involved in the study of the Wall at this time, Birley was the only real professional. Simpson was a shoe-factory owner and Gibson a photographer.
[69] Freeman (2007), 562–3.
[70] R. Birley (2009), 27. These lands were purchased during the selling off of the Clayton estate (Leach and Whitworth 2011, 17).

appointed lecturer at Armstrong College, Newcastle, then part of Durham University.[71]

Birley was later to move to the Durham part of the university where he established a powerful school of Roman study, becoming one of the most influential Wall scholars of the twentieth century.[72] He also followed Haverfield's campaign of the internationalization of research. The sixth Pilgrimage in 1930 had been attended by a number of archaeologists, including R. E. M. Wheeler, O. G. S. Crawford, M. V. Taylor, and James Curle.[73] Professor Gustav Behrens, a special delegate from the Limes-Commission, was also present; during the previous two years there had been increasing contact with researchers on the *Limes* and other Roman frontiers.[74] Birley was to build substantially on this cooperation with European frontier specialists, hosting the first Congress of Roman Studies in 1949, an event that attracted overseas colleagues to the conference in Newcastle.[75] He had originally planned the Congress for 1940, to follow the Pilgrimage due that year, although both had been cancelled due to the outbreak of the War.[76]

To return to Collingwood's 1931 paper, it summarized the new discoveries resulting from the detailed work of Wall scholars, including the determination that the curtain Wall was built in two contrasting forms, as a Broad Wall and a Narrow Wall, and that certain forts along the line of the Wall were constructed after the curtain Wall had been completed.[77] It was subsequently argued that the forts along the line of the Wall were secondary to the planning of the curtain Wall, but this was not evident to Collingwood at this time.[78] Collingwood's article also set out the evidence for the continuation of the system of forts and turrets along the Cumberland coast.[79] He continued to argue that the Vallum represented a frontier work, supplied with a number of forts, which predated the construction of the curtain Wall.[80] This interpretation was later overthrown when it was demonstrated that the line of the Vallum deviated to avoid elements of the stone Wall and, therefore, appeared to have been slightly later in date.[81]

Collingwood produced several additional papers that were to prove highly significant. In one article, he observed that the Roman sites along the Wall were referred to through the use of local place names but that a new, more systematic method of notation was now required.[82] He noted that:

> we know that Hadrian's Wall was divided into more or less equal lengths of about one Roman mile by its so-called milecastles (the place of a milecastle being

---

[71] E. Birley (1961), 66; R. Birley (2009), 28.
[72] Freeman (2007), 563; S. James (2002), 17–26.   [73] E. Birley (1961), 36.
[74] ibid., 36–7.   [75] E. Birley (1952).   [76] Anthony Birley (pers. comm.).
[77] Collingwood (1931), 47, 65.   [78] cf. RFa, 34.   [79] Collingwood (1931), 57–60.
[80] ibid., 59.   [81] E. Birley (1961), 122–3; Couse (1990), 71–3.
[82] Collingwood (1929), 108.

sometimes taken by a fort), and each mile into three more or less equal parts by two turrets, the place of a turret, again, sometimes taken by a fort. The present proposal is to use this ready-made system of divisions to facilitate references to the parts of the Wall itself and to the forts, milecastles, turrets and other structures on its line...Every turret and milecastle has its own number, and any point on the line of the Wall can be referred to as so many yards east or west of the center-line of the nearest milecastle or turret.

This scheme was adopted and adapted by later Wall scholars. Eric Birley argued that, but for Collingwood's numbering scheme, it would be 'all but impossible' to produce intelligible studies of the Wall's construction.[83] This scheme has been used on Ordnance Survey maps, in the various editions of the *Handbook,* and on the new map of the Wall produced by English Heritage in 2010.

THE FUNCTION OF THE WALL

Collingwood also used his methodological clear thinking to address the important problem of the 'precise object' of the builders of the Wall.[84] He argued that:

> It has always been assumed that the Wall was a military work in the fullest sense, a continuous fortification like the wall of a town, designed to repel or at least to check invading armies...The Roman troops have always been imagined lining the top of the Wall and from that strong position, entrenched as it were on the rampart-walk behind the parapet, repelling the attack of Caledonian armies that attempted to carry the work by breach or escalade.

He allowed that circumstances supported this defensive idea—including the height and size of the Wall and its position on top of raised ground in many places—but he argued that other observations did not. He identified four particular issues.[85]

First, with reference to Kipling's observations in *Puck of Pook's Hill,* Collingwood noted that the defensive function attributed to the Wall would require archers or artillery fighting to be stationed on top of the Wall. Like many young men of his generation, Collingwood had been gripped by Kipling's account of the Roman Wall,[86] but he specifically noted that there was little evidence to support the idea that archers were usually present along the line of the Wall.[87]

---

[83] E. Birley (1961), 67. [84] Collingwood (1921b), 4. [85] ibid., 4–6.
[86] Inglis (2009), 69. [87] Collingwood (1921b), 5.

Second, taking issue with Kipling's description of the curtain Wall, he argued that the Wall-walk could not have been more than three or four feet wide and would have provided, at the most, 'a very narrow fighting-front'. He noted that:

> It would be practically impossible to reinforce a threatened point, even in the most favourable conditions; wholly impossible to move wounded men. And a few corpses, or a couple of Caledonians who had effected an escalade, would block the walk entirely. . . . Let anyone try to imagine a front-line trench during an attack, with the conditions that the 'trench' is a wall-top fifteen feet from the ground and that access can only be had at points 500 yards apart, the turrets taking the place of communication trenches: and he will recognize the impossibility of fighting on the Wall in the traditional way.

These comments clearly reflect observations derived from trench warfare during the First World War, particularly the image of soldiers entrenched on the walkway.[88] Although Collingwood had worked at a desk job in the Admiralty for the course of the War,[89] he would have been all too aware of the character of trench warfare from survivors, which led him to conclude that the top of the Wall could not have provided an effective fighting platform.

Third, Collingwood noted that the top of the Wall would not be wide enough for the installation of artillery, catapults, and ballistas, contradicting the images of the Wall in *Puck* that had portrayed ballista on the top of the turrets (Figures 11.2 and 11.6). Drawing upon the images of turrets carved on Trajan's Column, he proposed that the Wall turrets were used for signalling.[90] He noted that some later Roman fortifications—including the Roman forts along the south and east coasts of Britain and a number of Roman town walls—had bastions that might have been used for artillery, but that these were never added to Hadrian's Wall.

Fourth and in conclusion, Collingwood proposed that the continuous line represented by the curtain Wall was designed at first to indicate where Roman territory ended, but this was supplemented by the 'secondary function . . . of being an obstacle to smugglers, or robbers, or other undesirables'.[91] He argued that the Vallum was a 'frontier-mark' and the Wall 'an elevated sentry-walk'.[92] Collingwood clearly considered that Roman soldiers were able to walk along the top of the Wall.[93] Arguing that the area through which the Wall ran was always more or less disturbed, he proposed that the patrolled Wall prevented minor disturbances from becoming more dangerous. If a substantial hostile force arrived, Collingwood proposed that the Roman army would move out to fight them beyond the Wall.[94] Therefore, as he was later to emphasize, the

[88] cf. Crow (2004b), 130.   [89] Collini and Williams (2004).
[90] Collingwood (1921b), 6.   [91] ibid., 7–8.   [92] ibid., 8–9.
[93] Breeze (2008a), 1.   [94] Collingwood (1921b), 9.

function of the Wall was to serve as 'an elevated sentry-walk and an obstacle to raiders'.[95] Collingwood also discussed the function of the Wall in his influential book, *Roman Britain*, stating that:

> In spite of the impressive appearance of this huge fortification . . . it was not in the ordinary sense a military work. It was not intended to stop invading armies of Caledonians, while Roman soldiers lined the parapet and repelled attempts at escalade. . . . The Wall was an obstacle, but an obstacle not so much to armies as to smugglers and raiding parties; and the troops stationed on it were there to patrol it on the watch for such parties, not to defend it against concerted attack. If we want an analogy in modern times, we shall find one not in the continuous lines of trench warfare but in the Indian 'customs-hedge' built by the English in 1843 for prevention of smuggling in salt, and patrolled for thirty-five years by 14,000 officers and men . . . [96]

The Indian Customs Hedge was a British colonial frontier that had been established during the 1840s as a line to manage the tax collected on salt and to deter smuggling,[97] consequently giving rise to salt starvation and the deaths of vast numbers of people.[98] It is clear that this frontier work was not a defensive barrier, since it was used specifically to control and tax the movement of salt rather than people. Henry Pelham had referred to the '"Customs Hedge" in India' as a potential parallel for the palisades of Roman date on a section of the German *Limes* and it is likely that Collingwood picked up his reference to this colonial frontier from this source.[99] Pelham observed that 'it is inconceivable that [this] palisade was ever intended as an effective defense in time of war'. Collingwood drew upon Pelham's observations to redefine the function of Hadrian's Wall as a less directly defensive structure than had formerly been supposed. Collingwood was also drawing on Lord Curzon's lecture on 'Frontiers', held at the Sheldonian Theatre in Oxford in 1907, which had provided a well-informed exploration of their historical contexts.[100]

Collingwood's argument for the Wall as a means of controlling smuggling and raiding had an immediate impact. Jessie Mothersole helped to popularize the idea of the Wall as an elevated sentry-walk in the third edition of her accessible book.[101] This idea was adopted by many later Wall scholars,[102] although the argument that Hadrian's Wall was a more directly defensive

---

[95] Collingwood (1927), 26.   [96] Collingwood (1923), 30–2.

[97] Moxham (2001), 70.

[98] ibid., 141–2. The Customs Hedge was abandoned later in the nineteenth century.

[99] Pelham (1906), 37–8.

[100] Curzon (1907). This lecture referred to the Roman frontiers and the Indian Customs Hedge as examples (Hingley 2000), 44–5.

[101] Mothersole (1924), xi–xii.   [102] Breeze (2008a); Couse (1990), 67.

frontier work has never entirely been abandoned and, indeed, has re-emerged during the past ten years,[103] as we shall see in Chapter 14.

SCIENTIFIC AND PRE-SCIENTIFIC UNDERSTANDINGS

Collingwood argued that the forty years after 1890 witnessed the introduction of scientific method for the study of the Roman Wall and he saw this as a period of professionalization, in which funding became available for a few archaeologists to commence full-time study, replacing the pre-existing tradition of the amateur. In Collingwood's terms, there was a transition from the amateur excavations of Clayton's generation to the professional problem-orientated work of Haverfield, Gibson, Simpson, and others. Phil Freeman has shown that Haverfield's excavations were not actually as well planned and recorded as Collingwood's comments would suggest,[104] but it is certainly true that, under the influence of Mommsen, Haverfield was the first to focus sustained interest on the disentanglement of the chronology of the individual elements of the Wall. Simpson, Collingwood, and others then adopted this analytical approach. It would have been difficult for earlier Wall scholars to establish the detailed chronology and sequence of the structures that made up the Roman frontier, since the important work that established the chronological sequence of Roman pottery only commenced during the later nineteenth century.[105]

In the writings of both Haverfield and Collingwood there is a conscious distancing from the antiquarian scholarship of previous generations. Collingwood characterized the pre-scientific work on the Wall as 'a tentative and amateurish . . . study of the subject, in which grave oversights and fundamental errors are expected and pardoned', while the scientific approach is characterized as 'an age of clear thinking'.[106] Under Collingwood's scientific approach to the Wall's structure, the focus was upon accounting for its detailed form and the sequence of its construction. The function of the Wall was determined through a comparable process and the individual elements along its line, the milecastles and turrets, were systematically numbered from east to west. Collingwood argued that his philosophy of question and answer was the best way to pursue such issues, while the methodology that he worked out for studying the Wall provided a scientific way to proceed. It is easy to see why Collingwood was so appreciative of the work of John Horsley, since the methods pursued from the 1890s drew on the analytical studies of some

---

[103] Bidwell (2008).   [104] Freeman (2007), 262–8.
[105] cf. C. R. Smith (1848); Maxfield (1982), 73–4.   [106] Collingwood (1921a), 52.

antiquaries.[107] Collingwood's systematic approach has focused the interests of architects, historians, and philosophers, and his contributions to the disciplines of history and philosophy have elevated his works on the Wall to a level of interest that has created an interdisciplinary audience.[108]

Collingwood posed the question 'why so elaborate a tissue of archaeological minutiae has been allowed to engage the writer's attention for ten more years' and answered with three reasons: 'First, the history of the Roman Empire is the history of the most important experiment known to us in conscious political co-operation among peoples widely differing in race, language, traditions and civilisations. At the present crisis in the history of the world, it concerns us to know how such an experiment succeeded and how it failed.'[109] The need to examine the sequence of the buildings of the Wall in such detail is because 'the Romans were always better at doing things than at talking about them'. It appears that the Roman example, and the archaeology of the Wall in particular, were useful for considering the difficult international situation developing during the early 1930s, since Collingwood argued that the issue of how the Roman provinces were civilized and defended could only be addressed through archaeological means. This echoes the earlier comments of Edwardian writers, including Kipling, about the significance of comparative studies that addressed the assimilation of colonial subjects and also those writings that had explored the defense of Roman frontiers.[110]

Collingwood's second and third reasons are more complex and they articulated the value of the study of the Wall in the establishment of the solidity and analytical structure of history.[111] Collingwood argued that the justification for the collection of the apparently 'pointless and fruitless minutiae of evidence' lay in the scientific and systematic approach to history.[112] He concluded:

> The more tedious the detail, the more apparently irrelevant the facts are to each other and to the whole, the more important it is to show that here, and not only in the visible symmetry of classical Greece or the intellectual glory of the Renaissance, reason still reigns; there is still a thread, if one can find it; there is not chaos, but order and intelligibility.[113]

Earlier in this article, Collingwood had made the claim that the real reason why the Wall had attracted particular notice in Britain during the early twentieth century is that previously work was so 'excellent in scientific quality, so well conceived in its methods and so well established in its result, that by degrees, it forced itself on the attention of archaeologists and historians outside the north of England'.[114] It will be argued below that it is rather

[107] cf. M. Hunter (1995), 181–200.
[108] cf. Bamford (2002), 250–1; Browning (1991); Browning (1995); Couse (1990).
[109] Collingwood (1931), 61.   [110] cf. Hingley (2000), 42–8.
[111] cf. Browning (1995).   [112] Collingwood (1931), 62.
[113] ibid., 63.   [114] ibid., 39.

more likely that the fame of the Wall resulted from the popularity of one particular piece of creative writing, Rudyard Kipling's *Puck of Pook's Hill*, but it is also doubtlessly true that the scholarly work from the 1890s to the 1930s added to the Wall's standing in the eyes of the public.

UNDERMINING CERTAINTY

Collingwood's writings demonstrate his considerable confidence in the fact that research on the Wall was producing clear thinking about its chronology, structure, and function, but subsequent commentators have attributed less value to this work. Eric Birley observed that Collingwood's contributions to the study of the Wall have not all stood the test of time,[115] while G. S. Couse observed that Collingwood remained 'confident as a matter of faith' that the 'complex problem of Hadrian's Wall would ultimately yield to rigorous investigation',[116] an idea that later research has not always supported.

Ian Richmond (1902–1965) had a deep interest in the Roman military and undertook significant research on Hadrian's Wall during the late 1920s.[117] He was appointed lecturer at Armstrong College in Newcastle in 1935 and conducted a number of excavations on the Wall and at other Roman sites in the north. Richmond argued that work upon the Wall between 1929 and 1939 had resulted in a situation in which 'the principal periods in the history of the monument were firmly fixed and the complicated relationship between its component parts was securely defined', and that more recent work had filled some gaps in knowledge.[118] David Breeze has observed that, once a number of specific issues about the Wall had been solved to Richmond's satisfaction, he turned his attention elsewhere, to the outpost forts and further north to the legionary fort at Inchtuthil in Scotland.[119]

Certainly, the work of the period between 1890 and 1939 did lead to a significant improvement in the available knowledge about the sequence and dating of the Wall and some conclusions remain relevant today, including the Hadrianic dating of much of the frontier complex. Nevertheless, it is difficult not to feel that, as more work has been conducted to address the physical structure of the Wall, questions have become more and more specific and detailed. The systematic and careful study of the structure and sequence of Wall elements is certainly warranted, but this does not necessarily improve understanding and certainly does not create comprehensive answers. David Breeze has argued that by the mid 1930s those leading the work on Hadrian's

---

[115] E. Birley (1961), 67.   [116] Couse (1990), 74.
[117] Birley revised by Todd (2004).   [118] Richmond (1950), 43.
[119] Breeze (2003), 13; cf. Crow (1991), 51.

Wall stated forcefully the belief that all the main problems of the frontier had been solved, an idea that still endures in the mind of the public.[120] Simon James has focused on a rather different interpretation but has also stressed the lack of innovation in Roman frontier studies since the 1970s.[121] The need for new approaches to the Wall reflects the observation that the archaeology of the monument is in reality not actually particularly well known.[122]

Subsequent work has demonstrated that the confidence shown by Collingwood, Richmond, and others in the security of knowledge about the Wall was at least partly misplaced. Matthew Symonds and David Mason have observed that:

> Establishing the chronological relationship between the key Wall elements was a major research priority in the first half of the twentieth century. While considerable progress was made, major gaps in knowledge still remain. The dating of many of the changes and adaptations to the Wall and its associated structures remains imprecise, while some relationships have become more complicated in the face of new discoveries.[123]

In addition to establishing the exact sequence and location of the features that make up Hadrian's Wall, archaeologists are far from confident about being able to answer some of the more important general questions raised by the works undertaken from the 1890s to 1940s. Couse has provided a list of some questions that remain puzzling: 'Why was a turf Wall originally built in the western sector? Why was the decision made to change the width of the curtain Wall or to move forts up to the line of the Wall? Why was the Hadrianic frontier composed of two barriers, the Wall and the Vallum?'[124] Recent work has explored the Vallum through field inspection and excavation, but this has not clearly replaced the understandings articulated by a number of earlier authors, including those of Simpson and Shaw in their innovative article of 1922.[125] We appear to be no closer to answering Couse's questions than was the case in the 1930s.

SUMMARY: ARCHAEOLOGICAL KNOWLEDGE

From the perspective adopted in this book, gaps in knowledge of the Wall—its form, sequence, meaning, and nature—provide an opportunity rather than a problem. It is vital to open the monument up once more to the type of lively

---

[120] Breeze (2008a), 3; cf. Breeze (2003), 13.
[121] S. James (2002), 5; S. James (2005); cf. Freeman (1996), 468; Hingley (2008b).
[122] Breeze (2008a), 3.   [123] RFb, 9.   [124] Couse (1990), 75.
[125] N. Hodgson (2009b), 29; Wilmott (2008), 127.

debate that occurred for much of the late nineteenth and early twentieth centuries—Hadrian's Wall is best served by viewing it as a 'Debatable land',[126] an area of debate that is not in the ownership of any one body of scholars. Indeed, stressing the uncertainty of our knowledge about the Wall increases, rather than decreases, the significance of the surviving remains of this living monument. Part of the process required to encourage lively research involves the continuing need to undermine the inherited idea that we have a comprehensively accurate and reliable understanding of the form, role, function, and character of Hadrian's Wall; it is far preferable to view knowledge and understanding as cumulative and ongoing. If the tradition of relative certainty is not critiqued, it will prove difficult to transform our knowledge of the monument.[127]

Jean Baudrillard has argued that the 'demand for authenticity is, strictly speaking...an obsession with certainty—specifically, certainty as to the origins, date, author and signature of a work.'[128] From the 1850s, the attention paid by Wall scholars to the authorship and Roman history of the Wall has placed a particular emphasis on separating its Roman history from its survival as a physical monument in post-Roman times. The true history of the Wall, from the perspective developed by Haverfield, Simpson, and Collingwood, focused upon its origins and its adaptation during Roman times. Once the Roman empire had fallen in the West and the Wall had become disused during the early fifth century, the significant history of the Wall as an archaeological structure is seen to have ceased. This form of reasoning contrasts markedly with the work of artists, illustrators, poets, novelists, and amateur antiquaries in reconstructing the Wall as a living phenomenon and emphasizes a growing divide between art and scholarship that evolved during the twentieth century. The archaeological focus on the origin, authorship, and signature of the monument contradicts the idea of the Wall as a living spirit and relegates mythical forms of knowledge to the status of folklore and art that can be set aside and ignored by analysts.

The archaeological exploration of Hadrian's Wall has drawn upon the techniques of field survey, mapping, excavation, stratigraphy, and artefact dating to construct knowledge of the monument's form and sequence. At the same time, this approach requires an absolute barrier to be constructed between past and present, in which the past is distinctly knowable but also 'closed', since it is viewed as entirely over and is perceived as existing on a different plane of reality.[129] The task for the archaeologist is to obtain the

---

[126] In addition to referring to the medieval border lands between England and Scotland, this term has been used in literary studies to address intellectual territories in which property rights are not firmly established (Lamont and Rossington 2007, 1–2).

[127] Hingley (2008c).   [128] Baudrillard (2005), 81.

[129] Blain and Wallis (2007), 33–4.

fullest possible knowledge of the past through a methodological exploration of the physical remains in the current landscape and to separate knowledge of these traces from myth, artistry, and speculation. The archaeological actions of survey, mapping, excavation, post-excavation, and interpretation bring the remains of the monument into a direct relationship with today, but these are separated off by the construction of a linear sense of time which isolates its Roman character from the present. The monument becomes effectively dead—a product of a past society, highly relevant and accessible in the present but also entirely closed to imaginative interpretation.

The archaeological focus on the 'closed' Wall ignores the issue that those who excavate and survey the Wall actively help to construct the monument, both metaphorically and physically. If the methods used by archaeologists in the actions of fieldwork and post-excavation are performed thoroughly and well, the Wall's physical characteristics have a considerable impact upon the conclusions that are drawn from detailed fieldwork and excavation. This is precisely why it is important to protect and manage the surviving traces of Hadrian's Wall, in order to retain as much of the Wall in an undisturbed condition so that it can retain its Roman character. It is also why the implementation of a systematic and clear methodology for archaeological research is vital, since this provides a series of standards for adoption in the field against which archaeological projects can be assessed.

The requirement to construct *absolute* archaeological certainty for the Wall reflects the need felt by concerned individuals, including archaeologists, to map, identify, and define the monument so that its nationally and internationally important remains can be protected, interpreted, and managed. This requires the demarcation of *the* Roman Wall from the later activities that have occurred along its line. Archaeologists usually view later actions that have impacted upon the Wall as unwarranted damage to the Roman structure, as in the example of the eighteenth-century military road. The role of archaeologists is perceived as disentangling *the* Roman Wall from later and irrelevant accretions and increasingly this function has taken on the need to defend these ancient remains from inappropriate modern development. The next chapter will explore a serious threat to the iconic section of the Wall on Whin Sill that emerged in 1930, which led to the strengthening of the measures available for the protection and management of this important landscape. The response of the establishment to this threat reflected the efforts of Haverfield and Collingwood to communicate the Wall's importance through the developing science of archaeology.

13

Whin Sill: Defending Ancient Springs

unless the island is conquered by some civilized nation, there will soon be
no trace of the Wall left. Nay, even the splendid whinstone crags on which
it stands will be all quarried away to mend the roads of our urban and
rural authorities.

Cadwallader Bates (1895), 47

INTRODUCTION

This chapter will focus upon two disputes that arose in 1930 and 1957
respectively, events that drew attention to the protection of the archaeological remains of the best-preserved section of Hadrian's Wall. The first
of these public arguments was over the threat posed by quarrying. Large-
scale extraction had commenced during the nineteenth century at several
sites along the central section of the Wall and in some areas substantially
destroyed the fabric of the Wall (Figure 13.1). In 1930 it was proposed that
stone should be extracted on a large scale at Shield on the Wall, six kilometres to the west of Housesteads. These works, if permitted, would have
created a very serious impact on the physical fabric and setting of the best-
preserved and most atmospheric part of the Wall, and the growing public
appreciation of the importance of these remains gave rise to a strong
resistance to the scheme. This chapter will initially assess the popularity of
the Wall and the response of the establishment to the threat of quarrying,
which swiftly led to a strengthening of the ancient monument legislation in
order to protect the monument. It will also explore the subsequent designation, management, consolidation, and display of this increasingly famous
section of the Wall, including an assessment of the current significance of
this iconic landscape.

Fig. 13.1. A section of the Wall that has been destroyed by quarrying just to the east of Carvoran. The Wall formerly ran through the area just to the right of the lake. Photograph by Richard Hingley, 2011.

QUARRYING AND PROTECTING THE WALL

Casual robbing of the Roman Wall for stone had occurred since the seventh century, its material reused in the building of the monasteries at Hexham, Jarrow, and Monkwearmouth. Extensive robbing continued during medieval times through to the eighteenth century, when Wall stone was used for constructing castles, churches, and country houses on and close to its line.[1] In the 1750s, a large quantity of stone from the monument was incorporated into the bottoming of the new military road that ran from Newcastle to Carlisle. Stukeley attempted to have the new military road moved to avoid damage to the monument and William Hutton tried to dissuade a local landowner from destroying a section of the curtain Wall during his visit in 1801.[2] Cadwallader Bates argued that the process of quarrying would, eventually, lead to the entire destruction of the whinstone Crags on which the Wall stands.[3]

Prior to the late 1920s, the Wall had little or no legal protection and its remains were almost entirely in private ownership. By this time, many sections had been destroyed, levelled, and obscured as a result of agricultural operations and urban developments, particularly in the lowland areas to the east and west of the Wall's line. Extensive damage through quarrying had also occurred

---

[1] Eaton (2000), 25–6; Whitworth (2000), 7–14.
[2] Hutton (1802), 202–6.   [3] Bates (1895), 47.

at several places in the central section.[4] Just to the east of Carvoran, the ninth edition of the *Handbook* notes the destruction of a turret and a considerable length of curtain Wall by Greenhead Quarry Company.[5] Alfred Wainwright noted in *A Pennine Journey* (1938) that at this place 'a vast quarry is eating into the hill with great bites'.[6]

Measures had been taken to protect the Wall and its landscape since the mid nineteenth century. John Clayton had acquired considerable areas of the central section, undertaking extensive excavation work and consolidating what came to be known as the 'Clayton Wall'. At South Shields in 1880, the Town Council turned the excavated remains of the fort into a 'Roman Remains and People's Park'. Housesteads and the sections of the Wall nearby remained in the hands of Clayton's successors after his death and continued to be protected until 1929 when these parts of the estate were auctioned following the financial difficulties of John Morris ('Jack') Clayton.[7] Housesteads fort and a section of the Wall were gifted to the National Trust, while Professor Trevelyan, who had purchased Housesteads Farm, donated it to the Trust, of which he was vice-president, in 1934.[8]

The parts of the monument not owned by the National Trust, however, had little or no protection. The initial Ancient Monument legislation was enacted in 1882 but the first section of Hadrian's Wall was not added until the production of the Fifth List of Ancient Monuments. An article in *The Illustrated London News* of 16 August 1924 noted that 'The Office of Works has taken steps to have the Roman Wall officially "scheduled" for preservation. This means that owners and occupiers of land over which it extends cannot interfere with it, except by authority of the Department, and are liable for any damage done to it'.[9] In December 1928, much of the Wall was scheduled under a joint entry for Cumberland and Northumberland.[10] Nevertheless, this legislation had little impact on the rights of landowners.

Early in 1930, the serious quarrying threat to the Wall emerged. This danger to the Wall was the result of the purchasing of the mineral rights for much of the land in the Wall's central section by John Wake of Darlington.[11] Wake's company, called 'Roman Stones Limited', planned to quarry for road stone at Shield on the Wall and to extract up to 200,000 tons of whinstone a year from the area that included Shield on the Wall, Peel Crag, and Housesteads.[12] Despite the promise of local jobs and considerable local support for the quarrying plans, a substantial campaign was organized to oppose the development. Jim Crow

---

[4] Leach and Whitworth (2011), 15.   [5] J. C. Bruce (1933), 160–1.
[6] Wainwright (1987), 127; cf. Breeze (2006a), 279.
[7] Woodside and Crow (1999), 92; Leach and Whitworth (2011), 12.
[8] ibid, 17.   [9] ibid.
[10] Whitworth (2000), 52; Leach and Whitworth (2011), 15.
[11] Allason-Jones and McIntosh (forthcoming); Woodside and Crow (1999), 93.
[12] Crow (2004a), 137.

has called this a 'remarkable display of establishment support' for the preservation of the Wall and its landscape. As a result of lengthy deliberations, the quarrying was prohibited.

PUBLIC APPRECIATION

In a letter to *The Times* of 19 April 1930, the eminent historian Professor George Macaulay Trevelyan raised serious concerns about the new proposal to extract substantial quantities of stone from a proposed quarry close to Housesteads.[13] Trevelyan (1876–1962) was a historian, public educator, and conservationist.[14] His father had inherited Wallington Hall in 1886, a formative influence on Trevelyan's attitude to the landscape. In 1927 he was appointed Regius Professor of modern history at Cambridge and Trevelyan became deeply involved in conservation during the 1930s, including important work for the National Trust. In his letter Trevelyan observed that:

> For a generation past public interest about the Romans in Britain has been growing in this island in all classes of community. 'Puck of Pooks Hill' has made 'the Wall' dear and familiar to children and grown-ups. The study of Roman Britain, conducted under great archaeologists like Haverfield and his successors, has become a principal part of the historical sciences and our popular culture. The number of visitors to, and walkers along, the Wall is increasing by leaps and bounds.[15]

The following year, Collingwood picked up on the second of Trevelyan's reasons for the growing popularity of the Wall when he argued that the growth in public appreciation resulted from the high quality of the scientific archaeological work that had been undertaken by Haverfield and his successors. He remarked, 'It is because of this growing appreciation of the work done on the Wall, among persons qualified to judge of its merits, that the Wall itself is more talked of and thought about among the public at large; and [that] there is now general consternation in the country that the Wall is insufficiently protected against wanton destruction.'[16] There is little quantitative information to indicate how many people were visiting the Wall at this time, although it is known that Housesteads Roman fort received 15,000 visitors in 1935.[17] This demonstrates that a wider public appreciation of the monument had developed during the early twentieth century.

Rudyard Kipling's *Puck of Pook's Hill* was circulating very widely at this time, enthusing many of its readers,[18] including artists, archaeologists, politicians, and

---

[13] G. Trevelyan (1930).   [14] Cannadine (2004).   [15] G. Trevelyan (1930).
[16] Collingwood (1931), 39.   [17] Crow (2004a), 140.   [18] Whittaker (1994,) 2.

military men. Charles Carrington remarked that the three stories of Roman centurions defending Hadrian's Wall presented a 'panegyric of military duty and service' which strengthened the resolve of many young soldiers in the 'dark days of 1915 and 1941'.[19] Letters sent by Major Reggie Chenevix Trench to his relatives from the Western Front in 1917–1918 clearly demonstrate the power of this particular novel, particularly the stories of the Roman centurion Parnesius, defending Hadrian's Wall against the assault of the barbarians.[20]

Kipling's work inspired other published accounts of the Wall. Maria Hoyer's book of reminiscences of a holiday on the Wall contains a poem that mused on the contemporary imperial significance of the Wall.[21] Jessie Mothersole produced a popular book entitled *Hadrian's Wall* in which she noted that she had followed in Kipling's steps by staying at the George Inn at Chollerford.[22] Arthur Weigall's *Wanderings in Roman Britain* also shows the growing popularity of Roman Britain with the general public. The individual chapters were first serialized in the *Daily Mail* and the book went through four editions during its first year of publication. Weigall aimed to encourage the British public to visit Roman monuments, including a substantial discussion of Hadrian's Wall, 'one of the most awe-inspiring relics of the power of Rome in the whole world'.[23] The book's popularity reflects Weigall's commitment to communicate the significance of Roman Britain to as wide an audience as possible.

The same year saw the publication of the first edition of R. G. Collingwood's *A Guide to the Roman Wall*. Earlier authors, including Warburton and Bruce, had attempted to provide conveniently sized accounts of the Wall for visitors, but Collingwood's short and inexpensive paperback guide was aimed at a far wider audience. Collingwood observed that:

> In the past its visitors have been mostly historians and antiquaries, and it has been for their use that previous descriptions have generally been designed. But lately it has ceased to be a preserve of scholars and has become a resort of the general public. It is now attracting year by year an increasing number of people who, without any claim to being archaeologists, take an interest in the relics of the past; and so happily does it combine the imaginative appeal of its fabric and history with the fascination of its varied and picturesque scenery that the visitor must be hard to please who does not think his visit well spent.[24]

DEFENDING ANCIENT SPRINGS

The growing prominence of the Wall and its landscape during the first thirty years of the twentieth century explains the response of the establishment to the

---

[19] Carrington (1955), 381.   [20] Fletcher (2004), 31–2.   [21] Hoyer (1908), vi.
[22] Mothersole (1924), 82.   [23] Weigall (1926), 106.   [24] Collingwood (1926), 3.

threat posed by the new quarry. Several articles of opposition appeared in *The Times* from April to July 1930, including one letter sent in April headed 'Strong protest by Antiquaries'.[25] This noted that 'Hadrian's Wall, which in ancient days withstood the inroads of barbarism and for centuries has offered a stout resistance to time and weather, is now threatened with violence in a new form.' The Society of Antiquaries of Newcastle had raised 'local concern' but the paper noted that the threat was 'national' because of the significance of the Wall. By 26 April, *The Illustrated London News* had picked up the story, featuring a short item accompanied by photographs of the Wall and a very impressive double-spread reconstruction of the fort at Housesteads.[26] On 21 June 1930, the *News* contained a short article entitled 'Defending Hadrian's Wall from Other Perils Than Quarrying: A Raid', accompanied by a coloured reprint of Robert Spence's painting of barbarians storming Housesteads.[27] On 29 July, *The Times* published a further letter—signed by Rudyard Kipling, Charles Oman, H. A. L. Fisher, Josiah C. Wedgewood, John Buchan, George Macdonald, and Philip E. Pilditch—requesting that the government minister, Mr Lansbury, should protect the Wall from the quarrying, noting that 'tentative' quarrying operations had already begun.[28]

Under considerable pressure, Lansbury agreed to organize a conference for archaeologists and interested Members of both Houses of Parliament.[29] This was held in the House of Commons at Westminster on the 4 November and a note from the Parliamentary Correspondent of *The Times* recorded the proceedings.[30] Many supporters demonstrated their opposition to the quarry by sending 'letters of sympathy' or by attending the meeting. They included all the signatories to the letter previously published in *The Times* and a number of additional famous names, including Stanley Baldwin, Lloyd George, Mortimer Wheeler, and R. G. Collingwood. Lansbury noted at the meeting that he had 'every hope' that the new Ancient Monuments Bill would be passed during this session of Parliament.[31] On 11 June 1931, an Amending Act had been passed to strengthen the Ancient Monuments Act.[32] The 'Roman Wall and Vallum Preservation Order' gave some measure of effective legal protection to extensive areas of the monument and the immediate quarrying threat to the west of Housesteads was removed.[33]

---

[25] *The Times* (1930a). Leach and Whitworth provide a detailed discussion of the response to the quarrying threat (2011, 18–52).

[26] *Illustrated London News* (1930a).

[27] *Illustrated London News* (1930b).

[28] *The Times* (1930b); see Allason-Jones and McIntosh (forthcoming) and Leach and Whitworth (2011), 48–9.

[29] Crow (2004a), 138.   [30] *The Times* (1930c).

[31] ibid; Leach and Whitworth (2011), 50.

[32] Crow (2004a), 138.   [33] Ewin (2000), 43–4.

Despite this strengthening of the legislation, quarrying continued on the line of the Wall at Walltown close to Carvoran until 1943, when further extraction was only prevented by costly compensation provided by the government.[34] At this time, a photograph taken by the influential photographer, Bill Brandt, illustrated a *Picture Post* article on the 'The Threat to the Great Wall'.[35] Through the strengthening of the Ancient Monuments Acts, the protection of the Wall had become the responsibility of the state.[36] The discussions of the significance of the Wall and the need to preserve its remains led to the taking into care of many sections of the Wall by the National Trust and the state antiquity service between the 1930s to the 1970s.[37] The site of the Roman fort and town at Corbridge had seen substantial excavations during the early part of the twentieth century and this area was donated to the state in 1933.[38] A number of additional sections of the monument were taken into state care, including the Benwell Vallum crossing (in 1934), and the temple to Antenociticus at Benwell (in 1936). Today, the Ministry's successor, English Heritage, has a range of monuments under its guardianship, including sites that remain in private ownership.[39] In 1942, the National Trust acquired Hotbank Farm, giving this organization ownership of a substantial part of the best-preserved central section of the Wall.[40] During the 1970s, the Trust's holdings of sections of the Wall were increased substantially and today this organization owns much of the most impressive part of the Wall,[41] including the fort at Housesteads, two of the six milecastles that have substantial displayed remains, and eight kilometers of the best-preserved section of the curtain Wall.[42]

CHARACTERIZING THE CURTAIN WALL

In the post-War period, the National Trust developed a more specific role as the guardian of English country houses, and in 1951 the sections of the Wall in their ownership were placed in the guardianship of the Ministry of Public Buildings and Works.[43] In 1957 a conflict in the preservation of the Wall arose between the National Trust and the Ministry,[44] derived from the history and character of two different traditions of consolidation.

---

[34] Woodside and Crow (1999), 93; Leach and Whitworth (2011), 58–60.
[35] Witcher (2010a), 134.   [36] Ewin (2000), 43.
[37] Leach and Whitworth (2011, 72–137) provide a detailed discussion.
[38] Whitworth (2009b), 50–1.   [39] MP, 23.
[40] Woodside and Crow (1999), 93.   [41] ibid., 95.
[42] MP, 23.   [43] Woodside and Crow (1999), 94.
[44] Whitworth (2009b), 67–9.

Jim Crow has described the methods for consolidating the curtain Wall that had been established by John Clayton and developed by F. G. Simpson during the early twentieth century:

> The Roman Wall was excavated of its accumulated tumble and the fallen facing stones were set aside. These were re-laid dry in level courses on the surviving wall and core, without the use of mortar or cement. New core was built up using some of the small rubble left from the clearance. The new facing was laid level on both sides and the top was then capped with turf, taken from the adjacent grassland.[45]

This method required only the materials available on site and could be conducted by Clayton's estate workers who were practised in the maintenance of stone dykes. After 1930, the National Trust continued this approach, since it fitted with their general ethos, maintaining the Wall as an attractive turf-topped feature that blended in with the surrounding landscape.[46] In addition, any mortar used in this work was kept well back from the faces of the stones that made up the Wall.

Prior to 1931 the main parts of the Wall that had been displayed and consolidated had been uncovered by John Clayton's workmen on Housesteads Crags, Peel Crag, and Steel Rigg.[47] After this time, a programme of work was undertaken to remove the soil, trees, and fences, and to consolidate the remains of the Wall at Birdoswald, Willowford, Walltown, Cawfields, Winshields, Peel Crag, and Sycamore Gap.[48] The Ministry and its successors, the Department of the Environment, adopted a contrasting approach to the consolidation of these sections of the curtain Wall from the 1930s to 1980s.[49] This reconstruction of the Wall is sometimes titled the 'DOE Wall', to distinguish it from both the Clayton Wall and the original Roman curtain Wall. This method derived from the techniques adopted to maintain some other monuments that were cared for by the state, including medieval abbeys and castles. It aimed to consolidate the Wall as found with the aim of incorporating no new stones; any necessary restoration of the stonework was to be kept to a minimum or clearly marked as modern where it was necessary.[50] Alan Whitworth had characterized this approach, noting that:

> After clearing the top of the Wall of any trees, accumulated soil and associated debris down to the original Roman core, the Wall face was then exposed to its foundations. It was often the case that the core of the Wall survived better than the pointing of the face, so that the task of building a modern mortar and stone capping to protect the core and to provide a water run off was of some skill.

[45] Crow (2004a), 141.   [46] Whitworth (2009b), 66–7.
[47] Leach and Whitworth (2011, 13).   [48] ibid.
[49] Crow, (2004a), 141. For a detailed discussion of the consolidation of the Wall between 1931 and 1987, see Leach and Whitworth (2011).
[50] Crow, (2004a), 141.

Fig. 13.2. The section of consolidated curtain Wall just to the west of Sycamore Gap, close to Castle Nick Milecastle (*MC 39*). Photograph by Richard Hingley, 2011.

> About 18 in (457 mm) of the top of the core stones were removed, cleaned and reset in a mortar bedding mix of Portland cement and sand . . . This was designed to shed water from the top of the Wall and prevent percolation of moisture into the remaining Roman core.[51]

Despite the general presumption that no restoration of stonework should take place, this process required the removal of several of the top courses of masonry facing-stones. These were removed with care, numbered, washed, cleaned, and bedded in a mortar mix comparable to that used for the core. The joints in the face of the Wall were lime-pointed. Whitworth notes that this was considered to be an appropriate method to use on national monuments of such considerable significance.[52] It had a more dramatic physical impact on the monument, but the Ministry and the DOE were evidently less concerned than the National Trust about the visual impact of their reconstruction works. In some places, as for example on the east side of Sycamore Gap, the curtain Wall was deliberately rebuilt in a way that emphasizes its ruined nature (Figure 13.2).

During the 1950s, the Ministry and the National Trust cared for different sections of the Wall, using these two contrasting approaches to its preservation. The Ministry's extensive consolidation works on Walltown Crags, Winshields, and Cawfields was capably supervised by Charles Anderson, but without the presence of an archaeologist.[53] Anderson (1909–98) spent most of his working life helping to consolidate various sections of the Wall, in the

---

[51] Whitworth (2009b), 64.   [52] ibid., 67.   [53] Crow (1991), 52.

employment of the Ministry and the DOE.[54] In 1957, a serious dispute arose over the consolidation method to be used, since the Trust wished to maintain the turf capping on the walls at Housesteads while the Ministry intended to consolidate the walls with a mortar capping.[55] Jacquetta Hawkes took the Trust's side in the debate and publicized the issue in an article in *The Observer* on 9 February 1958, entitled 'Battle of Hadrian's Wall'.[56]

Hawkes, who had visited the Wall to inspect the work, attacked the Ministry's approach and observed that the National Trust's policy is 'as far as possible to leave the Wall alone'. This was not entirely the case since the maintenance of the Clayton Wall involved occasional rebuilding. She also commented that the Ministry wanted to assume guardianship over the entire length of the Wall, including the Trust's holdings, ending a regime of management which 'in their eyes is sadly out of date and tainted with romanticism'. Hawkes argued that the unsupervised rebuilding undertaken by the Ministry destroyed evidence for the subsequent history of the Wall. In particular, she noted that stones were removed and not replaced exactly where they had been found and that 'the Roman mortar, which varied in colour from one age to the next and therefore shows repairs and alterations, is destroyed without record.' She concluded that the Wall emerging from this reconstruction was 'not Hadrian's Wall at all. It is a copy—and one which has lost all the gifts of time'. She called the work of the Ministry 'an Aladdinesque policy of *new* walls for old.'

It is clear that the construction of the 'Clayton Wall' also had a marked physical impact upon the character of the Roman curtain Wall. It is likely that, in places, quite substantial parts of the monument were effectively refaced and rebuilt. At Peel Gap, close to Steel Rigg car park, extensive excavations in 1911 had revealed the foundations of a medieval tower, or peel (Figure 4.5).[57] This medieval structure had evidently resulted in the partial demolition of the Roman curtain Wall but inspection of the rear face of the Clayton Wall close to this location today reveals no change in the fabric of its inner face (Figure 13.3). The Clayton Wall has been rebuilt here in a way that hides all traces of the medieval activities that damaged the Roman curtain Wall. The Clayton Wall also looks more like a managed feature of the landscape and less like the ruins of the original curtain Wall that it replaced. In some parts of its course, the DOE Wall certainly provides a better appreciation of its former character as a ruined stone structure.

The Trust and some local archaeologists supported Hawkes' campaign but the university establishment in Durham and Newcastle supported the Ministry. Anthony Birley recalls that, during this controversy, the BBC sent Alan Whicker, unannounced, to interview his father, Eric Birley at their house in Corbridge. Eric was at the Roman site, as the training excavation was underway. Anthony recalls

---

[54] Whitworth (2009b).   [55] ibid., 67; Leach and Whitworth (2011), 129–34.
[56] Hawkes (1958); cf. Crow (2004a), 142.   [57] Simpson (1976), 109.

Fig. 13.3. The Clayton Wall at Peel Gap, showing the modern rebuilding of the inner face of the curtain that had been damaged through the construction of the medieval peel. Photograph by Richard Hingley, 2011.

that, when Alan Whicker rang the door bell 'I opened the door (being at home during the Long Vac) and at once recognised who it was. I then took him to Corstopitum (as everyone then called it) to meet Eric Birley.'[58] This highly public debate was raised in the House of Commons during April 1958, but did not result in a clear resolution.[59] After this discussion, the Ministry and its successor, the Department of the Environment, continued its approach to the consolidation of the Wall and archaeologists were not involved to observe or record the remains that were being consolidated for some time.[60] Archaeological supervision of this consolidation work was initiated by Ian Stewart at Sewingshields Milecastle (*MC 35*).[61] Today the National Trust continues to use their own approach to the preservation of the Wall, drawing upon John Clayton's methods.

A graphic account of the scale and nature of the consolidation work conducted by the Ministry and the DOE was provided by Hunter Davies' popular account of the Wall. During his walk along the Wall, Davies witnessed the uncovering and conservation of the curtain Wall close to Cawfields Milecastle (*MC 42*), interpreting this act, in a direct contrast to Hawkes, as evidence for the Wall's continuing vitality.[62] Davies had been brought up in Carlisle and educated in Durham, where he had taken a degree that included a course on Romano-British archaeology and Hadrian's Wall. He remarked that he 'always found the subject incredibly boring', but that, 'Slowly, with age, I've come to appreciate that it was a living Wall, then as well as now'.[63] Davies was

---

[58] Anthony Birley (pers. comm.).   [59] Whitworth (2009b), 67–9.
[60] Crow (2004a), 142.   [61] David Breeze (pers. comm.).
[62] H. Davies (1974), 155.   [63] ibid., vii.

deeply influenced by William Hutton in representing the people of the Wall and the region's social condition as much as telling the tale of the Wall itself.[64]

On the crags in the centre of the Wall's line, close to Cawfields, Davies came across a party of workmen from the DOE opening up a new section of the Wall. He observed that:

> So much is happening on the Wall these days that the Ordnance Survey's archaeological map of the Wall, first produced in 1964, which is very recent as maps go, is already out of date. All along the Wall I'd been discovering new stretches and new turrets not on the map. I'd got the 1964 map without realizing a new one had come out in 1972. It's strange to think that an archaeological map, a map solely concerned with structures almost two thousand years old, has dated in less than ten years.[65]

Davies drew upon the discoveries made during the DOE's clearing work to argue that 'Hadrian's Wall is a living wall, not just for the local inhabitants, but for tourists and archaeologists, a living, breathing, expanding, growing wall'.

At an earlier stage in his explorations, Davies had visited the Roman site at Vindolanda. Writing about the construction of an entirely new section of the curtain Wall, he noted that 'a life-size hunk of Hadrian's Wall [was] taking shape before my eyes'.[66] Formed in 1970, the Vindolanda Trust was in the process of building a section of the stone curtain Wall accompanied by a turret and also a length of the turf Wall (Figure 1.6).[67] The stone curtain Wall and turret were built out of stone that ultimately derived from the Roman buildings on the site,[68] but they were constructed away from the Roman remains. Davies observed that:

> There was a stone mason working on it, fixing some hand-made wooden scaffolding which had been roped together and erected in the same way as the Romans must have done. For the first time in almost two thousand years, here was a workman building Hadrian's Wall...I couldn't understand why it had never been done before.[69]

Davies noted that the stone curtain Wall at Vindolanda was being built with the proper tools and methods, leading to genuine insights into how the original curtain Wall was constructed in Roman times. The Vindolanda Trust's objective was to recreate a realistic section of Hadrian's Wall. Robin Birley has explained that many visitors to the Wall were unaware of the substantial character of the Roman constructions along its line since only the foundations of these structures remain.[70] Although some sections of the curtain Wall survive to a considerable height, nowhere along its length could its original scale be fully appreciated. Despite this, the Vindolanda Trust

---

[64] Ewin (2000), 62–3.   [65] H. Davies (1974), 155.   [66] ibid., 121.
[67] R. Birley (2009), 36.   [68] ibid., 37.
[69] H. Davies (1974), 121.   [70] R. Birley (2009), 36.

encountered opposition from the planning authorities over this reconstruction, which was felt not to be entirely in keeping with Northumbrian rural architecture.[71]

From Davies' perspective, the Roman curtain Wall, the 'Clayton Wall', the 'DOE Wall', and the sections at Vindolanda were elements in the evolving structure of a 'living, breathing, expanding, growing wall'.[72] Extensive archaeological excavations, directed by Jim Crow between 1982 and 1988, were soon to add support to this idea by showing just how complex the curtain Wall could be. Crow's excavations for the National Trust were undertaken as a result of the severe erosion of the footpath along Whin Sill, especially between Highshields Crags and Peel Crag, east of Steel Rigg.[73] A section of the curtain Wall about 400 metres long was excavated, together with a milecastle and the turret at Peel Gap. The careful excavation and recording of this length of curtain Wall indicated a complex sequence of construction and rebuilding during Roman times.[74] The work uncovered significant evidence for a sequence of building periods, including a narrow rebuilding of the Wall, apparently undertaken during the late second century, which may well date to the reign of Severus.

Crow's work brought into sharp focus the fact that the earlier consolidation works on the curtain Wall had not usually been accompanied by archaeological exploration. As a result, important archaeological information about the form of the curtain Wall and its various phases of construction and alteration had undoubtedly been lost.[75] It was now apparent that more detailed recording was required during works to consolidate the curtain Wall.

During the 1980s there was also an assessment to determine the best type of mortars to be used in the consolidation of the curtain Wall. Alan Whitworth has noted that 'conflicting views' remain today about the best way to preserve the remains of the curtain Wall, but a consensus has since been reached between the Trust and the Ministry's successors, English Heritage.[76] The National Trust has accepted that all new ground disturbances and consolidation works on the Roman remains should follow the guidelines that are provided by English Heritage. The current management regime also recognizes that the 'Clayton Wall' has its own character and that it is to be protected, conserved, and managed in its own right.[77] English Heritage has accepted that these parts of the curtain Wall should be maintained with a turf topping and that any repairs to the fabric should blend in with the adjacent stonework.[78] Since the turf cap is a feature of the 'Clayton Wall' rather than of the original Roman curtain Wall, this indicates that the reconstructed Wall is

---

[71] ibid., 36–7.   [72] H. Davies (1974), 155.

[73] Crow 1991, 53; Crow (2004a), 112.   [74] Crow (1991).

[75] ibid., 52.   [76] Whitworth (2009b), 64–9.

[77] MP, 52–3.   [78] Whitworth (2009b), 69.

now considered to be an integral element of what has become effectively a composite curtain Wall, part Roman and part modern. All exposed Roman masonry is regularly monitored and coordinated action is taken to ensure its appropriate conservation and repair.[79] The exposed areas of stonework along the Wall require maintenance, and methods of consolidation will continue to develop in the future.

To set these observations on the excavation, maintenance, and management of the curtain Wall in context, Paul Bidwell and Peter Hill have provided some statistics that indicate that, although Hadrian's Wall is one of the most extensively excavated frontiers of the Roman empire, only around 159 metres of the entire curtain Wall (about 0.13 per cent of the total length) has been excavated under modern conditions since the late 1970s.[80] Around 2,416 metres (2.04 per cent) of the surviving curtain Wall constitutes the 'Clayton Wall', sections that were restored during the nineteenth century, while 6,055 metres (5.12 per cent) is DOE Wall that was cleared without archaeological supervision or recording during the mid twentieth century. This leaves a length of around 108,210 metres (91 per cent) of the curtain Wall that may have been destroyed or survives as buried remains or upstanding earthworks. In addition, a total of at least 1,440 metres (1.22 per cent) of the monument was destroyed during the late nineteenth and twentieth centuries.

THE ICONIC WALL

It is in this central upland section of the Wall that Hunter Davies appears to have experienced its living spirit most clearly. Robert Witcher has observed that some walkers on the Hadrian's Wall Path National Trail expressed disappointment with the first forty kilometres from Wallsend because of the lack of tangible traces and then 'delight' at 'finally reaching the Wall' once they arrive at this upland sector.[81] It often appears to be felt that the 'real' Hadrian's Wall is the section that lies in the rural uplands of Northumberland, where its best-preserved remains are situated.[82] Paul Usherwood has written of the rise of the concept of the 'Rustic Wall' during the twentieth century—the idea of the monument as an 'embellishment of the Northumbrian countryside'.[83] The Wall's course may include the urban lands of Tyneside and the low-lying areas of the Solway Basin to the west,[84] but the most authentic Wall experience is often perceived to be in its central section, since this is where its remains are

---

[79] MP, 52.   [80] RFa, 40.
[81] Witcher (2010a), 143.   [82] cf. Samuel (1994), 169; Barlow (2007), 141.
[83] Usherwood (1996), 158.   [84] MP, Appendix 2.2.

most complete, continuous, and most recognizable. Usherwood has argued that visitors have long been attracted to this central section—the area of Walltown Crags, Housesteads, and Chesters—and there is plenty of evidence to support this claim.[85] The majority of photographs of Hadrian's Wall published in the guides and on the internet show sections of the curtain Wall surviving in this rural upland landscape, while other written accounts often emphasize the remains of precisely this area.

The focus of interest on the length of Hadrian's Wall that is the most visually impressive, most scenic, and the best preserved is entirely logical. In the upland area, the Wall in its most famous section has often been preserved as a field and property boundary between estates, accounting for its good survival.[86] The substantial clearing and partial rebuilding of the curtain Wall that has occurred since Clayton's time allows the monument to be clearly appreciated by the visitor, who can study the details of the Wall and the turrets, milecastles, forts, and *vici* along its line. In this area, the Wall seems 'woven into the fabric of the landscape'.[87] By contrast, in the urban areas of Tyneside to the east, the archaeological remains of the Wall, where they are visible at all, have often been effectively dislocated from the broader landscape as the result of agricultural operations and extensive urban and industrial developments.[88] In built-up areas, the continuous nature of the monument has been fragmented by the complication of the overlying urban form. It is difficult for visitors to comprehend the Wall's unity across the lowland sections to its east and west, where most of its obvious physical features have been lost.

An emphasis on the scope, extent, and sophistication of the frontier,[89] certainly helps to explain the archaeological popularity of this central section of the Wall, but is this the only reason for the prominence of the landscape along Whin Sill in public appreciation of the Wall? This area is fairly remote from modern population centres.[90] Tourist guides often appear to suggest that Hadrian's Wall ends to the west of urban Tyneside and an overriding emphasis has been placed on the rural nature of the Wall since the 1980s as the government has promoted tourism to solve the region's economic problems.[91] This suggests that the publicizing of the Wall as a tourist destination has led to a valuation of the central section as a superior visitor experience, although it will be seen in Chapter 14 that extensive excavations at South Shields and Wallsend since the 1970s have sought to challenge this view by uncovering, displaying, and reconstructing Roman sites in urban Tyneside.

The prominence of the Wall's central section is not an entirely modern phenomenon.[92] William Stukeley referred to Housesteads as 'the Tadmor of

---

85 Usherwood (1996), 159.   86 MP, 13.
87 Usherwood (1996), 159.   88 MP, Appendix 2.2, Character Area 14.
89 MP, 27–8.   90 Usherwood (1996), 159.
91 ibid., 160.   92 Witcher *et al.* (2010), 110.

Britain',[93] evoking the idea of travel and otherness through a grandiose allusion to Palmyra.[94] This eastern city is a highly impressive Roman ruin, very remote from Western Europe, and had only recently been discovered in the Syrian Desert. Stukeley's comparison drew upon the marginal and unruly nature of the landscape of Whin Sill during the period prior to the seventeenth century, invoking a marginality that is broadly comparable to that of Palmyra. The sense of the marginality of this section of the Wall continued to inspire a feeling of awe in visitors.[95] William Hutton was cowed by the view from close to Housesteads, observing that on the Crag opposite Crag Lough, the 'prospects are not grand, but extensive and rather awful'.[96] The same prospect adds to the popularity of this section of the Wall with visitors today, but drawing upon rather different associations.

Jim Crow has argued that the open Northumbrian landscape around Housesteads appeals to the visitor because it provides a relief from the claustrophobia of modern urban life, but the genealogy of place is also vital here.[97] Woodside and Crow have observed that imperial Rome clearly left its 'hefty sandalprint' in this frontier landscape,[98] while Crow has argued that 'the archaeological remains of the Roman Wall are combined with the majestic sweep of the impressive natural contours of Whin Sill'.[99] He has written that 'It still feels like a frontier: to the south are farms and roads and the distant security of modern civilized life, to the north of the Wall is emptiness, shadowed only by the plantations of the Kielder Forest.' The section of Wall from Steel Rigg to Sewingshields is a part-wild but part-domesticated landscape in which the historical associations of this ancient frontier remain greatly in evidence. This landscape has become 'iconic' since the mid nineteenth century, illustrated and photographed to address the image of the curtain Wall rising and descending the Crags.[100] For example, the Wallington Hall painting draws upon this landscape for the setting of its imperial Wall (Figure 9.1), an engraving of this scenery is featured in Bruce's *The Wallet-Book* (Figure 13.4), and this view is one of the most common in modern photographs of the Wall (Figure 2.5).[101]

Some visitors may see this as the 'real' Wall, the section in which its physical remains may be appreciated most fully in relation to its landscape. Woodside and Crow have noted, however, that this landscape probably owes more to the nineteenth century than to the Roman period.[102] The area was settled and cultivated from medieval times, leading to substantial robbing of the Wall and changes to the landscape, but the farming landscapes of the central sections of the Wall, including the area around Housesteads, are predominantly nineteenth-century in character, comprising scattered farms and stone field walls.[103] We have seen that John Clayton had established a substantial

---

[93] Stukeley (1776), 61.   [94] Crow (2004a), 8.   [95] ibid., 9–11.
[96] Hutton (1802), 240.   [97] Crow (2004a), 10.
[98] Woodside and Crow (1999), 10.   [99] Crow (2004a), 10.
[100] Witcher (2010a), 132.   [101] J. C. Bruce (1863), 143; Witcher (2010a), 132.
[102] Woodside and Crow (1999), 11.   [103] MP, 11–12.

Fig. 13.4. An engraving of the Wall on Milking Gap from Bruce's *The Wallet-Book*. From J. C. Bruce (1863), 143.

archaeological 'park' in this area, while he had 'improved' the land, farms, and Roman remains across a substantial part of this landscape.[104] Clayton had uncovered and displayed these remains in an attempt to clarify the character of the Wall for visitors. The National Trust, the Ministry of Public Buildings and Works, the Department of the Environment, and English Heritage have all built upon Clayton's example.

This process of management and display continues today. Robert Witcher has observed of the central section of the Wall that:

> Today, the landscape is intensively managed...'Desire lines' are mown in the grass-sward in order to limit erosion by subtly guiding visitors elsewhere; weed-killer suppresses vegetation which would otherwise have long ago reclaimed stone structures; linesmen, rangers, and volunteers move along the Wall repairing damage and picking litter.[105]

Indeed, over 400 years this landscape has been transformed from dangerous and marginal into the most visited and photographed area of the Northumberland National Park,[106] a living and vital landscape. These management measures cannot, however, preserve this landscape in time, since constant change typifies all the areas through which the Wall runs.[107]

---

[104] Woodside and Crow (1999), 86–8.
[105] Witcher (2010a), 137.   [106] Witcher *et al.* (2010), 110.
[107] Woodside and Crow (1999), 124.

The management regime for the Wall has, however, had an effect on the recent history of archaeological discovery. Along the prominent basal intrusion of Whin Sill, where hill farming occurs alongside the well-preserved sections of the Wall, the emphasis of current planning policy is on the protection of the Wall and its setting.[108] Most of the surviving archaeological elements of Hadrian's Wall are scheduled under the *Ancient Monuments and Archaeological Areas Act 1979.*[109] The 1979 Act provides far greater protection to Scheduled Ancient Monuments than the earlier versions of the legislation, requiring owners and developers to obtain Scheduled Monument Consent before undertaking works that might damage the Wall's physical remains or environs. Consent can be refused if the developments are felt to have too negative an impact on the archaeological remains. Since the planning policy in this landscape emphasizes conservation, the opportunities for new discoveries resulting from archaeological excavations are more restricted than in the urban areas of Tyneside and Carlisle, where the Wall has been flattened and survives buried beneath modern industrial and urban development.[110] In these lowland areas of the western and eastern ends of the Wall, the excavation of buried remains is often required in advance of development, a theme that will be explored in Chapter 14. In the upland area, when excavations occur at all, they are usually carried out on a limited scale as a result of the erosion of the monument or to provide information about how the resource might be managed more adequately.[111]

Despite the increasing emphasis on the conservation and management of the upland sections of the Wall, a number of Roman sites were fairly extensively excavated during the final decades of the twentieth century. At Housesteads, excavations between 1974 and 1981 added vital new information about one of the best-preserved and most fully studied forts of the Roman empire (Figure 2.12).[112] Excavations at Birdoswald between 1987 and 1992, and in 1997 produced important information about the Roman fort but also the communities that continued to occupy this site for several centuries after the decline of Roman rule,[113] a pattern that now appears to be repeated at a number of other forts on the Wall.[114] The only major long-term excavations in the upland section that continue today are at Vindolanda, where continuous work since 1970 has focused on uncovering and displaying the Roman remains. This has led to significant discoveries that have transformed the understanding of the Roman fort (Figure 2.13).[115] Extensive areas of the fort and *vicus* have been uncovered and a variety of extremely important finds have been made, including the Vindolanda letters, a series of records written

---

[108] C. Young (1999a), 36.   [109] MP, 7.
[110] N. Hodgson (2009b), 5.   [111] ibid.; cf. Wilmott (2009a), 6–7.
[112] Crow (2004a); Rushworth (2009).   [113] Wilmott (1997); Wilmott (2001).
[114] RFa, 167–70; Wilmott (2010).   [115] R. Birley (2009).

on slivers of wood (alder and birch) by the Roman occupants of the fort during the decades before the construction of Hadrian's Wall.[116] At Vindolanda, we also have an excellent knowledge of the sequence of forts and the occupation of the *vicus*, unrivalled at any of the other Roman sites along the Wall. Here again, a community remained on the site long after the end of Roman rule and a small building that may have been a Christian church has been found. The idea that communities survived beyond the end of Roman rule at Birdoswald and Vindolanda is a concept that appeals to archaeologists because it is evocative and romantic, although on present evidence it is impossible to prove a continuity of population.[117] This idea, however, communicates with the romantic view of the persisting landscape, connecting with earlier ideas that linked the present population with the ancient people of the Wall. As a result of the scale of the work undertaken here over the past forty years, Vindolanda provides an exciting visitor experience.

SUMMARY: DEFENDING A LIVING WALL

The popularity of the Wall during the 1930s led to the taking of substantial sections into the protective custody of the National Trust and the state, helping to ensure the survival of the internationally important remains of the Wall across its central section, particularly at the time of the significant quarrying threat of 1930. The need to preserve the Wall led successively to the statutory protection of its remains through scheduling, the acquiring of extensive landholdings by public bodies and private charitable trusts and, in 1987, to the inscription of the Wall as a World Heritage Site.[118] The growing interest in visiting the remains has encouraged the development of visitor facilities on the central section of the Wall. The next chapter will turn to the contrasting history of the management, protection, and display of the eastern section of Hadrian's Wall.

---

[116] Primo Levi (1996) wrote a short story, *Cara mamma*, inspired by the socks and underpants letter (Anthony Birley pers. comm.).
[117] Nick Hodgson (pers. comm.).
[118] C. Young (1999b).

14

The Gateway at South Shields: The Romanization of Tyneside

Roman Wallsend ... is replete with paradox, caught in strange transitional position between celebration and melancholic connoisseurship of decay; locked in the assertion of Rome as the fount of industrial engineering and equally as the epitome of a post-industrial economy of retail.

Paul Barlow (2007), 140

INTRODUCTION[1]

The south-west gateway of the hinterland fort at *Arbeia* (South Shields), comprises another iconic image of the Wall (Figure 14.2). Opened in 1988 with considerable ceremony, it is one of the most impressive of the

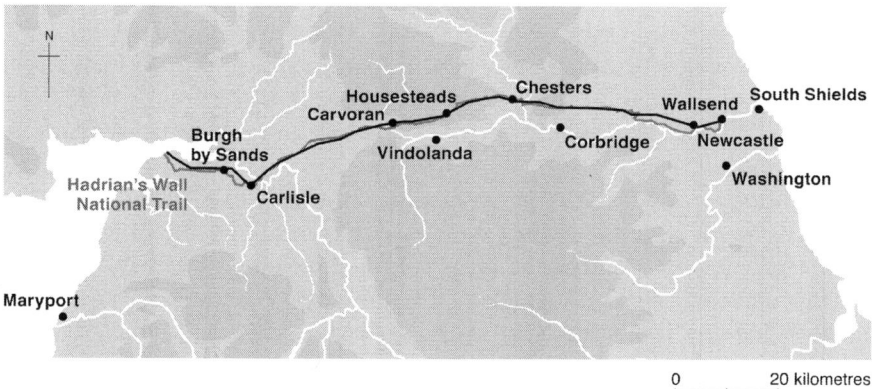

Fig. 14.1. Places mentioned in Chapters 14 and 15. The Hadrian's Wall Path National Trail is marked in grey. Drawn by Christina Unwin.

[1] I am particularly grateful to Paul Bidwell for considerable help and advice with this chapter.

Fig. 14.2. The reconstructed south-west gate at *Arbeia* Fort and Museum. Photograph by Richard Hingley, 2009. Reproduced by permission of Tyne and Wear Museums on behalf of North Tyneside Council.

reconstructed Roman structures along the Wall. It was built directly on top of the foundations of the Roman gateway of the fort and represents part of a substantial programme of works that has uncovered and displayed Roman remains across urban Tyneside. Since the mid 1970s, the Roman forts at South Shields and Wallsend have been extensively excavated and the remains displayed on site, with adjoining museums and reconstructed Roman military buildings. This chapter will explore these attempts to reconstruct elements of Hadrian's Wall, which forms part of a process that Barlow has called 'the Romanization of the Tyne'.[2] He has observed that the radical deindustrialization of Tyneside since the 1970s has led to a disassociation with the important recent industrial heritage of the area and the drawing of a connection with the more ancient legacy of the Roman empire. Barlow has also argued that this new identity allows for a distinctive negotiation between modern leisure-based businesses and the idealization of the lost heavy industry of this urban landscape.

Hunter Davies has seen the new section of Roman curtain Wall at Vindolanda as an addition to a living and evolving Wall, a concept that casts the

---

[2] Barlow (2007), 138–9.

Fig. 14.3. Hadrian's House, the Wallsend job centre. Photograph by Richard Hingley, 2010.

authoritative reconstructions of Roman buildings in a positive light.[3] The reconstructed buildings on the sites of the South Shields and Wallsend forts have been built with considerable care and have drawn in detail upon the archaeological knowledge that was derived from the excavation of the foundations of the structures from which they derive their forms. The recreation of Romanness on Tyneside includes examples of urban redevelopment that have little in the way of a specific physical or historical connection with the remains of the Wall, including the Hadrian's House Wallsend job centre employment agency (Figure 14.3) and the Forum shopping centre.[4] This chapter will explore references to Rome in modern Tyneside in order to set these buildings and structures in context. It will be argued that the recreation of an idea of 'Romanness' has helped to keep the remains of the Wall alive within the developing urban landscapes of Tyneside, an issue also emphasized by the recent history of archaeological discovery in this area.

[3] H. Davies (1974), 121.
[4] cf. Usherwood (1996), 160–1.

RESTORING *ARBEIA*

The reconstructed gateway at South Shields draws extensively on the archaeological knowledge derived from this Roman site over the previous 100 years. The remains of the Roman station at South Shields were first recorded during the eighteenth century.[5] The hilltop on which the Roman site is situated was laid out for the construction of houses in 1874.[6] John Collingwood Bruce described the Roman remains on this site as 'feeble',[7] but when ancient finds were uncovered during initial building works, an excavation committee was formed to discover as much as possible about the fort before it was built over.[8] The excavations, which drew upon labour provided by the building contractors, were extensively reported in local papers and were of considerable interest to the local population (Figure 10.10).[9] The outlines of the fort were soon uncovered, together with a substantial building at its centre,[10] thought at the time to represent a forum. A new 'Museum of Natural History, Antiquities, &C.' was opened as part of the Library at South Shields in 1876 and modified in 1893 to display the remains from the excavations.[11] Significant parts of the site were excluded from the development and in 1880 were designated by the town council as a 'Roman Remains and People's Park',[12] the first acquisition and presentation in Britain of a Roman fort to the public.[13] These works coincided with the discovery of the impressive tombstones dedicated to Regina and Victor in 1878 and 1885 respectively, which were displayed in the museum in the new library.[14] Together, the park and library presented these important remains to local people and visitors and the finds were well publicized, indicating the considerable investment made to preserve and interpret this Roman site.

During the early twentieth century, the condition of the site deteriorated and, in 1949, the corporation of South Shields consolidated the remains and built a new museum at the entrance to the Park. Ian Richmond was entrusted with the supervision of the archaeological work, which enabled some further excavation to be conducted.[15] Mortimer Wheeler opened the new museum in 1953, allowing local people and visitors to examine the archaeological site and the finds.[16] The demolition of areas of housing in 1966–7 allowed further explorations and the programme of excavations that began in 1975 continues today.[17] The development of these visitor facilities has also resulted in the building of

---

[5] E. Birley (1961), 152.   [6] Allason-Jones and Miket (1984), 9–10.

[7] Bruce (1863), 218.

[8] Bidwell and Speak (1994), 1; E. Birley (1961), 154; Ewin (2000), 30.

[9] E. Birley (1961), 154; Ewin (2000), 30.   [10] E. Birley (1961), 154.

[11] Allason-Jones and Miket (1984), 13; Ewin (2000), 30.

[12] Allason-Jones and Miket (1984), 12; E. Birley (1961), 154.

[13] Breeze (2006a), 115–16.   [14] J. C. Bruce (1907), 244.

[15] E. Birley (1961), 155.   [16] Ewin (2000), 31.   [17] Breeze (2006a), 116.

reconstructions of Roman structures over the past twenty-five years, including the gateway, the commanding officer's house, and a barrack block.

During the 1980s, it was proposed to reconstruct the south-west gateway of the fort on top of the foundations of the original structure. This proposal provoked considerable controversy. Some Roman frontiers specialists argued that this reconstruction would compromise future excavations on the site and was also unlikely to provide an accurate view of what had once existed at this location.[18] The Historic Buildings and Monuments Commission for England,[19] the state antiquity service that had taken over from the Department of the Environment, objected on the grounds that to carry out the scheme would be a major departure from the accepted procedures for looking after ancient monuments and because it was felt that the remains should be conserved as found.[20] Ancient Monument legislation has long emphasized the idea of reconstructing archaeological structures off-site, away from the scheduled and protected remains on which they are based.

To understand why this is so, it is useful to consider the history of the reconstruction of Roman military buildings. At the end of the nineteenth century, the Roman fort at Saalburg (Germany) was reconstructed under the orders of Kaiser Wilhelm II and the site was inaugurated in 1900 (Figure 14.4).[21] David Breeze has suggested that the reconstruction is a 'solid' and 'not quite correct' structure, but that it has, in turn, become a monument in its own right, since it provides a unique example of a nineteenth-century image of a Roman fort.[22] At Vindolanda, the reconstructed section of the curtain Wall built during the early 1970s was deliberately located beyond the edge of the Roman site. Despite the educational potential of this structure, the Vindolanda Trust experienced considerable problems in persuading the planning authorities of the veracity of this work.[23] The South Shields proposal was, therefore, bound to raise controversy.

A public local inquiry was held at South Shields from 27 to 30 November 1984, to debate the proposal to build a reconstruction of the gateway.[24] This resulted in reassurances that the underlying archaeological remains would be protected from disturbance through the provision of a concrete foundation. Permission for the building work was given soon afterwards, on the basis that the detailed proposals were to be reviewed by as many 'students of Roman military architecture as possible'. A seminar at South Shields considered how to create the most authentic Roman gateway for the site, resulting in the publication of a substantial monograph, containing a lengthy paper providing a detailed justification for the methods and materials used in this reconstruction.[25]

---

[18] Bidwell *et al.* (eds. 1988), i.   [19] Now known as English Heritage.
[20] Ewin (2000), 31.   [21] Obmann (2011); Struck (2001), 105.
[22] Breeze (2008b), 141.   [23] R. Birley (2009), 36–7.
[24] Bidwell *et al.* (1988).   [25] Ibid.

Fig. 14.4. The gateway of the reconstructed Roman fort at Saalburg, Germany. Photograph by David Breeze.

Archaeological excavation undertaken on the remains of the gateway in 1875, 1966, 1980, and 1985 had already provided the ground plan, evidence for the building materials used in its construction, and some detailed knowledge of its appearance. The elevated elements also drew upon evidence derived from the surviving gateways of Roman forts on the African frontier at Bu Ngem and Gheriat el-Garbia in Libya, and upon military gateways represented on Roman sculptures.[26] The resulting reconstruction was therefore a blend of knowledge deriving from the excavation of the surviving foundations of this particular gateway and the comparative analysis of frontier structures that survive as standing buildings elsewhere in the empire. Whereas earlier reconstructions—including Clayton's Victorian Wall and the reconstructed section of curtain Wall at Vindolanda—had recycled the Roman building materials, the South Shields gateway was built entirely of concrete, although newly quarried local sandstone has been used to face the walls.[27]

The external facade was designed to look authentic, but the building of the underlying structure utilized modern techniques and materials, particularly concrete. The interior arrangement of the spaces within the gateway also had to be modified to allow for fire and safety regulations, since these areas are accessible to the public and are used for display.[28] The gateway drew a realistic

[26] Bidwell *et al.* (1988), 156–7, 171–6.   [27] ibid., 224.   [28] ibid.

Fig. 14.5. The reconstructed barracks and commanding officer's house at *Arbeia* Fort and Museum, showing the foundations of excavated Roman buildings in the foreground. Photograph by Richard Hingley, 2010. Reproduced by permission of Tyne and Wear Museums on behalf of North Tyneside Council.

image from the Roman remains on which it is based, but is built in a contemporary way to serve current needs. Its authenticity was emphasized by the insertion of a new Latin dedicatory inscription into the exterior face, above the gate. This ascribes the building of the fort to the Governor Calpurnius Agricola for the emperors Marcus Aurelius and Lucius Verus in AD 161–3, drawing upon archaeological knowledge about the date at which the fort was initially constructed.[29] It is also one of a number of modern inscribed stones in urban Tyneside that draw upon Roman models.

A number of other military buildings have since been fully or partially reconstructed at South Shields, including the early fourth-century house of the commanding officer and a barrack block (Figure 14.5). As with the south-west gateway, these buildings have been built directly on top of the original foundations of the Roman structures, drawing on archaeological knowledge of the elevations and structure of such buildings. Again, evidence from the excavation has been used in the reconstructions. For example, the decorative style of the wall plaster in the commanding officer's house derives from archaeological finds made during the excavations.[30] All of these reconstructed buildings and structures at South Shields are built from modern materials and use modern construction techniques, including advertising for the fort and interpretation centre, located 250 metres beyond the eastern edge of the site

---

[29] Breeze (2006a), 122.   [30] ibid., 127.

Fig. 14.6. Advertising signage for the museum and fort at South Shields which draws upon the motif of Roman legionary shields, to the east of the site. Photograph by Richard Hingley, 2009.

(Figure 14.6). A re-enactment group called *Quinta* is based at the site, based on the *Cohors quinta Gallorum*, the Fifth Cohort of Gauls, a military unit that was stationed here from AD 213 to 222. *Quinta* forms part of the *Arbeia* Society and has been set up to promote interest in the Romans at South Shields.[31] The fort is run, managed, excavated, and interpreted by Tyne and Wear Archives and Museums, who act for the local authority that owns the site. *Quinta* aims to research, reconstruct, and display to the public aspects of military and civilian life from early third-century Britain. Membership of this group is open to anyone who is interested and, at particular times, it effectively repopulates this partly reconstructed fort.

AUTHENTIC EXPERIENCES?

The reconstructions at Vindolanda and South Shields provide concrete manifestations of the scale and magnificence of Roman structures along the Wall, an impression that the archaeological remains alone cannot convey. The reconstructions provide an insight into the ways that buildings might have appeared during the Roman period, helping visitors to understand how

---

[31] *Quinta* (2010); MP, 22; Paul Bidwell (pers. comm.).

life may have been lived in the past.[32] They bring the Wall to life for visitors, but their recreation on actual archaeological sites remains a problematic issue. David Breeze has argued that, 'The basic premise was and is straightforward: that the archaeological remains should be left to speak for themselves; to remain accessible for re-examination and re-interpretation; that any form of restoration must involve a significant element of guesswork and therefore that it is better not to undertake any restoration *in situ* at all.'[33] The full reconstruction of individual buildings on the original site of their excavation is usually felt to be inappropriate,[34] since all the archaeological remains of nationally and internationally significant monuments should be conserved as fully as possible 'as found'.[35] This explains why a public inquiry was held to debate the reconstruction of the South Shields gateway.

When archaeological excavations uncover and explore the buried remains of Hadrian's Wall, the preferred policy is to restore only the remains that are found during excavation *in situ*, using original materials wherever possible, and not to recreate any part of the original structure above these foundations; this is the policy that was pursued with regard to the DOE Wall.[36] Once uncovered, these buried remains are often kept open for display to the public, as on the fort sites along the Wall (Figure 14.5). When they have been exposed, however, the remains of Roman structures require conservation and management, but—as we have seen with the Clayton and DOE Walls—such acts of consolidation change the material nature of the remains.[37] The clearing and partial restoration of particular sections of the curtain Wall on Whin Sill by Clayton and later by the DOE has effectively changed the nature of these parts of the monument and successive acts of conservation have continued to accumulate change. The idea of the living Wall outlined by Hunter Davies provides a way of conceptualizing this process. As such, the 'Clayton Wall', which has been discussed in detail above, is now conserved as a monument in its own right as an element of the composite curtain Wall warranting its own conservation and management techniques. The DOE Wall, by contrast, is felt to be too recent to require conservation to preserve its own particularly distinctive character, although it does comprise a relevant theme for research.[38]

This raises a contradiction between two forms of reasoning—a strict form of conservation ethos that stresses the need to conserve structures as found and *in situ*, and a more creative concept of the Wall as an evolving and developing entity that needs to be maintained and restored if it is to remain alive and accessible to visitors. Jaap Lengkeek has noted that, although 'authenticity' is a

---

[32] cf. Brisbane and Wood (1996), 38; P. Wilson (2011).
[33] Breeze (2008b), 143.   [34] MP, 69.   [35] Breeze (2008b), 144.
[36] see MP, 52; cf. Brisbane and Wood (1996), 36.
[37] Breeze (2008b), 144; cf. P. Wilson (2011), 265.
[38] Whitworth (2009b), 50–65.

key concept in discussions of tourist experiences, it is also a highly problematic term.[39] Attractions made purposefully for tourists are often considered by visitors not to be authentic. Lengkeek has argued that only when the past can be presented 'as it was' is the tourist able to see something 'real'.[40] This explains the careful design policy that strove for authenticity for the Vindolanda curtain Wall and the South Shields gateway. In the case of the reconstructions at South Shields, the buildings are built on top of the remains of the original structures on which they are based. From a strict conservation viewpoint, the gateway and the other buildings cannot be authentic since they are modern constructions that are inevitably based on guesswork and incorporate contemporary health and safety concerns. For the planning officers who allowed the South Shields gateway to be built, the structure's authenticity and its historical respectability is a direct result of the serious work undertaken by its designers to create a realistically Roman appearance. For certain visitors, authenticity can relate closely to the spirit of a particular place.[41] Reconstructed Roman buildings, from the Saalburg to South Shields, have often been built upon Roman foundations, an approach that some visitors feel provides a historical link that would not exist if the reconstructed building was built on an entirely new site well away from the original monument.[42]

Evidently, the concept of 'authentic' may be imbued with different meanings. For many archaeologists, the authentic remains of the Wall are those that are experienced in the ground during excavation. From this viewpoint, the consolidated remains of the curtain Wall on Whin Sill and the managed remains on fort sites, such as South Shields, Vindolanda, and Housesteads, cannot be absolutely entirely authentic.[43] They may contain an element of their original character, particularly because they are conserved with care, but this does not make them entirely 'real' as Roman structures. In the case of reconstructed buildings, however much effort goes into their perceived authentication, they are modern constructions and this is clearly indicated by the contemporary materials from which the gateway and other buildings at South Shields are built. These buildings are interpretations and projections, or receptions, of how Roman material culture might once have appeared.

Each individual attempt to physically reconstruct the past is, as Paul Bidwell has emphasized, 'A product of archaeological reasoning and its validity depends entirely on the soundness of that reasoning and the reliability, relevance and range of the archaeological evidence'.[44] Our understanding of how Roman buildings and structures might have looked is transformed as academic knowledge is constructed and, as we have seen, this process is

---

[39] Lengkeek (2008); cf. Labadi (2010).   [40] Lengkeek (2008), 37.
[41] cf. Blain and Wallis (2007), 36.   [42] cf. Baudrillard (2005), 81.
[43] cf. Pearson and Shanks (2001), 114.   [44] Bidwell *et al.* (1988), 155.

ongoing.[45] This is why the Saalburg reconstruction is now dated; a current rebuilding of this fort would look rather different to the late nineteenth-century structure because archaeological concepts of authenticity and value have changed as knowledge has developed as a result of further archaeological excavation and study. The Saalburg reconstruction survives, however, as a physical manifestation of German late nineteenth-century ideas about Roman frontier forts. It has been argued that a tension exists between the production of experiences for tourists and the conservation of heritage, and the question of the authentic cannot be answered simply, since the meaning of this concept varies according to the experience and interests of the individual who explores the remains.[46]

RESTORING *SEGEDUNUM*

The remains of the forts at Wallsend have had a very different history of re-commemoration, although the site and its museum is also managed by Tyne and Wear Archives and Museums as a means of interpreting the past and providing an attraction for visitors and the local community.[47] The Roman remains here constituted part of the open field system until 1778, when a coal shaft was sunk in the vicinity.[48] In the late eighteenth century, John Brand visited the site and remarked that, 'The fire engines and workings of a new colliery adjoining to *Segedunum*, will soon, it is probable, deface every vestige of this station, so that future antiquaries will search for the foundations in vain.'[49] Nevertheless there were still substantial remains across the south of the fort that were visible to Bruce as grassy mounds in 1851, although the whole rampart of the northern section had been lost and a number of industrial structures, including a colliery railway and an engine house, had been constructed both over and around the remains, while the Wallsend Pit was situated just to the west (Figure 14.7).[50] Small-scale excavations were undertaken during the later nineteenth and early twentieth centuries,[51] but in 1884 the street plan for new houses was laid out and by 1907 much of the site was covered in housing.[52] Three modern inscriptions, which commemorate the site, have subsequently been built into a stone memorial close to the museum at the fort of Wallsend (Figure 14.8).

The first inscription was carved in 1895 and originally placed at the south-eastern corner of the fort by the owner of the site, Frank Buddle Atkinson. He

---

[45] cf. Pearson and Shanks (2001), 115.   [46] Lengkeek (2008).
[47] MP, 21, 24; Paul Bidwell (pers. comm.).   [48] E. Birley (1961), 159.
[49] Brand (1789), 604.   [50] J. C. Bruce (1851), 113–16.
[51] E. Birley (1961), 160.   [52] J. C. Bruce (1907), 39; Spain and Simpson (1930), 488.

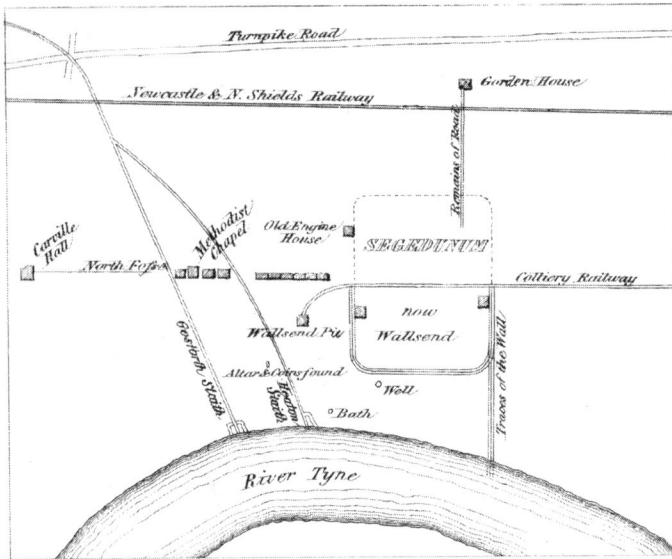

Fig. 14.7. A plan of the Roman site at Wallsend during the mid-nineteenth century. From J. C. Bruce (1851), 112.

Fig. 14.8. The modern memorial at *Segedunum* Roman Fort, Baths and Museum, which includes three modern commemorative inscriptions in Roman style. Photograph by Richard Hingley, 2010. Reproduced by permission of Tyne and Wear Museums on behalf of North Tyneside Council.

noted the presence of a 'Roman Camp', believed to be *Segedunum*, to the north-west. The inscription reads, 'THE INHABITANTS OF WALLSEND ARE REQUESTED TO CO-OPERATE FOR THE PROTECTION OF THIS INTERESTING MEMORIAL OF ANTIQUITY FROM WHICH THE TOWN DERIVES ITS NAME.' For decades, this stone stood in a garden on this site. A second stone, decorated in the manner of a Roman inscription, records the discovery of a portion of the east end of the curtain Wall in April 1903. Nearby lie the remains of the 'branch Wall', the foundations of a section of curtain Wall that used to run from the corner of the fort south-eastwards to the River Tyne. This section of curtain Wall had been found during works in the shipyard and was subsequently moved to Wallsend Park, accompanied by the inscription.[53] Both were returned to their current site in 1991, when the section of Wall was rebuilt on the site of the branch Wall, but not, it should be noted, exactly in its original location. A third inscription records the discovery of the east gateway of the fort, found in 1912 during the construction of a house, it was formerly built into Simpson's Hotel once located on the site of the present museum and heritage centre car park.

During the early twentieth century, this site was entirely covered by streets, houses, and shipyards. In 1929 the plan of the fort was established and the Wallsend Corporation marked its outline in the streets with white paving stones.[54] Hunter Davies has provided a vivid account of the site,[55] noting that:

> Today, there is not a scrap of the Fort left and I wouldn't advise anyone to try to look for it either. Wallsend Corporation has the limits of the fort marked out in white-washed cobble stones, which is kind of them, but they're hard to find. I was almost knocked over several times as I stooped in gutters, attempting to see which cobbles were less filthy than the others. The whole area seemed to be in the process of being knocked down. There was rubble everywhere and it looked as if a bomb had fallen.[56]

This situation was about to change in a very dramatic fashion. The terraced housing was demolished and almost the entire area of the fort was excavated between 1975 and 1984, with the Roman remains laid out for public display during the 1990s. The proposal for the new museum and reconstructions at Wallsend was put together during the late 1980s and the on-site work was carried out during the 1990s.[57] The visible Roman remains are accompanied by a substantial viewing platform and an extensive museum. More recently, a reconstructed Roman bath-house has been added, based on the substantial remains of the building excavated by John Clayton at Chesters (Figure 14.9).[58] In addition, a length of the stone curtain Wall has been reconstructed immediately adjacent to the main site, close to the displayed remains of the

---

[53] J. C. Bruce (1933), 38.   [54] Spain and Simpson (1930), 488; J. C. Bruce (1933), 38.
[55] H. Davies (1974), 6–11.   [56] ibid., 9.   [57] Paul Bidwell (pers. comm.).
[58] Breeze (2006a), 136. This new building was reconstructed just outside the remains of the Roman fort in order to avoid any direct impact upon its physical remains.

Fig. 14.9. The reconstructed bath-house at *Segedunum* Roman Fort, Baths and Museum. Photograph by Richard Hingley, 2010. Reproduced by permission of Tyne and Wear Museums on behalf of North Tyneside Council.

excavated foundations on which it was based (Figure 2.7). This reconstruction was built close to the site of the original structure but not on top of it, so that visitors could compare it with the Roman remains. Different types of pointing and plastering were used on the south face of the replica curtain Wall in order to emphasize that the Wall was maintained for a long period and that it was subject to modification. Neither of these two reconstructions generated controversy comparable to that occasioned by the proposal to construct the gateway at South Shields.[59]

During the construction of the visitor centre, the three modern inscriptions discussed above were fixed onto one side of a new memorial with the names of the centurions who had supervised the building work on the Wall on the other.[60] Below, space is provided for the addition of names from future discoveries of centurial stones. Barlow has suggested that this resembles a war memorial and commemorates the decline of the industry that once made Wallsend famous.[61] At the time the memorial was put in place, the massive cranes and slipways of the Swan Hunter Shipyard were visible just behind the remains of the Roman fort, and the construction of the memorial was part of the deliberate paradox of the new *Segedunum* created in the context of the contemporary decline of Wallsend's riverside industries.[62]

---

[59] Paul Bidwell (pers. comm.).   [60] ibid.
[61] Barlow (2007), 141.   [62] ibid.; Paul Bidwell (pers. comm.).

When this new visitor centre opened in 2000, Wallsend Metro station was installed with images of an imaginary view of a Roman town centre, in which road signs, street names, and shops were named in Latin.[63] As Barlow has recalled, the family-orientated local attraction at *Segedunum* opened shortly after the initial success of Ridley Scott's popular and successful movie *Gladiator*.[64] The film initially focuses on the savage fighting during the later second century as Rome attempted to bring the barbaric Germanic peoples to the north of the Rhine into the Roman empire.[65] It is possible that Ridley Scott's early years at South Shields, close the east end of Hadrian's Wall, inspired his interest in this theme. *Gladiator* was an immense box-office success and this new visitor experience drew upon the film's popularity through advertising.[66]

Gladiator has been the subject of considerable critical analysis and it is tempting to draw on this to consider the *Segedunum* development.[67] For example, Sandra Joshel and her co-authors have described the representation of the city of Rome in the film in the following terms: 'The new "real" Rome in *Gladiator* is a pastiche of a seventeenth-century Spanish fort on Malta (rebuilt by Napoleon in classical style), pictures of classical buildings from all over Europe, and computer-generated effects. Thus its physical setting is formed by pasting together different Roman buildings in different places...images [which]...would seem to re-process other pop-culture Romes.'[68] Barlow has suggested that the pop-culture version of Rome created through *Gladiator* impacted upon Tyneside, helping to create a fantasy of the kind represented by some alternative history novels in which Rome has never fallen.[69] In this fantasy, Barlow has suggested that Wallsend can reclaim its former role as the 'final outpost of Western civilisation confronting the wild wilderness to the north'.[70] This is a rather unfair representation of the new *Segedunum*, since the intention here was to develop Wallsend's main cultural asset and to improve its economy and ambience.[71] The Swan Hunter Shipyard has now closed and the cranes and slipways have been partly dismantled and cleared away but, as Paul Bidwell has noted, 'in fifty years' time the river may be as busy as it was fifty years ago'.

Other new buildings at Wallsend, including an employment agency called 'Hadrian House' (Figure 14.3) and the 'Forum' Shopping Centre, project the power of the image of the restoration of Roman order.[72] These elements of the urban infrastructure draw upon classical branding, however loosely the theme is interpreted. Through their facades, these buildings help to project a Roman identity that draws upon the location of Hadrian's Wall, while also raising

---

[63] Barlow (2007), 139–40.   [64] ibid., 139.
[65] Eckstein (2005), 54.   [66] Barlow (2007), 139–40.
[67] e.g. Joshel *et al.* (2001); Winkler (2005).   [68] Joshel *et al.* (2001), 1.
[69] cf. Willis (2007).   [70] Barlow (2007), 140.
[71] Paul Bidwell (pers. comm.); cf. Daniels and Cowell (2011), 110.
[72] Barlow (2007).

again the problematic issue of authenticity. The reconstructed buildings at the forts of Vindolanda, South Shields, and Wallsend were all built to create a realistically Roman experience for visitors, an approach that draws upon archaeological knowledge of the design and appearance of such structures.[73] A different motivation lay behind the design and construction of the employment agency and shopping centre since these did not aim to create an authentic cultural experience.

A COMPOSITE WALL

Barlow's claim for the Romanization of Tyneside may be extended to encompass much of the landscape through which the Wall runs since this is merely the most extensive of the various attempts to draw on the spirit of Rome through a widespread re-commemoration of *Britannia's* northern frontier (Figure 14.10).[74] Robert Witcher has observed that,

> Along the route of the Wall, there has been a long-term trend for 'Romanizing' the names of pubs, restaurants, and guesthouses (e.g. the Milecastle Inn at Cawfields, formerly the Common House). Over the past 15 years this trend has accelerated markedly leading to a new prominence of 'Roman-ness' in the landscape. There is a particular concentration in areas of urban regeneration such as Wallsend (e.g. Hadrian Mews), Byker (e.g. Hadrian Square), and Haltwhistle (e.g. Hadrian Business Park).[75]

The most dramatic examples of this practice of renaming is provided by the three Roman forts and visitor centres at Vindolanda, *Arbeia*, and *Segedunum*, since these places have been renamed in modern times by drawing upon their former Roman titles, recovered from classical sources. Local businesses draw more generally on the identity of the Wall, as in the case of the Hadrian Brewery, located in Newcastle, and Hadrian's Air Conditioning & Refrigeration Ltd., based in Washington (Tyne and Wear). The widespread use of the identity of the Wall attributes a particular popular valence to its remains.

It has already been suggested that many of the most impressive stone remains along the Wall—including lengths of the curtain Wall and the milecastles, turrets, and forts along its line—are composite in character, partly Roman and partly modern in structure and spirit. Since the mid nineteenth century, turrets, milecastles, forts, and buildings in *vicus* settlements have been uncovered, consolidated, and displayed and are subject to ongoing actions in

---

[73] Mortimer (2007, 20) suggests that the modern reconstruction of the bath-house at *Segedunum* has been 'renovated' rather than created.

[74] cf. Whitworth (2000), 35–6.

[75] Witcher (2010a), 145.

Fig. 14.10. A Romanized name on the Wall, at Haltwhistle. Photograph by Richard Hingley, 2011.

order to ensure that their remains do not deteriorate. In this process of the cultural reconstruction of the Wall, the modern versions of Roman buildings at Vindolanda, South Shields, and Wallsend constitute the most thoroughly rebuilt elements of this composite monument—structures that have been consciously built from the foundations as part of the interpretation and display of particular sites for visitors. In many other places, the composite elements of the Wall are partly Roman and partly later in date and, indeed, what we are looking at is often difficult to entirely ascertain.

Two examples of the rebuilding of the curtain Wall are the late medieval structure at Hare Hill close to Lanercost (see Chapter 4) and an early eighteenth-century refacing of the Wall between Carrow and Walwick (Chapter 6). Other sections may well also have been rebuilt prior to the nineteenth century and, since little recording occurred when the Clayton and the DOE Walls were constructed, it is likely that there has been significant reconstruction to the face and top of the curtain Wall. The Wall has been rebuilt on numerous occasions for a variety of reasons, including the prevention of raiding, as a field boundary, and to conserve and display its remains.

Intentional remodelling and reconstruction of turrets, milecastles, and forts may have been far less common. Despite this, the stone remains of these structures have been consolidated and managed since they were uncovered, resulting in changes in the form and character of the remains that are displayed. This is inevitable and the only way to avoid this issue would be to rebury excavated remains swiftly, but this would prevent visitors from being able to study and appreciate these parts of the Wall. Today, all of the uncovered stone remains visible along the line of the Wall provide information about its origins, transformation, and history, from the second century to the present day. For example, various details of the structure of the curtain Wall remain visible where Clayton and the DOE have consolidated it. It is unlikely that any of the reconstruction and consolidation work that has occurred along the Wall would have been so fundamental as to have substantially altered the width of the curtain Wall itself. The exact locations, shapes, dimensions, and details of the consolidated turrets, milecastles, and forts also incorporate vital evidence for the character and sequence of the construction of the Wall. The Hadrian's Wall *Handbook* describes and explains the significance of these features,[76] which can also be investigated on site. This does not detract, however, from the composite nature of all visible stone elements of the Wall. By contrast, many of the earthwork elements of the frontier—the Vallum, northern ditch, the turf Wall, and the unexcavated sections of the stone curtain Wall with its turrets and milecastles—may have been little altered since Roman times. These remains have been eroded, filled in, and in some cases, partly cleared and re-excavated, but often without substantial changes being made to their original characters.

Neither of the two extreme positions with regard to the authenticity of the Wall addressed above, therefore, is entirely supportable. Hunter Davies' idea that the Wall is a living entity growing with each new endeavour, if taken to an extreme, may justify forms of rebuilding that might intentionally damage or destroy the character of the surviving monument; not, it should be said, that this was what Davies intended. A 'pop culture' reconstruction of a section of the curtain Wall or of a building from a fort would have little value for visitors and might actively damage and obscure any archaeological remains over which it was built. The neo-Roman employment agency and shopping centre at Wallsend are built well away from the remains of the Roman Wall and have no direct impact on the monument. On the other hand, a strict insistence on the archaeological veracity of the evidence for a particular section of Hadrian's Wall would deny the fact that the acts of uncovering, consolidating, and displaying archaeological remains inevitably impact on the surviving structure of what has become composite through time. It would also suggest that the values pursued in archaeological study are in some way timeless and objective, that they are not in any way related to the social contexts in which each archaeologist operates.

Archaeological theories and methods often remove the material traces of past society, including artefacts and buildings, from the context of the present in which they are studied; this is achieved by placing these ancient materials in a linear sequence of time.[77] This is based on an archaeological approach that has erected a conceptual barrier between the physical evidence for the 'real' Roman monument and modern manifestations along the line of the Wall,

---

[76] Breeze (2006a).   [77] cf. Pearson and Shanks (2001), 114.

including the reconstructed buildings, re-enactments, and representations in novels, in the cinema, and the internet. The archaeological study of the Wall since the 1890s has usually been based on the idea that an authentic monument can be recovered through the collection of evidence for its origin, date, sequence, authorship, and signature.[78] This creates a sequence for the Roman history of the monument, outlined in Chapter 2,[79] a story that ends in immediately post-Roman times.

The dominant approach to the interpretation of the Wall has emphasized the creation of 'certainty' through the accumulation of secure and reliable knowledge.[80] Efforts have been made to establish a Roman system of frontier structures that is perceived as authentic and to distance the monument from the context of the present in which its remains persist. This process of interpretation has promoted the idea of a 'real' Wall on which the policies for its protection and management have been based.[81] Given the past and present threats to the material structure of the monument and the need to justify refusing development proposals, an emphasis on the definition of the Wall as a Roman monument is understandable. Nevertheless, the determination of definitive knowledge of a closed monument may also effectively kill 'the Wall', both detracting from the potential to collect new information and to challenge existing knowledge.

It has been emphasized in this book that the post-Roman elements of the Wall are, in themselves, part of the monument's character. In the act of becoming composite, the Wall has taken on new values that increase its significance and help to keep its remains alive. The example of the Clayton Wall clearly demonstrate that the activities of consolidation and display radically alter the elements of the monument on which they are based, eventually resulting in the need to conserve and interpret the neo-Roman reconstruction itself. The composite nature of Hadrian's Wall also increases the range of values it incorporates today and does not erode its significance as a Roman construction.[82] The attempts that are made to define and protect the Wall from inappropriate development should not prevent the uncovering of new evidence, since this helps to keep knowledge of the monument alive for contemporary communities, including local people, visitors, and archaeologists.

The various acts of renaming and rebuilding referenced here appear to suggest the erosion of a clear concept of *the* Roman Wall, since neo-Roman manifestations are proliferating across its landscape. Although this book is attempting to excavate and erode the idea of Hadrian's Wall as an entirely Roman phenomenon, it is important to realize that internationally significant Roman deposits survive at the core of its remains, since these justify the

---

[78] cf. Baudrillard (2005), 81.   [79] cf. N. Hodgson (2008).
[80] Breeze (2003), 13.   [81] cf. Blain and Wallis (2007), 33–4.   [82] cf. Labadi (2007).

considerable significance attributed to this ancient frontier. It is essential to be able to at least partly disconnect modern representations of Rome—including the reconstructed Roman gateway at South Shields, or the employment agency and shopping centre at Wallsend—from the material remains on which they are drawing, however literally or loosely.[83] In urban Tyneside, archaeological excavations since 1998 have provided important new information about the character and function of the monument, but in many cases these remains are deeply buried and require intricate physical and metaphorical excavation.

VALUING RESEARCH POTENTIAL

The partial reconstruction of the Roman forts at Wallsend and South Shields indicate that the urban sections of the Wall have the potential to continue to evolve in planned ways. This is more problematic for the upland sections of the monument, where the emphasis is upon landscape conservation. It has been seen that the protection of Hadrian's Wall and its landscape in the upland sections has the potential to prevent future excavation, since the priority here is upon the conservation of the archaeological and landscape values of the monument. For the past ten years, much of the new research on the Wall has depended on urban redevelopment and has been conducted as a result of developer-funded archaeology. Around ten per cent of Hadrian's Wall underlies the modern urban conurbations of Carlisle and Tyneside.[84] In these areas the Wall is often deeply buried and occasionally quite well preserved. New urban developments in the past three decades have resulted in important new discoveries at Carlisle and urban Tyneside,[85] enabling the understanding of Hadrian's Wall to continue to evolve.

Nick Hodgson has noted that many of the sites excavated in advance of urban development today are small in scale, but several have provided important information about the location of the curtain Wall in Tyneside where it had been lost for centuries.[86] The most notable discovery has been the location at a number of places in urban Tyneside of systems of cut features on the berm between the curtain Wall and northern ditch (Figure 14.11). In 1998, an excavation at Buddle Street, Wallsend, produced evidence for such a 'system of obstacles',[87] post pits arranged in three rows, possibly originally installed with the timbers with sharpened ends (*cippi*) mentioned by Julius Caesar in *de Bello Gallico* (VII, 73).[88] Since 2000, comparable systems of pits have been found on the berm of the Wall at ten sites on its easternmost section and it is

---

[83] cf. Baudrillard (no date).   [84] C. Young (1999a), 36.
[85] N. Hodgson (2009b); Newman (2008), 32; Wilmott (2009a), 1–5.
[86] N. Hodgson (2009b), 5.   [87] Bidwell and Griffiths (1999).   [88] ibid., 96.

Fig. 14.11. Obstacles on the berm of Hadrian's Wall at Shields Road, Byker, Newcastle. Reproduced by permission of Tyne and Wear Museum Services.

likely that they occurred intermittently along the Wall's length, from Wallsend to Bowness-on-Solway.[89] Presumably these obstacles were not previously located because no-one had specifically looked for archaeological features along the berm. There is some evidence that they were replaced at several sites and Paul Bidwell has argued that they were an original aspect of the Wall's design due to the berm's exceptional width.[90] These features were probably intended as an impenetrable barrier against anyone approaching the Wall.[91]

Nick Hodgson has noted that these obstacles are the 'first addition to the repertoire of regular Wall-works' to have been located in modern times and that their discovery has reignited the discussion of the Wall's function.[92] It has been seen that the discussion of the potential function of the Wall was a popular topic in Victorian times and also during the early twentieth century. In particular, R. G. Collingwood championed the idea of the Wall as an elevated sentry-walk, an argument that appears to have been widely accepted.[93] The dominant perspective since this time has stressed the impracticality of the Wall as a military line of defence, emphasizing its role as a monitor of people and controller of their movement.[94] From the 1950s, Eric Birley supported this

---

[89] RFa, 44; N. Hodgson (2009b), 25–6.   [90] RFa, 44.
[91] Bidwell and Griffiths (1999), 96.   [92] N. Hodgson (2009b), 43.
[93] Collingwood's (1921b).   [94] cf. Breeze (2008a).

interpretation, which was subsequently explored by his colleagues and former students.[95] In the first edition of *Hadrian's Wall*, published in 1976, David Breeze and Brian Dobson argued that the Wall was 'a barrier indeed, but a non-defensive barrier, for Hadrian's Wall was not a medieval town or castle wall'.[96] They re-emphasized Collingwood's argument that the top of the curtain Wall had not acted as a fighting platform,[97] concluding that there was no specific evidence that Roman soldiers could even patrol along its top.

In 1990 John Mann built on the doubts of Breeze and Dobson about the existence of a Wall-walk,[98] which was pursued by Peter Hill and Brian Dobson in a later paper.[99] These authors argued that the Broad Wall, about ten feet wide, may originally have been intended to support a Wall-walk but that it is unlikely that an effective patrol could have been maintained along the Narrow Wall, which was only six to eight feet wide. Since the amount of Broad Wall surviving along the line of Hadrian's Wall appears to be very small,[100] this effectively undermined the idea that a Wall-walk was provided along the top of the entire length of the stone structure. On the Narrow Wall, the walkway could only be around 1.4 metres wide and, although adequate for a single soldier to walk along behind a parapet, it would have been difficult for two soldiers carrying shields to pass each other, since there would have been a substantial drop to the rear and possibly no parapet on this side.[101] Hill and Dobson discussed several possibilities for the Wall top, including the idea that it was a sloping structure allowing rainwater run off, but they preferred the idea that the Wall was flat-topped with a low parapet and no crenellations.[102] This suggests that a Wall-walk may originally have been intended for Hadrian's Wall but that this plan was probably not carried forward after the reduction in the Wall-width.

Breeze and Dobson have argued that Hadrian's Wall is 'a barrier indeed, but not designed to thwart an attack in strength'.[103] Many of the other frontiers of the Roman empire consisted of timber palisades or narrow walls without walkways, which these authors have taken to indicate that the purpose of Hadrian's Wall was to 'allow the army to supervise small-scale movements of people, prevent petty raiding, hinder large-scale attacks and so encourage the peaceful development of the province'.[104] The surveillance of the ground in front and behind the Wall was conducted from the turrets and milecastle towers, and unauthorized crossing of the frontier by raiding parties prevented, while more serious problems would require the use of soldiers from the forts positioned along the Wall line.[105] It is therefore probable that the Wall was

---

[95] A point emphasized by Daniels (1979), 360 and Bidwell (2008), 129.
[96] Breeze and Dobson (1976), 143.   [97] ibid., 39.   [98] Breeze (2008a), 1.
[99] Hill and Dobson (1992).   [100] ibid., 28; cf. RFa, 37.
[101] Hill and Dobson (1992), 28.   [102] ibid., 29–33.
[103] Breeze and Dobson (2000), 149.   [104] ibid., 26.   [105] ibid., 39.

designed to control the movement of people and, perhaps, also to control and tax trade.[106]

The provision of many gateways through the Wall may support the idea that the main purpose of the barrier was to control access to and from the province, not to prevent it. It is sometimes considered that civilians could pass through on payment of customs dues, drawing on the writing of Tacitus about customs regulations that existed on the River Rhine.[107] This is a possibility that was first raised by R. G. Collingwood, when he compared Hadrian's Wall to the Indian Customs Hedge.[108] To summarize the protective explanation for the Wall, Breeze has argued that it had a range of functions, from controlling access to and from the province, to taxing exports and imports, and acting as a base for the Roman army to mass and combat serious threats. He has argued, however, that the Wall was protective rather than purely defensive, since the Roman army was not intending to fight determined attackers from any battlements that the Wall may have possessed.

Despite the domination of the idea that the Wall represented an observation and policing measure, some still argue for a directly defensive purpose.[109] Paul Bidwell has pointed out that we do not actually know that civilians were able to pass through the milecastle gates and there is also some debate about whether there were causeways across the northern ditch outside these gateways, since these are not very apparent today.[110] Even if regular causeways were shown to exist outside the northern gateways of all the milecastles, this would not settle the question of the function of the Wall, since the issue of civilian access across its line was dependant on the policy pursued by the Roman frontier forces.[111] Jim Crow has proposed that it is quite possible that access through the Wall was only allowed at the two points where main Roman roads passed through its line, which would suggest that the construction of the Wall had a highly significant impact upon local people.[112]

Bidwell defined his recent paper as an account that aims to 'give fuller voice to this muted dissent', and to argue that the Roman army intended to defend the Wall from a crenellated walkway, an explanation that its sheer size might well support.[113] The discovery of obstacles on the berm between the Wall and the ditch constitutes part of the evidence that Bidwell used to emphasize the potentially defensive nature of this frontier. A number of other detailed observations are also marshalled, including the reassessment of the width and detailed structure of the Wall as revealed in several places through

---

[106] Isaac (2000), 414.   [107] Breeze and Dobson (2000), 15–16, 40.
[108] Collingwood (1923), 30–2.
[109] Including Daniels (1979), 360–1; Crow (1991), 53; Bidwell (1999b), 31–5.
[110] Bidwell (1999b), 35.   [111] N. Hodgson (2009b), 23–4; RFa, 46.
[112] Crow (2004b), 131.   [113] Bidwell (2008), 129.

excavation, comparisons with Roman defensive architecture elsewhere in the empire, and a reconsideration of Roman defensive weaponry.

The function of the Wall remains a contested issue and the discovery of the obstacles on the berm appears to have reignited a difference of opinion that has existed for much of the past century. Bidwell has argued that every aspect of the design of Hadrian's Wall is entirely consistent with the idea of a Wall-walk and crenellated parapet,[114] while Breeze has proposed that the obstacles merely represent another element of control along the frontier, analogous to the trip-wires along the line of the Berlin Wall.[115] In this context, Breeze has mentioned that the purpose of frontier walls built since the 1960s, including the Berlin Wall and the Israeli Separation Wall, is to control the movement of people and not armies. Collingwood used the Indian Customs Hedge as an aid to his reinterpretation of the purpose of Hadrian's Wall, and Breeze has drawn upon other modern parallels for the same purpose. The use of analogy remains a vital part of any effective interpretation of the Wall, but it should also be kept in mind that modern frontier walls are built in very different contexts from that of the Roman frontier of second-century Britain.[116] Breeze has summarized his protective argument by observing, with regard to the Wall-walk and parapet, that:

> Unfortunately, no piece of evidence is conclusive, and in coming to a conclusion each of us falls back on our own interpretations of the function of Hadrian's Wall. My own preference is to envisage the Wall without a walkway along the top, but I cannot prove this. It simply fits more closely my view of the function of the artificial barriers on Roman frontiers.[117]

As Paul Bidwell has observed, the question of function is an archaeological problem that can only be answered through further archaeological work.[118] Effectively, however, even if the existence of a Wall-walk and crenellations could be conclusively demonstrated through excavation, this would not necessarily lead to a fuller comprehension of the Wall's function. This is because it could be argued that any such features were primarily symbolic rather than functional. Using the example provided by Roman city walls, Hadrian's Wall might, perhaps, have drawn on specifically defensive architectural features not necessarily for reasons that were primarily defensive.[119] Indeed, if it proved possible to demonstrate conclusively that crenellations and a walkway existed, this would only return the argument to the position

---

[114] ibid., 142; cf. N. Hodgson (2009b), 44.   [115] Breeze (2008a), 3.

[116] Paul Bidwell (pers. comm.) has observed to me that the East German government called the Berlin Wall the '*Antifaschistischer Schutzwall*', a wall that protected their population from the fascist West German state.

[117] Breeze (2008a), 1.

[118] Bidwell (1999b), 35.

[119] cf. Adams (2007).

outlined in 1921, when Collingwood proposed that the walkway along the Wall was not used as a fighting platform but as a means of patrolling the line. It is also quite possible that the function of the Wall changed over time, with a highly symbolic frontier work developing a more specifically defensive role in troubled times.

Clearly, the debate about the Wall's function will continue—and this, in itself, demonstrates the vitality of contemporary research on the Wall and the need for future excavation. It is possible that, one day, excavations will produce evidence to enable the significant issue of the Wall's function to be addressed more conclusively and it is likely that any significant new information will derive from the urban areas of the Wall rather than from the scenic upland sections.

SUMMARY: A COMPOSITE ROMAN WALL

The consolidation, reconstruction, and rebuilding of elements of the Wall represent attempts to recreate the monument's elemental 'Romanness'. Doubts continue to exist about the ethics of reconstructing Roman buildings on site, but the recent projects at Wallsend and South Shields have gone ahead without dispute or even debate. Reconstructions along the Wall have been based on the fullest assessment of contemporary knowledge. The discovery of the obstacles on the berm indicates that the understanding of the basic form of Hadrian's Wall as a barrier is likely to change in future, as the result of excavations and further detailed study. Changes in knowledge of the Wall will lead, in turn, to new forms of reconstruction. Archaeologists often work to establish a clear chronological division between the Roman remains of the Wall and its manifestation as a modern heritage and tourism asset. This book has emphasized that it *is* important to retain the idea of an authentic Roman Wall, but that we need to recognize that such an ideal is an abstraction that requires detailed metaphorical and physical excavation in each of the particular contexts in which the monument is experienced. Protection of the remains of the Wall is vital in order to conserve these significant deposits for future study, but it is also important that archaeological excavations continue, since these help to drive the changes in interpretation that keep the Wall alive through the transformation of knowledge.

The regional and international significance of the monument is emphasized by the way that Wallsend has drawn upon the image of the Roman Wall in order to remake itself. Attempts have been made to undermine the Roman credentials of this particular attempt at urban regeneration, but it is also important to recognize the living significance of the Roman Wall. Roman Wallsend now provides so much more for the archaeologist and the visitor to study than was the case when Hunter Davies visited the site during the early 1970s. Roman sites in urban Tyneside also attract tourists away from the better-known upland sections of the monument, helping to prevent erosion to some of the most popular sites and provide a distinctly different experience for the visitor.

15

The Hadrian's Wall Path National Trail: The Inclusive Monument

To think with ruins of empire is to emphasize less the artifacts of empire as dead matter or remnants of a defunct regime than to attend to their reappropriations and strategic and active positioning within the politics of the present.

Ann Laura Stoler (2008), 196

INTRODUCTION

The Hadrian's Wall Path National Trail opened in May 2003. This long-distance footpath from Wallsend to Bowness-on-Solway mainly follows the line of Hadrian's Wall. From the memorial in the *Segedunum* Museum (Figure 14.8), it runs for eighty-three miles until it reaches a small modern shrine at the west end of the Wall at Bowness (Figure 15.1). From the perspectives of this chapter, the Trail fulfils two fundamental role: firstly, it serves to recreate Hadrian's Wall as a linear monument, reconnecting elements that have been broken up by development and agricultural operations over 1,600 years and, second, it serves an inclusive function by channelling foot traffic along the line of the Wall.[1] This chapter will discuss a new and more socially inclusive role for the Wall that has come to prominence during the past two decades in academia, popular culture, and tourism.[2] It is at the interface between the ancient past and the contemporary world that the Wall continues to play a particularly prominent role.

The Great War and the problems emerging in Europe during the 1930s gave rise to more open criticisms of imperial force and armed combat that have influenced views of the Roman military for much of the past century.[3] The poet Wilfrid Gibson, son of the archaeologist John Pattison Gibson from Hexham,[4] wrote a number of poems that referred to the landscape of the

---

[1] Witcher *et al.* (2010), 122.   [2] cf. Hingley (2010b), 238–40.
[3] S. James (2002), 13.   [4] Currey revised by Basu (2004).

Fig. 15.1. The modern shrine at the west end of the Hadrian's Wall trail at Bowness. Photograph by Richard Hingley.

Wall. In 'Stillchesters,' Gibson imagined himself a farmer whose 'best pasture' contains the remains of a Roman fort. A team of archaeologists arrive to excavate the site and they disturb the spirit of one of the fort's Spanish auxiliary soldiers, who, having possessed the narrator's son, drives him crazy.[5] Joseph O'Neill's novel *Land Under England* (1935) draws upon a Roman underworld that is physically buried under Hadrian's Wall in order to provide a stern warning about the current dangers of Fascism. In 1937, W. H. Auden wrote the script for a BBC radio programme entitled *Hadrian's Wall from Caesar to the National Trust*, which was broadcast from the BBC studios at Newcastle upon Tyne on 25 November.[6] Auden wrote in the *Radio Times* that the Wall 'stood as a symbol for certain imperialistic conceptions of life, for military discipline and an international order; in opposition to the Celtic and Germanic tribal loyalties which over-whelmed it... The front of history now lies elsewhere, but the same issue of order versus liberty... still remain'.[7]

[5] Gibson (1926). I am grateful to Nick Hodgson for this reference.

[6] Carpenter (1981), 231–2. A highly contrasting view of the Roman occupation of Britain was provided by a book on Roman Britain by the Italian author C. M. Franzero (1936), which includes a chapter on Hadrian's Wall and a dedication to Benito Mussolini.

[7] Quoted in Carpenter (1981), 231.

This programme included Auden's poem 'Roman Wall Blues'

> Over the heather the wet wind blows,
> I've lice in my tunic and a cold in my nose.
>
> The rain comes pattering out of the sky,
> I'm a Wall soldier, I don't know why.
>
> The mist creeps over the hard grey stone,
> My girl's in Tungria; I sleep alone.
>
> Aulus goes hanging around her place,
> I don't like his manners, I don't like his face.
>
> Piso's a Christian, he worships a fish;
> There'd be no kissing if he had his wish.
> She gave me a ring but I diced it away;
> I want my girl and I want my pay.
>
> When I'm a veteran with only one eye
> I shall do nothing but look at the sky.[8]

Auden deliberately inverted Kipling's sentiments in his poem 'The Roman Centurion Speaks'.[9] Kipling's centurion has been called back to Rome but feels deeply that he belongs in *Britannia* where his wife and child are buried, while Auden's Roman soldier does not know why he is serving on the Wall and is desperate to return to his girlfriend in Tungria.

The Second World War and the dismantling of the British empire caused further critical reflection on the nature of Roman imperialism, as did the construction of the Berlin Wall during the 1960s.[10] Hunter Davies wrote that the Vallum served as, 'a prototype Berlin Wall, stopping any native British tribesmen who'd been pressganged into serving on the Wall from escaping south to their homes'—evidently, this is not an entirely positive image.[11] The abandonment and dismantling of the Berlin Wall in 1989 demonstrated that physical works do not last forever, but it also generated disputes over the creation of the Berlin Wall Memorial Site.[12] The construction of highly divisive physical and political frontiers in the modern world, such as those between the US and Mexico, and in Palestine, has raised worrying contemporary parallels for those who wish to reflect positively on Hadrian's Wall. These modern frontiers are reminders of the physical and military force used today to prevent the free movement of people throughout the world.[13]

These negative reflections have been countered over the past decade by emphasizing an aspect of Hadrian's Wall that helps to separate this Ancient

---

[8] Auden (1937).　　[9] Kipling (1911).
[10] cf. Hingley (2005), 37.　　[11] H. Davies (1974), 16.
[12] Camphausen (1999); Trotnow (1999).　　[13] Hingley (2008c), 27.

Monument from contemporary frontier works. Since Victorian times, the variety of people from different parts of the Roman empire that are known to have served on the Wall has been used to reflect on the apparently multicultural nature of those who built and lived in this landscape. Since the 1880s, visitors have been encouraged to explore the monument through the excavation, conservation, display, and the interpretation of the places along its line and, more recently, through re-enactment events. The image of Hadrian's Wall as a divisive structure is reversed by projects that address it effectively as a socially inclusive monument,[14] a concept that draws upon the idea that Rome brought various disparate peoples within the ambit of its culture. This concept draws on the Wall's role as a World Heritage Site, a highly accessible modern landscape. The geographically widespread origin of the people who lived on the Wall in Roman times helps to market it as an inclusive monument for all to visit and appreciate.

In this chapter, it will be argued that the issue of social inclusion requires detailed consideration, since it serves to sideline apparently less attractive themes, including the essentially divisive role played by all military fortifications throughout history. The negative impact of the Wall upon the communities of this area of Britain throughout time should not be ignored, as the past cannot only represent a source for positive reflection.[15] This chapter will address the extent to which the Wall may be seen to have been both divisive and inclusive, since the nature of its role depends on whose point of view is being taken into account.[16]

RE-ESTABLISHING THE UNITY OF THE WALL

Much of the Wall is scheduled under the Ancient Monuments and Archaeological Areas Act 1979, but a further level of designation was granted in 1987 when it was inscribed as a World Heritage Site (WHS) by UNESCO. This development enabled a more integrated approach to the monument's management. Under *The Ancient Monuments and Archaeological Areas Act 1979*, ancient sites are defined as of 'national importance', institutionalizing the close association that already existed between Hadrian's Wall and English national identity.[17] We have seen that this Ancient Monument has long played a powerful role in English society as a referent for the northern frontier of national space and as a signifier for the frontier of the civilized.[18]

---

[14] Hingley (2010b), 238.   [15] Hingley (2010c); Morley (2010).
[16] Hingley (2010b), 239; cf. Warnaby, Medway and Bennison (2010), 1377–9.
[17] Witcher *et al.* (2010), 114; cf. Harvey (2003).   [18] Hingley (2010a), 25.

The progressive scheduling of the Wall's remains effectively confirmed and perpetuated these national valuations.[19]

When it was first inscribed as a WHS, Hadrian's Wall was defined as the most complex and best preserved of the frontiers of the Roman empire.[20] Its inscription effectively redefined the Wall's national significance as international or global, since World Heritage Sites are considered to be of universal importance to humanity.[21] Christopher Young has observed that 'Recognition by UNESCO of the site as being of universal significance to the peoples of the world helped to raise its profile and the sense of its importance locally and among decision makers.'[22] Following its inscription, the first *Management Plan* for Hadrian's Wall was produced. UNESCO promotes the idea that each WHS requires a unified management plan and the production process of this formal document has helped to emphasize and communicate the essential unity of Hadrian's Wall to those involved in its management, interpretation, and marketing. Young has also observed that the Wall's inscription as a WHS served to emphasize its unity, including the sections in the urban areas of Tyneside and Carlisle, where most of the physical traces of its course have been lost and are not scheduled. Considerable promotional work carried out since this time has presented the Wall as a unified phenomenon.

The Hadrian's Wall *Management Plan* has now moved through three stages and the latest, which covers the years from 2008 to 2014, was published in 2009 and is widely available on the internet. This is the work of a substantial *Management Plan* Committee that was deliberately brought together to include representatives of all organizations and bodies with responsibilities and interests in the WHS.[23] This document intends to integrate the interests of the various stakeholders involved in the Wall, including planning authorities, Trusts, agencies, local landowners, archaeologists, environmentalists, and businesses. It emphasizes the advantages of the coordinated management, interpretation, and the marketing of the Wall and its setting, effectively helping to integrate the remains along its entire course into a unified whole.[24] In the *Management Plan's* terms, 'management . . . is the mechanism through which we strive to understand the history of the site, and its use and values for the present and the future'.

A non-profit organization, *Hadrian's Wall Heritage Ltd* (HWHL), was formally incorporated in 2006 to oversee and promote the implementation of the third iteration of the *Management Plan*, including taking on responsibility for overseeing the recently opened National Trail.[25] HWHL initially had core funding from the two regional development agencies and from English Heritage

---

[19] Witcher *et al.* (2010), 114.
[20] MP, 2; C. Young (1999a), 35; C. Young (1999b), 66–72.
[21] MP, 2; Witcher et al (2010), 115.   [22] C. Young (1999b), 66–7.
[23] MP, 3.   [24] cf. Warnaby, Medway and Bennison (2010).
[25] Breeze (2009b), 59; MP, 5. Unfortunately this organization was closed in Summer 2014.

Fig. 15.2. Produce from Hadrian's Wall Country. Reproduced by permission of Hadrian's Wall Heritage Ltd.

and Natural England. Its main focus is to coordinate and direct the contribution that the WHS can make to the economic and social benefit of local and regional communities, mainly through sustainable tourism.[26] This includes an aim to develop, manage, and deliver 'Wall-wide strategic initiatives'.[27] A number of projects are underway, including an ambitious programme to improve interpretation and visitor facilities within the WHS.[28] HWHL has also been promoting and relaunching the 'Hadrian's Wall Country' brand, which includes local produce created in and around the corridor of the Wall (Figure 15.2). The *Management Plan* notes 'A strong brand based on true, pertinent and desirable values can deliver positive messages to potential visitors. The 'Hadrian's Wall Country' brand was introduced in 2002/2003, and it continues to convey and reinforces values that encourage visitors.'[29]

In addition to the archaeological structures of the Wall, many of which are well protected, the setting of the monument is also vital and its management is one of the objectives of the *Management Plan*.[30] During the eighteenth century, antiquaries began to draw attention to the significance of the Wall's

---

[26] Breeze (2009b), 59.   [27] MP, 5.
[28] Interpretational Framework (2010).   [29] MP, 76.
[30] ibid., 10; cf. Witcher *et al.* (2010), 109–10.

setting and the policy for the protection of the monument during the twentieth century has gradually come to emphasize the importance of its context in the wider landscape.[31] Although a single monument, the Wall's character and landscape context varies along its line, as has been shown in the last two chapters. The well-preserved and iconic character of the upland section of the Wall explains the care taken to preserve its remains since Clayton's time. Further east and west, sections have been leveled and, in some areas, built over, but some of the Wall's remains on urban Tyneside have been uncovered and displayed for the public. The complex of earth and stone elements that make up the Wall is far simpler to comprehend in the central section on the Whin Sill that in the urban areas of Carlisle and Tyneside. As a consequence, the area defined through the current *Management Plan* seeks to protect the setting of the monument in addition to its physical and archaeological elements, in order to ensure that the context of the monument is not lost along particular parts of its course.[32]

ACCESSING THE WALL

An interest had developed in exploring the remains of the Wall from the late sixteenth century and, since the travels of Hutton and Skinner at the start of the nineteenth century, people have become interested in walking the Wall from sea to sea.[33] In fact, Hutton and Skinner very much followed in the footsteps of Camden, Cotton, Gordon, Warburton, and Stukeley, who had visited particular parts of the monument in order to create their itineraries. Hutton's successful book of his experiences was followed up by other accounts. *Jenkinson's Practical Guide to Carlisle, Gilsland, Roman Wall and Neighbourhood* provided instructions for 'A walk along the Roman Wall from coast to coast'.[34] Jessie Mothersole's *Hadrian's Wall* gave an account of her journey along the monument that was inspired by Hutton's example.[35] Hunter Davies' popular *A Walk along the Wall* also encouraged visitors to follow in the footsteps of Hutton.[36]

Since the 1930s, the development of an entitlement to holidays, increasing prosperity, the improvement of the road system, and wider car ownership, has led to a substantial increase in the number of visitors to the Wall.[37] The number of people exploring Housesteads Roman fort rose to around 15,000 in 1935, when Queen Mary visited the site, and between 2002 and 2007 visitor

---

[31] C. Young (1999a), 37.   [32] MP, 10–12, 43–5.
[33] Burton (2003), 1; Newman (2008), 29.   [34] Jenkinson (1875), 172–212.
[35] Mothersole (1924).   [36] H. Davies (1974).
[37] Newman (2008), 29; C. Young (1999a), 37.

numbers averaged around 108,000 a year.[38] At Birdoswald, visitors increased from around 4,000 in 1987 to over 45,000 in 2000, mainly because of the archaeological excavations conducted at this site, the display of the remains, and the provision of a new exhibition.[39] Over the past 100 years, development at various archaeological sites along the line of the Wall—at South Shields, Wallsend, Chesters, Corbridge, Housesteads, Carvoran, Vindolanda, and Maryport—has served to make these places accessible to visitors and to provide the necessary infrastructure for them to appreciate and enjoy the experience. In recent times the Hadrian's Wall Tourist Partnership and its successors, including HWHL, have overseen these developments, since visitors provide a vital source of income to communities along the line of the Wall, particularly in the central section.[40] HWHL is currently coordinating a Wall-wide programme of investment to improve interpretation and visitor facilities. This programme is underpinned by an *Interpretational Framework* that advocates an inclusive approach through which visitors are enabled to explore and understand the monument in their own terms rather than exclusively through the eyes of archaeologists and academics.[41]

The Hadrian's Wall Path National Trail was planned as a reaction to the problems of accessing certain sections of the Wall and to the dangers of erosion of the monument caused by the number of visitors. The Trail has already proved a significant success and the *Management Plan* observes that:

> It has fulfilled its purpose of providing a recreational facility and increasing access to the archaeological remains of the WHS, and the number of walkers using it has made a significant contribution to the local economy. Whereas previous Management Plans were focused on the development and construction of the Trail, now that it is open as a Public Right of Way, this Plan needs to focus on its proactive and reactive management so that it continues to fulfil its objectives in a sustainable way.[42]

The opening of the Trail had a marked physical impact on the Wall through the creation of an extensive network of gates, styles, directional signs, and the occasional bridge (Figure 15.3).[43] It has also resulted in a process that Robert Witcher has described as a significant 're-presencing of the Wall' through street furniture and art installations that help to link the disparate parts of the monument into a linear visitor experience.[44] In places, the pre-existing path has been moved away from the line of the curtain Wall to avoid impacts on visible or buried archaeological remains.[45] The maintenance of the Path requires an active management regime to preserve the greensward wherever

[38] Crow (2004a), 140.   [39] Wilmott (2001), 20.
[40] Newman (2008), 29; MP, 66–70; C. Young (1999a), 40.
[41] *Interpretational Framework* (2010); Nigel Mills (pers. comm.).
[42] MP, 35.   [43] Newman (2008), 34.
[44] Witcher (2010a), 145.   [45] Newman (2008), 34–5.

Fig. 15.3. 'Pathway to Heaven': a directional sign connected with the Trail at Heavenfield. Photograph by Richard Hingley, 2011.

possible.[46] Problems of erosion exist in some places along the line and remedial action is required from time to time, a management regime that is overseen by HWHL.[47] Where the erosion problems are too severe, the least invasive engineering solutions are used to prevent damage to the monument.[48]

The *Management Plan* and Trail constitute just two of the elements that seek to reconnect the various surviving sections and elements of Hadrian's Wall and to promote widespread access. In 2006 the Hadrian's Wall Cycleway (National Cycle Route 72) was established along much of the length of the Wall.[49] This runs from Ravenglass along the Cumbrian coast and along the Wall corridor to South Shields. Another way of visiting the Wall between Newcastle and Carlisle during the summer is the 'Hadrian's Wall Country Bus' service, which stops regularly at the major monuments and modern villages and towns (Figure 15.4). The *Management Plan* notes that this provides a 'central role' in developing integrated and sustainable travel for visitors and those local people who work in businesses along the Wall.[50] In addition, Northern Rail now promotes the Tyne Valley railway line from Carlisle to Hexham and Newcastle as the 'Hadrian's Wall Country' line and certain trains carry the Hadrian's Wall Country livery to encourage passengers to travel along the Wall.[51]

There is a variety of places along its line where visitors can experience the displayed remains of the Roman archaeology of Hadrian's Wall. The Trail

[46] ibid., 29.　　[47] Breeze (2009b), 60.
[48] MP, 62.　　[49] MP, 35; Witcher *et al.* (2010), 115.
[50] MP, 61.　　[51] ibid., 61–2.

Fig. 15.4. The Hadrian's Wall Country Bus at Once Brewed. Reproduced by permission of Hadrian's Wall Heritage Ltd.

gives free access to various sections of stone curtain Wall, ditch, Vallum, and to the remains of forts, milecastles, turrets, bridges, and other structures. Heritage centres, museums, and archaeological sites drawing on the Roman Wall include the Roman forts at South Shields, Wallsend, Chesters, Housesteads, Vindolanda, and Maryport, the Roman Army Museum at Carvoran, the Great North Museum in Newcastle, Tullie House Museum and Art Gallery in Carlisle, and the Roman fort and urban site at Corbridge. These are all linked together by the transport infrastructure along the Wall.

At Chesters, South Shields, and Wallsend, forts have been excavated and displayed, while recent excavations in the upland sections of the Wall at Vindolanda and Birdoswald have focused on providing new experiences for visitors. The only major ongoing excavations on Hadrian's Wall that have continued for the past thirty or more years are at Vindolanda and South Shields. Excavations will continue for management purposes where remains are being eroded or threatened, such as at the western cemetery of Birdoswald that was partly excavated in 2009 in advance of erosion.[52] Research excavations on the well-preserved sections of the monument are, however, likely to be rare for the foreseeable future as a result of management issues and the availability of funding. Ambitious plans are underway to develop a major new interpretation centre at Camp Farm, Maryport, involving a new museum and a substantial programme of archaeological excavation.[53] This initiative promises an even higher profile for Hadrian's Wall, an approach that will add to its living spirit, although the plans are currently under review following the substantial funding cuts implemented by the government.[54]

---

[52] Tony Wilmott (pers. comm.).

[53] Breeze (2009b), 59; Interpretational Framework (2010).

[54] For a lively but poorly informed debate in Parliament about the current situation on Hadrian's Wall, see Hansard (2011). I am very grateful to Lindsay Allason-Jones for this reference. These cuts also threaten the management, marketing, and interpretation of the whole of the WHS.

The *Management Plan* contains details of the policies to make these attractions widely accessible to sustainable tourism and to coordinate the experience of visitors travelling between the Roman attractions of the Wall.[55] Guides available to visitors include the English Heritage guidebook, *Hadrian's Wall,* that provides a well-illustrated and accessible introduction and is regularly republished and kept up-to-date, while the *Handbook of the Roman Wall* provides a more detailed study of the individual elements of the monument.[56] In 2010, English Heritage published an excellent map of Hadrian's Wall that marks all the main features for visitors exploring the remains, replacing the older Ordnance Survey maps of the Wall, which have long been out of print. There is a wealth of other popular works on the Wall today, in a variety of media.[57]

The development of tourist attractions along the Wall has had a substantial economic impact during the past forty years, providing employment and extra income to local businesses, including bed and breakfasts. Tourism on the Wall provides a major contribution to the local economy.

THE INCLUSIVE WALL

As the British empire went into decline, authors rarely discussed the significance of the mixed communities that had served on the Wall in Roman times. In *The People of Roman Britain*, Anthony Birley used the evidence of the inscriptions to consider the men who came from across the empire to serve in Britain, including Africans, but he did not seek to identify the character of these people in any greater detail.[58] David Breeze and Brian Dobson discussed the recruitment of soldiers from various parts of the empire but not the potential ethnicity of these people.[59] Illustrators also appear to have retreated from dealing with such issues.[60] For example, although Frank Graham discusses the geographical origins of the soldiers who served on the Wall, only white-skinned soldiers are present in Ronald Embleton's iconic illustrations.[61] One of Embleton's images (Figure 15.5) does show two apparently dark-skinned soldiers involved in building the Wall, but they appear as such probably because they are depicted as standing in the shadows.

Despite this, the study of Roman frontiers has broadened since the 1940s, as research extended to new areas of the empire. The Centenary Pilgrimage visited the Wall in 1949 and Eric Birley arranged a new venture, the Congress

---

[55] MP, 65–71.   [56] Breeze (2006a); Breeze (2006b).
[57] N. Hodgson (2009b), 9.   [58] A. Birley (1979), 65–71, 76–81.
[59] Breeze and Dobson (1976), 148–53.   [60] Hingley (2010b), 238.
[61] Embleton and Graham (1984). For the way in which Embleton incorporated archaeological detail into his many paintings of life on the Wall, see Ewin (2000, 52).

Fig 15.5. Ronald Embleton's image of the *Building the Wall*. Reproduced by permission of Frank Graham.

of Roman Frontier Studies (Limes Congress) that same year.[62] The aim was to allow academics from other countries to attend the Pilgrimage, but the first *Limes* Congress proved to fill a real need for international Roman frontiers specialists.[63] The *Proceedings*, which included eight papers by continental, and three by British scholars, were published in 1952. Since then, eighteen further Roman Frontiers Congresses have been held in various countries, the twentieth being held in Newcastle in August 2009. This event, which has grown into a very substantial international conference that occurs every

---

[62] E. Birley (1952); E. Birley (1961), 40; E. Birley (1974).   [63] E. Birley (1952), v–vii.

three or four years, has led to a far more international focus on the frontiers of the Roman empire.[64]

The academic perspectives on the communities living along the line of Hadrian's Wall have also been changing, as the focus has transformed from a fixation upon the Roman frontier as the dividing line between the civilized and the barbarians to a new perspective that emphasizes the landscape as a zone of interaction and cultural transformation.[65] In particular, the recent rise of interest in the idea of 'the Roman army as community' has reconsidered the evidence for the identity and ethnicity of the Roman auxiliary soldiers, exploring their lives and identities.[66] For much of the twentieth century the dominant image was upon the way that membership of the Roman auxiliary and legionary forces helped to create a unified Roman military culture, one in which ethnic differences appear to have been submerged. Writers often emphasized the soldiers' mixed cultural roots as demonstrated by their religious dedications, while also stressing the relatively unified character of the military.[67] During the past thirteen years, a body of work has developed that explores the lives and culture of the soldiers of the Roman empire, addressing the ways in which they were recruited and subsumed into the empire, and also the extent to which they may have continued to maintain their own cultural identities within the unified military body.[68]

These approaches place a particular emphasis on the people who built and occupied the Wall, emphasizing daily life and community alongside military identity. In particular, returning to some earlier ideas, the Wall was evidently built by an extensive and multi-ethnic military community that was derived from across the Roman empire. As has already been shown, this may well have involved some assistance from the southern *civitates* at some stage during its construction or reconstruction,[69] indicating that the Wall was not entirely a military Roman structure. The civil population of the south of the province presumably also helped to supply men for the Wall, especially during late Roman times. Perhaps the accuracy of the accounts of Gildas and Bede may be reassessed in this regard. The forts and *vici* are usually supposed to have been populated by military units from overseas and by the groups of civilians who followed them, but some of the *vici* are so extensive that they must, presumably, have included members of the local population as well as people from across the province of *Britannia*.[70]

Recent accounts of the Roman army have proposed that military identities may have incorporated the different cultures from which the soldiers were

---

[64] cf. Freeman (1996); S. James (2005).   [65] Whittaker (1994), 2–9.

[66] Goldsworthy and Haynes (eds. 1999).

[67] e.g. Huskinson (2002), 119–20; S. James (2001), 78–80.

[68] S. James (1999); S. James (2001), 79–80.   [69] Fulford (2006).

[70] Local recruitment became the normal situation later in the history of the Roman empire, which will have helped to develop a mixed local population along the line of the Wall.

recruited. For example, Simon James has explored the nature of the Roman army as 'multiple military communities'. He writes:

> Given the diverse ethnic and national origins of Roman regiments, especially the auxilia but also at least some of the legions... the imperial military was always ethnically very mixed, and it is likely that the culture of each of these regimental communities was a unique interplay of Roman or Italian and other cultural traditions, even before we being to consider how they may have interacted with 'host' communities in the frontier zones.[71]

The *Agenda* of the Hadrian's Wall *Research Framework* stresses the importance of considering the 'ethnic composition' of individual military units along the Wall, arguing that the information for which units were present at which location is partial at best.[72] It is suggested that ethnic identity can be pursued most directly through the excavation of cemeteries and the study of diet, food supply, and pottery.

Turning to the occupants of *vici*, the *Research Framework* stresses that there is a fundamental issue of the clarification of the 'origins and identities' of these people.[73] There is still relatively limited evidence from the excavation of the *vici*. Important excavations occurred at Housesteads during the earlier part of the twentieth century and the ongoing excavations at Vindolanda are producing vitally important information about the *vicus* and its relationship to the successive stages of the fort.[74] Since the late 1990s, a series of extensive geophysical surveys have provided graphic evidence for the extent and complexity of these sites,[75] and the high number of inscriptions along the Wall provides an important source of information for future research on these topics. Some recent studies have built interesting new perspectives by drawing on archaeological materials to study the particular identities of military and civil communities across Britain, including ideas of diasporic populations.[76]

The developing academic agendas often appear to reconceive Hadrian's Wall as an inclusive structure coinciding with the policies of the agencies that encourage people to visit the monument from both the urban centres of northern England and from overseas, and coordinate these experiences.[77] Issues of gender along the Roman Wall appear to be less well served by traditional scholarship and interpretation. Three decades ago, Frances Horovitz was inspired by the objects in the museum at Chesters Roman fort to write 'Poem found at Chesters Museum, Hadrian's Wall'. She explored the 'balance between masculine and feminine', on the Wall and the author's monologue mentions that it draws, in particular, on the images of the nymph Coventina but also upon other artefacts in this collection.[78]

---

[71] S. James (2002), 43.   [72] RFb, 13.   [73] ibid., 15.
[74] R. Birley (2009).   [75] N. Hodgson (2009b), 35–6.
[76] Cool (2004); Eckardt (2010).   [77] MP, 22; Newman (2008), 29.
[78] Horovitz (1982) explains the inspiration that lay behind this poem.

For Horovitz, the Wall was 'great, dominant and striding', but the objects in this museum allowed a balance to be established in her poem. The reader of this book will have noticed the masculine bias in the works of many antiquaries, artists, and archaeologists prior to the late twentieth century, but some recent works of art have aimed to reconceive the Wall in less masculine terms. It is clear that the landscape of the Wall during Roman times was full of women and children, but this point often appears to have been difficult to communicate to the public and even to specialists.[79]

Another manifestation of broadening access to the Wall is evident in arts projects and exhibitions. One of the most impressive of these ventures is 'Writing on the Wall', which has encouraged artists to write about Hadrian's Wall.[80] The project drew upon literary approaches to borderlands as landscape contexts for multiple alternative histories, a theme addressed through the elucidation of the diverse cultures of border regions in the modern world.[81] Created by Steve Chettle, 'Writing on the Wall' was an international creative writing project that aimed to link the local communities along the line of Hadrian's Wall with writers from the provinces that had contributed troops to the Roman frontier. Running from 2001 to 2006, the project was partly funded by the Regional Development Agency One North-East and the Hadrian's Wall Tourist Partnership.[82] Chettle has noted that it was inspired by a number of earlier writings on Hadrian's Wall, including W. H. Auden's 'Roman Wall Blues,' and a media report on the Vindolanda tablets. The project included a series of educational and community-based workshops that took place along the route of the Wall, including people of all ages and abilities. Some of the writers involved came from Cumbria, Northumberland, Tyne and Wear, and Scotland, but the project also actively pursued contributors from countries from whose areas auxiliary units for Hadrian's Wall had been derived, including poets from Morocco, Romania, Iraq, the Netherlands, and Bulgaria,[83] projecting the Wall in phenomenological terms as a multinational monument, open to all.[84]

The first contribution in the published volume was by Sean O'Brien, who explains that the Wall has a special role as a place 'where people of all kinds, often drawn from remote places...have wandered, fought, loved and worked during two thousand years.'[85] In another contribution, Margaret Lewis remarks that the individual poets involved in the project reflected their own histories in a multitude of ways by writing of contemporary concerns.[86] She noted that some found it easy to imagine life among the settlements:

---

[79] Lindsay Allason-Jones (pers. comm.); cf. Culham (1997).
[80] Chettle (ed. 2006).   [81] cf. Vaquera-Vásquez (2006), 703.
[82] Chettle (ed. 2006), 2.   [83] M. Lewis (2006), 16.
[84] Hingley (2010b), 239.   [85] O'Brien (2006), 10.   [86] M. Lewis (2006), 16.

especially the life of women and ordinary soldiers. The idea of the Wall as a
barrier became significant to several poets, and also the lingering sense of a lost
empire, withering away. The land beyond the Wall has always presented as a
defining force. All these poets found their own work was being enhanced by the
interweaving of contemporary issues with a response to the landscape and the
historical events connected with it.

Here, once again, is a clear statement of how art draws directly upon the
physical archaeological remains, transporting Roman culture directly into the
context of contemporary concerns. The sense of a lost empire, withering away,
reflects on the ruination of the Wall, drawing on a tradition that originated
during the eighteenth century. The experiences expressed in this volume,
however, are far wider.

The Iraqi poet Hashem Shafiq visited a school in Newcastle and found the
experience of reading to and listening to primary children 'unique' and
'enchanting', observing that the children brought him back to his childhood
and closer to his poetry.[87] Margret Lewis asked 'So who does own the Stones?'
and replied: 'Every writer, every artist, every musician, every visitor who has
stopped to wonder and to respond to this World Heritage Site. This heritage
is for us all'.[88] As Sean O'Brien observed in his contribution, Hadrian's frontier is open to numerous different readings, 'It is capacious, mysterious,
hospitable to multiple and contradictory interpretations, as much at home
to the individual—the Roman legionary, the Victorian antiquary, the present-
day walker—as to the imperial strategy which ordered the vast and ingenious
labour which went into its construction' (Figure 15.6).[89]

One of the projects that arose from 'Writing on the Wall' was a specially
commissioned play, *Off the Wall*, written by Peter Mortimer. The playwright
and a group of six actors toured the line of the Wall on foot from west to east
in August 2004, arriving each evening at a rural location along the Wall's line
to hold a performance.[90] The play was a satire focused on an attempt by a local
entrepreneur to turn the Wall into the world's longest theme park, but the
action was also partly based in Roman times. Mortimer notes:

> The idea seemed organic and took on energy of its own; we decided that
> each small venue, as well as hosting the play would be closely involved before-
> hand. We would ask visual artists to go into these small communities, and work
> with them creating an individual backdrop for each performance. Each backdrop
> would fit onto our specially made frame, so that each performance was unique to
> its venue.[91]

The emphasis on the Wall as an inclusive monument for all to experience,
visit, and enjoy appears to be growing in popularity. As part of the *Tales of the*

---

[87] ibid., 18.   [88] ibid., 20.   [89] O'Brien (2006), 9.
[90] Mortimer (2007).   [91] ibid., 10.

Fig. 15.6. A cartoon by Jorodo titled 'Obsessives anonymous'- 'My name is Hadrian and I build walls'. Reproduced by permission of the *Evening Standard*, reference Jdo 0575.

Frontier project, the initiative that led to the production of this book, an exhibition entitled 'An archaeology of "race": exploring the Northern frontier in Roman Britain' sought to address the mixed nature of the peoples of the Roman Wall.[92] In an introduction to the exhibition catalogue, Mike Crang observed:

> The wall was garrisoned not by toga-draped Latin speakers but by a polyglot mix of recruits drawn from around the Roman world. The Roman empire served to allow people, things and ideas to move over great areas and mingle in new

---

[92] Tolia-Kelly and Nesbitt (2009); cf. Tolia-Kelly (2010).

combinations. Near Eastern religions from the cult of Mithras to Christianity were brought to the region, while classical gods were fused with local ones. Far from the empty rural and isolated landscape we now see, the military zone of the Wall was an area of thriving activity, economic and cultural innovation and pluralism.[93]

This exhibition attracted over 11,000 visitors while installed at Wallsend and Carlisle during the summer and autumn of 2009 and this initiative was also part of an educational programme from 2009 to 2010, addressing the themes of citizenship and Englishness.[94] Richard Paul Benjamin and Alan M. Greaves are investigating some broadly comparable issues in their project 'The archaeology of Black Britain', which is addressing the genetic origins of the black people who came to settle in the Roman province and is raising issues of contemporary interest.[95] Benjamin observes that: 'One archaeological site in particular could herald the discipline of black British archaeology. Many black British lifestyle and history websites refer to a unit of North African Moors, *Numerus Maurorum Aurelianorum*, stationed at the Roman military garrison at Burgh-by-Sands (ancient *Aballava/Aballaba*) at the western end of Hadrian's Wall in Cumbria.'[96] A number of initiatives build on a desire to use the evidence from Hadrian's Wall to help to communicate a more complex idea of the history and identity of Britain, indicating that it has been home to diasporic communities for millennia.[97]

Some of the archaeological studies of the Roman army as community, together with the works of art and exhibitions, emphasize the mixed population of the Wall in Roman times. They draw a direct contrast with the older ideas that lay behind the Picts' Wall and the Roman Wall, approaches that stressed the frontier as a monument that dominated and excluded the uninvited and the unassimilated. It would be mistaken, however, to imply that these divisive ideas have entirely disappeared, since some contemporary accounts continue to express highly exclusionary perspectives. For example, there are a few proposals on the internet that Hadrian's Wall should be rebuilt as a means to prevent the immigration of certain groups of people into England. This theme will not be explored further here, except to remark that newspapers continue to draw upon the Wall to reflect on the divisions between the countries to the south and north of the monument's line (Figure 15.7).[98]

---

[93] Crang (2009), 1.   [94] Divya Tolia-Kelly (pers. comm.).
[95] Benjamin and Greaves (no date); cf. Benjamin (2004).   [96] Benjamin (2004), 1.
[97] cf. Eckardt (2010), 7; Moving People Changing Places (2011).
[98] The 'British Cartoons Archive' contains seven additional newspaper cartoons from the 1970s to the 2000s that reflect upon border affairs by drawing upon Hadrian's Wall <http://www.cartoons.ac.uk/search/cartoon_item/>.

Fig. 15.7. A cartoon by Michael Cummings titled 'Pandora's box', from *The Times*, 1 March, 1997. Courtesy of *The Times*, Mrs Annie Cummings, and the British Cartoon Archive, University of Kent. <http:www.cartoons.ac.uk>.

PICTURES ON THE WALL

Despite the dominant emphasis in 'Writing on the Wall' on the monument as inclusive, some contributors to that book cast a critical gaze on colonization and oppressive power. In fact, 'Writing on the Wall' directed a certain amount of critical attention to Hadrian's Wall as a cultural statement, since the concept behind the project's title draws upon literary and artistic works inspired by acts of resistance to the Berlin Wall and to other contemporary political and military barriers. Ron English has noted that during the mid 1980s, many artists 'registered their visions, hope and anger' on the façade of the Berlin Wall;[99] indeed, wall-pickers pulled this frontier work apart during the course of 1989.[100] In December 2007, this approach to resistance through art was exported to the Israeli Separation Wall by a group of artists led by Banksy and the London-based organization Pictures on Walls.[101] The works executed on the Berlin Wall provided an interesting context for the 'Writing on the [Hadrian's] Wall' project—a theme that some of the contributors in that volume reflected.

Samuel Shimon, an Iraqi writer now living in London, considered his experience while visiting the mouth of the Tyne:

---

[99] English (2010), 6.   [100] Rose (2005), 88–93.   [101] Parry (2010), 9.

I was eating fish and chips and hearing a voice telling me: 'Your Ancestors were working here. They were ferrymen from the Tigris'. I was nodding my head and saying, yes, my ancestors were slaves here. Slaves under the same sky.[102]

The Tigris boatmen were not slaves in literal terms, but Roman auxiliary soldiers. Contemporary ways of viewing such people are, however, at least in part, a reflection of the dominant perspective in writings about the Roman empire, which perceives imperial assimilation—often called Romanization or 'becoming Roman'—from a directly positive perspective.[103] Roman auxiliary soldiers were recruited in ways that exploited their own natural abilities, but they were also marginalized through the creation of an imperial system of order that worked to the benefit of certain dominant participants.[104]

This suggests that it is important to consider the political context in which the more inclusive ideas about Hadrian's Wall are being generated—for empires, both ancient and modern, have effectively enslaved many.[105] As Angela Locke has suggested in her poem, 'After the Raj; Last Outpost of Empire':

> Yet, Empire to Empire, some things
> More enduring than the track
> Of ancient Walls
> Have stayed the same.[106]

The frontier between the US and Mexico, and the Israeli Separation Wall in Palestine both project and recreate the grossly unequal power relations that exist on either side. This situation requires consideration when addressing the idea of Hadrian's Wall as an inclusive landscape. In a study of colonial frontiers, Lynette Russell has remarked that boundaries and frontiers have particular significance as 'spaces, both physical and intellectual, which are never neutrally positioned, but are assertive, contested and dialogic'.[107] A literary and artistic approach to the US—Mexico border has explored this landscape as containing many different histories,[108] setting out to illuminate the diverse cultures of this region.[109] This provides a context for those accounts of the Roman Wall that seek to reconstruct it as a means of consensus and community building.

Another of England's most famous ancient monuments, Stonehenge, has more clearly been addressed in detail as a contested landscape, largely because of its role with regard to contemporary druids.[110] Is Hadrian's Wall necessarily actually less political in contemporary terms? The creation of an archaeological

---

[102] Shimon (2006), 77.
[103] van Driel-Murray (2002); Mattingly (2006); Hingley (2010c).
[104] Hingley (2010c).   [105] Hingley (2010b), 239–40.
[106] Locke (2006), 61.   [107] Russell (2001), 1.
[108] Vaquera-Vásquez (2006), 703.   [109] cf. Juffer (2006); Manzanas Calvo (2006).
[110] Bender (1998); Blain and Wallis (2007).

conception of certainty with regard to the Wall was explored in Chapter 12 and this tradition has perhaps served to sideline the deeply political significance of Hadrian's Wall in the contemporary age, a theme that requires further exploration.[111] Ann Laura Stoler has argued that, 'To think with ruins of empire is to emphasize less the artifacts of empire as dead matter or remnants of a defunct regime than to attend to their reappropriations and strategic and active positioning within the politics of the present.'[112] It is time to consider Hadrian's Wall in the context of other territorial frontiers in order to develop more cross-disciplinary perspectives.

TRANSNATIONAL HERITAGE

The inscription of Hadrian's Wall as a WHS enabled various measures that helped to reconnect the surviving elements of the Wall, while recent measures have grasped a broader geographical perspective in order to create a transnational monument across multiple states. The European Union's Culture 2000 programme, 'Frontiers of the Roman Empire', championed a proposal to create a WHS to encompass all the frontiers of the former Roman empire, including those in Europe, the Middle East, and North Africa (Figure 15.8).[113] In 2005, UNESCO inscribed the Frontiers of the Roman Empire World Heritage Site, which included both the German *Limes* and Hadrian's Wall, forming an international network of Roman frontiers across Europe.[114] In 2008 UNESCO inscribed the Antonine Wall frontier in Scotland as part of this new WHS. Hadrian's Wall, as a consequence, now forms part of an extensive transnational WHS. The measures agreed to manage the WHS are currently starting the process of integrating the interpretation and management of the entire Roman frontier in Europe into a single coordinated policy.[115] Recent exhibitions and a web-portal have provided public access to information on the European frontiers of the empire.[116]

The concept of Roman frontiers as World Heritage, however, is problematic.[117] Sophia Labadi has explored the nature of the sites inscribed by UNESCO in order to 'present the main values for which a selection of sites has been nominated for inclusion on the World Heritage List and to discuss how these values have been used to construct and represent the past, the nation, and cultural identity and diversity within official and national

---

[111] Hingley (2008c); cf. Interpretational Framework (2010), 26.
[112] Stoler (2008), 196.　　[113] Breeze *et al.* (2005), 20; Breeze (2008c).
[114] Breeze and Jilek (2008), 7; N. Hodgson (2009b), 7; MP, 2.
[115] cf. Breeze and Jilek (2008), 7; MP, 18.　　[116] Breeze and Jilek (eds. 2008).
[117] Witcher *et al.* (2010), 115.

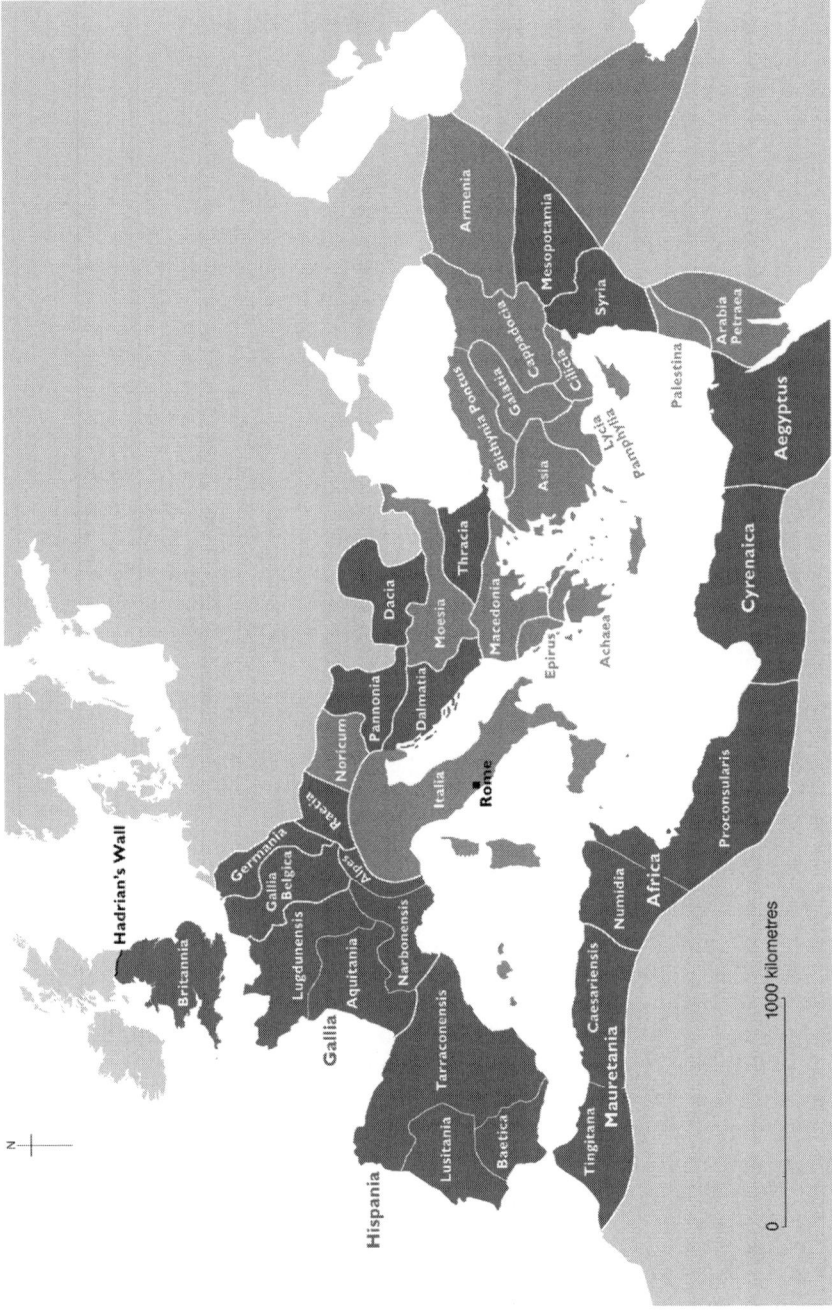

Fig. 15.8. The frontiers of the Roman empire; the more darkly shaded areas indicate those provinces that provided Roman soldiers for Hadrian's Wall. Drawn by Christina Unwin using information provided by Robert Witcher.

discourses on World Heritage.'[118] She has observed that, 'These constructions and representations have been based on mythical notions of origins, timelessness, stability, traditions and homogeneity of the nation and its population'. Labadi has also explored the problems 'engendered by these constructions and representations... such as the exclusion of specific groups of the population as well as their histories and values'.

It can be argued that frontiers are, by their very nature, divisive and this means that their promotion as universal heritage appears to be problematic.[119] The inclusive agenda that has been developed for Hadrian's Wall aims to challenge the idea of the divisive frontier, making the monument more palatable as a WHS, but it is questionable whether such a perspective can be entirely justified. In his study of the walled city as World Heritage, Oliver Creighton has commented upon social inclusion and exclusion in a way that is relevant to the Roman frontiers. In particular, he has argued that:

> The meanings of city walls and the identities they represent are not passive but active, and have inherent potential to be written and re-written through their treatment and presentation as heritage. No matter how sensitive the actions of agencies responsible for the fabric of monuments, neutral handling of city walls which are the very embodiment of 'living' heritage is simply impossible, and many of the case studies examined here expose the difficulties of converting into practice the principle of the 1994 Nara Declaration that 'The cultural heritage of each is the cultural heritage of all'.[120]

It is presumed that Hadrian's Wall was built to exclude and control the access of indigenous people and settlers across the frontier. The multiple gateways in the Wall that have been recognized since the time of Clayton have made it increasingly possible to see Hadrian's Wall as fairly permeable, but access across its line for civilians, if possible at all, is likely to have been strictly controlled by the Roman army. However inclusive we seek to make the Wall in the contemporary world, it evidently continued to serve as an exclusionary concept in medieval times.[121] W. H. Auden viewed Hadrian's Wall as a symbol for 'a certain imperialistic conception of life'.[122] Auden's observation that 'the same issue of order versus liberty' that Hutton had raised, and which persisted in his day, raises difficulties that are hard to ignore in the contemporary world. Can and should we necessarily write such imperialistic conceptions out of current interpretations of the role of the Roman frontiers, especially in the context of the events that have occurred across the world since the beginning of the twenty-first century?[123]

---

[118] Labadi (2007), 148.
[119] Witcher et al (2010), 115; Robert Witcher (pers. comm.).
[120] O. Creighton (2007), 351.　　　[121] cf. Hutton (1802), 90–1.
[122] quoted by Carpenter (1981), 231.　　　[123] cf. Morley (2010).

In the context of the idea of the Roman frontiers as structures that incorporated communities into the Roman empire, it is highly significant that not all countries that have such remains have yet responded to the European Community initiative by proposing their frontier remains for inscriptions as part of the WHS. David Breeze has observed that a number of European countries have expressed an interest in nominating their sections of the Roman frontier for inscription within the transnational WHS, but the countries of North Africa and the Near East have yet to follow;[124] indeed, they clearly have more urgent political and economic concerns at the present time. In the countries to the south and east of the Mediterranean, the Roman empire is often associated with the idea of Western imperialism, reflecting the fact that Western powers in the nineteenth and twentieth centuries drew directly on Roman imperial models for their colonial policies in North Africa and the Near East.[125] This has made the idea of the former Roman domination of these territories particularly problematic for many contemporary resident populations and governments although efforts continue to be made to encourage the inclusion of these non-European sections of the Roman frontiers in the Frontiers of the Roman Empire World Heritage Site.[126]

SUMMARY: DEBATABLE LANDS

Making Hadrian's Wall more inclusive may be achieved by measures to encourage people from both Britain and overseas to visit the monument by walking, traveling by bus, or cycling along its line. It can also be explored through art projects, excavations, exhibitions, re-enactments, and reading popular or scholarly publications—but the Wall's example always needs to be considered in context. One way to achieve this is by addressing the complex network of forces that lay behind the incorporation of peoples into the Roman empire and their movements between provinces, including the ways in which these colonized peoples reacted to control and manipulation. Through such analyses, new understandings of the Roman Wall may arise that reflect upon the imperial context of dictatorial government, oppression, and violence that constitute imperial order.[127]

---

[124] Breeze (2009b), 59.
[125] Ball (2000), 447–8; Mattingly (1996); Hingley (2005), 28–9.
[126] David Breeze (pers. comm.). The value of Roman remains as tourist assets may help eventually to encourage this process.
[127] Hingley (2010b), 240.

As Neville Morley has argued, one of the reasons for studying the Roman Empire is: 'not as a means of understanding better how to run an empire and dominate other countries, or finding a justification for humanitarian or military intervention, but as a means of understanding and questioning modern conceptions of empire and imperialism, and the way they are deployed in contemporary political debates.'[128] This chapter has explored Hadrian's Wall as an inclusive monument, an image that challenges earlier understandings of it as a highly divisive construction. Changing knowledge and new discoveries have helped to inform transforming ideas about the Wall and the character of its population. Yet all attempts to interpret the Wall's significance are interpretative in nature and relate to the interests of the contemporary age, and so these concepts become outdated with time, rather than because new discoveries necessarily require different understandings.[129] Some of the reflections in the art project 'Writing on the Wall' provide a model for the type of critical and reflective perspective that some archaeologists, classicists, and ancient historians are now seeking to apply to the study of Roman world.[130] They also provide various contrasting views that help to keep this living frontier alive and relevant today as the focus for new research, interpretation, and debate.[131]

[128] Morley (2010), 10.   [129] Hingley (2010b), 240.
[130] Hingley (2010b); Hingley (2010c); Morley (2010); Witcher (2010b); Witcher *et al.* (2010).
[131] cf. Blain and Wallis (2007).

16

Conclusions: The Archaeological Imagination

At its most intense the archaeological imagination can fuse, as no written or oral history does, a sense of the past as unbridgeably other with a sense of the past, in its silent immediacy, challenging or teasing us into the re-creating response that is, in a complex of senses, reading.

Donald Mackenzie (1983, xiv)

INTRODUCTION

This book has explored the life of Hadrian's Wall and addressed the ways that texts and images have drawn upon the physical nature of the monument, while also considering how the monumentality of the Wall has been altered through the ages. Certain concepts inherited from the past have been transformed by changing political, religious, and social circumstances. Some of the materials drawn upon to address the three 'ages' of the Wall in this book will now be summarized through a consideration of the semantic shifts that accompanied the changing names for the Wall. Finally, the inclusive Wall shall be discussed.

THE PICTS' WALL

In medieval times, the monument was often known by the name 'Picts' Wall'. It was apparently generally recognized that the monumental remains of the Wall were linked to the Roman occupation of Britain. Gildas and Bede provided an explanation and historical context for the Wall's construction during the period that witnessed the end of Roman rule. This name emphasized the Wall's role as a physical frontier work that was intended to prevent the Picts from gaining access to the rich lowlands of the former Roman province to the south. Gildas and Bede interpreted the Wall's construction as a response to the crisis of social and military collapse, an attempt to build an impenetrable fence to prevent the movement of barbarians from the north. This swiftly failed because the indolent British were unable to defend its battlements effectively. In the context of the gradual tenth- to twelfth-century formation of the medieval border between the two kingdoms of England and Scotland just north of the Wall's surviving remains, this Roman frontier had a distinct role. Its physical scale and widespread fame recreated it as a signifier for the frontier of the space of English nationhood, the substantial scale of its surviving remains continuing to hinder access across much of its line well into post-medieval times and beyond.

Physical intervention was mainly restricted to the robbing of the stone elements of the Wall for building projects. In the case of some religious sites along its line and in the hinterland, this robbing of Roman masonry probably had a symbolic dimension, creating Christian structures out of the ruins of Roman civilization. In the political and military realm, the possible evidence for the reuse of elements of the Wall by the mid sixteenth-century night watches along the border is not clear-cut. The surviving documentation suggests that the line of the Wall was used as a useful location for surveillance at three points along its line. In the nineteenth century, William Hutton took this to represent an effective re-manning of the Wall to defend the English border, but this was not the case, and the practice of watching the borderlands extended over a far wider landscape well to the north and south of the line. Despite this, there are hints in the accounts of Camden, Drayton, and the anonymous *Epystle* that these late Elizabethan and Jacobean authors equated the sixteenth-century night watch with the role of the Picts' Wall in immediately post-Roman times. Camden and Drayton wrote of watch and ward being kept by the Roman soldiers, while the *Epystle* argued the need for a new fortification along the English border as the basis for the continued watch. The chorographical approach pursued by these authors effectively created eddies in time that focused on the space of the Wall.

The Wall had a significant conceptual role in the minds of such writers, but its main practical purpose prior to the late sixteenth century was as a quarry for the stone required in order to build churches, castles, and houses. Despite this, its remains largely survived in the upland landscapes—Camden mentions that only the 'battlements' were missing from some of the surviving portions in 1599. For Camden and his contemporaries, the remains of the Wall were indicative of an ancient period of civility and order across these northern borderlands. The Roman monumental remains provided a model for the creation of contemporary order as the unification of England and Scotland entered the political agenda. Antiquaries and poets drew upon the Wall's remains as a precursor of King James I's efforts to create peace and order across these debatable lands. The recovery of Roman inscriptions and the traces of ancient towns and buildings in this landscape provided an idea of the civility of the Wall-zone in Roman times, which set the accounts of Gildas and Bede of a crisis in the immediately post-Roman period in context. This is why Michael Drayton's living spirit is characterized as 'aged *Pictswall*'—the role of the monument in 1622 was less significant than it had been a generation before, but concerns over both border security and union had not entirely disappeared.

The late sixteenth and early seventeenth centuries also witnessed the initial stages of the separation of scholarly knowledge of the Wall from its artistic representation. Camden specifically chose not to record many of the fables of the common people, but some of the stories included in *Britannia* would today be considered as folklore. Drayton's image of *Pictswall* is more complex, since it draws on Camden's historical scholarship but also creates a living spirit of place. Developing scholarship was gradually to lead to a changing appreciation of the Wall, and the name of the monument changed. Camden refers to it primarily as the 'Picts' Wall'. Although he does record the potential role of Septimius Severus in its construction, he considered that the most substantial stone elements were built during and after the departure of the Romans. Bede's account was too old and too famous for Camden to be able to mount a convincing challenge, despite the wealth of Roman inscriptions that had been found. In turn, this ancient idea about the Wall's origins was repeated in the new editions of *Britannia* published in 1695 and 1722.

By the early eighteenth century, it was becoming clear that the Picts were unlikely to have constituted the motive for the building of the Wall, since it was evidently constructed earlier than had been supposed. The popular argument that the curtain Wall was built in the late second or early third centuries by Severus, suggesting that it was already two centuries old by the time of the collapse of Roman rule, was promoted by John Horsley and came to be accepted by many. After this time the monument is addressed as the 'Roman Wall' in many antiquarian accounts, although the older name occasionally recurs. In particular, in the early nineteenth century, certain English writers drew upon the Picts' Wall to consider the immigration of the Scots and Irish into England. New ideas about the Wall often take some time to be accepted, as old traditions live on in popular, political, and scholarly writings.

THE ROMAN WALL

Until the early eighteenth century the curtain Wall was, therefore, commonly interpreted as of immediately post-Roman date. The Vallum of Severus was thought to constitute an earlier fortification along much the same line, comparable to the turf rampart of the Antonine Wall. The growth of interest in England's Roman Wall during the early eighteenth century drew upon the political and cultural analogy that was increasingly being drawn between Augustan Rome and contemporary England. The English Lowlands contained no substantial classical ruins that could be compared to those of the city of Rome, and although the buried remains of Roman monuments were found on occasion—for example in London, York, and Bath—the Roman Wall was by far the most impressive of the surviving Roman structures. As a result, John Warburton and William Stukeley drew upon these impressive remains as the English counterpart of the grand imperial ruins of the city of Rome, although it is also relevant that neither author had actually visited Italy. The ruination of the Picts' Wall was emphasized in political pamphlets, novels, and poems in the context of the unification of Great Britain, but antiquaries countered this argument by emphasizing the scale and monumentality of its surviving remains. Visitors explored the Wall in increasing numbers during the early eighteenth century, producing impressive publications that provided detailed accounts of its physical presence.

The works of Gordon, Horsley, Warburton, and Stukeley emphasized the significance of the Latin inscriptions found in the remains of the Wall during the previous century and a half. The mapping of the surviving physical traces by Horsley and others led to an increasing appreciation of the character and complexity of the Wall and excavations began to uncover the remains of Roman buildings at a few points along its line. These reinforced the view, initially expressed by William Camden, that the impact of Rome across this frontier area was on a large scale. These writings, illustrations, and maps reconstructed the Wall as evidence for the former glory of imperial Rome, reflecting Britain's contemporary greatness as an increasingly significant imperial power. In troubled times, the Wall could also serve as an example of the physical manifestation of Roman control on the English northern frontier. The events of 1745–6 resulted in the creation of a new military road, constructed, in both physical and metaphorical terms, on the foundations of the Roman Wall.

The Wall's military and imperial associations prevented the rise of a sustained tradition of Romantic antiquarianism comparable to the growing late eighteenth-century interest in the megalithic monuments and abbeys of Britain. William Hutton aimed to bring the monument to life through his account of the long-term history of the frontier and by musing upon its contemporary significance. In this context, the peace of the early nineteenth-century borderlands was a cause for celebration and Rome is now usually seen in the guise of a violent and dictatorial invader. Later travellers who also wished to bring the remains of the Wall to life in their work drew upon Hutton's example.

HADRIAN'S WALL

A further semantic shift took place when antiquaries began to find and interpret evidence for the Hadrianic date of the main elements of the Wall. The mid-nineteenth century witnessed a growing emphasis on the excavation of substantial parts of the monument and its associated infrastructure. Earlier antiquaries had undertaken small-scale excavations at various stations along the line of the Wall, often as part of a search for inscriptions, but Hodgson, Bruce, and Clayton began a more analytical study of the monument's physical form. Clayton's work, in particular, led to the uncovering of lengthy sections of the curtain Wall, together with the remains of milecastles, forts, and turrets. This enabled a fuller appreciation of the physical form of the Wall, while the excavations conducted at Chesters and Housesteads began to provide a better understanding of the monumental buildings within the stations along the Wall, recovering highly impressive inscribed stones and other artefacts that could be easily displayed to visitors.

Disputes over the dating of the curtain Wall continued for 80 years until a Hadrianic date was clearly demonstrated by the excavations undertaken during the period of 'scientific' study at the beginning of the twentieth century. The attribution of the Wall to Hadrian helped to draw a distinction between this monument and the northern Roman Wall, the Antonine Wall, which was the work of Hadrian's successor. In the context of an increasing appreciation of the international context of the Roman frontiers of Britain and Germany, this monument could no longer be called *the* Roman Wall. The process of detailed archaeological research during the early twentieth century also helped to distance conclusively the building of the Wall from its context as a contemporary focus of study by elaborating a clear understanding of the temporal divisions between the Roman past, the medieval age, and present times. For many artists, poets, and antiquaries, the Wall had a relatively immediate relevance—in social, political, religious, and cultural terms—indicated by the reconstructions created in narrative from and imagery. From the early twentieth century, the intellectual tools of clear thinking and question and answer effectively served to separate the surviving physical remains of Hadrian's Wall from the later history of the use of the border landscape and from the mythical accounts of the monument. It was now possible to consider the nature and function of the Wall through a comparison with other frontier works, such as the Indian Customs Hedge and the German *Limes*, but the Roman history of Hadrian's Wall no longer had any relevance to the medieval activities along its line, while folk tales were perceived as having limited relevance by archaeologists. It became important to document specifically the details of the Wall as an elementally Roman monument, one that was disused and ruined but survived in the form of an 'Ancient Monument'. It also became paramount to uncover and display the Roman elements and to remove later structures and accretions.

In the writings of Robert Forster, the separation of knowledge from tale led to the definition of two forms of antiquarian study, the pedantic and the imaginative.[1] The pedantic antiquary focused on the details of inscriptions and, perhaps, on the minutiae of the recorded evidence for the Wall, while its imaginative counterpart was more interested in telling tales by drawing on the particular archaeological remains that had been derived from the Wall. Forster drew upon Hutton and Bruce to define his imaginative approach to reconstructing the Wall, just as Kipling, Auden, and Hunter Davies were inspired by Hutton's example during the twentieth century. By reconstructing the Wall in 'ethnographic time', these artistic and popular accounts sought to breath life into its remains, animating it as a living monument. The later inhabitants of the Wall-line, together with folk tales and myth, are highly relevant from this perspective. The living presence of the monument has been continued in projects such as 'Writing on the Wall' and 'Illuminating Hadrian's Wall'.

The concept of time exhibited in these works has been explored in some detail above. In these terms, a focus on place—whether this be the entire length of the Wall or a particular place along its line—serves to define local topography, not exclusively as it exists in the present moment, but also as it has existed historically.[2] Case studies, such as Drayton's 'aged *Pictswall*', Hunter Davies' living Wall, and the reconstructed buildings at South Shields, created eddies in time which link the Roman monument to its current manifestation as an animate entity. Another tradition of Wall scholarship, with roots in the detailed antiquarian study of John Horsley and his contemporaries, effectively aimed to create an oppositional form of time focused on chronological logic. This was intended to erode nebulous thinking by focusing scientific reasoning onto the problems raised by the Wall, including its exact structure, the date of its component parts, and the purposes for which it was constructed. This perspective focused the interest of twentieth-century archaeologists on the unraveling of the problems of the Wall, leading, on occasions, to an unwarranted assumption of the certainty of archaeological knowledge, a development that has, in turn, served to hold back debate.

This programme of archaeological work during the first half of the twentieth century has made Hadrian's Wall the best-known frontier work of the Roman empire, but it has also left many important issues unanswered,[3] or even unstudied. This focus on an analytical comprehension of definitive knowledge appears to have distanced the scholarly study of the Wall from a wider public appreciation. The concept of the 'authentic Wall' required the establishment of a clear chronological barrier between the Roman Wall and the activities that have drawn upon its remains since the sixth century.

This archaeological focus effectively kills the Wall's living significance today.[4] The very particular focus on the exact form, location, and sequence of the various elements that constituted the Wall reflects a strategy that dwells

---

[1] Forster (1899).   [2] Marchitello (1997), 79.   [3] RFb.
[4] cf. Pearson and Shanks (2001), 114–15.

on a need for secure and unchallengeable knowledge, but this is also an approach that has served to prohibit broader discussions of function and meaning by relegating them to the level of speculation.[5] The creation of the idea of an authentic Roman Wall is an important abstraction—an idea that is vital in all attempts to justify the protection and management of the monument and its landscape. What is problematic, in these terms, is *not* the idea that the Roman phases of the Wall are internationally important but that the claim that archaeological knowledge is absolute, since this can help to generate an image of a dead and static monument that is effectively owned, as a research topic, by the archaeological community and not open for broader public debate. To paraphrase Gary Warnaby, Dominic Medway, and David Bennison's words, this suggests that 'the kaleidoscopic and multifaceted nature of place may become hidden behind one-dimensional . . . approaches.'[6]

An alternative direction is to see all antiquarian and archaeological work on the Wall as part of the social, political, religious, and cultural context of the society in which it has taken place. The Wall is studied because it appears particularly relevant today, just as all antiquarian and archaeological studies reflect the context of their times.

AN INCLUSIVE WALL?

The first decade of the twenty first century has witnessed the development of a new image for Hadrian's Wall, which is reinvigorating scholarship and making a substantial contribution to the local economy. Since its inscription as a World Heritage Site in 1987, an integrated agenda for the management and interpretation of the Wall has been developed that focuses on its contemporary role as an inclusive structure for all who wish to visit its remains and also those who live close by.[7] It is important that this role draws on the Roman identity of the Wall as a structure that was built and patrolled by men from communities across the Roman empire who were integrated into a relatively unified frontier society. The mixed nature of this community has been recognized since the mid-nineteenth century, but the significance has changed

---

[5] Lindsay Allason-Jones (pers. comm.) notes that the public often appears to want certainty and become confused when alternative views are expressed.

[6] Warnaby, Medway, and Bennison (2010), 1379. This reference addresses marketing approaches for the Wall, but I have adapted it to relate to the intellectual tradition of archaeological studies.

[7] This developing framework for the Wall fits the agenda of the 2005 Faro Convention, which is a 'Framework Convention on the Value of Cultural Heritage for Society', published by the Council of Europe and yet to be adopted in Britain (cf. heritagetalks.org 2011; Michael Shanks pers. comm.).

as Britain's position in the world has altered and it has become a more multi-ethnic nation.

The inclusive agenda is, however, rather more extensive than this. For centuries, stone robbing, agricultural operations, and building works have flattened and obscured what survives of the Wall, fragmenting its remains so that the monument is harder to follow and comprehend. Its most substantial and impressive remains are situated in the central part of its course. Projects that have re-emphasized the former unity of the Wall include the building of the Newcastle to Carlisle military road during the eighteenth century, and the construction of the Newcastle and Carlisle Railway in the nineteenth. This emphasis has gathered significant momentum since the late 1980s, with an inclusive agenda for the Wall expressed through the strategy for integrated management and interpretation, the creation of the National Trail, and the establishment of the Hadrian's Wall bus service. This integration of management and interpretation coincided with the definition of an archaeological *Research Framework*, commissioned by English Heritage, and produced by the community of archaeologists involved in the study of the monument.[8] It is interesting, in the terms explored here, that the *Management Plan* actively seeks to involve all interested individuals but the archaeological *Research Framework* predominantly drew upon archaeologists who were actively involved in research on the Wall. Perhaps one day the two strategies will be fully integrated.

The planning emphasis on integration and inclusion in the management, interpretation, and marketing of the Wall coincides with many of the academic priorities identified in the *Research Framework*. Works on the Roman army as community and ideas of diasporic populations within the Roman empire link neatly with current ideas for marketing and publicizing the monument,[9] but some problems remain. In the last chapter, the masculine bias of past research on the Wall was addressed and it is worth considering whether other voices might communicate alternative valuations today. As a result of recent discussions about Stonehenge, it has become possible to explore conceptions of Hadrian's Wall that contradict its apparent character as a ancient military landscapes which is imagined to have possessed a fairly pragmatic function (or functions).

William Camden, John Collingwood Bruce, and Charles Roach Smith explored some of the myths that adhered to Hadrian's Wall in former times. These represent ideas that have gradually been written out of academic accounts, in much the same way that scholarly writings on Stonehenge have often sidelined alternative valuations.[10] Mythical ideas about Hadrian's Wall have, however, continued to been produced. In Joseph O'Neill's novel *Land*

---

[8] RAa; RAb.   [9] Hingley (2010b), 238.
[10] Blain and Wallis (2007), 33–5.

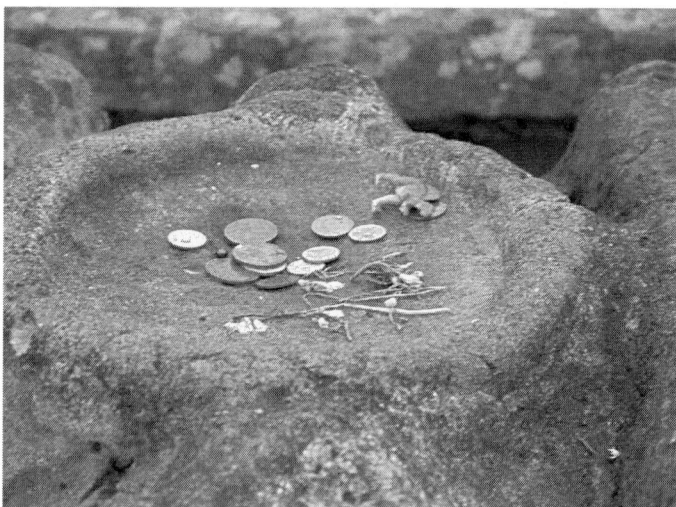

Fig. 16.1. Ritual offerings of coins, flowers, and a dinosaur on a reproduction of a Roman altar at the Carrawburgh mithraeum, close to the site of Coventina's Well. Photograph by Richard Hingley, 2011.

Under England (1935), the narrator falls through a trapdoor close to the line of Hadrian's Wall and into an underground world peopled by living Romans. This world draws on the problematic contemporary analogy of Fascist Italy and Germany, but the landscape that O'Neill describes is also heavily mythologized.[11] In Neil Gaiman's cult novel *Stardust* (1999), a stone wall forms the division between semi-rational Victorian England and a mythical land called 'faerie'.[12] Certain references in the novel suggest that Gaiman draws metaphorically on Hadrian's Wall in creating his two distinct lands.

Generations of antiquaries and archaeologists have removed the carved stones and inscriptions from the line of Hadrian's Wall to place them with care in museums where they can be protected from the weather. This has effectively resulted in a rationalized Wall where most of the elements of Roman ritual have been removed from public inspection, leaving in place the remains of the curtain Wall with its fairly regularly placed forts, milecastles, and turrets. In a few places, traces of temple buildings can be inspected and at three sites along the Wall's line altars remain visible. In these places, offerings of coins, flowers, and other items are often made (Figure 16.1). These offerings are comparable to the items that are deposited at other special places in the contemporary landscape of Britain, such as trees, springs, and

[11] O'Neill (1935). I am grateful Norman Vance and Anthony Birley for this reference.
[12] Gaiman (1999).

megalithic monuments.[13] Occasionally these items on the Hadrian's Wall altars may relate directly to the renewed worship of certain ancient spirits. Coventina (from Carrawburgh), and Antenociticus (from Benwell) have quite a following on the internet,[14] and it is possible that neo-pagan interest in the spirit of the Wall is increasing.

Changing perspectives on the meaning of the Wall do not mean that more traditional archaeological works that focus on the mapping, excavation, chronology, form, and sequence of the Wall have less value today. These aspects of the monument should continue to be researched in order to evolve understanding of the Wall as a living and developing monument. It is necessary to find a balance between developing and conserving the monument in order to ensure that it is not changed in inappropriate or damaging ways while not being prevented from continuing its life, a process best served through archaeological excavation and research.[15]

In particular, it is important that the visible evidence for the monumental nature of Hadrian's Wall does not undermine the debatable physical, economic, religious, and intellectual landscapes through which it passes.[16] New directions for studying the Wall are required in order to keep its remains alive, both as a theme for future generations of archaeologists to research, and also for the general public. In the past, ideas about the Wall often appear to have become firmly established and, on occasions, they have proved very difficult to challenge. Perhaps the apparent stability of knowledge is, in itself, a metaphorical reflection of the scale and relative permanence of the monument's imposing physical structure. The debates about the naming and chronology of the Wall illustrate the way that knowledge has tended to become fossilized, as does the development of an attitude of scholarly certainty about the Wall throughout much of the twentieth century. This book has sought to demonstrate that knowledge and understanding are constantly transforming, and that it is the task of all who take an interest in Hadrian's Wall to add their voices to this living, mutating, and growing monument of transnational significance.

---

[13] Blain and Wallis (2007), 9, 42.

[14] Seamus Heaney's poem 'Grotus and Coventina' is a rare literary expression of this ancient cult (Heaney 1984).

[15] Archaeologists should also take a direct interest in the management of the Wall because they need to ensure that their archaeological resource remains as intact as possible.

[16] For the use of 'debatable lands' to address conceptual territories where rights are disputed, see Christianson (2002) and Lamont and Rossington (2007). This literary concept draws upon the disputed territory on the border between England and Scotland, reviewed above.

Published accounts of the Wall

David Breeze and Brian Dobson's *Hadrian's Wall* presents a detailed account of the building of the Wall, its context, and the history of its use during the Roman period.[1] An English Heritage guidebook to the Wall provides a popular and well-illustrated introduction to the Wall and a guide to many of the major monuments along its line.[2] An edited book arising from a conference held at South Shields in 2006 contains a number of papers that address recent research on the Wall, including issues of interpretation, research, and management.[3] For a very detailed summary of the current position with archaeological research along the Wall, the two volumes of the *Research Framework* contain vital information and also ideas for future targeted research.[4] Another volume, edited by Rob Collins and Lindsay Allason-Jones, assesses the significance of material culture on the Wall during the fourth and fifth centuries.[5]

The most recent *Handbook* provides a useful resource for exploring the monument and also an account of its construction and use.[6] The *Official National Trail Guide to the Hadrian's Wall Path* provides an accessible guide to the monument and landscape.[7] Regular Pilgrimages occur along the line of the Wall, the latest in August 2009, and the little volume that was produced for the latest of these journeys contains an assessment of research on the Wall between 1999 and 2009.[8] There are numerous articles and volumes on individual sites along the length of the Wall.[9]

Rather less has been written about the post-Roman history of the Wall. Eric Birley provided a definitive history of antiquarian and archaeological research and, although this is now out of date, it continues to represent an important source.[10] Leslie Hepple produced an important collection of papers about the history of the collections of Roman inscribed stones that were made along the Wall from the late sixteenth century to the seventeenth.[11] Alan Whitworth has explored the post-Roman impact of the Wall on its landscape, addressing a variety of relevant topics.[12] Stephen Leach and Alan Whitworth provide a detailed account of the conservation and consolidation of the Wall.[13] Woodside and Crow have written a useful study of the Wall as a historic landscape,[14] but this is restricted in its geographical scope to the central upland

---

[1] Breeze and Dobson (2000).   [2] Breeze (2006b).   [3] Bidwell (ed. 2008).
[4] RFa; RFb.   [5] Collins and Allason-Jones (eds. 2010).
[6] Breeze (2006a).   [7] Burton (2010).
[8] Hodgson (ed. 2009). For another recent volume that addresses archaeological research, including some important summaries of research on the earthwork elements of the monument, see Wilmott (ed. 2009).
[9] For example, for South Shields, see Bidwell and Speak (1994); for Vindolanda, see R. Birley (2009); for Corbridge, see Bishop (1994); for Housesteads, see Crow (2004a) and Rushworth (2009); for Birdoswald, see Wilmott (1997; 2001).
[10] E. Birley (1961).   [11] e.g. Hepple (2003a).   [12] Whitworth (2000).
[13] Leach and Whitworth (2011).   [14] Woodside and Crow (1999).

sections. W. D. Shannon discusses a variety of early medieval and medieval texts and maps that refer to the Wall.[15] The most general social history of the Wall is by Alison Ewin,[16] but this only provides a brief account of a vast topic and is stronger on the nineteenth and twentieth centuries than the earlier centuries. For the current management of the Wall, the recent *Management Plan* provides a full consideration of the management, interpretation, and marketing of the monument. A recent volume on the *Frontiers of the Roman Empire* sets the publicizing of Hadrian's Wall in a broader context.[17] Two articles by Robert Witcher address the ways that contemporary people experience and explore the Wall,[18] while Warnaby, Medway, and Bennison provide an assessment of the marketing of the monument.[19]

[15] Shannon (2007).   [16] Ewin (2000).
[17] Breeze and Jilek (eds. 2008).   [18] Witcher (2010a; 2010b).
[19] Warnaby, Medway, and Bennison (2010).

Table 1 Hadrian's Wall: a timeline

Vallum Aelium

120s	Initial construction of the Wall on the orders of the Emperor Hadrian.
140s	The frontier is moved to the Antonine Wall; Hadrian's Wall is probably mothballed for around twenty years.
160s	The frontier is moved back to Hadrian's Wall and the Wall installation is reconditioned.
190s/200s	The curtain Wall may have been reconstructed under the Emperor Septimius Severus.
200s	The growth of civil settlements and maintenance of forts and Wall instillations.
300s	The decline of civil settlements but continued maintenance of many forts and Wall instillations.
400s	Continued activity on many fort sites (including Vindolanda, South Shields, and Birdoswald) but gradual abandonment of frontier system.

The Picts' Wall

500–550	Gildas writes about the Wall, ascribing it to the immediate post-Roman period.*
635	The battle of Heavenfield is fought close to the remains of the Wall.
731	Bede writes about the Wall, describing the Vallum as Severus' fortification and the stone curtain Wall as immediately post-Roman.*
900s–1100s	Formation of border between England and Scotland.
c.1169	Foundation of Lanercost Priory, close to the Wall.
c.1250	Matthew Paris' maps of Britain illustrates the location of the Walls.
1550s	The night watch in the border region reused the remains of the Wall in three locations.
1580s	Two proposals are made to build new fortifications on the English frontier with Scotland, ideas that drew upon the Wall for inspiration.
1580s	John Senhouse begins to collect Roman inscribed stones at Ellenborough (Maryport).
1586	William Camden produces his first account of the Wall in Latin in his *Britannia*.*
1599	William Camden and Robert Cotton visit the Wall.
1599 & 1601	Reginald Bainbrigg visits the Wall.
1603–9	King James I attempts to settle the frontier lands and to impose metropolitan order.
1610	The first detailed account of the Wall written in English is published in William Camden's *Britannia*. The Vallum is thought to be the work of Severus and the curtain Wall is argued to be immediately post-Roman in date.*
1622	Michael Drayton gives voice to 'aged *Pictswall*' in his poem *Poly-Olbion*.
1695	A new revised edition of Camden's *Britannia* raises renewed interest in the Wall.*

(continued)

Table 1 (continued)

The Roman Wall

c1702	Christopher Hunter visits the Wall.
1707	The Act of Union unites England and Scotland into Great Britain.
1707	The first graphic reconstruction of the Picts' Wall is produced by J. Goeree.
1708–9	Robert Smith visits the Wall.
1715	A rebellion by Jacobite forces causes concern in the frontier region.
1715–6	As a result of the rebellion, John Warburton surveys the Wall, producing an authoritative map.*
1724	Sir John Clerk and Alexander Gordon visit the Wall.
1725	William Stukeley and Roger Gale visit the Wall.
1726	Alexander Gordon's account of the Wall is published.*
1732	John Horsley's influential account of the Wall is published in his monograph on Roman Britain. The Vallum is ascribed to Hadrian and the stone curtain Wall to Severus.*
1741	Susana Maria Appleby excavates a bath-house at Castlesteads, which is described and illustrated in print by George Smith. +
1745	A second Jacobite rebellion penetrates the line of the Wall as the rebels march south to Derby.
1746	George Smith calls on the spirit of the Roman Wall in order to preventing further problems in the frontier regions.
1749–50	Dugal Campbell and Hugh Debbieg produce a detailed survey of the remains of the Wall as part of the planning for the new road between Newcastle and Carlisle.*
1751	An Act of Parliament is passed to require the construction of this new military road.
1753	John Warburton publishes the first book entirely dedicated to the Wall. He writes of the 're-edification' of the Roman Wall through the building of the new military road.*
1754	William Stukeley attempts to get the line of the new road moved to avoid the serious damage that is currently occurring to the Wall.
1776.	William Stukeley's account of the Wall is published posthumously.*
1801	William Hutton may have been the first person to walk the entire length of the Wall and his experiences are published in a small but influential book.*
1813	The foundation of the Society of Antiquaries of Newcastle upon Tyne focuses renewed attention on the Wall.
1815	Walter Scott narrates the 'celebrated' Roman Wall in his novel *Guy Mannering*.
1822	John Hodgson writes an account of the excavation of the Mithraeum at Housesteads. +
1840	John Hodgson publishes an influential account of the Wall, includes a detailed argument for the building of the curtain Wall by Hadrian.*
1843–1890	John Clayton excavates much of the site at Chesters, next to his country house. +
1848	Clayton starts to excavate the Roman site at Housesteads. +
1848	Clayton's excavation at Cawfields milecastle locate a gateway through the curtain Wall, indicating that the Wall may have been more permeable than was previously thought. +

1848–1873	Clayton has the curtain Wall on Whin Sill rebuilt, creating the 'Clayton Wall'.
1849	John Collingwood Bruce leads the First Pilgrimage to the Wall and presents a lecture on imperial comparison at Housesteads.
1851	Bruce publishes *The Roman Wall*.*
1851–1854	The growth of interest in the Roman frontiers in Germany stimulates new interest in the Roman Wall.
1851–1858	The Duke of Northumberland hopes to promote a significant project on the Roman Wall, but this does not succeed.
1857	William Bell Scott paints the *Building of the Roman Wall* for Wallington Hall.
1863	Bruce publishes *The Wallet-Book*, providing a handy volume for visitors to take with them along the Wall.*
1866	The foundation of the Cumberland and Westmorland Society focused attention on the west end of the Wall
1876–1877	Discovery and excavation of Coventina's Well. +
1870–1880	Excavations undertaken at the Roman site at South Shields resulted in the creation of an archaeological Park. +
1880–1883	The Glasgow Archaeological Society conducts a programme of work on Roman sites along the Antonine Wall in Scotland.
1885	The German ancient historian Theodor Mommsen describes England's Roman Wall as the 'best known' Roman military work.
1892	The German Limes-Commission is founded and members visit the Roman Walls of Britain during the following year.
1894–1906	A significant programme of work commences on the Wall, exploring its constituent elements, dating, and sequence. +
1895	Discovery of the Turf Wall close to Birdoswald.*
1898	Reginald Bosanquet conducts extensive excavations at Housesteads in an effort to uncover the entire plan of the fort.*
1899	Francis Haverfield reviews the first five years of the major excavation programme. He is still uncertain about the dating of the Wall, arguing in a subsequent article that the Vallum was built by Hadrian and the curtain Wall by Severus.*
1899	Robert Forster publishes an imaginative book about the Wall, entitled *The Amateur Antiquary*.*

Hadrian's Wall

1906	Rudyard Kipling writes about the Wall in *Puck of Pook's Hill*, a novel which influences generations of school children.*
1906–1914	Significant excavations are undertaken at the Roman site at Corbridge. +
1920	Kipling uses the Wall as a metaphor for Englishness in a lecture to the Royal Society of St George.
1921	R. G. Collingwood writes an article summarizing the state of play with the ongoing research into the Wall and a second article on the function of the Wall. He argues that most elements of the Wall, including the curtain Wall are Hadrianic in date.*
1926	Collingwood publishes a popular guide to the Wall.*
1929	Eric Birley acquires the farm at Vindolanda.*
1930	A quarrying threat to the central sections of the Wall leads to a strengthening of the Ancient Monuments legislation.
1930s	Significant sections of the Wall are acquired by the National Trust and by the Ministry of Public Buildings and Works, guaranteeing its protection and public access to its remains.

(continued)

Table 1 (continued)

Hadrian's Wall

1931	Collingwood argues for the existence of a system of Roman frontier defenses along the Cumbrian coast at the west of the Wall.
1937	W. H. Auden writes 'Roman Wall Blues', an ironic reflection on the Wall's imperial purpose.*
1949	The first international Congress of Roman Frontier Studies is organized by Eric Birley at Newcastle upon Tyne.*
1950	Ian Richmond argues that the principle questions about the Wall have been answered.
1957	A major dispute arises about the best way to conserve the curtain Wall.
1960s	The construction of the Berlin Wall casts a negative light on Hadrian's Wall.
1970	The Vindolanda Trust is founded and excavation and reconstruction work commences. +
1974	Hunter Davies published a popular account that seeks to animate the Wall.*
1975–1984	Excavation at Wallsend uncover the plan of the fort, which had been covered in housing. +
1982–1988	Significant excavation work is conducted on the curtain Wall on Whin Sill by Jim Crow, indicating that the Hadrianic Wall was rebuilt, probably under Severus. +
1984	The remains of Hadrian's Wall are inscribed as a World Heritage Site.
1987–1992	Significant excavations at Birdoswald by Tony Wilmott produced important information for the post-Roman history of the site. +
1988	The reconstructed Roman gateway at South Shields is opened.
1989	The dismantling of the Berlin Wall.
1998	The discovery of 'obstacles' on the berm between the curtain Wall and northern ditch during excavations at Buddle Street, Wallsend reignites the debate about the function of the Wall. +
1999	The Roman fort, museum, and interpretation centre at Wallsend is opened to the public.

An inclusive Wall

2002–2003	The creation of the 'Hadrian's Wall Country Brand' aims to help local businesses to recover from an outbreak of foot-and-mouth disease.
2003	The opening of the Hadrian's Wall National Trail provides coordinated access to the remains of the Wall.
2003	The discovery of Ilam Pan, a Roman patera, which includes text related to Hadrian's Wall.
2005	The Roman *Limes* in Germany are inscribed as part of the Frontiers of the Roman World Heritage Site.
2006	Hadrian's Wall Heritage Ltd is formed to supervise and manage the Wall.
2006	The Hadrian's Wall National Cycle Route is opened.
2006	A collection of art works inspired by the Wall, 'Writing on the Wall', is published.*
2006	The fourteenth *Handbook* to the Roman Wall, edited by David Breeze, is published.*
2007–2011	The Arts and Humanities Research Council funds the *Tales of the Frontier* project, the initiative from which this book arose.*
2008	The Antonine Wall is inscribed as part of the Frontiers of the Roman Empire World Heritage Site.
2009	The latest *Management Plan* for Hadrian's Wall is published.*

2009	The Archaeological *Research Framework* for Hadrian's Wall is published.*
2009	The Thirteenth Pilgrimage explores the remains of Hadrian's Wall.
2009	The twenty-first Congress of Roman Frontier Studies is held at Newcastle upon Tyne.
2010	The English Heritage map of Hadrian's Wall is published.*
2010–2011	Ambitious proposals are developed to undertake major excavation and create a visitor experience at Maryport. +

Notes: * = an influential publication or an important map
+ = a significant excavation or excavation programme

Bibliography

Abbreviations used in text

RIB = Collingwood, R. G. and R. P. Wright (1995). *The Roman Inscriptions of Britain, Volume 1*, New edition (Stroud, Allan Sutton).

MP = *Management Plan* (2009). *Frontiers of the Roman Empire World Heritage Site: Hadrian's Wall Management Plan 2008–2014* (Hexham, Hadrian's Wall Heritage). Also available on line <http://www.hadrian's-wall.org/page.aspx//About-the-World-Heritage-Site/Management Plan>.

RFa = Symonds, M. F. A. and D. A. Mason (2009a). *Frontiers of Knowledge: A Research Framework for Hadrian's Wall, Volume I: Resource Assessment* (Durham, Durham County Council).

RFb = Symonds, M. F. A. and D. A. Mason (2009b). *Frontiers of Knowledge: A Research Framework for Hadrian's Wall, Volume II: Agenda and Strategy* (Durham, Durham County Council).

Other references

Abbatt, R. (1849). *A history of the Picts or Romano-British Wall and of the Roman Stations and Vallum; with an account of their present states, taken during a pilgrimage along that part of the island in the month of June, 1849* (London, George Bell).

Act of Parliament (1750). *A BILL for laying out, making, and keeping in Repair, a Road from the City of Carlisle to the Town of Newcastle-upon-Tyne*, 11 June, 1750. *House of Commons Parliamentary Papers* <http://parlipapers.chadwyck.co.uk./> Accessed March 2011.

Adams, J.-P. (2007). 'Murailles de la peur, murailles de prestige, murrailles du plaisir', in A. Rodríguez Colomenero and I. Rodá de Llanza (eds.) *Murallas de Ciudades Romanas en al Occidente del Imperio* (Lugo, Museo de Lugo), 21–46.

Allason-Jones, L. and McIntosh, F. (forthcoming). 'The Wall, a Plan and the Ancient Monuments Acts', *Archaeologia Aeliana*.

——and B. McKay (1985). *Coventina's Well: A shrine on Hadrian's Wall* (Oxford, Oxbow).

——and R. Miket (1984). *The Catalogue of Small Finds from South Shields Roman Fort* (Newcastle upon Tyne, Society of Antiquaries of Newcastle upon Tyne).

Alston, R. (2010). 'Dialogues in Imperialism: Rome, Britain and India', in E. Hall and P. Vasunia (eds), 51–78.

Anon. (1708). *The Union-Proverb: viz. If Skiddaw has a Cap, Scruffell wots full well of that* (London, J. Morphew).

Anon. (1857). 'The Parliamentary Session', *The Englishwoman's Review and Home Newspaper*, Saturday, December 5, 1857, 241–2.

——(1867). 'The Roman Wall', The *Daily Review*, Edinburgh, Monday June 17, 1867.

——(1876). 'Cilurnum', *Belgravia*, Third Series 9, 213–17.

——(1885). 'Report of the Society of Antiquaries of Newcastle-upon-Tyne', *Archaeologia Aeliana* Second series, 11 (1886), iii–vii.

——(1909). *A Suggested History Course for the Elementary School. Standards I-VII* (London: Goldsmith's College).

——(1913). 'Report of the Council for 1912', *Archaeologia Aeliana* Third Series 9, ix–xvi.

Arnold, D. (1998). 'The Illusion of Grandeur? Antiquity, Grand Tourism and the Country House', in D. Arnold (ed.) *The Georgian Country House: Architecture, Landscape and Society* (Stroud, Sutton), 100–16.

Ash, M. (1983). 'A Past "Filled with Living Men": Scott, Daniel Wilson, and Scottish and American Archaeology', in J. H. Alexander and D. Hewitt (eds.) *Scott and his Influence: The Papers of the Aberdeen Scott Conference, 1982* (Aberdeen, Association for Scottish Literary Studies), 432–42.

Auden, W. H. (1937). 'Roman Wall Blues', in E. Mendelson (ed.) *W.H. Auden, Collected Poems* (London, Faber and Faber), 121.

Ayres, P. (1997). *Classical Culture and the Idea of Rome in Eighteenth-Century England* (Cambridge, Cambridge University Press).

Ayris, I. (1997). *A City of Palaces: Richard Grainger and the making of Newcastle upon Tyne* (Newcastle upon Tyne, Newcastle Libraries & Information Services).

Baatz, D. (2000). *Der Römische Limes: Archäologische Ausflüge zwischen Rhein und Donau*, Revised edition (Berlin, Mann Verlag).

Babington, C. (1869). *Polychronicon Ranulphi Higden Monachi Cestrensis, Volume 2* (London: Longmans, Green, and Co.).

Baillie, J. (1801). *An Impartial History of the Town and County of Newcastle upon Tyne* (Newcastle upon Tyne, Vint and Anderson).

Bain, J. (1894). *The Border Papers: Calendar of Letters and Papers relating to the affairs of the Borders of England and Scotland preserved in Her Majesty's Public Record Office London* (Edinburgh, HMSO).

Ball, W. (2000). *Rome in the East: the transformation of an empire* (London, Routledge).

Ballantyne, T. (2002). *Orientalism and Race: Aryanism in the British Empire* (Basingstoke, Palgrave Macmillan).

Bamford, G. (2002). 'From analysis/synthesis to conjecture/analysis: a review of Karl Popper's influence on deign methodology in architecture', *Design Studies* 23, 245–61.

Barlow, P. (2007). 'Tyneside's Modern Rome: The North-East's Image of it's Roman Past and it's Lost Englishness', in H. Fawcett (ed.) *Made in Newcastle: Visual Culture* (Newcastle upon Tyne, Northumbria University Press), 135–52.

Barnett, L. (2007). *Jonathan Swift in the Company of Women* (Oxford, Oxford University Press).

Batchelor, J. (2004). 'Scott, William Bell', *Oxford Dictionary of National Biography, online edition* <http://www.oxforddnb.com/view/article/24938> Accessed February 2010.

——(2006). *Lady Trevelyan and the Pre-Raphaelite Brotherhood* (London, Chatto & Windus).

Bates, J. C. (1895). *The History of Northumberland* (London, Elliot Stock).

Baudrillard, J. (2005). *The System of Objects*, New edition (London, Verso).

——(no date) 'Simulacra and Simulations – I: The procession of Simulacra'. <http://www.egs.edu/faculty/jean-baudrillard/articles/simulacra-and-simulations-i-the-precession-of-simulacra/>. Accessed April 2011.

Bede. *Bede's Ecclesiastical History of the English People*. Edited by B. Colgrave and R. Mynors (Oxford, Clarendon Press, 1969).

Beeverell, J. (1707a). *Les Delices de la Grand' Bretagne & de l'Irelande, Volume 6* (Leiden, Van der Aa).

——(1707b). *Les Delices de la Grand' Bretagne & de l'Irelande*, Volume 1 (Leiden, Van der Aa).

Bell, T. (2005). *The Religious Reuse of Roman Structures in Early Medieval England* (Oxford, British Archaeological Reports, British Series 390).

Bell, W. (1854). 'The German Roman Wall', in C. R. Smith *Collectanea Antiqua, Etchings and Notices of Ancient Remains illustrative of the Habits, Customs, and History of Past Ages, Volume III* (London, published for the subscribers only), 210–13.

Bellhouse, R. L. (1969). 'Roman Sites on the Cumberland coast, 1966–1967', *Transactions of the Cumberland and Westmorland Antiquarian and Archaeological Society* New Series 69, 54–101.

Bender, B. (1998). *Stonehenge: Making Space* (Oxford, Berg).

Benjamin, R. (2004). 'Roman wall: Barrier or bond', *British Archaeology* 77, July 2004 <http://britarch.ac.uk/ba/ba77/feat1.shtml> Accessed December 2009.

——and A. Greaves (no date) *The Archaeology of Black Britain*. <http://www.channel4.com/history/microsites/B/blackhistorymap/arch.html> Accessed November 2010.

Betts, R. F. (1971). 'The Allusion to Rome in British imperialist thought of the late nineteenth and early twentieth centuries', *Victorian Studies* 15, 149–59.

Bidwell, P. (ed. 1999). *Hadrian's Wall 1989–1999* (Kendal, Titus Wilson and Son).

——(1999a). 'The Pilgrimages of Hadrian's Wall', in P. Bidwell (ed.), 1–6.

——(1999b). 'A summary of Recent Research on Hadrian's Wall', in P. Bidwell (ed.), 7–36.

——(2008). 'Did Hadrian's Wall have a Wall-walk?', in P. Bidwell (ed.), 129–43.

——(ed. 2008). *Understanding Hadrian's Wall*. Arbeia Society (Kendal, Titus Wilson).

——(2010). 'A survey of the Anglo-Saxon crypt at Hexham and its reused Roman stonework', *Archaeologia Aeliana* Fifth Series 39, 53–146.

——and W. Griffiths (1999). 'The Wall at Buddle Street', in P. Bidwell (ed.), 95–7.

——and N. Holbrook (1989). *Hadrian's Wall Bridges* (London, Historic Buildings and Monuments Commission for England).

——and S. Speak (1994). *Excavations at South Shields Roman Fort, Volume 1* (Newcastle upon Tyne, The Society of Antiquaries of Newcastle upon Tyne).

Bidwell, P., R. Miket and B. Ford (1988). 'The Reconstruction of a gate at the Roman fort of South Shields', in P. Bidwell, R. Miket and B. Ford (eds.), 155–231.

——(eds. 1988). *Portae cum turribus: Studies of Roman fort gates* (Oxford, British Archaeological Reports, British Series 206).

Birkholz, D. (2004). *The King's Two Maps: Cartography and Culture in Thirteenth-Century England* (London, Routledge).

Birley, A. R. (1979). *The people of Roman Britain* (London, Batsford).

——(1997). *Hadrian: The restless emperor* (London, Routledge).

——(2005). *The Roman Government of Britain* (Oxford, Oxford University Press).

Birley, E. (1935). 'Nine years ago' [poem sent to R. G. Collingwood, Christmas 1935] (Birley familly archive, Vindolanda, Northumberland).

——(1952). 'Introduction, in E. Birley' (ed.) *The Congress of Roman Frontier Studies 1949* (Kendal, Titus Wilson), v–vii.

——(1961). *Research on Hadrian's Wall* (Kendal, Titus Wilson).

——(1974). 'Introduction', In J. Horsley *Britannia Romana: or the Roman Antiquities of Britain*, New edition (Newcastle, Frank Graham), iii–v.

Birley, E. revised by M. Todd (2004). 'Richmond, Sir Ian Archibald', *Oxford Dictionary of National Biography, online edition* <http://www.oxforddnb.com/view/article/35744> Accessed March 2011.

Birley, R. (2009). *Vindolanda: A Roman Frontier Fort on Hadrian's Wall* (Stroud, Amberley).

Bishop, M. C. (1994). *Corstopitum: An Edwardian Excavation* (London, English Heritage).

Blain, J. and R. Wallis (2007). *Sacred Sites: Contested Rites/Rights* (Eastbourne, Sussex Academic Press).

Bohun, E. (1693). *A geographical dictionary representing the present and ancient names and states of all the countries, provinces, remarkable cities, universities, ports, towns, mountains, seas, streights, fountains, and rivers of the whole world* (London, Charles Brome).

Bosanquet, R. C. (1904). 'Excavations on the line of the Roman Wall in Northumberland. The Roman Camp at Housesteads', *Archaeologia Aeliana* Second Series 25, 193–299.

——(1926). 'The Roman Wall from Rudchester Burn to Matfen Piers', in M.H. Dodds (ed.) *A History of Northumberland, Volume 12* (Newcastle upon Tyne, Andrew Reid & Company), 17–50.

——(1929). 'Dr John Lingard's notes on the Roman wall', *Archaeologia Aeliana* Fourth Series 6, 130–62.

——(1956). 'Robert Smith and the "Observations upon the Picts Wall"', *Transactions of the Cumberland and Westmorland Antiquarian and Archaeological Society* New Series 55, 156–71.

Bowersock, G. W. (2009). *From Gibbon to Auden: Essays on the Classical Tradition* (Oxford, Oxford University Press).

Bradley, A. G. (1913). *The Romance of Northumberland*, Third edition (London, Methuen and Co.).

Brand, J. (1789). *The History and antiquities of the town and county of the town of Newcastle upon Tyne, Volume 1* (London, B. White and Son).

Breeze, D. (2003). 'John Collingwood Bruce and the Study of Hadrian's Wall', *Britannia* 34, 1–18.

——(2006a). *J. Collingwood Bruce's Handbook to the Roman Wall, Fourteenth edition* (Newcastle upon Tyne, Society of Antiquaries of Newcastle upon Tyne).

——(2006b). *Hadrian's Wall: A souvenir guide to the Roman Wall* (London, English Heritage).

——(2006c). *The Antonine Wall* (Edinburgh, John Donald).

——(2008a). 'To study the monument: Hadrian's Wall 1848–2006', in P. Bidwell (ed.), 1–4.

——(2008b). 'Presenting Roman Military Sites to the Public', in D. Breeze and S. Jilek (eds.), 141–7.

——(2008c). 'Preface', in D. Breeze and S. Jilek (eds.), 5.

——(2009a). 'Did Hadrian design Hadrian's Wall', *Archaeologia Aeliana* Fifth series 38, 87–103.

——(2009b). 'The Management of Hadrian's Wall', in N. Hodgson (ed.), 59–60.

——(in press). *The First Souvenirs: Enamelled vessels from Hadrian's Wall* (Cumberland and Westmorland Antiquarian and Archaeological Society, Tract Series, 23).

Breeze, D. and B. Dobson (1976). *Hadrian's Wall* (Harmondsworth, Penguin).

——(2000). *Hadrian's Wall*, Revised edition (London, Allen Lane).

Breeze, D. and S. Jilek (2008). 'The Frontiers of the Roman Empire World Heritage Site', in D. Breeze and S. Jilek (eds.), 25–8.

——(eds. 2008). *Frontiers of the Roman Empire: The European Dimension of a World Heritage Site* (Edinburgh, Historic Scotland).

Breeze, D., S. Jilek and A. Thiel (2005). *Frontiers of the Roman Empire* (Historic Scotland/Deutsche Limeskommission, Edinburgh/Esslingen).

Brennan, M. G. (2004). *The Origins of the Grand Tour: The travels of Robert Montagu, Lord Mandeville (1649–1654), William Hammond (1655–1658), Banaster Maynard (1660–1663)* (London, The British Library).

Brink, J. R. (1990). *Michael Drayton Revisted* (Boston, Twayne).

Brisbane, M. and J. Wood (1996). *A Future for our Past? An introduction to heritage studies* (London, English Heritage).

Brown, I. G. (1987). 'Modern Rome and Ancient Caledonia: the Union and the Politics of Scottish Culture', in A. Hook (ed.) *The History of Scottish Literature, 2, 1660–1800* (Aberdeen, Aberdeen University Press), 33–49.

——(2004). 'Gordon, Alexander', *Oxford Dictionary of National Biography, online edition* <http://www.oxforddnb.com/view/article/11021> Accessed March 2011.

Browning, M. (1991). 'Archaeology historicized: Romano-British frontier studies and German historiography at the turn of the century', in V. A. Maxfield and M. J. Dobson (eds.) *Roman Frontier Studies 1989: Proceedings of the XVth International Congress of Roman Frontier Studies* (Exeter, University of Exeter Press), 354–7.

——(1995). 'A Baconian Revolution: Collingwood and Romano-British Studies', in D. Boucher, J. Connelly and T. Modood (eds). *Philosophy, History and Civilization: Interdisciplinary Perspectives on R. G. Collingwood* (Cardiff, University of Wales Press), 330–63.

Bruce, G. (1905). *The Life and Letters of John Collingwood Bruce, LL.D, D.C.L., F.S.A. of Newcastle-upon-Tyne* (London, William Blackwood).

Bruce, J. C. (1850). 'On the Roman Wall from the Tyne to the Solway', *Journal of the British Archaeological Association* 5, 201–6.

——(1851). *The Roman Wall: A Historical, Topographical and Descriptive account of the Barrier of the Lower Isthmus, extending from the Tyne to the Solway* (London, John Russell Smith).

——(1857a). 'An account of the Excavations made at the Roman Station of Bremenium during the summer of 1855', *Archaeologia Aeliana* Second Series 1, 69–85.

——(1857b). 'Catalogue of the inscribed and sculptured Roman stones in the possession of the Society of Antiquaries of Newcastle-upon-Tyne', *Archaeologia Aeliana* Second Series 1, 221–70.

——(1863). *The Wallet-Book of the Roman Wall* (London, Longman).

——(1865). 'Mural Notes', *Archaeologia Aeliana* Second Series 6, 220–4.

——(1875). *Lapidarium Septentrionale: or, a Description of the Monuments of Roman Rule in the North of England* (London/Newcastle, Bernard Quaritch/William Dodd).

——(1876). 'On the Forum of the Roman Station at Cilurnum', *Archaeologia* 46 (1881), 1–8.

——(1879). 'An account of the excavation of the south gateway of the station of Cilurnum', *Archaeologia Aeliana* Second Series 8 (1880), 211–21.

——(1885). *The Hand-Book to the Roman Wall: A Guide to tourists traversing the barrier of the lower isthmus*, Third edition (London/Newcastle, Longmans, Green & Co./Andrew Reid).

——(1887). 'The Chairman', *Proceedings of the Society of Antiquaries of Newcastle upon Tyne* 3 (1889), 265–6.

——(1888). 'The Wall of Antonine', *Journal of the British Archaeological Association* 45 (1889), 131–4.

——(1892). 'Obituary Notices of deceased members: John Clayton', *Archaeologia Aeliana* Second Series 15, 90–5.

——(1907). *The Hand-Book to the Roman Wall, Fifth edition*. Revised and corrected by R. Blair (London, Longmans).

——(1933). *The Handbook to the Roman Wall, Ninth edition*. Edited by R. G. Collingwood (London, Longmans).

Buchner, J. A. (1822). 'Extract from a German Pamphlet, intitled "A Tour along the Devil's Wall," published as a Specimen of a projected History of Bavaria', *Archaeologia Aeliana*, 1, 219–30.

Budge, E. A. W. (1903). *An Account of the Roman Antiquities preserved in the Museum at Chesters, Northumberland* (London, Gilbert & Rivington).

Bullion, J. L. (2004). 'Augusta, princess of Wales', *Oxford Dictionary of National Biography, online edition* <http://www.oxforddnb.com/view/article/46829> Accessed March 2011.

Burnham, B. C. and J. Wacher (1990). *The 'Small Towns' of Roman Britain* (London, Routledge).

Burton, A. (2003). *Hadrian's Wall Path* (London, Aurum Press).

——(2010). *Hadrian's Wall Path*, Revised edition (London, Aurum Press).

Buzard, J. (2002). 'The Grand Tour and after (1660–1840)', in P. Hulme and T. Youngs (eds.), 37–52.

Camden, W. (1586). *Britannia sive florentissimorvm regnorum, Angliæ, Scotiæ, Hiberniae* (London, Radulphurn Newbery).

——(1607). *Britannia sive florentissimorvm regnorvm, Angliæ, Scotiæ, Hiberniæ* (London, Georgii Bishop).

——(1610). *Britain, or a Chorographicall description of the most flourishing King-domes, England, Scotland, and Ireland. Translated into English by Philémon Holland* (London, Georgii Bishop & Ioannis Norton).

——(1695). *Camden's Britannia, Newly Translated into English: with large additions and improvements. Published by Edmund Gibson* (London, F. Collins).

——(1722). *Britannia: or a Chorographical Description of Great Britain and Ireland, together with the Adjacent Islands ... The Second Edition, Volume II. Revised, Digested, and Published, with Large Additions, by Edmund Gibson* (London, Mary Matthews).

Campbell, D. and H. Debbieg (1750). *A Survey of the Country between Newcastle and Carlisle, Representing the several present Roads and the Tract which is proposed for the New Intended Road of Communication between these Towns. As also the Course of the Roman Wall with all the Military Stations, Castella and Military Ways that lye upon this survey* (British Library, Map, K. Top.5.103).

Campbell, J. (1978). 'Bede's Words for Places', in P.H. Sawyer (ed.) *Names, Words, and Graves: lectures delivered in the University of Leeds, May 1978* (Leeds, University of Leeds), 34–54.

Camphausen, G. (1999). 'The Monument on the Berlin Wall Memorial Site: A Process of Development', in *Berlin Wall: Memorial Site, Exhibition Centre and the Chapel of Reconciliation on Bernauer Strasse* (Berlin, Jaron Verlag), 18–22.

Cannadine, D. (2004). 'Trevelyan, George Macaulay'. *Oxford Dictionary of National Biography, online edition* <http://www.oxforddnb.com/view/article/36554>. Accessed March 2011.

Canny, N. (1998). 'The Origins of Empire: An Introduction', in N. Canny (ed.) *The Oxford History of the British Empire, Volume 1: The Origins of Empire* (Oxford, Oxford University Press), 1–33.

——(2000). *Making Ireland British, 1580–1650* (Oxford, Oxford University Press).

Carlyle, E. I., revised by C. M. Fraser (2004). 'White, Robert', *Oxford Dictionary of National Biography, online edition* <http://www.oxforddnb.com/view/article/29269> Accessed March 2011.

Carpenter, H. (1981). *W. H. Auden: A Biography* (London, George, Allen and Unwin).

Carrington, C. (1955). *Rudyard Kipling: His Life and Work* (London, Macmillan).

Casey, P. J. (2002). 'The fourth century and beyond', in P. Salway (ed.), 75–106.

Charlton, B. and J. Day (1984). 'Henry MacLauchlan: Surveyor and Field Archae-ologist', in R. Miket and C. Burgess (eds.), 4–37.

Chettle, S. (ed. 2006). *Writing on the Wall: An International writing project for Hadrian's Wall 2001–2006* (Newcastle upon Tyne, ARTS UK).

Christianson, A. (2002). 'Gender and nation: debatable lands and passable boundaries', in G. Norquay and G. Smyth (eds.) *Across the margins: cultural identity and change in the Atlantic archipelago* (Manchester, Manchester University Press), 67–82.

Clayton, J. (1855). 'Account of the Excavations at the Mile Castle of Cawfields, on the Roman Wall', *Archaeologia Aeliana* 4 (1855), 54–9.

——(1876). 'Description of Roman Remains discovered near to Procolitia, a Roman Station on the Wall of Hadrian', *Archaeologia Aeliana* Second series, 8 (1880), 1–19.

——(1877). 'Continuation of Description of, and Remarks on, the Temple of Coventina and its Contents', *Archaeologia Aeliana* Second series, 8 (1880), 20–39.

Clerk, J. (1742). 'Sir John Clerk to Roger Gale, relating his Journey to Whitehaven, the Coal Works there, Antiqutys at Boulnesse, and the Picts Wall', in W. C. Lukis (ed. 1883) *The Family Memoirs of the Rev. William Stukeley, M.D. and the Antiquarian and other Correspondence of William Stukeley, Roger & Samuel Gale, etc., Volume 2* (Durham, Surtees Society, Volume 76, 1883), 90–7.

Cobbett, W. (1807). 'Summary of Politics', *Cobbett's Weekly Political Register, no. 13* Saturday September 26, 1807, 491.

Colgrave, B. (1969). 'Historical Introduction', in B. Colgrave and R. A. B. Mynors, xvii–xxxviii.

Colgrave, B. and R. A. B. Mynors (eds. 1969). *Bede's Ecclesiastical History of the English People* (Oxford, Clarendon Press).

Collingwood, R. G. (1921a). 'Hadrian's Wall: A History of the Problem', *Journal of Roman Studies* 11, 37–66.

——(1921b). 'The Purpose of the Roman Wall', *The Vasculum* 8(1), 4–9.

——(1923). *Roman Britain* (London, Oxford University Press).

——(1926). *A Guide to the Roman Wall* (Newcastle, Andrew Reid and Company).

——(1927). 'The Roman Frontier in Britain', *Antiquity* 1, 15–30.

——(1929). 'A system of numerical references to the parts of Hadrian's Wall and the structures along its line', *Transactions of the Cumberland and Westmorland Antiquarian and Archaeological Society* Second Series 30 (1930), 108–15.

——(1931). 'Hadrian's Wall: 1921–1930.' *Journal of Roman Studies*, 21, 36–64.

——(1939). *An Autobiography* (Oxford, Oxford University Press).

Collini, S. and B. Williams (2004) 'Collingwood, Robin George', *Oxford Dictionary of National Biography, online edition* <http://www.oxforddnb.com/view/article/32503> Accessed March 2011.

Collins, R. and L. Allason-Jones (eds. 2010) *Finds from the Frontier: Material Culture in the 4th-5th Centuries* (York, Council for British Archaeology, Research Report 162).

Colls, R. (2002). *Identity of England* (Oxford, Oxford University Press).

Cool, H. E. M. (2004). *The Roman cemetery at Brougham, Cumbria: excavations 1966–67* (London, Society for Promotion of Roman Studies).

Cooper, T., revised by M. J. Mercer (2004). 'Baillie, John', *Oxford Dictionary of National Biography, online edition* <http://www.oxforddnb.com/view/article/1063> Accessed July 2011.

Copeland, E. (2001). 'Crossing Oxford Street: Silverfork Geopolitics', *Eighteenth-Century Life* 25(2), 116–34.

Corfe, T. (1997). 'The Battle of Heavenfield', in T. Corfe (ed.) *Before Wilfrid* (*Hexham Historian*, 7), 65–86.

Couse, G. S. (1990). 'Collingwood's Detective Image of the Historian and the Study of Hadrian's Wall', *History and Theory* 29(4), 57–77.

Cowper, W. (1872). 'Boadicea, an Ode', in J. D. Baird and C. Ryskamp (eds.) *The Poems of William Cowper, Volume 1: 1748–1782* (Oxford, Clarendon Press, 1980), 431–2.

Crang, M. A. (2009). 'World Heritage and world heritages', in D. Tolia-Kelly and C. Nesbitt *An Archaeology of 'race': Exploring the northern frontier in Roman*

Britain. <http://www.dur.ac.uk/resources/roman.centre/TotFArchaeologyOfRace-Catalogue.pdf.> Accessed March 2011.

Creighton, J. (2000). *Coins and Power in Late Iron Age Britain* (Cambridge, Cambridge University Press).

Creighton, O. (2007). 'Contested townscapes: the walled city as world heritage', *World Archaeology* 39, 339–54.

Crow, J. G. (1991). 'A Review of Current Research on the Turrets and Curtain of Hadrian's Wall', *Britannia* 22, 51–63.

——(2004a). *Housesteads: A fort and garrison on Hadrian's Wall*. Second edition (Stroud, Tempus).

——(2004b). 'The Northern Frontier of Britain from Trajan to Antoninus Pius: Roman Builders and Native Britons', in M. Todd (ed.), 114–35.

——(2007). 'Tracing the Busy Gap Rogues', *International Journal of Historical Archaeology* 11, 322–35.

Culham, P. (1997). 'Did Roman Women have an empire'? In M. Golden and P. Toohey (eds.) *Inventing Ancient Culture: Historicism, Periodization, and the Ancient World* (London, Routledge), 192–204.

Currey, R. N. revised by S. Basu (2004). 'Gibson, Wilfrid Wilson', *Oxford Dictionary of National Biography*, online edition <http://www.oxforddnb.com/view/article/33392> Accessed July 2011.

Curzon, G. N. (1907). *Frontiers: The Romanes Lecture 1907, delivered in the Sheldonian Theatre, Oxford* (Oxford, Clarendon Press).

Daniel, S. (1603). *A Panegyrike Congratvlatorie Delivered to the Kings Most Excellent Maistie at Burleigh Harrington in Rutlandshire* (London, Edward Blount).

Daniels, C. (1979). 'Fact and Theory on Hadrian's Wall', *Britannia* 10, 357–64.

Daniels, S. and B. Cowell (2011). 'Living Landscapes', in J. Bate (ed.) *The Public Value of the Humanities* (London, Bloomsbury), 105–17.

David, S. (2002). *The Indian Mutiny* (London, Viking).

Davies, G. (1997). 'Sir Robert Cotton's collection of Roman stones: a catalogue with commentary', in C. J. Wright (ed.), 129–67.

Davies, H. (1974). *A Walk along the Wall* (London, Weidenfeld and Nicolson).

Davis, G. (2000). 'The Irish in Britain, 1815–1939', in A. Bielenberg (ed.) *The Irish Diaspora* (Harlow, Pearson), 19–37.

Dawson, J. (1769). 'A MS. Diary of John Dawson of Brunton, beginning 8 March and ending 31 December, 1769', *Proceedings of the Society of Antiquaries of Newcastle upon Tyne* Third Series 3 (1909), 46–55.

Defoe, D. (1709). *The History of the Union of Great Britain* (Edinburgh, the heirs and successors of Andrew Anderson).

——(1719). *The Farther Adventures of Robinson Crusoe, Being the Second and Last Part of his Life and Strange Surprising Accounts of his Travels Round three Parts of the Globe* (London, W. Taylor).

——(1726). *A Tour Thro' the Whole Island of Great Britain, Volume III* (London, G. Strahan).

de Montluzin, E. L. (2004). 'George Smith of Wigton: *The Gentleman's Magazine* Contributor, Unheralded Scientific Polymath, and Shaper of the Aesthetic of the Romantic Sublime', *Eighteenth-Century Life* 28, No, 3, 66–89.

Devine, T. M. (1999). *The Scottish Nation 1700–2000* (London, Allen Lane).

Doubleday, T. (1822). 'The Roman Wall', *Blackwood's Magazine* 12, 409–12.

Dowling, L. (1985). 'Roman Decadence and Victorian historiography', *Victorian Studies* 28, 579–607.

Drayton, M (1622). *The Second Part, or a Continuance of Poly-Olbion from the Eighteenth Song* (London, Augustine Mathews).

Dumville, D. N. (1984). 'The Chronology of *De Excidio Britanniae*, Book 1', in M. Lapidge and D. Dumville (eds.), 61–84.

Duncan, D. (1993). 'Introduction', in J. Clerk. *History of the Union of Scotland and England: Extracts from his MS 'De Imperio Britannico'* (Edinburgh, Scottish History Society), 1–29.

Eaton, T. (2000). *Plundering the Past: Roman Stonework in Medieval Britain* (Stroud, Tempus).

Ebbatson, L. (1994). 'Context and Discourse: Royal Archaeological Institute Membership 1845-1942', in B. Vyner (ed.) *Building on the Past: papers celebrating 150 years of the Royal Archaeological Institute* (London, Royal Archaeological Institute), 22–74.

Eckardt, H. (2010). 'Introduction: Diasporas in the Roman world', in H. Eckardt (ed.), 7–12.

——(ed. 2010). *Roman Diasporas: Archaeological Approaches to Mobility and Diversity in the Roman Empire* (Portsmouth, Rhode Island, Journal of Roman Archaeology, supplementary series No. 78).

Eckstein, A. M. (2005). 'Commodus and the Limits of the Roman Empire', in M. M. Winkler (ed.), 53–72.

Edwards, B. (2001). 'Reginald Bainbridgg: scholemaister and his stones', in N. Higham (ed.) *Archaeology of the Roman Empire: a tribute to the life and works of Professor Barry Jones* (Oxford, British Archaeological Reports, International 940), 25–34.

Ellis, S. G. (1988). *The Pale and the Far North: Government and Society in two early Tudor borderlands. The O'Donnell Lecture, 1986* (Galway, National University of Ireland).

——(1999). 'The English State and its Frontiers in the British Isles, 1300–1600', in D. Power and N. Standen (eds.), 153–81.

Elrington, C. R. (2004). 'Hutton, William', *Oxford Dictionary of National Biography, online edition* <http://www.oxforddnb.com/view/article/14317> Accessed March 2011.

Embleton, R. and F. Graham (1984). *Hadrian's Wall in the Days of the Romans* (Newcastle upon Tyne, Frank Graham).

English, R. (2010). 'Foreword', in W. Parry, 6–7.

English Heritage (2010). *An Archaeological Map of Hadrian's Wall* (London, English Heritage).

Ewell, B. C. (1978). 'Drayton's *Poly-Olbion*: England's Body Immortalized', *Studies in Philology* 75, 297–315.

Ewin, A. (2000). *Hadrian's Wall: A Social and Cultural History* (Lancaster, University of Lancaster).

Ferguson, R. S. (1893). 'Part II: Hardknott Castle', *Transactions of the Cumberland and Westmorland Antiquarian and Archaeological Society* 12, 376–90.

Ferguson, W. (1977). *Scotland's Relations with England: A survey to 1707* (Edinburgh, John Donald).

Fletcher, A. (2004). 'An Officer on the Western Front', *History Today* 54, 31–7.

Fletcher, C. R. L. and R. Kipling (1911). *A School History of England* (Oxford, Clarendon Press).

Floyd-Wilson, M. (2002). 'Delving to the root: *Cymberline*, Scotland, and the English race', in D. J. Baker and W. Maley (eds.) *British Identities and English Renaissance Literature* (Cambridge, Cambridge University Press), 101–15.

Forster, R. H. (1899). *The Amateur Antiquary: His Notes, Sketches, and Fancies concerning the* ROMAN WALL *in the Counties of Northumberland and Cumberland* (London, Gay & Bird).

——(1901). 'Some Notes on Hadrian's Wall', *Journal of the British Archaeological Association* New Series 7, 69–75.

Fowler, J. T. (1878). 'A Remarkable Speaking-tube', *Notes and Queries* Fifth Series 10, 357.

Franzero, C. M. (1936). *Roman Britain* (London, George Allen & Unwin).

Freeman, P. W. M. (1996). 'Roman Frontier Studies: What's new?' *Britannia* 27, 465–70.

——(2007). *The Best Training-Ground for Archaeologists: Francis Haverfield and the Invention of Romano-British Archaeology* (Oxford, Oxbow).

Frodsham, P. (2004). '"Long ago in the land of the far horizons . . ." An introduction to the archaeology of the Northumberland National Park', in P. Frodsham (ed.) *Archaeology in the Northumberland National Park* (York, Council for British Archaeology Research Report 136), 2–152.

Fulford, M. (2006). 'Corvées and the *civitates*', in R. J. A. Wilson (ed.) *Romanitas: Essays on Roman archaeology in honour of Sheppard Frere on the occasion of his ninetieth birthday* (Oxbow, Oxford), 65–71.

——(2007). 'The Grand Excavation Projects of the Twentieth Century', in S. Pearce (ed.), 353–82.

Gaiman, N. (1999). *Stardust* (London, Headline).

Gale, R. (1726). 'Roger Gale to Sir John Clerk . . . London, June 24th, 1726', in W. C. Lukis (ed. 1887), 86–91.

Gazin-Schwartz, A. and C. Holtorf (1999). '"As long as I have ever known it . . .": on folklore and archaeology', in A. Gazin-Schwartz and C. Holtorf (eds.) *Archaeology and Folklore* (London, Routledge), 3–25.

Gibbon, E. (1776). *The History of the Decline and Fall of the Roman Empire: Volume 1* (London, Penguin, 1994).

Gibson, W. (1926). 'Stillchesters', in W. Gibson *Collected Poems, 1905–1925* (London, Macmillan and Co.), 761–2.

Gildas, *The Ruin of Britain and other works*, Edited and translated by M. Winterbottom, 1978 (London, Phillimore).

Gilmour, D. (2002). *The Long Recessional: The Imperial Life of Rudyard Kipling* (London, John Murray).

Glazier, D. (2007). 'Telling Tales: Folklore, Archaeology and the Discovery of the Past in the Present', in S. Grabow, D. Hull and E. Waterton (eds.) *Which Present, Whose*

Future? Treatments of the Past at the start of the 21st Century (Oxford, British Archaeological Reports International Series 1633), 41–9.

Glendening, J. (1997). *The High Road: Romantic Tourism, Scotland and Literature, 1720–1820* (Basingstoke, Macmillan).

Goldsworthy, A. and I. Haynes (ed. 1999). *The Roman Army as a Community* (Portsmouth, Rhode Island , Journal of Roman Archaeology, Supplementary Series 34).

Goodwin, G. and F. Horsman (2004). 'Hunter, Christopher', *Oxford Dictionary of National Biography, online edition* <http://www.oxforddnb.com/view/article/14216> Accessed March 2011.

Gordon, A. (1726). *Itinerarium Septentrionale: or, a Journey Thro' most of the counties of Scotland and those in the north of England* (London, Printed for the author).

Gore, C. G. F. (1831). *Pin Money; a novel, Volume 1* (London, Henry Colburn and Richard Bentley).

Gray, W. (1649). *Chorographia, or a survey of Newcastle upon Tyne* (London, J. B).

Griffiths, A. (2004). 'Hole, William', *Oxford Dictionary of National Biography, online edition* <http://www.oxforddnb.com/view/article/13503> Accessed March 2011.

Griffiths, H. (2003). 'Britain in Ruin', *Rethinking History* 7, 89–105.

Guardian (2008). 'Pathway to Heavenfield', <http://www.guardian.co.uk/travel/2008/aug/16/walkingholidays.adventure> Accessed March 2011.

Hall, E. (2010). 'British Refractions of India and the 1857 'Mutiny' through the prism of ancient Greece and Rome', in E. Hall and P. Vasunia (eds.), 33–49.

——and P. Vasunia (eds. 2010). *India, Greece, & Rome 1757–2007* (London, Insitute of Classical Studies).

Hansard (2011). 'Hadrian's Wall', *Hansard, Commons Debates, June 22nd, 2011, Column 126WH to 133WH* <http://www.publications.parliament.uk/pa/cm201011/cmhansrd/cm110622/halltext/110622h0002.htm> Accessed June 2011.

Hardin, R. F. (1973). *Michael Drayton and the Passing of Elizabethan England* (Lawrence, University Press of Kansas).

Harris, B. (2002). *Politics and the Nation: Britain in the Mid Eighteenth-Century* (Oxford, Oxford University Press).

Harvey, D. (2003). '"National identities" and the Politics of the Ancient Heritage: Continuity and Change at Ancient Monuments in Britain and Ireland, *c.*1675–1850' *Transactions of the Institute of British Geographers* 28, 473–87.

Haverfield, F. (1899a). 'Five Years excavation on the Roman Wall', *Transactions of the Cumberland and Westmorland Antiquarian and Archaeological Society* 15, 337–44.

——(1899b). *A catalogue of the Sculptured and Inscribed Stones in the Cathedral Library, Durham* (Durham, Thomas Coldcleugh).

——(1904). 'Obituary notices: Theodor Mommsen, Honorary Member', *Archaeologia Aeliana* Second Series 25, 185–8.

——(1906). 'The Romanization of Roman Britain', *Proceedings of the British Academy* 2, 185–217.

——(1911). 'Cotton Iulius F.VI. Notes on Reginald Bainbrigg of Appleby, on William Camden and on some Roman Inscriptions', *Transactions of the Cumberland and Westmorland Antiquarian and Archaeological Society* New series, 11, 343–78.

——(1912). *The Romanization of Roman Britain*, Second edition (Oxford, Clarendon Press).

——(1914). 'Introduction to J. B. Bailey's "Catalogue of Roman Inscribed and Sculptured Stones, Coins, Eathernware, etc., discovered in and near the Roman Fort at Maryport, and preserved at Nethehall"', *Transactions of the Cumberland and Westmorland Antiquarian and Archaeological Society* New series, 15, 135.

——(1924a). 'The Permanent Military Occupation of Britain', in F. Haverfield (1924b), 125–70.

——(1924b). *The Roman Occupation of Britain*, Revised by G. Macdonald (Oxford, Clarendon Press).

Hawkes, J. (1958). 'Battle of Hadrian's Wall', *Observer*, February 9, 1958, 7.

Haycock, D. B. (2002). *William Stukeley: Science, Religion and Archaeology in eighteenth-century England* (Woodbridge, Boydell Press).

——(2004). 'Horsley, John', *Oxford Dictionary of National Biography, online edition* <http://www.oxforddnb.com/view/article/13819> Accessed March 2011.

Haynes, H. W. (1890). 'The Roman Wall in Britain', *Journal of the American Geographical Society* 22, 157–210.

Heaney, S. (1984). 'Grotus and Coventina', in S. Heaney *Hailstones* (Dublin, The Gallery Press), 20.

Helgerson, R. (1988). 'The Land Speaks: Cartography, Chorography and Subversion in Renaissance England', in S. Greenblatt (ed.) *Representing the English Renaissance* (London, University of California Press), 327–61.

——(1992). *Forms of Nationhood: The Elizabethan Writing of England* (London, University of Chicago Press).

Henig, M. (1984). *Religion in Roman Britain* (London, Batsford).

Hepple, L. W. (1999). 'Sir Robert Cotton, Camden's *Britannia*, and the Early History of Roman Wall Studies', *Archaeologia Aeliana* Fifth Series 27, 1–19.

——(2002). 'Lord William Howard and the Naworth-Rokeby Collection of inscribed Roman Stones', *Transactions of the Cumberland and Westmorland Antiquarian and Archaeological Society* Third Series 11, 87–101.

——(2003a). 'William Camden and early collections of Roman antiquities in Britain', *Journal of the History of Collections* 15(2), 159–74.

——(2003b). 'John Horsley, James Jurin and the Royal Society Metrological Network', *Archaeologia Aeliana* Fifth series, 32, 153–70.

——(2004). '"The Camden Connection": Revisiting the origins of Romano-British archaeology and its historiography', in B. Croxford, H. Eckardt, J. Meade and J. Weekes (eds.) *TRAC2003: Proceedings of the Thirteenth Annual Theoretical Roman Archaeology Conference, Leicester 2003* (Oxford, Oxbow), 147–56.

Herendeen, W. (2007). *William Camden: a life in context* (Woodbridge, Boydell).

heritagetalks.org (2011). *The ratification of the Faro Convention* <http://heritagetalks.org/index.php/archives/71>. Accessed July 2011.

Hicks, D. and L. McAtackney (2007). 'Introduction: Landscapes as Standpoints', in D. Hicks, L. McAtackney and G. Fairclough (eds.), 13–29.

Hicks, D., L. McAtackney and G. Fairclough (eds. 2007). *Envisioning Landscapes: Situations and Standpoints in Archaeology and Heritage* (Walnut Creek, California, Left Coast Press).

Higham, N. J. (1991). 'Gildas, Roman Walls, and British Dykes', *Cambridge Medieval Celtic Studies* 22, 1–14.

——(2006). *(Re-)Reading Bede: The Ecclesiastical History in context* (London, Routledge).

Hill, P. R. (2000). 'Appendix 1: The Possible Re-use of Roman Stones in the Priory', in H. Summerson and S. Harrison (eds.), 191–2.

——(2006). *The Construction of Hadrian's Wall* (Stroud, Tempus).

——and B. Dobson (1992). 'The design of Hadrian's Wall and its Implications', *Archaeologia Aeliana* Fifth Series 20, 27–52.

Hingley, R. (2000). *Roman Officers and English Gentlemen: The imperial origins of Roman archaeology* (London, Routledge).

——(2004). 'Rural Settlement in Northern Britain', in M. Todd (ed.), 327–48.

——(2005). *Globalizing Roman Culture: Unity, diversity and Empire* (London, Routledge).

——(2007a). 'The Society, its Council, Membership and Publications, 1820–50', in S. Pearce (ed.), 173–98.

——(2007b). 'Francis John Haverfield (1860–1919): Oxford, Roman archaeology and Edwardian imperialism', In C. Stray (ed.) *Oxford Classics: Teaching and Learning 1800–2000* (London, Duckworth), 135–53.

——(2008a). *The Recovery of Roman Britain 1586–1906: 'A Colony so Fertile'* (Oxford, Oxford University Press).

——(2008b). 'Hadrian's Wall in Theory: Pursuing new agendas?', in P. Bidwell (ed.), 25–8.

——(2010a). '"The most ancient Boundary between England and Scotland": Genealogies of the Roman Walls', *Classical Reception Journal* 2, 25–43.

——(2010b). 'Tales of the frontier: diasporas on Hadrian's Wall', in H. Eckardt (ed.), 227–43.

——(2010c). 'Cultural Diversity and Unity: Empire and Rome', in S. Hales and T. Hodos (eds.) *Material Culture and Social Identities in the Ancient World* (New York, Cambridge University Press), 54–75.

——and R. Hartis (2011). 'Contextualizing Hadrian's Wall: The Wall as "debatable lands,"' in O. Hekster and T. Kaizer (eds.) *Impact of Empire* 13: *Frontiers of the Roman World* (Leiden, Brill), 79–96.

——and Nesbitt, C. (2008). 'A Wall for All Times', *British Archaeology* 102, 44–9.

——and C. Unwin (2005). *Boudica: Iron Age Warrior Queen* (London, Hambledon and London).

Hodgkin, T. (1883). 'The Pfahlgraben', *Archaeologia Aeliana* Second Series 9, 73–161.

——(1892). 'Obituary notice of the Rev. J. C. Bruce', *Archaeologia Aeliana* Second Series 15, 364–70.

Hodgson, J. (1822). 'Observations on the Roman Station of Housesteads, and on some Mithraic Antiquities discovered there', *Archaeologia Aeliana* 1, 263–320.

——(1840). *History of Northumberland, Part II, Volume III* (Newcastle, for the author).

Hodgson, N. (2008). 'After the Wall-periods', in P. Bidwell (ed.), 11–24.

——(2009a). 'Previous Pilgrimages', in N. Hodgson (ed.), 1–4.

——(2009b). 'A Review of Research on Hadrian's Wall 1999–2000', in N. Hodgson (ed.), 5–51.

——(ed. 2009). *Hadrian's Wall 1999–2009* (Kendal, Titus Wilson and Son).

——(2011). 'The Provenance of RIB 1389 and the Rebuilding of Hadrian's Wall in AD 158', *Antiquaries Journal* 91, 1–13.

——and J. McKelvey (2006). 'An excavation on Hadrian's Wall at Hare Hill, wall mile 53, Cumbria', *Transactions of the Cumberland and Westmorland Antiquarian and Archaeological Society* 6, 45–60.

Hooper, G. (2002). 'The Isles/Ireland: the wilder shore', in P. Hulme and T. Youngs (eds.), 174–90.

Hooppell, R. E. (1878). 'Results of the Recent Exploration of the Roman Station at South Shields', *Journal of the British Archaeological Association* 34, 373–83.

Horovitz, F. (1982). 'Audio recording: "Poem found at Chesters Museum, Hadrian's Wall"', in F. Horovitz *Collected Poems* <http://www.bloodaxebooks.com/titlepage. asp?isbn = 1852249250> Accessed June 2011.

Horsley, J. (1732). *Britannia Romana: or the Roman Antiquities of Britain* (London, John Osborn and Thomas Longman).

Howarth, D. (1997). 'Sir Robert Cotton and the commemoration of famous men', in C. J. Wright (ed.), 40–67.

Hoyer, M. A. (1908). *By the Roman Wall: notes on a summer holiday* (London, David Nutt).

Hübner, E. (1884). 'The Roman Annexation of Britain', *Archaeologia Aeliana* Second Series 11 (1886), 82–116.

Hudson, K. (1981). *A Social History of Archaeology* (London, Macmillan).

Hulme, P. and T. Youngs (eds. 2002) *The Cambridge Companion to Travel Writing* (Cambridge, Cambridge University Press).

Hunter, C. (1702a). 'Part of Some Letters from Mr. Christopher Hunter to Dr. Martin Lister, F.R.S. concerning Several Roman Inscriptions, and other Antiquities in Yorkshire', *Philosophical Transactions*, 23 (1702–3), 1129–32.

——(1702b). [untitled letter] (Durham Cathedral, *Rayne Collection, 117*).

Hunter, M. (1995). *Science and the Shape of Orthodoxy: Intellectual Change in Late Seventeenth-Century Britain* (Woodbridge, Boydell Press).

Hunter Blair, C. H. (1956). 'The armorials upon *A new map of Northumberland*, by John Warburton, 1716', *Archaeologia Aeliana* Third Series 34, 27–56.

Huskinson, J. (2002). 'Culture and social relations in the Roman province', in P. Salway (ed.), 107–40.

Hutchins, F. G. (1967). *The Illusion of Permanence: British Imperialism in India* (Princeton NJ, Princeton University Press).

Hutchinson, W. (1778). *A view of Northumberland with an Excursion to the Abbey if Mailroos in Scotland, 1776* (Newcastle, T. Saint).

Hutton, W. (1802). *The History of the Roman Wall, which crosses the island of Britain, from the German Ocean to the Irish Sea. Describing its antient state, and its appearance in the year 1801* (London, John Nichols and Son).

Hynes, S. (1991). *The Edwardian Turn of Mind*, Reprinted (London, Pimlico).

Illustrated London News (1843). 'The Cartoon, additional prizes', *Illustrated London News*, August 12th, 1843, 105.

——(1851). 'Nooks and Corners of Old England: Remains of the Wall of Severus, Walltown Crags, Cumberland', *Illustrated London News*, September 6th, 1851, 285.

——(1861). 'Mr. W. Bell Scott's Pictures Illustrative of English Border Life', *Illustrated London News*, July 20, 1861, 64.

——(1911). 'The Making of the Modern Englishman. No. 1: England under the Roman Empire', *Illustrated London News*, April 1, 1911, 468–9.

——(1924). 'Coming under Office of Works Protection: The Roman Wall', *Illustrated London News*, August 16, 1924, 301.

——(1930a). 'Hadrian's Wall and Quarrying', *Illustrated London News*, April 26, 1930, 735–7.

——(1930b). 'Defending Hadrian's Wall from Other Perils Than Quarrying: A Raid', *Illustrated London News*, June 21, 1930, 1139.

Inglis, F. (2009). *History Man: the Life of R. G. Collingwood* (Oxford, Princeton).

Interpretational Framework (2010). *Frontiers of the Roman Empire, Hadrian's Wall, Interpretational Framework* (Hexham, Hadrian's Wall Heritage).

Isaac, B. H. (2000). *The Limits of Empire: The Roman Army in the East*. Reprinted (Oxford, Clarendon Press).

Ivic, C. (2002). 'Mapping British identities: Speed's *Theatre of the Empire of Great Britaine*', in D. J. Baker and W. Maley (eds.) *British Identities and English Renaissance Literatures* (Cambridge, Cambridge University Press), 135–57.

Jackson, A. (2004). 'Wyndham, George', *Oxford Dictionary of National Biography*, online edition <http://www.oxforddnb.com/view/article/37052> Accessed March 2011.

James, E. (2001). *Britain in the First Millennium* (London, Arnold).

James, S. (1999). 'The Community of the Soldiers', in P. Baker, C. Forcey, S. Jundi and R. Witcher (eds.) *TRAC 98: Proceedings of the Eighth Annual Theoretical Roman Archaeology Conference Leicester 1998* (Oxford, Oxbow), 14–25.

——(2001). 'Soldiers and civilians: identity and interaction in Roman Britain', in S. James and M. Millett (eds.) *Britons and Romans: advancing an archaeological agenda* (York, Council for British Archaeology Research Report 125), 77–89.

——(2002). 'Writing the Legions: the Development and Future of Roman Military Studies in Britain', *Archaeological Journal* 159, 1–58.

——(2005). '*Limesfreunde* in *Philadelphia*: a Snapshot of the State of Roman Frontier Studies', *Britannia* 36, 499–502.

James, I. (1603). 'A Speech, as it was delivered in the Vpper Hovse of the Parliament to the Lords Spirituall and Temporall, and to the Knights, Citizens and Burgesses there assembled', in *The Political Works of James I: Reprinted from the edition of 1616* (Cambridge, Harvard University Press, 1918), 269–80.

Jenkinson, H. I. (1875). *Jenkinson's Practical Guide to Carlisle, Gilsland, Roman Wall and Neighbourhood* (London, Edward Stanford).

Jones, M. E. (1996). *The End of Roman Britain* (London, Cornell University Press).

Joshel, S. R., M. Malamud and M. Wyke (2001). 'Introduction', in S. R. Joshel, M. Malamud and D. T. McGuire. *Imperial Projections: Ancient Rome in Modern Popular Culture* (Baltimore, Johns Hopkins University Press), 1–22.

Juffer, J. (2006). 'Introduction', in J. Juffer (ed.), 663–80.

——(ed. 2006) *The Last Frontier: The Contemporary Configuration of the U.S.-Mexico Border* (Durham, Duke University Press, The South Atlantic Quarterly 105(4)).

Jurin, J. (1718). 'Remarks on a Fragment of an old Roman Inscription lately found in the North of England, and transcribed by the Curious and Learned Dr James Jurin', *Philosophical Transactions* 30 (1718–1719), 813–14.

Kemble, J. M. (1849). *The Saxons in England: A History of the English Commonwealth till the period of the Norman Conquest, Volume 1* (London, Longman, Brown, Green and Longmans), v–viii.

Keppie, L. (1998). *Roman Inscribed and Sculptured Stones in the Hunterian Museum, University of Glasgow* (London, Society for the Promotion of Roman Studies Britannia Monograph Series 13).

Kerlouégan, F. (2004). 'Gildas [St Gildas]', *Oxford Dictionary of National Biography, online edition* <http://www.oxforddnb.com/view/article/10718> Accessed March 2011.

Kidd, C. (1999). *British Identities before Nationalism: Ethnicity and Nationhood in the Atlantic World, 1600–1800* (Cambridge, Cambridge University Press).

Kipling, R. (1897). 'To Charles Eliot Norton, 16–17 December 1897', in T. Pinney (ed.) *The Letters of Rudyard Kipling*, Volume 2 1890–99 (1990) (London, Macmillan), 323–6.

——(1906). *Puck of Pook's Hill* (London, Macmillan and Co.).

——(1911). 'The Roman Centurion Speaks', in C. R. L. Fletcher and R. Kipling. *A School History of England* (Oxford, Clarendon Press), 19–20.

——(1920). 'England and the English, 'Royal Society of St. George: April 1920', in R. Kipling *A Book of Words: Selections from speeches and addresses delivered between 1906 and 1927* (1928) (London, Macmillan and Co.), 175–87.

Kirby, M. W. (2004). 'Stephenson, George', *Oxford Dictionary of National Biography, online edition* <http://www.oxforddnb.com/view/article/26397> Accessed March 2011.

Klein, B. (2001). 'Imaginary journeys: Spenser, Drayton, and the poetics of national space', in A. Gordon and B. Klein (eds.) *Literature, Mapping and the Politics of Space in Early Modern Britain* (Cambridge, Cambridge University Press), 204–23.

Kopperman, P. E. (2004). 'Debbieg, Hugh', *Oxford Dictionary of National Biography, online edition* <http://www.oxforddnb.com/view/article/7402> Accessed September 2008.

Kumar, K. (2003). *The Making of English National Identity*. Cambridge, Cambridge University Press.

Kunst, C. (1995). 'William Camden's *Britannia*: History and historiography', in M. H. Crawford and C. R. Ligota (ed.) *Ancient History and the Antiquarian: essays in memory of Arnaldo Momigliano* (London, Warburg Institute), 117–31.

Labadi, S. (2007). 'Representations of the nation and cultural diversity in discourses on World Heritage', *Journal of Social Archaeology* 7, 147–70.

——(2010). 'World Heritage, autenticity and post-authenticity: international and national perspectives', in S. Labadi and C. Long (eds.) *Heritage and Globalization* (London, Routledge), 66–84.

Lamont, C. and M. Rossington (2007). 'Introduction', in C. Lamont and M. Rossington (eds.), 1–12.

——and M. Rossington (eds. 2007) *Romanticism's Debatable Lands* (Basingstoke, Palgrave Macmillan).

Lapidge, M. and D. Dumville (eds. 1984) *Gildas: New approaches* (Woodbridge, Boydell).

Larson, V. T. (1999). 'Classics and the Acquisition and Validation of Power in Britain's "Imperial Century" (1815–1914)', *International Journal of the Classical Tradition* 6, 185–225.

Lawson, W. (1966). 'The origin of the Military Road from Newcastle to Carlisle', *Archaeologia Aeliana* Fourth Series 44, 185–207.

Lax, A. and K. Blood (1997). 'The earthworks of the Maryport fort: an analytical field survey by the Royal Commission on the Historic Monuments of England', in R. J. A. Wilson (ed.), 52–66.

Leach, S. and A. Whitworth (2011). *Saving the Wall: the conservation of Hadrian's Wall 1746–1987* (Stroud, Amberley).

Lengkeek, J. (2008). 'The authenticity discourse of heritage', in D. Breeze and S. Jilek (eds.), 37–51.

Lenihan, P. (2004). 'O'More, Rory [Roger Moore]', *Oxford Dictionary of National Biography, online edition* <http://www.oxforddnb.com/view/article/20762> Accessed March 2011.

Levi, P. (1996). 'Cara mamma', in P. Levi *I racconti: storie naturali Vizio di forma Lilít* (Turin, Einaudi).

Levine, J. M. (1987). *Humanism and History: origins of modern English historiography* (London, Cornell).

Lewis, E. (2007). 'Lost and Found', in *Making History: Antiquaries in Britain, 1707–2007* (London, Royal Academy of Arts), 109–21.

Lewis, M. (2006). 'Who Owns the Stones?' In S. Chettle (ed.), 16–20.

Locke, A. (2006). 'After the Raj; Last Outpost of the Empire'. in S. Chettle (ed.), 61.

Low, G. C.-L. (1996). *White Skins/Black Masks: Representation and Colonialism* (London, Routledge).

Lowenthal, D. (1985). *The Past is a Foreign Country* (Cambridge, Cambridge University Press).

Lukis, W. C. (ed. 1887). *The Family Memoirs of the Rev. William Stukeley, M.D. and the Antiquarian and other Correspondence of William Stukeley, Roger & Samuel Gale, etc., Volume 3* (Durham, Surtees Society, Volume 80, 1885).

Macdonald, G. (1933). 'John Horsley: Scholar and Gentleman', *Archaeologia Aeliana*, Fourth Series 10, 1–57.

Mack, D. S. (2006). *Scottish Fiction and the British Empire* (Edinburgh, Edinburgh University Press).

Mackenzie, D. (1993). 'Introduction', in R. Kipling, *Puck of Pooks Hill* and *Rewards and Fairies* (Oxford, Oxford University Press), xiii–xxxii.

Manzanas Calvo, A. M. (2006). 'Contested Passages: Migrants Crossing the Río Grande and the Mediterranean Sea', in J. Juffer (ed.), 759–75.

Marchand, S. (2003). *Down from Olympus: archaeology and philhellenism in Germany, 1750–1970* (London, Princeton University Press).

Marchitello, H. (1997). *Narrative and meaning in early modern England: Browne's skull and other histories* (Cambridge, Cambridge University Press).

Markham, S. (1984). *John Loveday of Caversham 1711–1789: The Life and Tours of an Eighteenth-Century Onlooker* (Salisbury, Michael Russell).

Marshall, T. (2000). *Theatre and empire: Great Britain on the London stages under James VI and I.* (Manchester, Manchester University Press).

'Martia' (1899). 'The Roman Wall', *Country Life*, August 26th, 1899, 236–8.

Mattingly, D. (1996). 'From one colonialism to another: imperialism and the Maghreb', In J. Webster and N. Cooper (eds.) *Roman Imperialism: Post-colonial perspectives.* (Leicester, School of Archaeological Studies, University of Leicester), 49–70.

——(2006). *An Imperial Possession: Britain in the Roman empire* (London, Allen Lane).

Maxfield, V. A. (1982). 'Mural Controversies', in B. Orme (ed.) *Problems and Case Studies in Archaeological Dating* (Exeter, Exeter Studies in History 4), 57–82.

Maxwell, G. (1989). *The Romans in Scotland.* (Edinburgh, James Thin).

McConnell, A. (2004). 'Laurie, Sir Peter', *Oxford Dictionary of National Biography, online edition* <http://www.oxforddnb.com/view/article/16133> Accessed March 2011.

McCord, N. (2004). 'Doubleday, Thomas', *Oxford Dictionary of National Biography, online edition* <http://www.oxforddnb.com/view/article/7848> Accessed March 2011.

——and R. Thompson (1998). *The Northern Counties from 1000* (London, Longmans).

McEachern, C. (1996). *The poetics of English nationhood, 1590–1612* (Cambridge, Cambridge University Press).

McKitterick, D. (1997). 'From Camden to Cambridge: Sir Robert Cotton's Roman inscriptions, and their subsequent treatment', in C. J. Wright (ed.), 105–28.

Meikle, M. M. (2004). *A British Frontier? Lairds and Gentlemen in the Eastern Borders, 1540–1603.* (East Linton, Tuckwell Press).

Merriman, M. (1982). 'Introduction: The Scottish Border', in H. M. Colvin (ed.) *The History of the King's Works, Volume IV 1485–1660, Part 2.* (London, HMSO), 607–13.

——(1984). '"The Epystle to the Queen's Majestie" and its "Platte"', *Architectural History* 27, 25–32.

Mikalachki, J. (1998). *The Legacy of Boadicea: Gender and nation in early modern England* (London, Routledge).

Miket, R. (1984). 'John Collingwood Bruce and the Roman Wall Controversy: The Formative Years, 1848–1858', in R. Miket and C. Burgess (eds.), 243–63.

——and C. Burgess (eds. 1984) *Between and Beyond the Walls: Essays on the Prehistory and History of North Britain in Honour of George Jobey* (Edinburgh, Edinburgh University Press).

Miller, D. (1995). *On Nationality* (Oxford, Clarendon Press).

Minto, W. (ed. 1892). *Autobiographical Notes of the Life of William Bell Scott, Volume 2* (London, James R. Osgood).

Mitchell, R. (2004). 'Skinner, John', *Oxford Dictionary of National Biography, online edition* <http://www.oxforddnb.com/view/article/25680> Accessed March 2011.

Mitchison, R. (2004). 'Clerk, Sir John of Penicuik', *Oxford Dictionary of National Biography, online edition* <http://www.oxforddnb.com/view/article/5617> Accessed March 2011.

Moore, W. H. (1968). 'Sources of Drayton's Conception of *Poly-Olbion*', *Studies in Philology* 65, 783–803.

Morley, N. (2010). *The Roman Empire: Roots of Imperialism* (New York, Pluto Press).

Morrell, J. (2004). 'Trevelyan, Sir William Calverley', *Oxford Dictionary of National Biography, online edition* <http://www.oxforddnb.com/view/article/27718> Accessed April 2011.

Morris, J., (1978). 'Historical Introduction', in M. Winterbottom (ed.) *Gildas, The Ruin of Britain and other works* (London, Phllimore), 1–4.

Morse, M. (2005). *How the Celts came to Britain: Druids, ancient skulls and the birth of archaeology* (Stroud, Tempus).

Mortimer, P. (2007). *Off the Wall: The Journey of a Play* (Nottingham, Five Leaves).

Mothersole, J. (1924). *Hadrian's Wall*. Third edition (London, Bodley Head).

Mouritsen, H. (1998). *Italian unification: a study in ancient & modern historiography* (London, Institute of Classical Studies).

Moving People, Changing Places (2011). *Moving People, Changing Places* <http://www.movingpeoplechangingplaces.org/migration-histories/black-romans.html> Accessed June 2011.

Moxham, R. (2001). *The Great Hedge of India*. (London, Constable).

Nagai, K. (2005). 'The Writing on the Wall: The Commemoration of the Indian Mutiny in the Delhi Durbar and Rudyard Kipling's "The Little House at Arrah"', *Interventions* 7, 84–96.

Nesbitt, C. and D. P. Tolia-Kelly (2009). 'Hadrian's Wall: Embodied Archaeologies of the Linear Monument', *Journal of Social Archaeology* 9, 368–90.

Newman, R. (2008). 'Whose Wall is it? The value of Hadrian's Wall as an archaeological resource', in P. Bidwell (ed.), 29–40.

Newton, D. (2006). *North-East England, 1569–1625: Governance, Culture and Identity* (Woodbridge, Boydell Press).

Nicolson, W. (1705). *Leges Marchiarum, or Border-Laws. Containing Several Original Articles and Treaties, Made and Agreed upon by the Commissioners of the Respective Kings of England and Scotland* (London, Tim Goodwin).

Oates, J. (2003). 'Responses in Newcastle upon Tyne to the Jacobite Rebellions of 1715 and 1745', *Archaeologia Aeliana* Fifth Series 32, 137–52.

Obmann, J. (2011). '"Sie muß den Kaiser auf der Saalburg sehen"—Die Feier zur Grundsteinlegung des wiedererrichteten Römerkastells am 11. Oktober 1900'. <http://www.archaeologie.uni-koeln.de/?q = node/172>. Accessed January 2011.

O'Brien, S. (2006). 'Writing on the Writing on the Wall', in S. Chettle (ed.), 8–11.

O'More, R. (1838). 'Sir Peter Laurie and the Irishry', *Bell's life in London and Sporting Chronicle*, Sunday October 21st, 1838, 1.

O'Neill, J. (1935). *Land Under England* (London, Victor Gollancz).

Orton, F. and I. Wood (2007). *Fragments of history: Rethinking the Ruthwell and Bewcastle monuments* (Manchester, Manchester University Press).

Ovenden, R. and S. Handley. (2004). 'William Howard', *Oxford Dictionary of National Biography, online edition* <http://www.oxforddnb.com/view/article/13947> Accessed March 2011.

Painter, K. S. (1973). 'John Skinner's Observations on Hadrian's Wall in 1801', *The British Museum Quarterly* 37, 18–70.

Paminter, M. (2007). *St Oswald's Way: official guidebook* (Alnwick, Alnwick District Council).

Parchami, A. (2009). *Hegemonic Peace and Empire: The Pax Romana, Britannica, and Americana* (London, Routledge).

Parry, W. (2010). *Against the Wall: The Art of Resistance in Palestine* (London, Pluto Press).

Paxton, N. L. (1992). 'Mobilizing Chivalry: Rape in British Novels about the Indian Uprising of 1857', *Victorian Studies* 36, 5–30.

Pearce, S. (2007). 'Visions of Antiquity: Introduction', in S. Pearce (ed.), 1–10.

——(ed. 2007) *Visions of Antiquity: The Society of Antiquaries 1797–2007. Archaeologia* 111 (London, Society of Antiquaries).

Pears, R. (2008). 'Image, identity and allusions: the Ridley monuments in St Nicholas Catherdral, Newcastle upon Tyne', *The School of Historial Studies [Newcastle University] Postgratuate Forum E-Journal*, 6 (2007/08). <http://www.societies.ncl.ac.uk/shspgf/Ed_5/pears.pdf> Accessed September 2010.

Pearson, M. (2006). *'In Comes I': Performance, Memory and Landscape* (Exeter, University of Exeter Press).

——and M. Shanks (2001). *Theatre Archaeology* (London, Routledge).

Pearson, W. (1708). '[Letter] To the Revd. Mr Gale, Rector of Scruton, near Northallerton', in W. C. Lukis (ed. 1883) *The Family Memoirs of the Rev. William Stukeley, M.D. and the Antiquarian and other Correspondence of William Stukeley, Roger & Samuel Gale, etc., Volume 2* (Durham, Surtees Society, Volume 76, 1883): 61–5.

Pelham, H. F. (1906). 'A Chapter in Roman Frontier History', *Transactions of the Royal Historical Society* New Series 20, 17–47.

Piggott, S. (1976). *Ruins in a Landscape: Essay in Antiquarianism* (Edinburgh, Edinburgh University Press).

Pinney, T. (2004). 'Kipling, (Joseph) Rudyard', *Oxford Dictionary of National Biography, online edition* <http://www.oxforddnb.com/view/article/34334> Accessed October 2008.

Pittock, M. G. H. (1997). *Inventing and Resisting Britain: Cultural Identities in Britain and Ireland, 1685–1789* (London, Macmillan).

Pitt-Rivers, A. H. L. F. (1898). 'Address to the Archaeological Institute of Great Britain and Ireland', in A. H. L. F. Pitt-Rivers *Excavations in Cranborne Chase, near Rushmore, on the borders of Dorset and Wilts, 1893–1896*, Volume 4 (London, Privately printed), 5–30.

Porter, R. (1988). *Gibbon, making history* (London, Phoenix).

Power, D. (1999). 'Introduction: Terms, Concepts, and the Historians of Medieval and Early Modern Europe', in D. Power and N. Standen (ed.), 1–12.

——and N. Standen (eds. 1999) *Frontiers in Question: Eurasian Borderlands, 700–1700* (Basingstoke, MacMillan).

Prescott, A. L. (1990). 'Drayton's Muse and Selden's "Story": The interfacing of Poetry and History in *Poly-Olbion*', *Studies in Philology* 87, 128–35.

——(1991). 'Marginal Discourse: Drayton's Muse and Selden's "Story"', *Studies in Philology* 88, 307–28.

——(2004). 'Michael Drayton', *Oxford Dictionary of National Biography, online edition.* <http://www.oxforddnb.com/view/articles/8042> Accessed July 2011.

Probyn, C. (2004). 'Swift, Jonathan', *Oxford Dictionary of National Biography, online edition.* <http://www.oxforddnb.com/view/articles/26833> Accessed March 2011.

Quinn, D. B. (1966). *The Elizabethans and the Irish* (Ithaca N.Y., Cornell University Press).

Quinta (2010) 'Roman Re-Enactment' <http://www.arbeiasociety.org.uk/Quinta.htm> Accessed June 2010.

Reitan, E.A. (1985). 'Expanding Horizons: Maps in the *"The Gentleman's Magazine,"* 1731–1754', *Imago Mundi* 37, 54–62.

Richmond, I. A. (1950). 'Hadrian's Wall, 1939–1949', *Journal of Roman Studies* 40, 43–56.

Ricketts, H. (1999). *The Unforgiving Minute: A life of Rudyard Kipling* (London, Chatto & Windus).

Ricoeur, P. (1984). *Time and Narrative, Volume 1* (London, University of Chicago Press).

Ridpath, G. (1776). *The Border-History of England and Scotland, Deduced from the earliest times to the Union of the two Crowns. Revised and published by the Author's Brother, Mr. Philip Ridpath, Minister of Hutton* (London, T. Cadell, A. Donaldson, J. Balfour and R. Taylor).

Rivet, A. L. F. (1976). *Rudyard Kipling's Roman Britain: Fact and fiction* (Keele, Keele University Library).

——and C. Smith (1979). *The Place-Names of Roman Britain* (London, Batsford).

Robbins, K. (1998). *Great Britain: Identities, Institutions and the Idea of Britishness* (London, Longman).

Roberts, D. H. (2007). 'Reconstructed pasts: Rome and Britain, child and adult in Kipling's *Puck of Pook's Hill* and Rosemary Sutcliff's historical fiction', in C. Stray (ed.) *Remaking the Classics: Literature, Genre and Media in Britain 1800–2000* (London, Duckworth), 107–24.

——(2010). 'Water-jug and plover's feathers: Rudyard Kipling's India in Rosemary Sutcliff's Roman Britain', in E. Hall and P. Vasunia (eds.), 117–30.

Robertson, J. (1995). 'An elusive sovereignty: The course of the Union debate in Scotland 1698–1707', in J. Robertson (ed.) *A Union for Empire: Political Thought and the British Union of 1707* (Cambridge, Cambridge University Press), 198–227.

Rogan, J. (1954). 'Christopher Hunter: Antiquary', *Archaeologia Aeliana* Fourth Series 32, 116–25.

Rogers, A. (2011). *Late Roman Towns in Britain: Rethinking Change and Decline* (Cambridge, Cambridge University Press).

——and R. Hingley (2010). 'Edward Gibbon and Francis Haverfield: The Tradition of Imperial Decline', in M. Bradley (ed.) *Classics & Imperialism in the British Empire* (Oxford, Oxford Univesity Press), 189–209.

Rose, B. (2005). *The Lost Border: The Landscape of the Iron Curtain* (New York, Princeton Architectural Press).

Rushworth, A. (2009). *Housesteads Roman Fort—The Grandest Station: Volume 1, Structural Report and Discussion* (London, English Heritage).

Rusnock, A. A. (1996). 'James Jurin', in A. A. Rusnock (ed.) *The Correspondence of James Jurin (1684-1750); Physician and Secretary to the Royal Society* (Amsterdam, Rodopi), 8-61.

Russell, L. (2001). 'Introduction', in L. Russell (ed.) *Colonial Frontiers: Indigenous-European Encounters in settler societies* (Manchester, Manchester University Press), 1-15.

Sachs, J. (2010). *Romantic Antiquity: Rome in the British Imagination, 1789-1832* (Oxford, Oxford University Press).

Salway, P. (ed. 2002) *Short Oxford History of the British Isles: The Roman Era* (Oxford, Oxford University Press).

Samuel, R. (1994). *Theatres of Memory, Volume 1: Past and Present in Contemporary Culture* (London, Verso).

Scott, J. (2003). *The Pleasure of Antiquity: British Collectors of Greece and Rome* (London, Yale University Press).

Scott, W. (1797). 'To a lady, With Flowers from a Roman Wall', in J. Logie Robertson (ed.) *Scott, Poetical Works*. Reprinted (London, Oxford University Press, 1967), 695.

——(1813). *Rokeby: A Poem* (Edinburgh, John Ballantyne and Co).

——(1814). *The Border Antiquities of England and Scotland, Volume 1* (London, Longman, Hurst, Rees, Orme and Brown).

——(1815). *Guy Mannering; or, the astrologer, Volume 2*. Second edition (Edinburgh, James Ballantyne and Co.).

——(1816). *The Antiquary* (Edinburgh, B&W, 1993).

Scott, W. B. (1843). *Design for a Westminster Hall Cartoon: A battle between ancient Britons and Romans* (National Gallery of Scotland, Permanent collections, D4713.9 C).

——(1857a). [untitled letter to Walter Trevelyan, January 11, 1857], (Newcastle University Library, Special collection, WCT 73).

——(1857b). [untitled letter to to Lady Trevelyan, March 12, 1857], (Newcastle University Library, Special collection, WCT 73).

——(1857c). [untitled letter to Lady Trevelyan, March 15, 1857], (Newcastle University Library, Special collection, WCT 73).

——(1857d). [untitled letter to Lady Trevelyan, April 21, 1857], (Newcastle University Library, Special collection, WCT 73).

——(1857e). [untitled letter to Lady Trevelyan, May 26, 1857], (Newcastle University Library, Special collection, WCT 73).

——(1857f). [untitled letter to Walter Trevelyan, June 5, 1857], (Newcastle University Library, Special collection, WCT 73).

——(1879). [untitled letter to Walter Trevelyan, August 3, 1879], (Newcastle University Library, Special collection, WCT 80).

Sebald, W. G. (2002). *The Rings of Saturn*. Revised edition (London, Vintage).

Seymour, W. A. (ed. 1980). *A History of the Ordnance Survey* (Folkestone, Dawson).

Shannon, W. D. (2007). *Murus ille famosus (that famous wall): Depictions and Descriptions of Hadrian's Wall before Camden* (Cumberland and Westmorland Antiquarian and Archaeological Society, Transactions Series 22, Kendal, Titus Wilson & Son).

Shimon, S. (2006). 'Kika and the Ferryman', in S. Chettle (ed.), 77-80.

Shumate, N. (2006). *Nation, Empire, Decline: Studies in Rhetorical Continutity from the Roman to the Modern Era* (London, Duckworth).

Sibbald, R. (1707). *Historical Inquiries, concerning the Roman Monuments and Antiquities in the North-Part of Britain called Scotland.* (Edinburgh, James Watson).

Simpson, F. G. (1976). 'Military Works', in G. Simpson (ed.) *Watermills and Military Works on Hadrian's Wall: Excavations in Northumberland 1907–1913* (Kendal, Titus Wilson & Son), 75–163.

——and J. McIntyre (1933). 'Banks Burn to Randylands', *Transactions of the Cumberland and Westmorland Antiquarian and Archaeological Society* New Series 33, 262–70.

——and I. A. Richmond (1935). 'The Turf Wall of Hadrian, 1895–1935', *Journal of Roman Studies* 25, 1–18.

——and R. C. Shaw (1922). 'The Purpose and Date of the Vallum and its crossings', *Transactions of the Cumberland and Westmorland Antiquarian and Archaeological Society* New series 22, 353–433.

Sims-Williams, P. (1995a). 'Gildas and the Anglo-Saxons', in P. Sims-Williams *Britain and Early Christian Europe: Studies in Early Medieval History and Culture, Item 1* (Aldershot, Ashgate), 1–30.

——(1995b). 'The settlement of England in Bede and the *Chronicle*', in P. Sims-Williams *Britain and Early Christian Europe: Studies in Early Medieval History and Culture Item II* (Aldershot, Ashgate), 1–41.

Skinner, W. (1801). *Observations on the Roman Wall, being an account of a Tour from Broadstairs to Newcastle by Sea, and through Northumberland and Cumberland* (British Library Manuscript Collection, 33,638. Vol. VI [ff. 244]).

Smiles, S. (1994). *The Image of Antiquity: Ancient Britain and the Romantic Imagination* (London, Yale University Press).

Smith, C. R. (1848). 'The Red Glazed Pottery of the Romans, found in this country and on the Continent', *Journal of the British Archaeological Association* 4 (1849), 1–10.

——(1852). *Collectanea Antiqua, Etchings and Notices of Ancient Remains illustrative of the Habits, Customs, and History of Past Ages, Volume II* (London, J. Russell Smith).

——(1883). *Retrospections, Social and Archaeological, Volume I* (London, George Bell and Sons).

——(1891). *Retrospections, Social and Archaeological, Volume III* (London, George Bell and Sons).

——(no date). *Collectanea Antiqua, Etchings and Notices of Ancient Remains, illustrative of the Habits, Customs and History of Past Ages, Volume III* (Printed for subscribers and not published, printed in 1857 or 1858).

Smith, G. (1741). 'The *Roman* Altar lately found at *Cast Steeds* in Cumberland with other curiosities there; Little Pedestals, like Portable Altars, found also at *Cast Steeds*', *The Gentleman's Magazine* 11, 650.

——(1742a). 'The Inscription on the *Roman* Altar, and an Account of the other Figures. p. 627', *The Gentleman's Magazine* 12, 30.

——(1742b). 'A letter from *G. Smith*, Esq; concerning the Altar, &c.', *The Gentleman's Magazine* 12, 76.

——(1746a). 'A Letter to a friend, containing an account of the march of the rebels into England, a description of the castle of *Carlisle*, and a dissertation on the old Roman wall; with respect to the map of it, and the adjacent country, the plan of *Carlisle*, and a view of its castle, just publish'd in two sheets; the draughts of which were favourably received by the duke of *Cumberland* on his forming the attack on *Carlisle* castle; and now are dedicated to his royal highness', *The Gentleman's Magazine* 16, 233–5.

——(1746b). 'Letter relating the Map and Plan of Carlisle, and the Retreat of the Rebels . . . Description of *Carlisle* castle', *The Gentleman's Magazine* 16, 300–2.

——(1746c). 'A Dissertation on the Roman Wall, relating to the Map and plan, see p. 300', *The Gentleman's Magazine* 16, 357–8.

——(1746d). 'A Map of the Countries Adjacent to Carlisle showing the Route of the Rebels with their principal fords over ye rr Eden. By George Smith', *The Gentleman's Magazine* 16, facing 233.

Spain, G. R. B. and F. G. Simpson (1930). 'The Roman frontier works from Wallsend to Rudchester Burn', in M. H. Dodds (ed.) *A History of Northumberland, Volume 13*, 484–564.

Speck, W. A. (2004). 'William Augustus, Prince', *Oxford Dictionary of National Biography, online edition* <http://www.oxforddnb.com/view/article/29455> Accessed January 2010.

Speidel, M. P. (1998). 'The Risingham *Praetensio*', *Britannia* 29, 356–9.

Stafford, F. (2007). 'Writing on the Borders', in C. Lamont and M. Rossington (eds.), 13–26.

Stearn, R. T. (2004). Woodville, Richard Caton. *Oxford Dictionary of National Biography, online edition* <http://www.oxforddnb.com/view/article/68891> Accessed April 2011.

Stevens, C. E. (1941a). 'The British Sections of the Notitia Dignitatum', *Archaeological Journal* 97 (1940), 125–54.

——(1941b). 'Gildas Sapiens', *English Historical Review* 56, 353–73.

Stoler, A. L. (2008). 'Imperial Debris: Reflections on Ruins and Ruination', *Cultural Anthropology* 23, 191–219.

Stray, C. (1998). *Classics Transformed: Schools, Universities, and Society in England, 1830–1960* (Oxford, Oxford University Press).

Streets, H. (2004). *Martial races: The Military, race and masculinity in British imperial culture, 1857–1914* (Manchester, Manchester University Press).

Struck, M. (2001). 'The *Heilige Römische Reich Deutscher Nation* and Hermann the German', in R. Hingley (ed.) *Images of Rome: Perceptions of ancient Rome in Europe and the United States in the modern age* (Portsmouth, Rhode Island, *Journal of Roman Archaeology. Supplementary Series 44*), 91–112.

Stukeley, W. (1754a). '[Diary extract], 15th July 1754', in W C. Lukis (ed. 1887), 139–40.

——(1754b). '[Diary extract], 19 Oct. 1754', in W C. Lukis (ed. 1887), 140–1.

——(1754c). '[Diary extract], 23 Oct. 1754', in W. C. Lukis (ed. 1887), 141–3.

——(1754d). '[Diary extract], 16 Nov. 1754', in W. C. Lukis (ed. 1887), 143.

——(1776). *Itinerarium Curiosum. Or, an Account of the Antiquities and Remarkable Curiosities in Nature or Art, Observed in Travels through Great Britain, Centuria II* (London, Baker and Leigh).

Summerson, H. (2000). 'The History of Lanercost Priory', in H. Summerson and S. Harrison (eds.), 1–80.

——(2004). 'Dacre family', *Oxford Dictionary of National Biography, online edition* <http://www.oxforddnb.com/view/article/71861> Accessed April 2011.

——and S. Harrison (eds. 2000) *Lanercost Priory, Cumbria: A survey and documentary history.* (Carlisle, Cumberland and Westmorland Antiquarian and Archaeological Society, Research Series 10).

Sutherland, A. C. (1984). 'The Imagery of Gildas's *De Excidio Britanniae*', in M. Lapidge and D. Dumville (eds. 1984), 157–68.

Swann, M. (2001). *Curiosities and Texts: The culture of collecting in early modern England* (Philadelphia, University of Pennsylvania Press).

Sweet, R. (1997). *The Writing of Urban Histories in Eighteenth-Century England* (Oxford, Clarendon Press).

——(2004). *Antiquaries: the Discovery of the Past in Eighteenth-Century Britain* (London, Hambledon and London).

Swift, J. (1746). 'The Story of the *Injured Lady*. Written by Herself. In a Letter to her Friend, with his Answer', in J. Swift, *Miscellanies, The eleventh volume* (London, C. Hitch, C. Davis, R. Dodsley, and M. Cooper), 103–14.

The Times (1930a). 'Hadrian's Wall, quarry threat to countryside: Strong protest by Antiquaries', *The Times*, April 11, 1930, 14.

——(1930b). 'Hadrian's Wall, Continued danger of disfigurement: An invitation to Mr. Lansbury', *The Times*, July 29, 1930, 15.

——(1930c). 'Hadrian's Wall: Conference at House of Commons', *The Times*, November 4, 1930, 16.

Thompson, F. M. L. (2004) 'Percy, Algernon, fourth duke of Northumberland (1792–1865)', *Oxford Dictionary of National Biography, online edition* <http://www.oxforddnb.com/view/article/21924> Accessed April 2011.

Thorne, J. (2010). 'The "Indian Mutiny" and the "Gallic Revolt"', in E. Hall and P. Vasunia (eds.), 99–116.

Todd, J. M. (1997). 'Introduction', in J. M. Todd (ed.) *The Lanercost Cartulary (Cumbria County Record Office MS DZ/1)* (Gateshead, The Publication of the Surtees Society 203), 1–50.

——(2006). 'The boundary of the lands of Lanercost Priory at Hare Hill', in N. Hodgson and J. McKelvey (2006), 45–60.

Todd, M. (ed. 2004). *A Companion to Roman Britain* (Oxford, Blackwell).

Tolia-Kelly, D. P. (2010). 'Narrating the postcolonial landscape: Archaeologies of race at Hadrian's Wall', *Transactions of the Institute of British Geographers* 36, 71–88.

——and C. Nesbitt (2009). *An Archaeology of 'race': Exploring the northern frontier in Roman Britain.* <http://www.dur.ac.uk/resources/roman.centre/TotFArchaeologyOfRaceCatalogue.pdf.> Accessed March 2011.

Tomlin, R. S. O. (1999). 'Towards a new volume of *The Roman Inscriptions of Britain*', *Oxford University Centre for the Study of Ancient Documents* 8 (Autumn 1999), 1–2

<http://www.csad.ox.ac.uk/csad/newsletters/newsletter8/Newsletter8a.html> Accessed April 2011.

——and M. W. C. Hassall (2004). 'Inscription', *Britannia* 35, 335–49.

Trevelyan, G. M. (1930). 'Hadrian's Wall. Dignity and Beauty unregarded: A contrast with other countries', *The Times*, April 16, 15.

Trevelyan, R. (1978). *A Pre-Raphaelite Circle* (London, Chatto & Windus).

——(1994). *Wallington, Northumberland* (London, National Trust).

——(2009). *Wallington, Northumberland*. Revised edition (London, National Trust).

Trevelyan, W. C. (1857). '[note] Wallington Hall, during 1857', (Newcastle University Library, Special collection, WCT 78).

Trotnow, H. (1999). 'Understanding the Present by Looking Back at the Past: Bernard Strasse and the Berlin Wall Memorial Site', in *Berlin Wall: Memorial Site, Exhibition Centre and the Chapel of Reconciliation on Bernauer Strasse* (Berlin, Jaron Verlag), 8–12.

Ulmer, G. L. (1994). *Heuretics: the logic of invention* (London, John Hopkins University Press).

Usherwood, P. (1996). 'Hadrian's Wall and the New Romans', in T. E. Faulkner (ed.) *Northumbrian Panorama: Studies in the History and Culture of North East England* (London, Octavian Press), 151–62.

——(2007). 'Myths of Northumberland', in R. Colls (ed.) *Northumbria: History and Identity 574–2000* (Chichester, Phillimore), 239–55.

Vance, N. (1997). *The Victorians and Ancient Rome* (Oxford, Blackwell).

van Driel-Murray, C. 2002. 'Ethnic soldiers: the experience of the Lower Rhine tribes,' in T. Grünewald and S. Seibel (eds.) *Kontinuität und Diskontinuität: Germania inferior am Beginn und am Ende der römischen Herrschaft* (Berlin, de Gruyter), 200–17.

Vaquera-Vásquez, S. (2006). 'Notes from an Unrepentant Border Crosser', in J. Juffer (ed.), 699–716.

Voss, J. A. (1987). 'Antiquity Imagined: Cultural Values in Archaeological Folklore', *Folklore* 98, 80–90.

Wainwright, A. (1987). *A Pennine Journey: The Story of a Long Walk in 1938* (London, Penguin).

Wallace-Hadrill, J. M. (1988). *Bede's Ecclesiastical History of the English People: A Historical Commentary* (Oxford, Clarendon Press).

Waller, E. (1655). *A Panegyrick to My Lord Protector, By a Gentleman that Loves the Peace, Union, and Prosperity of the English Nation* (London, Thomas Newcomb).

Walpole, H. (1780). 'To Cole, Monday 13 March 1780', in W. S. Lewis and A. Dayle Wallace (eds.) *Horace Walpole's Correspondence with the Rev. William Cole, Volume II* (London, Oxford University Press), 203–6.

Walsh, S. (2010). *Kipling's Children's Literature: Language, Identity, and Constructions of Childhood* (Farnham, Ashgate).

Warburton, J. (1716). *A Map of the County of Northumberland* (British Library, Maps 183. N. 5).

——(1753). *Vallum Romanum: or, the History and Antiquities of the Roman Wall, commonly called the Picts Wall, in Cumberland and Northumberland, built by*

Hadrian and Severus, the Roman Emperors, Seventy Miles in Length, to keep out the Northern Picts and Scots (London, J. Millan, J. Robinson and R. Baldwin).

Ward, J. (1742). 'Explanation of the *Roman* Altar and Figures', *The Gentleman's Magazine* 12, 30–1.

Warnaby, G., D. Medway and D. Bennison (2010). 'Notions of materiality and linearity: the challenges of marketing the Hadrian's Wall place "product"', *Environment and Planning* 42, 1365–82.

Weigall, A. (1926). *Wanderings in Roman Britain* (London, Thornton Butterworth).

Welfare, H. (2000). 'Causeways, at Milecastles, across the Ditch of Hadrian's Wall', *Archaeologia Aeliana* Fifth series 28, 13–25.

Whitaker, H. (1949). *A Descriptive List of Maps of Northumberland, 1576–1900* (Gateshead on Tyne, Society of Antiquaries of Newcastle upon Tyne and The Public Libraries Committee of Newcastle upon Tyne).

White, R. (1867). 'To a Friend: on visiting the Roman Wall', in R. White *Poems: Including Tales, Ballads, and Songs* (Kelso, J. and J. H. Rutherfurd), 217–21.

Whittaker, C. R. (1994). *Frontiers of the Roman Empire: A Social and Economic Study* (London, Johns Hopkins University Press).

Whitworth, A. M. (2000). *Hadrian's Wall: Some Aspects of its Post-Roman Influence on the Landscape.* (Oxford, British Archaeological Reports, British Series 296).

——(2009a). 'A 19th-century condition survey of Hadrian's Wall: the James Irwin Coates archive, 1877–1896', in T. Wilmott (ed.), 8–49.

——(2009b). 'Charles Anderson and the consolidation of Hadrian's Wall', in T. Wilmott (ed.), 50–71.

Williams, H. (2008). 'Anglo-Saxonism and Victorian archaeology: William Wylie's *Fairford Graves*', *Early Medieval Europe* 16(1), 49–88.

Willis, I. (2007). 'The Empire Never Ended', in L. Hardwick and C. Gillespie (ed.) *Classics in Post-Colonial Worlds* (Oxford, Oxford University Press), 329–48.

Wilmott, T. (1997). *Birdoswald: Excavations of a Roman Fort on Hadrian's Wall and its successor settlements: 1987–92* (London, English Heritage).

——(2001). *Birdoswald Roman Fort: 1800 years on Hadrian's Wall* (Stroud, Tempus).

——(2008). 'The Vallum: how and why: A review of the evidence', in P. Bidwell (ed.), 119–28.

——(2009a). 'Introduction: English Heritage research work on Hadrian's Wall, 1976–2000', in T. Wilmott (ed.), 1–7.

——(2009b). 'Excavations at the Hadrian's Wall fort of Birdoswald (*Banna*), Cumbria: 1996–2000', in T. Wilmott (ed.), 203–95.

——(ed. 2009) *Hadrian's Wall: Archaeological Research by English Heritage 1976–2000* (London, English Heritage).

——(2010). 'The Late Roman frontier: A structural background', in R. Collins and L. Allason-Jones (eds.), 10–16.

——and J. Bennett (2009). 'The linear elements of the Hadrian's Wall complex: four investigations 1983–2000', in T. Wilmott (ed.), 72–136.

——H. Cool and J. Evans (2009). 'Excavations at the Hadrian's Wall fort of Birdoswald (*Banna*), Cumbria, 1996–2000', in T. Wilmott (ed.), 203–395.

Wilson, J. (1901). 'Introduction to the Cumberland Domesday, Early Pipe Rolls, and Testa de Nevill', in *The Victoria History of the County of Cumberland, Volume 1* (London, Archibald Constable), 295–335.

Wilson, K. (1998). *The sense of the People: Politics, culture and imperialism in England, 1715–1785* (Cambridge, Cambridge University Press).

Wilson, P. (2011). 'To Build or not to Build? Presenting Roman Sites in Britain', in M. Müller, T. Otten and U. Wulf-Rheidt (eds.), *Schutzbauten und Rekonstruktionen in der Archäologie. Von der Ausgrabung zur Präsentation* (Mainz, Xantener Berichte 19), 263–74.

Wilson, R. J. A. (ed. 1997). *Roman Maryport and its Setting* (Nottingham, Cumberland and Westmorland Antiquarian and Archaeological Society).

Winchester, A. J. L. (2004). 'Reginald Bainbrigg', *Oxford Dictionary of National Biography, online edition* <http://www.oxforddnb.com/view/article/1084> Accessed March 2010.

Winkler, M. M. (2005). 'Editor's Preface', in M. M. Winkler (ed.), xi–xii.

——(ed. 2005). *Gladiator: Film and History* (Oxford, Blackwell).

Witcher, R. (2010a). 'The Fabulous Tales of Common People, Part 1: Representing Hadrian's Wall', *Public Archaeology* 9, 126–52.

——(2010b). 'The Fabulous Tales of Common People, Part 2: Encountering Hadrian's Wall', *Public Archaeology* 9, 211–38.

Witcher, R., D. P. Tolia-Kelly and R. Hingley (2010). 'Archaeologies of Landscape: Excavating the Materialities of Hadrian's Wall', *Journal of Material Culture* 15: 105–28.

Witmore, C. L. (2007). 'Landscape, Time, Topology: An Archaeological Account of Southern Argolid, Greece', in D. Hicks, L. McAtackney and G. Fairclough (eds.), 194–225.

Woodcock, T. (2004). 'Warburton, John', *Oxford Dictionary of the National Biography, online edition.* <http://www.oxforddnb.com/view/articles/28673> Accessed April 2011.

Woodside, R. and J. G. Crow (1999). *Hadrian's Wall: An Historic Landscape* (London, The National Trust).

Wormald, J. (1994). 'The union of 1603', in R. A. Mason (ed.) *Scots and Britons: Scottish political thought and the union of 1603* (Cambridge, Cambridge University Press), 17–40.

Wright, C. J. (ed. 1997). *Sir Robert Cotton as Collector: Essays on an Early Stuart Courtier and his Legacy* (London, The British Library).

Wright, T. (1852). *The Celt, the Roman, and the Saxon: A history of the early inhabitants of Britain, down to the conversion of the Anglo-Saxons to Christianity* (London, Arthur Hall Virtue & Co.).

Wroth, W. W. revised by C. M. Fraser (2004). 'Bruce, John Collingwood', *Oxford Dictionary of the National Biography, online edition.* <http://www.oxforddnb.com/view/articles/3741> Accessed March 2011.

Wyndham, G. (1906). 'To Rudyard Kipling, Saighton, 5th October 1906', in J. W. Mackail and G. Wyndham (eds. no date) *Life and Letters of George Wyndham, Volume 2* (London, Hutchinson and Co.), 552–3.

Yates, J. (1858). 'On the Limes Rhæticus and the Limes Transrhenaus of the Roman Empire', *Memoirs chiefly illustrative of the History and Antiquities of Northumberland communicated to the Annual General Meeting of the Archaeological Institute of Great Britain and Ireland held at Newcastle-on-Tyne in August 1852, Volume 1, Miscellaneous papers* (London, Bell & Daldy), 97–134.

Young, B. (2000). 'Geology of Lanercost Priory', in H. Summerson and S. Harrison (eds.), 81–5.

Young, C. J. (1999a). 'Hadrian's Wall', in G. Chitty and D. Baker (eds.) *Managing Historic Sites and Buildings* (London, Routledge), 35–48.

——(1999b). 'The Management of Hadrian's Wall', in P. Bidwell (ed.), 65–72.

Young, R. J. C. (2008). *The Idea of English Ethnicity* (Oxford, Blackwell).

Index

Printed and bound by CPI Group (UK) Ltd, Croydon, CR0 4YY